Collins
gem

Hockey Facts & Stats

2009–10

Andrew Podnieks

Collins Gem Hockey Facts & Stats 2009–10
Copyright © 2009 by Andrew Podnieks.
All rights reserved.

First edition

Published by Collins, an imprint of HarperCollins Publishers Ltd.

HarperCollins books may be purchased for educational, business, or sales
promotional use through our Special Markets Department.

HarperCollins Publishers Ltd
2 Bloor Street East, 20th Floor
Toronto, Ontario, Canada
M4W 1A8

www.harpercollins.ca

ISBN: 978-1-55468-621-6

Library and Archives Canada Cataloguing in Publication data is available
upon request.

Printed and bound in Canada
WEB 9 8 7 6 5 4 3 2 1

Contents

INTERNATIONAL HOCKEY

Introduction

Well, Sidney Crosby and the Pittsburgh Penguins have lived up to the comparisons to the Edmonton Oilers—at least for one year. Just as the Oilers defeated the New York Islanders to win the Stanley Cup in 1984 after losing to the same team in the finals the previous year, so, too, did the Penguins win the Cup in the spring of 2009 after being manhandled by the Detroit Red Wings in June 2008. And they achieved their 2009 victory for all the expected reasons.

Captain Sidney Crosby was unstoppable in the playoffs, particularly in the seven-game showdown against Alexander Ovechkin and the Washington Capitals in the Eastern Conference semifinals; Evgeni Malkin, quiet in the first two rounds, was the dominant player in the final two rounds; and goalie Marc-Andre Fleury made big saves at the right time, none bigger than in game seven of the finals.

As the Penguins held to a 2–1 lead in Detroit while the last seconds ticked off the clock, Fleury bounded from one side of his goal to the other to make a great lunging save off Detroit captain Nicklas Lidstrom and preserved the victory. Crosby became the youngest captain in league history to win the Cup. Now, though, the talk turns to the future. Can the Penguins do it again? Is this an Oilers-like dynasty in the making?

The 2008–09 hockey season was chock full of significant events. It began with four teams opening the NHL season in Europe again, Pittsburgh playing Ottawa twice in Stockholm and the New York Rangers facing Tampa Bay in Prague. Days before these games, the Rangers were in Bern, Switzerland, to participate in the historic Victoria Cup. This one-game showdown pitted an NHL team—the Rangers—against the European champions, Metallurg Magnitogorsk.

Before a packed PostFinance Arena, the Rangers got the annual NHL–Europe challenge off to a great start, rallying from a 3–0 deficit to win 4–3 in the final minute on a goal by Ryan Callahan. The 2009–10 season will also begin with NHL teams competing in Europe, and the second Victoria Cup will pit the Chicago Blackhawks against Zurich, winners of the inaugural Champions Hockey League tournament.

Alexander Ovechkin was unquestionably the most dynamic player of the '08–09 season. His extraordinary wrist shot led him to a league-best 56 goals, and his showmanship earned him both support and criticism after his showboating celebration of goal number 50. Countryman Malkin led the league in scoring, and a third Russian, Pavel Datsyuk, won both the Lady Byng Trophy and Frank Selke Trophy, making it a very good year, indeed, for Russians.

The outdoor game—the Winter Classic—was held at Wrigley Field in Chicago and featured the local 'Hawks against the Detroit Red Wings. It was such a success that the NHL has vowed to make the outdoor game an annual event for the foreseeable future, and teams have lined up to host it. The 2010 game will take place in Boston's hallowed Fenway Park and feature the Bruins and Philadelphia Flyers.

Internationally, the World Championship in Switzerland featured a matchup all Canadians hope will be replicated in February 2010, albeit with a different outcome. For the second year in a row, the gold-medal game put Canada against Russia, but for the second year the Russians prevailed in a one-goal game, this time a nail-biting 2–1 finale. The re-emergence of Russia as a superpower augurs well for the 2010 Olympics in Vancouver, when the pre-tournament favourites are the host nation and its historic international adversary.

Of course, no summary of the last year would be complete without mentioning the name Jim Balsillie. He is attempting to bring NHL hockey to Hamilton, Ontario, most recently by buying and relocating the troubled Phoenix Coyotes. Whether he succeeds or fails is almost beside the point. What he has done in the last two years through this and previous failed attempts is to make clear how viable another team in southern Ontario would be. Before his arrival, there was only cursory talk about Hamilton. Today, it is clearly a matter of when, not if, a franchise will wind up at Copps Coliseum. For that, all Canadians should be grateful to Balsillie and his dogged pursuit of a seventh team in the motherland of the game.

The 2008–09 hockey season was a fantastic one, but the coming year promises even more fireworks. On the men's side, the Olympics could prove to be the greatest hockey tournament ever played. For the women, the Canada–United States rivalry has taken a turn. Canada was far and away the best team in 2006, then won the 2007 World Women's Championship, but has fallen off badly since then. They lost narrowly in 2008 and convincingly in 2009—all games against the Americans—making the U.S. the clear favourites heading to Vancouver. The 2009–10 NHL should be a good one—but the Olympics will be the real focus. Let the Games begin!

Andrew Podnieks
Toronto, August 2009

GLOSSARY OF ABBREVIATIONS

NHL Teams

ANA=Anaheim Ducks, ATL=Atlanta Thrashers, BOS=Boston Bruins, BUF=Buffalo Sabres, CAL=Calgary Flames, CAR=Carolina Hurricanes, CHI=Chicago Blackhawks, COL=Colorado Avalanche, CBJ=Columbus Blue Jackets, DAL=Dallas Stars, DET=Detroit Red Wings, EDM=Edmonton Oilers, FLO=Florida Panthers, LA=Los Angeles Kings, MIN=Minnesota Wild, MON=Montreal Canadiens, NAS=Nashville Predators, NJ=New Jersey Devils, NYI=New York Islanders, NYR=New York Rangers, OTT=Ottawa Senators, PHI=Philadelphia Flyers, PHO=Phoenix Coyotes, PIT=Pittsburgh Penguins, STL=St. Louis Blues, SJ=San Jose Sharks, TB=Tampa Bay Lightning, TOR=Toronto Maple Leafs, VAN=Vancouver Canucks, WAS=Washington Capitals

International

AUT	Austria	KAZ	Kazakhstan
BEL	Belgium	LAT	Latvia
BLR	Belarus	LTU	Lithuania
CAN	Canada	NED	Netherlands
CHN	China	NIG	Nigeria
CZE	Czech Republic	NOR	Norway
DEN	Denmark	POL	Poland
FIN	Finland	ROM	Romania
FRA	France	RUS	Russia
GBR	Great Britain	SLO	Slovenia
GER	Germany	SUI	Switzerland
HUN	Hungary	SVK	Slovakia
IRL	Ireland	SWE	Sweden
ITA	Italy	UKR	Ukraine
JPN	Japan	USA	United States

2010 OLYMPICS SCHEDULE—MEN

Tournament Format

Preliminary Round: All teams play a round robin within their group (three games each).

Qualification Playoff Round: All 12 teams are ranked in one group (D). The top four receive an automatic bye to the quarter-finals. The remaining eight teams play a one-game elimination for the other four places in the quarter-finals. These games will be scheduled thus: 5D vs. 12D (winner called 1E), 6D vs. 11D (2E), 7D vs. 10D (3E) and 8D vs. 9D (4E).

    The winners of the quarter-finals will be named 1F, 2F, 3F and 4F, the higher team from the Preliminary Round being the home team. These winners play in the semifinals and those winners in the finals, while the semifinal losers will play in the bronze-medal game.

Group A: Canada (CAN), United States (USA), Switzerland (SUI), Norway (NOR)
Group B: Russia (RUS), Czech Republic (CZE), Slovakia (SVK), Latvia (LAT)
Group C: Sweden (SWE), Finland (FIN), Belarus (BLR), Germany (GER)

February 16	12:00 p.m.	USA–SUI
	4:30 p.m.	CAN–NOR
	9:00 p.m.	RUS–LAT
February 17	12:00 p.m.	FIN–BLR
	4:30 p.m.	SWE–GER
	9:00 p.m.	CZE–SVK
February 18	12:00 p.m.	USA–NOR
	4:30 p.m.	SUI–CAN
	9:00 p.m.	SVK–RUS

February 19	12:00 p.m.	BLR–SWE
	4:30 p.m.	CZE–LAT
	9:00 p.m.	FIN–GER
February 20	12:00 p.m.	NOR–SUI
	4:30 p.m.	LAT–SVK
	9:00 p.m.	GER–BLR
February 21	12:00 p.m.	RUS–CZE
	4:30 p.m.	CAN–USA
	9:00 p.m.	SWE–FIN
February 23	12:00 p.m.	5D–12D
	4:30 p.m.	6D–11D
	7:00 p.m.	7D–10D
	9:00 p.m.	8D–9D
February 24	12:00 p.m.	1D–4E
	4:30 p.m.	2D–3E
	7:00 p.m.	3D–2E
	9:00 p.m.	4D–1E
February 26	12:00 p.m.	Semifinal 1
	6:30 p.m.	Semifinal 2
February 27	7:00 p.m.	Bronze-Medal Game
February 28	12:15 p.m.	Gold-Medal Game

All games will be played at GM Place except 7D–10D and 3D–2E, which will be played at Thunderbird Arena, UBC. Because General Motors is not an official Olympics sponsor, the arena will be called Canada Hockey Place for the tournament.

2010 OLYMPICS SCHEDULE—WOMEN

TOURNAMENT FORMAT

Preliminary Round: all teams play a round robin within their group (three games each).

The top two teams from each group advance to the semifinals, and the bottom two teams to a Placement Round. For the playoffs, 1A vs. 2B and 2A vs. 1B, and for the Placement Round, 3A vs. 4B and 4B vs. 3A. The semifinal winners will advance to the gold-medal game, the losers to the bronze-medal game.

Group A: Canada (CAN), Sweden (SWE), Switzerland (SUI), Slovakia (SVK)
Group B: United States (USA), Finland (FIN), Russia (RUS), China (CHN)

February 13	12:00 p.m.	SWE–SUI
	5:00 p.m.	CAN–SVK
February 14	12:00 p.m.	USA–CHN
	4:30 p.m.	FIN–RUS
February 15	2:30 p.m.	SUI–CAN
	7:00 p.m.	SWE–SVK
February 16	2:30 p.m.	RUS–USA
	7:00 p.m.	FIN–CHN
February 17	2:30 p.m.	CAN–SWE
	7:00 p.m.	SVK–SUI
February 18	2:30 p.m.	USA–FIN
	7:00 p.m.	CHN–RUS

February 20	2:30 p.m.	Placement 1
	7:00 p.m.	Placement 2
February 22	12:00 p.m.	Semifinal 1
	2:00 p.m.	Placement 3
	5:00 p.m.	Semifinal 2
	7:00 p.m.	Placement 4
February 25	11:00 a.m.	Bronze-Medal Game
	3:30 p.m.	Gold-Medal Game

All games will be played at Thunderbird Arena (UBC) except CAN–SVK and all playoff games (semifinal and medal games), which will be played at Canada Hockey Place (GM Place).

International A–Z Register—Men

The players who will represent Canada at the 2010 Olympics in Vancouver will almost certainly be among the names listed here, along with their statistics in international competition.

Legend: OG=Olympic Games, WM=World (men) Championships, U20=World Junior Championships, CC=Canada Cup, WCH=World Cup of Hockey, G=Gold Medal, S=Silver Medal, B=Bronze Medal

Player

YEAR	EVENT	NAT	GP	G	A	P	Pim	Finish

Goalie

YEAR	EVENT	NAT	GP	W-T-L	Mins	GA	SO	GAA	A	Pim	Finish

Beauchemin, Francois   b. Sorel, Quebec, June 4, 1980
• no international experience

Bergeron, Patrice   b. L'Ancienne Lorette, Quebec, July 24, 1985

YEAR	EVENT	NAT	GP	G	A	P	Pim	Finish
2004	WM	CAN	9	1	0	1	4	G
2005	U20	CAN	6	5	8	13	6	G
2006	WM	CAN	9	6	8	14	2	4th

Blake, Rob   b. Simcoe, Ontario, December 10, 1969

YEAR	EVENT	NAT	GP	G	A	P	Pim	Finish
1991	WM	CAN	2	0	2	2	0	S
1994	WM	CAN	8	0	2	2	6	G
1996	WCH	CAN	4	0	1	1	0	2nd
1997	WM	CAN	11	2	2	4	22	G
1998	OG	CAN	6	1	1	2	2	4th
1998	WM	CAN	5	1	0	1	6	6th
1999	WM	CAN	10	2	5	7	12	4th

| 2002 | OG | CAN | 6 | 1 | 2 | 3 | 2 | G |
| 2006 | OG | CAN | 6 | 0 | 1 | 1 | 2 | 7th |

Bouwmeester, Jay b. Edmonton, Alberta, September 27, 1983

2000	U20	CAN	7	0	0	0	2	B
2001	U20	CAN	7	0	2	2	6	B
2002	U20	CAN	7	0	2	2	10	S
2003	WM	CAN	9	3	4	7	4	G
2004	WM	CAN	9	2	1	3	0	G
2004	WCH	CAN	4	0	0	0	0	1st
2006	OG	CAN	6	0	0	0	0	7th
2008	WM	CAN	9	0	0	0	4	S

Boyes, Brad b. Mississauga, Ontario, April 17, 1982

2001	U20	CAN	7	1	3	4	2	B
2002	U20	CAN	7	5	4	9	16	S
2006	WM	CAN	9	4	4	8	4	7th

Boyle, Dan b. Ottawa, Ontario, July 12, 1976

| 2005 | WM | CAN | 9 | 0 | 3 | 3 | 6 | S |

Briere, Daniel b. Gatineau, Quebec, October 6, 1977

1997	U20	CAN	7	2	4	6	4	G
2003	WM	CAN	9	4	5	9	6	G
2004	WM	CAN	9	2	6	8	6	G

Brodeur, Martin b. Montreal, Quebec, May 6, 1972

1996	WM	CAN	3	0–1–1	140:00	8	0	3.43	0	0	S
1996	WCH	CAN	2	0–0–1	60:02	4	0	4.00	0	0	2nd
2002	OG	CAN	5	4–0–1	300:00	9	0	1.80	0	0	G
2004	WCH	CAN	5	5–0–0	300:00	5	1	1.00	0	2	1st
2005	WM	CAN	7	5–0–2	418:36	20	0	2.87	0	0	S
2006	OG	CAN	4	2–0–2	238:40	8	0	2.01	0	0	7th

Burns, Brent   b. Ajax, Ontario, March 9, 1985

2004	U20	CAN	6	0	6	6	20	S
2008	WM	CAN	9	3	6	9	16	S

Cammalleri, Mike   b. Richmond Hill, Ontario, June 8, 1982

2001	U20	CAN	7	4	2	6	2	B
2002	U20	CAN	7	7	4	11	10	S
2006	WM	CAN	8	1	4	5	4	4th
2007	WM	CAN	9	4	3	7	6	G

Campbell, Brian   b. Strathroy, Ontario, May 23, 1979

1999	U20	CAN	7	1	1	2	4	S

Carter, Jeff   b. London, Ontario, January 1, 1985

2004	U20	CAN	6	5	2	7	2	S
2005	U20	CAN	6	7	3	10	6	G
2006	WM	CAN	9	4	2	6	2	4th

Cleary, Dan   b. Carbonear, Newfoundland, December 18, 1978

2002	WM	CAN	7	2	1	3	2	6th

Crosby, Sidney   b. Cole Harbour, Nova Scotia, August 7, 1987

2004	U20	CAN	6	2	3	5	4	S
2005	U20	CAN	6	6	3	9	4	G
2006	WM	CAN	9	8	8	16	10	4th

Doan, Shane   b. Halkirk, Alberta, October 10, 1976

1999	WM	CAN	4	0	0	0	0	4th
2003	WM	CAN	9	4	2	6	12	G
2004	WCH	CAN	6	1	1	2	2	1st
2005	WM	CAN	9	1	3	4	2	S
2006	OG	CAN	6	2	1	3	2	7th
2007	WM	CAN	9	5	5	10	8	G

| 2008 | WM | CAN | 9 | 2 | 4 | 6 | 6 | S |
| 2009 | WM | CAN | 9 | 1 | 6 | 7 | 14 | S |

Doughty, Drew   b. London, Ontario, December 8, 1989

| 2008 | U20 | CAN | 7 | 0 | 4 | 4 | 0 | G |
| 2009 | WM | CAN | 9 | 1 | 6 | 7 | 4 | S |

Fleury, Marc-Andre   b. Sorel, Quebec, November 28, 1984

| 2003 | U20 | CAN | 5 | 4–0–1 | 267:28 | 7 | 1 | 1.57 | 1 | 0 | S |
| 2004 | U20 | CAN | 5 | 4–0–1 | 298:51 | 9 | 1 | 1.81 | 0 | 2 | S |

Gagne, Simon   b. Ste. Foy, Quebec, February 29, 1980

1999	U20	CAN	7	7	1	8	2	S
2002	OG	CAN	6	1	3	4	0	G
2004	WCH	CAN	6	1	1	2	0	1st
2005	WM	CAN	9	3	7	10	0	S
2006	OG	CAN	6	1	2	3	6	7th

Getzlaf, Ryan   b. Regina, Saskatchewan, May 10, 1985

2004	U20	CAN	6	3	3	6	4	S
2005	U20	CAN	6	3	9	12	8	G
2008	WM	CAN	9	3	11	14	10	S

Giguere, Jean-Sebastien   b. Montreal, Quebec, May 16, 1977

| 2002 | WM | CAN | 5 | 3–0–1 | 253:43 | 8 | 0 | 1.89 | 0 | 0 | 6th |
| 2004 | WM | CAN | 2 | 2–0–0 | 120:00 | 1 | 1 | 0.50 | 0 | 0 | G |

Green, Mike   b. Calgary, Alberta, October 12, 1985

| 2008 | WM | CAN | 9 | 4 | 8 | 12 | 2 | S |

Hamhuis, Dan   b. Smithers, British Columbia, December 13, 1982

| 2001 | U20 | CAN | 7 | 0 | 1 | 1 | 8 | B |

2002	U20	CAN	6	0	3	3	8	S
2006	WM	CAN	9	1	4	5	10	4th
2007	WM	CAN	9	1	2	3	2	G
2008	WM	CAN	9	1	1	2	8	S

Heatley, Dany   b. Freiburg, West Germany (Germany), January 21, 1981

2000	U20	CAN	7	2	2	4	4	B
2001	U20	CAN	7	3	2	5	10	B
2002	WM	CAN	7	2	2	4	2	6th
2003	WM	CAN	9	7	3	10	10	G
2004	WM	CAN	9	8	3	11	4	G
2004	WCH	CAN	6	0	2	2	2	1st
2005	WM	CAN	9	3	4	7	16	S
2006	OG	CAN	6	2	1	3	8	7th
2008	WM	CAN	9	12	8	20	4	S
2009	WM	CAN	9	6	4	10	8	S

Iginla, Jarome   b. St. Albert, Alberta, July 1, 1977

1996	U20	CAN	6	5	7	12	4	G
1997	WM	CAN	11	2	3	5	2	G
2002	OG	CAN	6	3	1	4	0	G
2004	WCH	CAN	6	2	1	3	2	1st
2006	OG	CAN	6	2	1	3	4	7th

Jovanovski, Ed   b. Windsor, Ontario, June 26, 1976

1995	U20	CAN	7	2	0	2	4	G
1998	WM	CAN	6	2	1	3	6	6th
2000	WM	CAN	9	1	1	2	8	4th
2002	OG	CAN	6	0	3	3	4	G
2004	WCH	CAN	1	0	0	0	0	1st
2005	WM	CAN	9	1	2	3	8	S
2008	WM	CAN	9	0	1	1	4	S

Keith, Duncan   b. Winnipeg, Manitoba, July 16, 1983

2008	WC	CAN	9	0	2	2	6	S

Lecavalier, Vincent   b. Ile Bizard, Quebec, April 21, 1980

1998	U20	CAN	7	1	1	2	4	8th
2001	WM	CAN	7	3	2	5	29	5th
2004	WCH	CAN	6	2	5	7	8	1st
2006	OG	CAN	6	0	3	3	16	7th

Lucic, Milan   b. Vancouver, British Columbia, June 7, 1988
• no experience in major international tournaments; played for Canada in Super Series vs. Team Russia, 2007

Luongo, Roberto   b. Montreal, Quebec, April 4, 1979

1998	U20	CAN	3	0–0–2	145:02	8	0	3.31	0	2	8th
1999	U20	CAN	7	4–1–2	405:13	13	2	1.92	1	0	S
2001	WM	CAN	2	2–0–0	83:36	2	0	1.44	0	0	5th
2003	WM	CAN	4	4–0–0	211:50	7	1	1.98	0	0	G
2004	WM	CAN	7	5–1–1	440:00	17	1	2.32	0	0	G
2004	WCH	CAN	1	1–0–0	63:45	3	0	2.82	0	0	1st
2005	WM	CAN	2	1–1–0	120:00	3	1	1.50	0	0	S
2006	OG	CAN	2	1–0–1	118:58	3	0	1.51	0	0	7th

Marleau, Patrick   b. Aneroid, Saskatchewan, September 15, 1979

1999	WM	CAN	7	1	1	2	0	4th
2001	WM	CAN	7	2	3	5	4	5th
2003	WM	CAN	9	0	4	4	4	G
2005	WM	CAN	9	2	2	4	4	S

Mason, Steve   b. Red Deer, Alberta, April 20, 1976

2008	U20	CAN	5	5–0–0	303:36	6	1	1.19	0	0	G

McDonald, Andy   b. Strathroy, Ontario, August 25, 1977

2002	WM	CAN	7	4	1	5	0	6th

Morrow, Brenden   b. Carlyle, Saskatchewan, January 16, 1979

1999	U20	CAN	7	1	7	8	4	S
2001	WC	CAN	1	0	0	0	0	5th
2002	WC	CAN	7	0	1	1	2	6th
2004	WC	CAN	9	0	3	3	12	G
2004	WCH	CAN	1	0	0	0	4	1st
2005	WC	CAN	9	0	1	1	6	S

Nash, Rick   b. Brampton, Ontario, June 16, 1984

2002	U20	CAN	7	1	2	3	2	S
2005	WM	CAN	9	9	6	15	8	S
2006	OG	CAN	6	0	1	1	10	7th
2007	WM	CAN	9	6	5	11	4	G
2008	WM	CAN	9	6	7	13	6	S

Niedermayer, Scott   b. Edmonton, Alberta, August 31, 1973

1991	U20	CAN	3	0	0	0	0	G
1992	U20	CAN	7	0	0	0	10	6th
1996	WCH	CAN	8	1	3	4	6	2nd
2002	OG	CAN	6	1	1	2	4	G
2004	WM	CAN	9	3	2	5	12	G
2004	WCH	CAN	6	1	1	2	9	1st

Perry, Corey   b. Peterborough, Ontario, May 16, 1985

2005	U20	CAN	6	2	5	7	6	G

Phaneuf, Dion   b. Edmonton, Alberta, April 10, 1985

2004	U20	CAN	6	2	2	4	29	S
2005	U20	CAN	6	1	5	6	14	G
2007	WM	CAN	7	0	8	8	2	G

Phillips, Chris   b. Fort McMurray, Alberta, March 9, 1978

1996	U20	CAN	6	0	0	0	0	G
1997	U20	CAN	7	0	1	1	4	G
2000	WM	CAN	9	0	0	0	2	4th
2005	WM	CAN	9	0	1	1	8	S
2009	WM	CAN	9	0	3	3	12	S

Pronger, Chris   b. Dryden, Ontario, October 10, 1974

1993	U20	CAN	7	1	3	4	6	G
1997	WM	CAN	9	0	2	2	12	G
1998	OG	CAN	6	0	0	0	4	4th
2002	OG	CAN	6	0	1	1	2	G
2006	OG	CAN	6	1	2	3	16	7th

Regehr, Robyn   b. Recife, Brazil, April 13, 1980

1999	U20	CAN	7	0	0	0	2	S
2000	WM	CAN	6	0	0	0	2	4th
2004	WCH	CAN	6	0	0	0	6	1st
2005	WM	CAN	9	0	0	0	4	S
2006	OG	CAN	6	0	1	1	2	7th

Richards, Brad   b. Montague, Prince Edward Island, May 2, 1980

2000	U20	CAN	7	1	1	2	0	B
2001	WM	CAN	7	3	3	6	0	5th
2004	WCH	CAN	6	1	3	4	0	1st
2006	OG	CAN	6	2	2	4	6	7th

Richards, Mike   b. Kenora, Ontario, February 11, 1985

2004	U20	CAN	6	2	3	5	2	S
2005	U20	CAN	6	1	4	5	2	G
2006	WM	CAN	9	3	2	5	10	4th

Robidas, Stephane   b. Sherbrooke, Quebec, March 3, 1977

2001	WM	CAN	7	0	1	1	0	5th
2006	WM	CAN	9	1	1	2	6	4th

Roy, Derek   b. Ottawa, Ontario, May 4, 1983

2003	U20	CAN	6	1	2	3	4	S
2008	WM	CAN	9	5	5	10	6	S
2009	WM	CAN	9	4	4	8	4	S

Savard, Marc   b. Ottawa, Ontario, July 17, 1977
• no international experience

Seabrook, Brent   b. Richmond, British Columbia, April 20, 1985

2004	U20	CAN	6	1	2	3	2	S
2005	U20	CAN	5	0	3	3	0	G
2006	WM	CAN	8	0	0	0	2	4th

Sharp, Patrick   b. Thunder Bay, Ontario, December 27, 1981

2008	WM	CAN	9	3	0	3	4	S

Smyth, Ryan   b. Banff, Alberta, February 21, 1976

1995	U20	CAN	7	2	5	7	4	G
1999	WM	CAN	10	0	2	2	12	4th
2000	WM	CAN	9	3	6	9	0	4th
2001	WM	CAN	7	2	3	5	4	5th
2002	OG	CAN	6	0	1	1	0	G
2002	WM	CAN	7	4	0	4	2	6th
2003	WM	CAN	9	2	2	4	2	G
2004	WM	CAN	9	2	2	4	2	G
2004	WCH	CAN	6	3	1	4	2	1st
2005	WM	CAN	9	2	1	3	6	S
2006	OG	CAN	6	0	1	1	4	7th

Spezza, Jason   b. Mississauga, Ontario, June 13, 1983

2000	U20	CAN	7	0	2	2	2	B
2001	U20	CAN	7	3	3	6	2	B
2002	U20	CAN	7	0	4	4	8	S
2008	WM	CAN	9	1	2	3	0	S
2009	WM	CAN	9	7	4	11	2	S

Staal, Eric   b. Thunder Bay, Ontario, October 29, 1984

2007	WM	CAN	9	5	5	10	6	G
2008	WM	CAN	8	4	3	7	6	S

Staal, Jordan   b. Thunder Bay, Ontario, September 10, 1988

2007	WM	CAN	9	0	2	2	0	G

Staal, Marc   b. Thunder Bay, Ontario, January 13, 1987

2006	U20	CAN	6	0	1	1	4	G
2007	U20	CAN	6	0	0	0	4	G

Stamkos, Steve   b. Markham, Ontario, February 7, 1990

2008	U20	CAN	7	1	5	6	4	G
2009	WM	CAN	9	7	4	11	6	S

St. Louis, Martin   b. Laval, Quebec, June 18, 1975

2006	OG	CAN	6	2	1	3	0	7th
2008	WM	CAN	9	2	8	10	0	S
2009	WM	CAN	9	4	11	15	2	S

Thornton, Joe   b. London, Ontario, July 2, 1979

1997	U20	CAN	7	2	2	4	0	G
2001	WM	CAN	6	1	1	2	6	5th
2004	WCH	CAN	6	1	5	6	0	1st
2005	WM	CAN	9	6	10	16	4	S
2006	OG	CAN	6	1	2	3	0	7th

Toews, Jonathan   b. Winnipeg, Manitoba, April 29, 1988

2006	U20	CAN	6	0	2	2	2	G
2007	U20	CAN	6	4	3	7	12	G
2007	WM	CAN	9	2	5	7	6	G
2008	WM	CAN	9	2	3	5	8	S

Turco, Marty   b. Sault Ste. Marie, Ontario, August 13, 1975

2002 WM	CAN	3	2–0–1	165:31	5	1	1.81	0	0	6th

Ward, Cam   b. Saskatoon, Saskatchewan, February 29, 1984

2007 WM	CAN	5	5–0–0	300:00	11	0	2.20	0	2	G
2008 WM	CAN	5	4–0–1	302:42	13	0	2.58	0	0	S

Weber, Shea   b. Sicamous, British Columbia, August 14, 1985

2005 U20	CAN	6	0	0	0	10	G
2007 WM	CAN	6	1	1	2	31	S
2009 WM	CAN	9	4	8	12	6	S

International A–Z Register—Women

The players who will represent Canada at the 2010 Olympics in Vancouver will almost certainly be among those listed here, along with their statistics in international competition.

Legend: OG–W=Olympic Games—Women, WWC=World Women's Championship

Player
YEAR	EVENT	NAT	GP	G	A	P	Pim	Finish

Goalie
YEAR	EVENT	NAT	GP	W-T-L	Mins	GA	SO	GAA	A	Pim	Finish

Agosta, Meghan   b. Windsor, Ontario, February 12, 1987

YEAR	EVENT	NAT	GP	G	A	P	Pim	Finish
2006	OG–W	CAN	5	3	1	4	2	G
2007	WWC	CAN	5	0	4	4	4	G
2008	WWC	CAN	5	3	0	3	8	S
2009	WWC	CAN	5	2	2	4	2	S
Totals			**20**	**8**	**7**	**15**	**16**	

Apps, Gillian   b. North York (Toronto), Ontario, November 2, 1983

YEAR	EVENT	NAT	GP	G	A	P	Pim	Finish
2004	WWC	CAN	5	4	0	4	10	G
2005	WWC	CAN	5	4	2	6	8	S
2006	OG–W	CAN	5	7	7	14	14	G
2007	WWC	CAN	5	1	3	4	6	G
2008	WWC	CAN	5	1	0	1	8	S
2009	WWC	CAN	5	2	1	3	4	S
Totals			**30**	**19**	**13**	**32**	**50**	

Bechard, Kelly　b. Sedley, Saskatchewan, January 22, 1978

2000	WWC	CAN	5	0	2	2	0	G
2001	WWC	CAN	5	1	9	10	8	G
2002	OG–W	CAN	5	0	1	1	2	G
2004	WWC	CAN	5	1	0	1	0	G
2005	WWC	CAN	5	2	4	6	2	S
2007	WWC	CAN	5	3	1	4	16	G
2008	WWC	CAN	5	1	1	2	4	S
Totals			**35**	**8**	**18**	**26**	**32**	

Bonhomme, Tessa　b. Sudbury, Ontario, July 23, 1985

2007	WWC	CAN	5	1	1	2	6	G
2009	WWC	CAN	5	0	3	3	0	S
Totals			**10**	**1**	**4**	**5**	**6**	

Botterill, Jennifer　b. Winnipeg, Manitoba, May 1, 1979

1998	OG–W	CAN	6	0	0	0	0	S
1999	WWC	CAN	5	1	3	4	0	G
2000	WWC	CAN	5	1	5	6	2	G
2001	WWC	CAN	5	8	2	10	4	G
2002	OG–W	CAN	5	3	3	6	8	G
2004	WWC	CAN	5	3	8	11	0	G
2005	WWC	CAN	5	1	6	7	4	S
2006	OG–W	CAN	5	1	6	7	4	G
2007	WWC	CAN	5	3	2	5	4	G
2008	WWC	CAN	5	4	4	8	4	S
2009	WWC	CAN	5	5	3	8	2	S
Totals			**56**	**30**	**42**	**72**	**32**	

Collins, Delaney　b. Pilot Mound, Manitoba, May 2, 1977

2000	WWC	CAN	5	1	1	2	0	G

2004	WWC	CAN	5	3	1	4	4	G
2005	WWC	CAN	5	0	4	4	2	S
2007	WWC	CAN	5	0	4	4	2	G
2008	WWC	CAN	5	0	1	1	4	S
Totals			**25**	**4**	**11**	**15**	**12**	

Ferrari, Gillian   b. Richmond Hill, Ontario, June 23, 1980

2004	WWC	CAN	5	0	2	2	6	G
2006	OG–W	CAN	5	0	0	0	0	G
2007	WWC	CAN	5	0	0	0	2	G
2008	WWC	CAN	5	0	1	1	2	S
2009	WWC	CAN	5	0	0	0	2	S
Totals			**25**	**0**	**3**	**3**	**12**	

Hefford, Jayna   b. Trenton, Ontario, May 14, 1977

1997	WWC	CAN	5	1	3	4	2	G
1998	OG–W	CAN	6	1	0	1	6	S
1999	WWC	CAN	5	5	6	11	0	G
2000	WWC	CAN	5	5	3	8	4	G
2001	WWC	CAN	5	2	2	4	6	G
2002	OG–W	CAN	5	3	4	7	2	G
2004	WWC	CAN	5	7	3	10	2	G
2005	WWC	CAN	5	6	2	8	0	S
2006	OG–W	CAN	5	3	4	7	0	G
2007	WWC	CAN	5	2	1	3	2	G
2008	WWC	CAN	5	3	5	8	8	S
2009	WWC	CAN	5	1	6	7	2	S
Totals			**61**	**39**	**39**	**78**	**34**	

Irwin, Haley   b. Thunder Bay, Ontario, June 6, 1988

| 2009 | WWC | CAN | 5 | 2 | 3 | 5 | 2 | S |

Johnston, Rebecca   b. Sudbury, Ontario, September 24, 1989

2008	WWC	CAN	5	0	0	0	0	S
2009	WWC	CAN	5	3	2	5	0	S
Totals			**10**	**3**	**2**	**5**	**0**	

Kellar, Becky   b. Hagersville, Ontario, January 1, 1975

1998	OG–W	CAN	6	1	2	3	2	S
1999	WWC	CAN	5	1	0	1	6	G
2000	WWC	CAN	5	2	2	4	0	G
2001	WWC	CAN	5	1	2	3	2	G
2002	OG–W	CAN	5	0	1	1	6	G
2004	WWC	CAN	4	0	0	0	0	G
2005	WWC	CAN	5	0	2	2	4	S
2006	OG–W	CAN	5	0	1	1	2	G
2008	WWC	CAN	5	1	4	5	0	S
2009	WWC	CAN	5	0	0	0	4	S
Totals			**50**	**6**	**14**	**20**	**26**	

Kingsbury, Gina   b. Uranium City, Saskatchewan, November 26, 1981

2001	WWC	CAN	4	2	2	4	0	G
2004	WWC	CAN	5	1	1	2	4	G
2005	WWC	CAN	5	2	0	2	4	S
2006	OG–W	CAN	5	0	3	3	2	G
2007	WWC	CAN	5	2	0	2	0	G
2008	WWC	CAN	5	1	3	4	0	S
2009	WWC	CAN	5	1	2	3	2	S
Totals			**34**	**9**	**11**	**20**	**12**	

Labonte, Charline   b. Greenfield Park, Quebec, October 15, 1982

2005	WWC	CAN	2	2–0–0	120:00	0	2	0.00	1	0	S
2006	OG–W	CAN	3	3–0–0	180:00	1	2	0.33	0	0	G
2007	WWC	CAN	2	2–0–0	130:00	4	1	1.85	0	0	G

2008	WWC	CAN	3	1–0–1	138:29	3	1	1.30	0	0	S
2009	WWC	CAN	3	2–0–1	179:04	5	2	1.68	0	0	S
Totals			**13**	**10–0–2**	**747:33**	**13**	**8**	**1.04**	**1**	**0**	

MacLeod, Carla b. Edmonton, Alberta, June 16, 1982

2005	WWC	CAN	5	1	2	3	0	S
2006	OG–W	CAN	5	2	2	4	2	G
2007	WWC	CAN	5	0	1	1	2	G
2008	WWC	CAN	5	1	3	4	2	S
2009	WWC	CAN	5	2	6	8	4	S
Totals			**25**	**6**	**14**	**20**	**10**	

Mikkelson, Meaghan   b. St. Albert, Alberta, January 4, 1985

2008	WWC	CAN	5	0	0	0	2	S
2009	WWC	CAN	5	0	3	3	6	S
Totals			**10**	**0**	**3**	**3**	**8**	

Ouellette, Caroline   b. Montreal, Quebec, May 25, 1979

1999	WWC	CAN	5	2	5	7	4	G
2000	WWC	CAN	5	0	2	2	2	G
2001	WWC	CAN	5	2	3	5	4	G
2002	OG–W	CAN	5	2	4	6	6	G
2004	WWC	CAN	5	3	6	9	0	G
2005	WWC	CAN	5	2	6	8	0	S
2006	OG–W	CAN	5	5	4	9	4	G
2007	WWC	CAN	5	1	3	4	2	G
2008	WWC	CAN	5	2	4	6	4	S
2009	WWC	CAN	5	3	5	8	6	S
Totals			**50**	**22**	**42**	**64**	**32**	

Piper, Cherie   b. Toronto, Ontario, June 29, 1981

2002	OG–W	CAN	5	3	2	5	0	G
2004	WWC	CAN	5	1	6	7	4	G
2005	WWC	CAN	5	3	1	4	2	S
2006	OG–W	CAN	5	7	8	15	0	G
2008	WWC	CAN	5	2	6	8	0	S
Totals			**25**	**16**	**23**	**39**	**6**	

Poulin, Marie-Philip   b. Beauceville, Quebec, March 28, 1991

2009	WWC	CAN	5	2	3	5	0	S

Sostorics, Colleen   b. Regina, Saskatchewan, December 17, 1979

2001	WWC	CAN	5	2	1	3	2	G
2002	OG–W	CAN	5	0	2	2	4	G
2004	WWC	CAN	5	1	1	2	2	G
2005	WWC	CAN	5	0	0	0	4	S
2006	OG–W	CAN	5	0	1	1	6	G
2007	WWC	CAN	5	0	3	3	2	G
2008	WWC	CAN	5	0	2	2	10	S
2009	WWC	CAN	5	1	1	2	2	S
Totals			**40**	**4**	**11**	**15**	**32**	

St. Pierre, Kim   b. LaSalle, Quebec, December 14, 1978

1999	WWC	CAN	2	2–0–0	120:00	1	1	0.50	0	0	G
2000	WWC	CAN	2	2–0–0	149:58	3	0	1.20	0	0	G
2001	WWC	CAN	3	3–0–0	180:00	2	2	0.67	0	0	G
2002	OG–W	CAN	4	4–0–0	240:00	5	2	1.25	1	0	G
2004	WWC	CAN	4	2–0–1	179:44	3	2	1.00	0	0	G
2005	WWC	CAN	3	2–0–1	200:00	0	3	0.00	0	0	S
2006	OG–W	CAN	2	2–0–0	120:00	1	1	0.50	0	0	G
2007	WWC	CAN	3	3–0–0	180:00	1	2	0.33	0	0	G

2008	WWC	CAN	3	2–0–1	160:00	7	0	2.63	0	0	S
2009	WWC	CAN	2	2–0–0	120:00	0	2	0.00	0	0	S
Totals			**28**	**24-0-3**	**1649:42**	**23**	**15**	**0.84**	**1**	**0**	

Vaillancourt, Sarah   b. Fleurimont, Quebec, May 8, 1985

2005	WWC	CAN	5	3	5	8	2	S
2006	OG–W	CAN	5	2	4	6	2	G
2007	WWC	CAN	5	2	4	6	4	G
2008	WWC	CAN	5	4	2	6	8	S
2009	WWC	CAN	5	3	4	7	8	S
Totals			**25**	**14**	**19**	**33**	**24**	

Ward, Catherine   b. Mt. Royal, Quebec, February 27, 1987

| 2009 | WWC | CAN | 5 | 0 | 4 | 4 | 2 | S |

Weatherston, Katie   b. Thunder Bay, Ontario, April 6, 1983

2006	OG–W	CAN	5	4	1	5	2	G
2007	WWC	CAN	5	3	1	4	0	G
2008	WWC	CAN	5	2	0	2	2	S
Totals			**15**	**9**	**2**	**11**	**4**	

Wickenheiser, Hayley   b. Shaunavon, Saskatchewan, August 12, 1978

1994	WWC	CAN	3	0	1	1	4	G
1997	WWC	CAN	5	4	5	9	12	G
1998	OG–W	CAN	6	2	6	8	4	S
1999	WWC	CAN	5	3	5	8	8	G
2000	WWC	CAN	5	1	7	8	4	G
2002	OG–W	CAN	5	7	3	10	2	G

Year	Event	Country						Medal
2004	WWC	CAN	5	3	2	5	2	G
2005	WWC	CAN	5	5	3	8	6	S
2006	OG–W	CAN	5	5	12	17	6	G
2007	WWC	CAN	5	8	6	14	0	G
2008	WWC	CAN	5	3	6	9	6	S
2009	WWC	CAN	5	4	4	8	4	S
Totals			**59**	**45**	**60**	**105**	**58**	

Sledge Hockey

The Origins

Sledge hockey was created in the early 1960s by two Swedes at a rehabilitation centre in Stockholm. It wasn't until 1969 that games between European nations took place. In 1981, Great Britain started a team, and the next year Canada joined. The United States entered the competition in 1990, and three years later Estonia and Japan joined. The year 1994 was a breakthrough year for the sport as it became part of the Paralympic Games, the quadrennial event that followed the Olympic Winter Games. In 2004, sledge hockey became a fully recognized sport by Hockey Canada.

The Rules

First drawn up in 1990 and based on Canadian hockey rules, sledge hockey rules are virtually identical, save for a few that specifically address players' needs. The sledge must consist of a metal frame with two blades under which the puck can pass. Entranceways to benches are at ice level so that players can slide on and off the ice easily. Sticks are curved at one end and have small picks at the other, so that players can push themselves around the ice using the butt end of the shaft. To this end, each player is allowed two sticks, one for each hand. Helmets are mandatory. Games consist of a standard three periods of 20 minutes each, and teams play five skaters a side (plus a goalie).

Results

Year	Event	Gold	Silver	Bronze	Host
1991	World Cup	CAN	SWE	NOR	Oslo, NOR
1992	World Cup	CAN	NOR	USA	Ottawa/Hull, CAN
1994	Paralympic Winter Games	SWE	NOR	CAN	Lillehammer, NOR
1996	World Championship	SWE	NOR	CAN	Nynashamn, SWE
1998	Paralympic Winter Games	NOR	CAN	SWE	Nagano, JPN
1999	Commemorative Games	CAN	NOR	SWE	Nagano, JPN
2000	World Championship	CAN	NOR	SWE	Salt Lake City, USA
2002	Paralympic Winter Games	USA	NOR	SWE	Salt Lake City, USA
2004	World Championship	NOR	USA	SWE	Ornskoldsvik, SWE
2006	Paralympic Winter Games	CAN	NOR	USA	Turin, ITA
2007	World Sledge Hockey Challenge	CAN	NOR	USA	Kelowna, CAN
2008	World Championship	CAN	NOR	USA	Marlborough, USA
2009	World Sledge Hockey Challenge	USA	NOR	CAN	Charlottetown, CAN

2009–10 National Men's Sledge Hockey Team Roster

Goal: Paul Rosen, Benoit St. Amand, Corbin Watson
Defence: Matthew Cook, Adam Dixon, Raymond Grassi, Jean Labonte (captain)
Forward: Jeremy Booker, Bradley Bowden, Billy Bridges, Marc Dorion, Herve Lord, Shawn Matheson, Graeme Murray, Todd Nicholson, Dany Verner, Greg Westlake, Derek Whitson,

The 2010 Paralympic Games run from March 13 to March 20 in Vancouver. The tournament schedule has yet to be finalized.

THE GAMES OF THE VII OLYMPIAD

ANTWERP, BELGIUM, April 23–September 12, 1920
(Winter Olympics held April 23–29, 1920)

FINAL PLACINGS

GOLD MEDAL	Canada
SILVER MEDAL	United States
BRONZE MEDAL	Czechoslovakia
Fourth Place	Sweden

THE FIRST OLYMPIC WINTER GAMES

CHAMONIX, FRANCE, January 25–February 5, 1924

FINAL PLACINGS

GOLD MEDAL	Canada
SILVER MEDAL	United States
BRONZE MEDAL	Great Britain
Fourth Place	Sweden
Fifth Place	Czechoslovakia
(tie)	France
Seventh Place	Belgium
(tie)	Switzerland

THE SECOND OLYMPIC WINTER GAMES

ST. MORITZ, SWITZERLAND, February 11–20, 1928

FINAL PLACINGS

GOLD MEDAL	Canada
SILVER MEDAL	Sweden
BRONZE MEDAL	Switzerland
Fourth Place	Great Britain
Fifth Place	France
Sixth Place	Czechoslovakia

Seventh Place	Belgium
(tie)	Austria
Ninth Place	Poland
Tenth Place	Germany
Eleventh Place	Hungary

THE THIRD OLYMPIC WINTER GAMES

LAKE PLACID, UNITED STATES, February 4–13, 1932

FINAL PLACINGS

GOLD MEDAL	Canada
SILVER MEDAL	United States
BRONZE MEDAL	Germany
Fourth Place	Poland

THE FOURTH OLYMPIC WINTER GAMES

GARMISCH–PARTENKIRCHEN, GERMANY, February 6–16, 1936

FINAL PLACINGS

GOLD MEDAL	Great Britain
SILVER MEDAL	Canada
BRONZE MEDAL	United States
Fourth Place	Czechoslovakia
Fifth Place	Germany
(tie)	Sweden
Seventh Place	Austria
(tie)	Hungary
Ninth Place	Italy
(tie)	France
(tie)	Japan
(tie)	Poland
Thirteenth Place	Belgium
(tie)	Latvia
(tie)	Switzerland

THE FIFTH OLYMPIC WINTER GAMES

ST. MORITZ, SWITZERLAND, January 30–February 8, 1948

FINAL PLACINGS

GOLD MEDAL	Canada
SILVER MEDAL	Czechoslovakia
BRONZE MEDAL	Switzerland
Fourth Place	United States
Fifth Place	Sweden
Sixth Place	Great Britain
Seventh Place	Poland
Eighth Place	Austria
Ninth Place	Italy

THE SIXTH OLYMPIC WINTER GAMES

OSLO, NORWAY, February 15–25, 1952

FINAL PLACINGS

GOLD MEDAL	Canada
SILVER MEDAL	United States
BRONZE MEDAL	Sweden
Fourth Place	Czechoslovakia
Fifth Place	Switzerland
Sixth Place	Poland
Seventh Place	Finland
Eighth Place	West Germany
Ninth Place	Norway

THE SEVENTH OLYMPIC WINTER GAMES

CORTINA d'AMPEZZO, ITALY, January 26–February 4, 1956

FINAL PLACINGS

GOLD MEDAL	Soviet Union
SILVER MEDAL	United States
BRONZE MEDAL	Canada
Fourth Place	Sweden

Fifth Place	Czechoslovakia
Sixth Place	Germany
Seventh Place	Italy
Eighth Place	Poland
Ninth Place	Switzerland
Tenth Place	Austria

THE EIGHTH OLYMPIC WINTER GAMES

SQUAW VALLEY, UNITED STATES, February 19–28, 1960

FINAL PLACINGS

GOLD MEDAL	United States
SILVER MEDAL	Canada
BRONZE MEDAL	Soviet Union
Fourth Place	Czechoslovakia
Fifth Place	Sweden
Sixth Place	Germany
Seventh Place	Finland
Eighth Place	Japan
Ninth Place	Australia

THE NINTH OLYMPIC WINTER GAMES

INNSBRUCK, AUSTRIA, January 29–February 9, 1964

FINAL PLACINGS

GOLD MEDAL	Soviet Union
SILVER MEDAL	Sweden
BRONZE MEDAL	Czechoslovakia
Fourth Place	Canada
Fifth Place	United States
Sixth Place	Finland
Seventh Place	Germany
Eighth Place	Switzerland
Ninth Place	Poland
Tenth Place	Norway
Eleventh Place	Japan

Twelfth Place	Romania
Thirteenth Place	Austria
Fourteenth Place	Yugoslavia
Fifteenth Place	Italy
Sixteenth Place	Hungary

THE TENTH OLYMPIC WINTER GAMES

GRENOBLE, FRANCE, February 6–17, 1968

FINAL PLACINGS

GOLD MEDAL	Soviet Union
SILVER MEDAL	Czechoslovakia
BRONZE MEDAL	Canada
Fourth Place	Sweden
Fifth Place	Finland
Sixth Place	United States
Seventh Place	West Germany
Eighth Place	East Germany
Ninth Place	Yugoslavia
Tenth Place	Japan
Eleventh Place	Norway
Twelfth Place	Romania
Thirteenth Place	Austria
Fourteenth Place	France

THE ELEVENTH OLYMPIC WINTER GAMES

SAPPORO, JAPAN, February 5–12, 1972

FINAL PLACINGS

GOLD MEDAL	Soviet Union
SILVER MEDAL	United States
BRONZE MEDAL	Czechoslovakia
Fourth Place	Sweden
Fifth Place	Finland
Sixth Place	Poland
Seventh Place	West Germany
Eighth Place	Norway

Ninth Place   Japan
Tenth Place   Switzerland
Eleventh Place   Yugoslavia

THE TWELFTH OLYMPIC WINTER GAMES

INNSBRUCK, AUSTRIA, February 4–13, 1976

FINAL PLACINGS

GOLD MEDAL   Soviet Union
SILVER MEDAL   Czechoslovakia
BRONZE MEDAL   West Germany
Fourth Place   Finland
Fifth Place   United States
Sixth Place   Poland
Seventh Place   Romania
Eighth Place   Austria
Ninth Place   Japan
Tenth Place   Yugoslavia
Eleventh Place   Switzerland
(tie)   Norway
Thirteenth Place   Bulgaria

THE THIRTEENTH OLYMPIC WINTER GAMES

LAKE PLACID, UNITED STATES, February 13–24, 1980

FINAL PLACINGS

GOLD MEDAL   United States
SILVER MEDAL   Soviet Union
BRONZE MEDAL   Sweden
Fourth Place   Finland
Fifth Place   Czechoslovakia
Sixth Place   Canada
Seventh Place   Poland
Eighth Place   Romania
Ninth Place   Netherlands
(tie)   Norway

Eleventh Place	West Germany
(tie)	Yugoslavia
Thirteenth Place	Japan

THE FOURTEENTH OLYMPIC WINTER GAMES

SARAJEVO, YUGOSLAVIA, February 7–19, 1984

FINAL PLACINGS

GOLD MEDAL	Soviet Union
SILVER MEDAL	Czechoslovakia
BRONZE MEDAL	Sweden
Fourth Place	Canada
Fifth Place	West Germany
Sixth Place	Finland
Seventh Place	United States
Eighth Place	Poland
Ninth Place	Italy
Tenth Place	Norway
Eleventh Place	Austria
(tie)	Yugoslavia

THE FIFTEENTH OLYMPIC WINTER GAMES

CALGARY, CANADA, February 13–28, 1988

FINAL PLACINGS

GOLD MEDAL	Soviet Union
SILVER MEDAL	Finland
BRONZE MEDAL	Sweden
Fourth Place	Canada
Fifth Place	West Germany
Sixth Place	Czechoslovakia
Seventh Place	United States
Eighth Place	Switzerland
Ninth Place	Austria
Tenth Place	Poland
Eleventh Place	France
Twelfth Place	Norway

THE SIXTEENTH OLYMPIC WINTER GAMES

ALBERTVILLE, FRANCE, February 8–23, 1992

FINAL PLACINGS

GOLD MEDAL	Unified Team
SILVER MEDAL	Canada
BRONZE MEDAL	Czechoslovakia
Fourth Place	United States
Fifth Place	Sweden
Sixth Place	Germany
Seventh Place	Finland
Eighth Place	France
Ninth Place	Norway
Tenth Place	Switzerland
Eleventh Place	Poland
Twelfth Place	Italy

THE SEVENTEENTH OLYMPIC WINTER GAMES

LILLEHAMMER, NORWAY, February 13–27, 1994

FINAL PLACINGS

GOLD MEDAL	Sweden
SILVER MEDAL	Canada
BRONZE MEDAL	Finland
Fourth Place	Russia
Fifth Place	Czech Republic
Sixth Place	Slovakia
Seventh Place	Germany
Eighth Place	United States
Ninth Place	Italy
Tenth Place	France
Eleventh Place	Norway
Twelfth Place	Austria

THE EIGHTEENTH OLYMPIC WINTER GAMES

NAGANO, JAPAN, February 7–22, 1998 (Men);
February 8–17, 1998 (Women)

FINAL PLACINGS: MEN

GOLD MEDAL	Czech Republic
SILVER MEDAL	Russia
BRONZE MEDAL	Finland
Fourth Place	Canada
Fifth Place (tie)	Sweden
	United States
	Belarus
	Kazakhstan
Ninth Place	Germany
Tenth Place	Slovakia
Eleventh Place	France
Twelfth Place	Italy
Thirteenth Place	Japan
Fourteenth Place	Austria

FINAL PLACINGS: WOMEN

GOLD MEDAL	United States
SILVER MEDAL	Canada
BRONZE MEDAL	Finland
Fourth Place	China
Fifth Place	Sweden
Sixth Place	Japan

THE NINETEENTH OLYMPIC WINTER GAMES

SALT LAKE CITY, UNITED STATES, February 9–24, 2002 (Men);
February 11–21, 2002 (Women)

FINAL PLACINGS: MEN

GOLD MEDAL	Canada
SILVER MEDAL	United States
BRONZE MEDAL	Russia

Fourth Place	Belarus
Fifth Place	Sweden
Sixth Place	Finland
Seventh Place	Czech Republic
Eighth Place	Germany
Ninth Place	Latvia
Tenth Place	Ukraine
Eleventh Place	Switzerland
Twelfth Place	Austria
Thirteenth Place	Slovakia
Fourteenth Place	France

FINAL PLACINGS: WOMEN

GOLD MEDAL	Canada
SILVER MEDAL	United States
BRONZE MEDAL	Sweden
Fourth Place	Finland
Fifth Place	Russia
Sixth Place	Germany
Seventh Place	China
Eighth Place	Kazakhstan

THE TWENTIETH OLYMPIC WINTER GAMES

TURIN, ITALY, February 10–26, 2006 (Men);
February 11–20, 2006 (Women)

FINAL PLACINGS: MEN

GOLD MEDAL	Sweden
SILVER MEDAL	Finland
BRONZE MEDAL	Czech Republic
Fourth Place	Russia
Fifth Place	Slovakia
Sixth Place	Switzerland
Seventh Place	Canada

Eighth Place	United States
Ninth Place	Kazakhstan
Tenth Place	Germany
Eleventh Place	Italy
Twelfth Place	Latvia

FINAL PLACINGS: WOMEN

GOLD MEDAL	Canada
SILVER MEDAL	Sweden
BRONZE MEDAL	United States
Fourth Place	Finland
Fifth Place	Germany
Sixth Place	Russia
Seventh Place	Switzerland
Eighth Place	Italy

ANAHEIM DUCKS

(name changed from Mighty Ducks of Anaheim on June 22, 2006)
First Game Played: October 8, 1993
Detroit Red Wings 7 at Mighty Ducks of Anaheim 2
Nickname Provenance: Owners, Disney, named team after a
popular kids' movie, *The Mighty Ducks* (1992)
Mascot: Wild Thing
Arena History: Arrowhead Pond, 1993–2006; Honda Centre
2006–present (capacity 17,174)
Retired Numbers: none
Hall of Famers: Players (1): Jari Kurri
Website: www.anaheimducks.com
Minor League Affiliate(s): Bakersfield Condors (ECHL)
Stanley Cups: (1) 2006–07
Hosted All-Star Game: none
1st Overall Draft Choices: none

ATLANTA THRASHERS

First Game Played: October 2, 1999
New Jersey Devils 4 at Atlanta Thrashers 1
Nickname Provenance: The Brown Thrasher is the state bird
of Georgia
Mascot: Thrash (b. September 4, 1999)
Arena History: Philips Arena, 1999–present (capacity 18,545)
Retired Numbers: Dan Snyder (43, unofficial)
Hall of Famers: none
Website: www. atlantathrashers.com
Minor League Affiliate(s): Chicago Wolves (AHL), Gwinnett
Gladiators (ECHL)
Stanley Cups: none

Hosted All-Star Game: (1) 2008
1st Overall Draft Choices: 1999 (Patrik Stefan), 2001 (Ilya Kovalchuk)

BOSTON BRUINS

First Game Played: December 1, 1924
Montreal Maroons 1 at Boston Bruins 2
Nickname Provenance: Named by owner Art Ross for the brown bear
Mascot: Blades (b. October 9, 2000)
Arena History: Boston Arena, 1924–28; Boston Garden, 1928–95; FleetCenter, 1995–2003; TD Banknorth Garden (formerly known as the FleetCenter), 2005–present (capacity 17,565)
Retired Numbers: Eddie Shore (2), Lionel Hitchman (3), Bobby Orr (4), Dit Clapper (5), Phil Esposito (7), Cam Neely (8), Johnny Bucyk (9), Milt Schmidt (15), Terry O'Reilly (24), Ray Bourque (77)
Hall of Famers: Players (47): Marty Barry, Bobby Bauer, Leo Boivin, Ray Bourque, Frank Brimsek, Johnny Bucyk, Billy Burch, Gerry Cheevers, Dit Clapper, Sprague Cleghorn, Paul Coffey, Roy Conacher, Bun Cook, Bill Cowley, Cy Denneny, Woody Dumart, Phil Esposito, Fern Flaman, Frank Fredrickson, Harvey Jackson, Tom Johnson, Duke Keats, Guy Lapointe, Brian Leetch, Harry Lumley, Mickey MacKay, Sylvio Mantha, Joe Mullen, Cam Neely, Harry Oliver, Bobby Orr, Bernie Parent, Brad Park, Jacques Plante, Babe Pratt, Bill Quackenbush, Jean Ratelle, Art Ross (inducted as Player, associated with Boston as Builder), Terry Sawchuk, Milt Schmidt, Eddie Shore, Babe Siebert, Hooley Smith, Allan Stanley, Nels Stewart, Tiny Thompson, Cooney Weiland; Builders (6): Charles Adams, Weston Adams, Walter Brown, Bud Poile (played with Boston, inducted as Builder), Glen Sather (played with Boston, inducted as Builder), Harry Sinden
Website: www.bostonbruins.com
Minor League Affiliate(s): Providence Bruins (AHL), Reading Royals (ECHL—shared with Toronto)

Stanley Cups: (5) 1928–29, 1938–39, 1940–41, 1969–70, 1971–72
Hosted All-Star Game: (2) 1971, 1996
1st Overall Draft Choices: 1982 (Gord Kluzak),
1997 (Joe Thornton)

BUFFALO SABRES

First Game Played: October 10, 1970
Buffalo Sabres 2 at Pittsburgh Penguins 1
Nickname Provenance: a contest determined the name Sabres
Mascot: Sabre-Tooth
Arena History: Memorial Auditorium ("The Aud"), 1970–96;
Marine Midland Bank Arena, 1996–2000; HSBC Arena (formerly
known as the Marine Midland Bank Arena), 2000–present
(capacity 18,690)
Retired Numbers: Tim Horton (2), Rick Martin (7), Gilbert Perreault
(11), Rene Robert (14), Pat LaFontaine (16), Danny Gare (18)
Hall of Famers: Players (8): Dick Duff, Tim Horton, Gilbert
Perreault, Dale Hawerchuk, Clark Gillies, Grant Fuhr, Pat
LaFontaine, Marcel Pronovost (inducted as Player, associated
with Buffalo as Builder); Builders (4): Scotty Bowman, Punch
Imlach, Seymour Knox III, Roger Neilson
Website: www.sabres.com
Minor League Affiliate(s): Portland Pirates (AHL)
Stanley Cups: none
Hosted All-Star Game: 1978
1st Overall Draft Choices: 1970 (Gilbert Perreault),
1987 (Pierre Turgeon)

CALGARY FLAMES

First Game Played:
As Atlanta Flames: October 7, 1972
Atlanta Flames 3 at New York Islanders 2
As Calgary Flames: October 9, 1980
Quebec Nordiques 5 at Calgary Flames 5

Nickname Provenance: Flames was chosen by contest, representative of Atlanta during the Civil War when much of it was burned to the ground

Mascot: Harvey the Hound

Arena History: The Omni (Atlanta), 1972–80; Stampede Corral, 1980–83; Olympic Saddledome, 1983–95; Canadian Airlines Saddledome, 1995–2001; Pengrowth Saddledome (same building as previous two Saddledomes), 2001–present (capacity 19,289)

Retired Numbers: Lanny McDonald (9), Mike Vernon (30)

Hall of Famers: Players (5): Lanny McDonald, Joe Mullen, Grant Fuhr, Brett Hull, Al MacInnis; Builders (2): Cliff Fletcher, Harley Hotchkiss

Website: www.calgaryflames.com

Minor League Affiliate(s): Abbotsford Heat (AHL)

Stanley Cups: (1) 1988–89

Hosted All-Star Game: 1985

1st Overall Draft Choices: none

CAROLINA HURRICANES

First Game Played:
As Hartford Whalers: October 11, 1979
Hartford Whalers 1 at Minnesota North Stars 4
As Carolina Hurricanes: October 1, 1997
Carolina Hurricanes 2 at Tampa Bay Lightning 4

Nickname Provenance: Whalers adopted because it contained the letters of the WHA and it was emblematic of the region

Mascot: Stormy

Arena History: Springfield Civic Center (Hartford), 1979–80; Hartford Civic Center (Hartford), 1980–97; Greensboro Coliseum, 1997–99; Raleigh Entertainment & Sports Arena, 1999–2003; RBC Center, 2003–present (capacity 18,730)

Retired Numbers: Glen Wesley (2), Ron Francis (10)

Hall of Famers: Players (5): Paul Coffey (Hartford/Carolina),

Gordie Howe (Hartford), Bobby Hull (Hartford), Dave Keon (Hartford), Ron Francis (Hartford/Carolina)
Website: www.carolinahcanes.com
Minor League Affiliate(s): Albany River Rats (AHL), Florida Everblades (ECHL—shared with Florida)
Stanley Cups: 2005–06
Hosted All-Star Game: 1986 (as Hartford Whalers)
1st Overall Draft Choices: none

CHICAGO BLACKHAWKS

First Game Played: November 17, 1926
Toronto St. Pats 1 at Chicago Blackhawks 4
Nickname Provenance: (spelling changed from "Black Hawks" to "Blackhawks" in 1986)
Mascot: Tommy the Hawk
Arena History: Chicago Coliseum, 1926–32; Chicago Stadium, 1932–94; United Center, 1995–present (opening of United Center delayed by disruption of 1994–95 NHL season, capacity 20,500)
Retired Numbers: Glenn Hall (1), Keith Magnuson (3), Pierre Pilote (3), Bobby Hull (9), Denis Savard (18), Stan Mikita (21), Tony Esposito (35)
Hall of Famers: Players (39): Sid Abel, Doug Bentley, Max Bentley, Georges Boucher, Frank Brimsek, Billy Burch, Paul Coffey, Lionel Conacher, Roy Conacher, Art Coulter, Babe Dye, Phil Esposito, Tony Esposito, Bill Gadsby, Charlie Gardiner, Herb Gardiner, Michel Goulet, Glenn Hall, George Hay, Bobby Hull, Duke Keats, Hugh Lehman, Ted Lindsay, Harry Lumley, Mickey MacKay, Stan Mikita, Howie Morenz, Bill Mosienko, Bert Olmstead, Bobby Orr, Pierre Pilote, Denis Savard, Earl Seibert, Clint Smith, Allan Stanley, Barney Stanley, Jack Stewart, Carl Voss (played for Chicago, inducted as Builder), Harry Watson; Builders (12): Al Arbour, Emile Francis (played for Chicago, inducted as Builder), Dick Irvin (played for Chicago, inducted as Builder), Tommy Ivan, John Mariucci (also played for Chicago), Major Frederic McLaughlin,

James Norris, James Norris, Jr., Rudy Pilous, Bud Poile (played for Chicago, inducted as Builder), Arthur Wirtz, William Wirtz
Website: www.chicagoblackhawks.com
Minor League Affiliate(s): Rockford IceHogs (AHL), Toledo Walleye (ECHL—shared with Detroit)
Stanley Cups: (3) 1933–34, 1937–38, 1960–61
Hosted All-Star Game: (4) 1948, 1961, 1974, 1991
1st Overall Draft Choices: Pat Kane

COLORADO AVALANCHE

First Game Played:
As Quebec Nordiques: October 10, 1979
Atlanta Flames 5 at Quebec Nordiques 3
As Colorado Avalanche: October 6, 1995
Detroit Red Wings 2 at Colorado Avalanche 3
Nickname Provenance: Team owners polled fans. Out of 8 names offered, Avalanche was the most popular.
Mascot: Howler
Arena History: McNichols Sports Arena, 1995–99; Pepsi Center, 1999–present (capacity 18,007)
Retired Numbers: J-C Tremblay (3), Marc Tardif (8), Michel Goulet (16), Peter Stastny (26), Patrick Roy (33), Ray Bourque (77)
Hall of Famers: Players (6): Ray Bourque, Patrick Roy, Michel Goulet (Quebec), Jari Kurri, Guy Lafleur (Quebec), Peter Stastny (Quebec)
Website: www.coloradoavalanche.com
Minor League Affiliate(s): Lake Erie Monsters (AHL), Johnstown Chiefs (ECHL—shared with Columbus), Charlotte Checkers (ECHL—shared with NY Rangers)
Stanley Cups: (2) 1995–96, 2000–01
Hosted All-Star Game: 2001
1st Overall Draft Choices: 1989 (Mats Sundin—Quebec Nordiques), 1990 (Owen Nolan—Quebec), 1991 (Eric Lindros—Quebec)

COLUMBUS BLUE JACKETS

First Game Played: October 7, 2000
Chicago Blackhawks 5 at Columbus Blue Jackets 3
Nickname Provenance: reflects patriotism and history of the Civil War
Mascot: Stinger
Arena History: Nationwide Arena, 2000–present (capacity 18,136)
Retired Numbers: none
Hall of Famers: none
Website: www. bluejackets.com
Minor League Affiliate(s): Syracuse Crunch (AHL), Johnstown
Chiefs (ECHL—shared with Colorado)
Stanley Cups: none
Hosted All-Star Game: none
1st Overall Draft Choices: 2002 (Rick Nash)

DALLAS STARS

First Game Played:
As Minnesota North Stars: October 11, 1967
Minnesota North Stars 2 at St. Louis Blues 2
As Dallas Stars: October 5, 1993
Detroit Red Wings 4 at Dallas Stars 6
Nickname Provenance: shortening of North Stars, consistent
with Texas as the Lone Star state
Mascot: none
Arena History: Metropolitan Sports Center (also known as the Met
Center), 1967–93; Reunion Arena, 1993–2001; American Airlines
Center, 2001–present (capacity 18,532)
Retired Numbers: Neal Broten (7), Bill Goldsworthy (8), Bill
Masterton (19)
Hall of Famers: Players (6): Mike Gartner (Minnesota), Harry
Howell (Minnesota), Brett Hull, Larry Murphy (Minnesota), Gump
Worsley (Minnesota), Leo Boivin (Minnesota); Builders (3): Herb
Brooks (coached Minnesota), Glen Sather (played for University

of Minnesota), John Mariucci
Website: www.dallasstars.com
Minor League Affiliate(s): Allen Americans (CHL), Idaho
Steelheads (ECHL), Texas Stars (AHL)
Stanley Cups: 1998–99
Hosted All-Star Game: 1972 (as North Stars); 2007
1st Overall Draft Choices: 1978 (Bobby Smith—Minnesota North
Stars), 1983 (Brian Lawton—Minnesota), 1988 (Mike Modano—
Minnesota)

DETROIT RED WINGS

First Game Played:
As Detroit Cougars: November 18, 1926
Boston Bruins 2 at Detroit Cougars 0
As Detroit Falcons: November 13, 1930
New York Rangers 0 at Detroit Falcons 1
As Detroit Red Wings: November 10, 1932
Chicago Blackhawks 1 at Detroit Red Wings 3
Nickname Provenance: Owner James Norris, a Montreal native,
used the Winged Wheel from his hometown team and combined
it with Detroit's place in America as a car-making centre
Mascot: Al the Octopus
Arena History: Windsor Arena (Border Cities Arena), 1926–27;
Olympia, 1929–79; Joe Louis Arena, 1979–present (capacity 20,066)
Retired Numbers: Terry Sawchuk (1), Ted Lindsay (7), Gordie
Howe (9), Alex Delvecchio (10), Sid Abel (12), Steve Yzerman (19)
Hall of Famers: Players (51): Sid Abel, Jack Adams (inducted as
Player, associated with Detroit as builder), Marty Barry, Andy
Bathgate, Johnny Bucyk, Paul Coffey, Charlie Conacher, Roy
Conacher, Alec Connell, Alex Delvecchio, Marcel Dionne, Bernie
Federko, Slava Fetisov, Frank Foyston, Frank Fredrickson, Bill
Gadsby, Ed Giacomin, Ebbie Goodfellow, Glenn Hall, Doug
Harvey, George Hay, Harry Holmes, Gordie Howe, Syd Howe, Brett
Hull, Duke Keats, Red Kelly, Brian Kilrea (played for Detroit,

inducted as Builder), Igor Larionov, Herbie Lewis, Ted Lindsay, Harry Lumley, Frank Mahovlich, Larry Murphy, Reg Noble, Brad Park, Bud Poile (played for Detroit, inducted as Builder), Marcel Pronovost, Bill Quackenbush, Luc Robitaille, Borje Salming, Terry Sawchuk, Earl Seibert, Darryl Sittler, Jack Stewart, Tiny Thompson, Norm Ullman, Jack Walker, Harry Watson, Cooney Weiland, Steve Yzerman; Builders (8): Al Arbour (played for Detroit, inducted as Builder), Leo Boivin (played for Detroit, inducted as Builder), Scotty Bowman, Tommy Ivan, Bruce Norris, James Norris, James Norris, Jr., Carl Voss (played for Detroit, inducted as Builder)

Website: www.detroitredwings.com

Minor League Affiliate(s): Grand Rapids Griffins (AHL), Toledo Walleye (ECHL—shared with Chicago)

Stanley Cups: (11) 1935–36, 1936–37, 1942–43, 1949–50, 1951–52, 1953–54, 1954–55, 1996–97, 1997–98, 2002–02, 2007–08

Hosted All-Star Game: (5) 1950, 1952, 1954, 1955, 1980

1st Overall Draft Choices: 1977 (Dale McCourt), 1986 (Joe Murphy)

EDMONTON OILERS

First Game Played: October 10, 1979
Edmonton Oilers 2 at Chicago Black Hawks 4

Nickname Provenance: from Alberta Oilers and later Edmonton Oilers of WHA, to refer to Alberta's place as an oil capital in Canada

Mascot: none

Arena History: Northlands Coliseum, 1979–99; Skyreach Centre, 1999–2003; Rexall Place, 2005–present (all three are the same building, capacity 16,839)

Retired Numbers: Al Hamilton (3), Paul Coffey (7), Glenn Anderson (9) Mark Messier (11), Jari Kurri (17), Grant Fuhr (31), Wayne Gretzky (99—leaguewide recognition)

Hall of Famers: Players (6): Glenn Anderson, Paul Coffey, Grant Fuhr, Wayne Gretzky, Jari Kurri, Mark Messier; Builders (1): Glen Sather

Website: www.edmontonoilers.com

Minor League Affiliate(s): Springfield Falcons (AHL), Stockton Thunder (ECHL)
Stanley Cups: (5) 1983–84, 1984–85, 1986–87, 1987–88, 1989–90
Hosted All-Star Game: 1989
1st Overall Draft Choices: none

FLORIDA PANTHERS

First Game Played: October 6, 1993
Florida Panthers 4 at Chicago Blackhawks 4
Nickname Provenance: named for the animal, which is common in Florida
Mascot: Stanley C. Panther
Arena History: Miami Arena, 1993–99; National Car Rental Center, 1999–2002; Office Depot Center, 2002–03; BankAtlantic Center, 2005–present (previous three are the same building, capacity 19,250)
Retired Numbers: none
Hall of Famers: Players (1): Igor Larionov
Website: www.floridapanthers.com
Minor League Affiliate(s): Rochester Americans (AHL), Florida Everblades (ECHL—shared with Carolina)
Stanley Cups: none
Hosted All-Star Game: 2003
1st Overall Draft Choices: 1994 (Ed Jovanovski)

LOS ANGELES KINGS

First Game Played: October 14, 1967
Philadelphia Flyers 2 at Los Angeles Kings 4
Nickname Provenance: named by owner Jack Kent Cooke to give the team a royal (i.e., important) sound to it
Mascot: Bailey
Arena History: Long Beach Arena, October 1967; Los Angeles Sports Arena, November–December 1967; The Forum, 1967–88;

Great Western Forum, 1988–99 (same building as The Forum); Staples Center, 1999–present (capacity 18,118)

Retired Numbers: Marcel Dionne (16), Dave Taylor (18), Luc Robitaille (20), Rogie Vachon (30), Wayne Gretzky (99—leaguewide recognition)

Hall of Famers: Players (14): Paul Coffey, Marcel Dionne, Dick Duff, Grant Fuhr, Wayne Gretzky, Harry Howell, Jari Kurri, Larry Murphy, Bob Pulford, Larry Robinson, Luc Robitaille, Terry Sawchuk, Steve Shutt, Billy Smith; Builders (1): Brian Kilrea (played for Los Angeles, inducted as Builder)

Website: www.lakings.com

Minor League Affiliate(s): Manchester Monarchs (AHL), Ontario Reign (ECHL)

Stanley Cups: none

Hosted All-Star Game: (2) 1981, 2002

1st Overall Draft Choices: none

MINNESOTA WILD

First Game Played: October 6, 2000
Minnesota Wild 1 at Mighty Ducks of Anaheim 3

Nickname Provenance: selected by fan contest

Mascot: Nordy

Arena History: Xcel Energy Center, 2000–present (capacity 18,064)

Retired Numbers: none

Hall of Famers: none

Website: www.wild.com

Minor League Affiliate(s): Houston Aeros (AHL)

Stanley Cups: none

Hosted All-Star Game: (1) 2004

1st Overall Draft Choices: none

MONTREAL CANADIENS

First Game Played:
In NHA: January 19, 1910
Montreal Canadiens 4 at Renfrew Millionaires 9
In NHL: December 19, 1917
Ottawa Senators 4 at Montreal Canadiens 7

Nickname Provenance: as a Canadian team based in Quebec, simply called Canadiens in French (they are also known as "the Habs," short for "*les habitants*," a name given to the early settlers of the province)

Mascot: Youppi

Arena History: Westmount Arena, 1909–1918; Jubilee Arena, 1918–20; Mount Royal Arena, 1920–24; Montreal Forum, 1924–96 (refurbished in 1968); Molson Centre, 1996–2002; Bell Centre, 2002–present (same building as Molson Centre, capacity 21,273)

Retired Numbers: Jacques Plante (1), Doug Harvey (2), Jean Beliveau (4), Bernie Geoffrion (5), Howie Morenz (7), Maurice Richard (9), Guy Lafleur (10), Yvan Cournoyer (12), Dickie Moore (12), Henri Richard (16), Serge Savard (18), Larry Robinson (19), Bob Gainey (23), Ken Dryden (29), Patrick Roy (33)

Hall of Famers: Players (50): Marty Barry, Harry Cameron, Gord Drillon, Dick Duff, Tony Esposito, Rod Langway, Roy Worters, Dick Irvin (inducted as Player, associated with Montreal as Builder), Howie Morenz, Georges Vezina, Aurel Joliat, Newsy Lalonde, Joe Malone, Sprague Cleghorn, Herb Gardiner, Sylvio Mantha, Joe Hall, George Hainsworth, Maurice Richard, Jack Laviolette, Didier Pitre, Bill Durnan, Babe Siebert, Toe Blake, Emile Bouchard, Elmer Lach, Ken Reardon, Tom Johnson, Jean Beliveau, Bernie Geoffrion, Doug Harvey, Dickie Moore, Jacques Plante, Henri Richard, Patrick Roy, Gump Worsley, Frank Mahovlich, Yvan Cournoyer, Ken Dryden, Jacques Lemaire, Bert Olmstead, Serge Savard, Jacques Laperriere, Guy Lafleur, Buddy O'Connor, Bob Gainey, Guy Lapointe, Steve Shutt, Larry Robinson, Denis Savard; Builders (12): Cliff Fletcher, William Northey, Hon. Donat

Raymond, Frank Selke, Ambrose O'Brien, Leo Dandurand, Tommy Gorman, Hon. Hartland de Montarville Molson, Joseph Cattarinich, Sam Pollock, Scotty Bowman, Glen Sather (played with Montreal, inducted as Builder)

Website: www.canadiens.com

Minor League Affiliate(s): Hamilton Bulldogs (AHL), Cincinnati Cyclones (ECHL—shared with Nashville)

Stanley Cups: (23) 1923–24, 1929–30, 1930–31, 1943–44, 1945–46, 1952–53, 1955–56, 1956–57, 1957–58, 1958–59, 1959–60, 1964–65, 1065–66, 1967–68, 1968–69, 1970–71, 1972–73, 1975–76, 1976–77, 1977–78, 1978–79, 1985–86, 1992–93

Hosted All-Star Game: (12) 1953, 1956, 1957, 1958, 1959, 1960, 1965, 1967, 1969, 1975, 1993, 2009

1st Overall Draft Choices: 1969 (Rejean Houle), 1971 (Guy Lafleur), 1980 (Doug Wickenheiser)

NASHVILLE PREDATORS

First Game Played: October 10, 1998
Florida Panthers 1 at Nashville Predators 0

Nickname Provenance: selected by fans

Mascot: Gnash

Arena History: Gaylord Entertainment Center, 1998–2006; Sommet Centre, 2007–present (capacity 17,113)

Retired Numbers: none

Hall of Famers: none

Website: www.nashvillepredators.com

Minor League Affiliate(s): Milwaukee Admirals (AHL), Cincinnati Cyclones (ECHL—shared with Montreal)

Stanley Cups: none

Hosted All-Star Game: none

1st Overall Draft Choices: none

NEW JERSEY DEVILS

First Game Played:
As Kansas City Scouts: October 9, 1974
Kansas City Scouts 2 at Toronto Maple Leafs 6
As Colorado Rockies: October 5, 1976
Toronto Maple Leafs 2 at Colorado Rockies 4
As New Jersey Devils: October 5, 1982
Pittsburgh Penguins 3 at New Jersey Devils 3
Nickname Provenance: selected by fans in reference to legend of a
demonic baby produced by one Mrs. Leeds in 1735, her 13th child
Mascot: The Devil
Arena History: Kemper Arena (Kansas City), 1974–76; McNichols
Sports Arena (Colorado), 1976–82; Brendan Byrne Arena, 1982–83;
Byrne Meadowlands Arena, 1983–92 (same building as Brendan
Byrne Arena); Meadowlands Arena (same building as Byrne
Meadowlands Arena), 1992–96; Continental Airlines Arena (same
building as Meadowlands Arena), 1996–2007; Prudential Center,
2007–present (capacity 17,625)
Retired Numbers: Ken Daneyko (3), Scott Stevens (4)
Hall of Famers: Players (5): Slava Fetisov, Igor Larionov, Lanny
McDonald (Colorado Rockies), Peter Stastny, Scott Stevens;
Builders (2): Herb Brooks, Lou Lamoriello
Website: www.newjerseydevils.com
Minor League Affiliate(s): Lowell Devils (AHL), Trenton Devils
(ECHL)
Stanley Cups: (3) 1994–95, 1999–2000, 2002–03
Hosted All-Star Game: 1984
1st Overall Draft Choices: 1979 (Rob Ramage—Colorado Rockies)

NEW YORK ISLANDERS

First Game Played: October 7, 1972
Atlanta Flames 3 at New York Islanders 2
Nickname Provenance: named, simply, because the team is
located on Long Island, New York

Mascot: none
Arena History: Nassau Veterans' Memorial Coliseum, 1972–present (capacity 16,234)
Retired Numbers: Denis Potvin (5), Clark Gillies (9), Bryan Trottier (19), Mike Bossy (22), Bob Nystrom (23), Billy Smith (31)
Hall of Famers: Players (6): Mike Bossy, Pat LaFontaine, Denis Potvin, Billy Smith, Bryan Trottier, Clark Gillies; Builders (2): Al Arbour, Bill Torrey
Website: www.newyorkislanders.com
Minor League Affiliate(s): Bridgeport Sound Tigers (AHL), Utah Grizzlies (ECHL), Odessa Jackalopes (CHL)
Stanley Cups: (4) 1979–80, 1980–81, 1981–82, 1982–83
Hosted All-Star Game: 1983
1st Overall Draft Choices: 1972 (Billy Harris), 1973 (Denis Potvin), 2000 (Rick DiPietro), 2009 (John Tavares)

NEW YORK RANGERS

First Game Played: November 16, 1926
Montreal Maroons 0 at New York Rangers 1
Nickname Provenance: Emerged when sportswriters in New York called the new franchise Tex's Rangers, in reference to Tex Rickard, the president of Madison Square Garden and the man who assembled the executive for the team in 1926
Mascot: none
Arena History: Madison Square Garden, 1926–68; Madison Square Garden, 1968–present (newly built, capacity 18,200)
Retired Numbers: Ed Giacomin (1), Brian Leetch (2), Harry Howell (3), Rod Gilbert (7), Andy Bathgate (9), Adam Graves (9) Mark Messier (11), Mike Richter (35)
Hall of Famers: Players (47): Glenn Anderson, Dick Duff, Howie Morenz, Lester Patrick, Bill Cook, Frank Boucher, Ching Johnson, Babe Siebert, Earl Seibert, Doug Bentley, Max Bentley, Babe Pratt, Neil Colville, Bryan Hextall, Bill Gadsby, Terry Sawchuk, Bernie Geoffrion, Doug Harvey, Charlie Rayner, Art Coulter, Johnny

Bower, Tim Horton, Andy Bathgate, Jacques Plante, Harry Howell, Lynn Patrick, Pat LaFontaine, Harry Lumley, Gump Worsley, Allan Stanley, Rod Gilbert, Phil Esposito, Jean Ratelle, Ed Giacomin, Guy Lafleur, Buddy O'Connor, Brad Park, Clint Smith, Marcel Dionne, Edgar Laprade, Bun Cook, Wayne Gretzky, Mike Gartner, Jari Kurri, Mark Messier, Brian Leetch, Luc Robitaille; Builders (9): Herb Brooks, Bud Poile (played with Rangers, inducted as Builder), Emile Francis (also played for Rangers), William Jennings, John Kilpatrick, Roger Neilson, Craig Patrick, Glen Sather (played with Rangers, inducted as Builder), Carl Voss (played with Rangers, inducted as Builder)
Website: www.newyorkrangers.com
Minor League Affiliate(s): Hartford Wolf Pack (AHL), Charlotte Checkers (ECHL—shared with Colorado)
Stanley Cups: (4) 1927–28, 1932–33, 1939–40, 1993–94
Hosted All-Star Game: (2) 1973, 1994
1st Overall Draft Choices: none

OTTAWA SENATORS

First Game Played: October 8, 1992
Montreal Canadiens 3 at Ottawa Senators 5
Nickname Provenance: from original team of same name from 1917–34
Mascot: Spartacat
Arena History: Civic Centre, 1992–96; Palladium, 1996; Corel Centre, 1996–2006; Scotiabank Place, 2006–present (same building as Palladium and Corel Centre, capacity 19,153)
Retired Numbers: Frank Finnigan (8)
Hall of Famers: none
Website: www.ottawasenators.com
Minor League Affiliate(s): Binghamton Senators (AHL), Elmira Jackals (ECHL)
Stanley Cups: none
Hosted All-Star Game: none

1st Overall Draft Choices: 1993 (Alexandre Daigle), 1995 (Bryan Berard), 1996 (Chris Phillips)

PHILADELPHIA FLYERS

First Game Played: October 11, 1967
Philadelphia Flyers 1 at Oakland Seals 5
Nickname Provenance: named by a nine-year-old in a fan contest
Mascot: none
Arena History: The Spectrum, 1967–96; CoreStates Center, 1996–98; First Union Center, 1998–2003 (same building as CoreStates Center); Wachovia Center, 2003–present (same building as First Union Center, capacity 19,523)
Retired Numbers: Bernie Parent (1), Barry Ashbee (4), Bill Barber (7), Bobby Clarke (16)
Hall of Famers: Players (7): Paul Coffey, Bernie Parent, Bobby Clarke, Bill Barber, Dale Hawerchuk, Darryl Sittler, Allan Stanley; Builders (2): Ed Snider, Keith Allen
Website: www.philadelphiaflyers.com
Minor League Affiliate(s): Adirondack Phantoms (AHL), Kalamazoo Wings (ECHL—shared with San Jose)
Stanley Cups: (2) 1973–74, 1974–75
Hosted All-Star Game: (2) 1976, 1992
1st Overall Draft Choices: 1975 (Mel Bridgman)

PHOENIX COYOTES

First Game Played:
As Winnipeg Jets: October 10, 1979
Winnipeg Jets 2 at Pittsburgh Penguins 4
As Phoenix Coyotes: October 5, 1996
Phoenix Coyotes 0 at Hartford Whalers 1
Nickname Provenance: the logo depicts a Kachina coyote, indigenous to the region
Mascot: Howler

Arena History: Winnipeg Arena (Winnipeg), 1979–96; America West Arena, 1996–98; Cellular One Ice Den (same building as America West Arena), 1998–99; America West Arena, 1999–2000; Alltel Ice Den, 2000–03; Glendale Arena, 2003–2008, Jobing.com Arena (same building as Glendale Arena, capacity 17,799)
Retired Numbers: Bobby Hull (9), Thomas Steen (25)
Hall of Famers: Players (5): Mike Gartner, Brett Hull, Bobby Hull (Winnipeg), Dale Hawerchuk (Winnipeg), Serge Savard (Winnipeg)
Website: www.phoenixcoyotes.com
Minor League Affiliate(s): San Antonio Rampage (AHL), Las Vegas Wranglers (ECHL), Arizona Sundogs (CHC)
Stanley Cups: none
Hosted All-Star Game: none
1st Overall Draft Choices: 1981 (Dale Hawerchuk—Winnipeg Jets)

PITTSBURGH PENGUINS

First Game Played: October 11, 1967
Montreal Canadiens 2 at Pittsburgh Penguins 1
Nickname Provenance: After the Pittsburgh arena opened in 1961, it was dubbed "The Igloo" for its shape. As a result, when Pittsburgh was awarded an NHL team in 1967, owners opted for a nickname compatible with "Igloo" and decided on "Penguins."
Mascot: Iceburgh
Arena History: Civic Arena ("The Igloo"), 1967–2000; Mellon Arena, 2000–present (same building as Civic Arena, capacity 16,940)
Retired Numbers: Michel Briere (21), Mario Lemieux (66)
Hall of Famers: Players (11): Leo Boivin, Paul Coffey, Tim Horton, Red Kelly (inducted as Player, associated with Pittsburgh as Builder), Andy Bathgate, Mario Lemieux, Larry Murphy, Bryan Trottier, Joe Mullen, Ron Francis, Luc Robitaille; Builders (4): Scotty Bowman, Bob Johnson, Craig Patrick, Glen Sather (played for Pittsburgh, inducted as Builder)
Website: www.pittsburghpenguins.com

Minor League Affiliate(s): Wilkes-Barre/Scranton Penguins
(AHL), Wheeling Nailers (ECHL)
Stanley Cups: (3) 1990–91, 1991–92, 2008–09
Hosted All-Star Game: 1990
1st Overall Draft Choices: 1984 (Mario Lemieux), 2003 (Marc-
Andre Fleury), 2005 (Sidney Crosby)

ST. LOUIS BLUES

First Game Played: October 11, 1967
Minnesota North Stars 2 at St. Louis Blues 2
Nickname Provenance: named to remember the city's place in
the history of music
Mascot: Louie
Arena History: St. Louis Arena, 1967–94; Kiel Center, 1994–2000; Savvis
Center, 2000–2008, Scottrade Center, 2008–present (same building as
Kiel Center and Savvis Center, capacity 19,022)
Retired Numbers: Al MacInnis (2), Bob Gassoff (3), Barclay Plager
(8), Brian Sutter (11), Brett Hull (16), Bernie Federko (24)
Hall of Famers: Players (15): Glenn Anderson, Grant Fuhr, Bernie
Federko, Dale Hawerchuk, Joe Mullen, Wayne Gretzky, Peter
Stastny, Guy Lapointe, Jacques Plante, Glenn Hall, Dickie Moore,
Doug Harvey, Al MacInnis, Scott Stevens, Brett Hull; Builders (7):
Roger Neilson, Al Arbour, Scotty Bowman, Emile Francis, Craig
Patrick (played for St. Louis, inducted as Builder), Lynn Patrick,
Glen Sather (played for St. Louis, inducted as Builder)
Website: www.stlouisblues.com
Minor League Affiliate(s): Peoria Rivermen (AHL),
Alaska Aces (ECHL)
Stanley Cups: none
Hosted All-Star Game: (2) 1970, 1988
1st Overall Draft Choices: none

SAN JOSE SHARKS

First Game Played: October 4, 1991
San Jose Sharks 3 at Vancouver Canucks 4
Nickname Provenance: named by team owners after a fan contest
Mascot: S.J. Sharkie (b. January 1992)
Arena History: Cow Palace, 1991–93; San Jose Arena, 1993–2001; Compaq Center, 2001–03; HP Pavilion, 2003–present (same building as Compaq Center and San Jose Arena, capacity 17,496)
Retired Numbers: none
Hall of Famers: (1) Igor Larionov
Website: www.sjsharks.com
Minor League Affiliate(s): Worcester Sharks (AHL), Kalamazoo Wings (ECHL—shared with Philadelphia), China Sharks (Asian Hockey League)
Stanley Cups: none
Hosted All-Star Game: 1997
1st Overall Draft Choices: none

TAMPA BAY LIGHTNING

First Game Played: October 7, 1992
Chicago Blackhawks 3 at Tampa Bay Lightning 7
Nickname Provenance: Tampa Bay is, statistically, the lightning capital of the world.
Mascot: Thunder Bug
Arena History: Expo Hall, 1992–93; ThunderDome, 1993–96 (five home games played at Orlando Arena); Ice Palace, 1998–2003; *St. Petersburg Times* Forum, 2003–present (same building as Ice Palace, capacity 19,758)
Retired Numbers: none
Hall of Famers: Players (1): Denis Savard
Website: www.tampabaylightning.com
Minor League Affiliate(s): Norfolk Admirals (AHL), Colorado Eagles (CHL)
Stanley Cups: 2003–04
Hosted All-Star Game: 1999

1st Overall Draft Choices: 1992 (Roman Hamrlik), 1998 (Vincent Lecavalier), 2008 (Steve Stamkos)

TORONTO MAPLE LEAFS

First Game Played:
As Toronto Arenas: December 19, 1917
Toronto Arenas 9 at Montreal Wanderers 10
As Toronto St. Pats: December 23, 1919
Toronto St. Pats 0 at Ottawa Senators 3
As Toronto Maple Leafs: February 17, 1927
New York Americans 1 at Toronto Maple Leafs 4
Nickname Provenance: named by owner Conn Smythe after a World War I regiment
Mascot: Carlton the Bear
Arena History: Arena Gardens (Mutual Street Arena), 1917–31; Maple Leaf Gardens, 1931–99; Air Canada Centre, 1999–present (capacity 18,819)
Retired Numbers: Bill Barilko (5), Ace Bailey (6)
Honoured Numbers: Turk Broda (1), Johnny Bower (1), Red Kelly (4), King Clancy (7), Tim Horton (7), Charlie Conacher (9), Ted Kennedy (9), Syl Apps (10), George Armstrong (10), Wendel Clark (17), Borje Salming (21), Frank Mahovlich (27), Darryl Sittler (27), Doug Gilmour (93)
Hall of Famers: Players (59): Jack Adams, Glenn Anderson, Syl Apps, Al Arbour, George Armstrong, Ace Bailey, Andy Bathgate, Max Bentley, Leo Boivin, Johnny Bower, Turk Broda, Harry Cameron, Gerry Cheevers, King Clancy, Sprague Cleghorn, Charlie Conacher, Rusty Crawford, Hap Day, Gord Drillon, Dick Duff, Babe Dye, Fern Flaman, Grant Fuhr, Mike Gartner, Eddie Gerard, George Hainsworth, Harry Holmes, Red Horner, Tim Horton, Syd Howe, Harvey Jackson, Red Kelly, Ted Kennedy, Dave Keon, Brian Leetch, Harry Lumley, Frank Mahovlich, Lanny McDonald, Dickie Moore, Larry Murphy, Frank Nighbor, Reg Noble, Bert Olmstead, Bernie Parent, Pierre Pilote, Jacques Plante, Babe Pratt, Joe Primeau,

Marcel Pronovost, Bob Pulford, Borje Salming, Terry Sawchuk, Sweeney Schriner, Darryl Sittler, Allan Stanley, Norm Ullman, Carl Voss, Harry Watson, Ron Francis; Builders (12): Harold Ballard, J.P. Bickell, Cliff Fletcher, Foster Hewitt, William Hewitt, Punch Imlach, Dick Irvin (played for Toronto, inducted as Builder), Frank Mathers (played for Toronto, inducted as Builder), Rudy Pilous, Bud Poile (played for Toronto, inducted as Builder), Frank Selke, Conn Smythe

Website: www.torontomapleleafs.com

Minor League Affiliate(s): Toronto Marlies (AHL), Reading Royals (ECHL—shared with Boston)

Stanley Cups: (13) 1917–18, 1921–22, 1931–32, 1941–42, 1944–45, 1946–47, 1947–48, 1948–49, 1950–51, 1961–62, 1962–63, 1963–64, 1966–67

Hosted All-Star Game: (8) 1947, 1949, 1951, 1962, 1963, 1964, 1968, 2000

1st Overall Draft Choices: 1985 (Wendel Clark)

VANCOUVER CANUCKS

First Game Played: October 9, 1970
Los Angeles Kings 3 at Vancouver Canucks 1

Nickname Provenance: continuation of WHL franchise nickname

Mascot: Fin the Whale

Arena History: Pacific Coliseum, 1970–95; General Motors (GM) Place, 1995–present (capacity 18,630)

Retired Numbers: Wayne Maki (11, unofficial, later worn by Mark Messier but not before or since), Stan Smyl (12), Trevor Linden (16)

Hall of Famers: (3) Igor Larionov, Cam Neely, Mark Messier

Website: www.canucks.com

Minor League Affiliate(s): Manitoba Moose (AHL), Victoria Salmon Kings (ECHL)

Stanley Cups: none

Hosted All-Star Game: (2) 1977, 1998

1st Overall Draft Choices: none

WASHINGTON CAPITALS

First Game Played: October 9, 1974

Washington Capitals 3 at New York Rangers 6

Nickname Provenance: so called because the team plays in the capital city of the USA

Mascot: Slapshot

Arena History: Capital Center, 1974–93; US Air Arena, 1993–95 (same building as Capital Center); MCI Center, 1995–present; Verizon Center (same building as MCI Center—capacity 18,277)

Retired Numbers: Rod Langway (5), Yvon Labre (7), Mike Gartner (11), Dale Hunter (32)

Hall of Famers: Players (4): Mike Gartner, Rod Langway, Larry Murphy, Scott Stevens; Builders (1): Craig Patrick (played for Washington, inducted as Builder)

Website: www.washingtoncaps.com

Minor League Affiliate(s): Hershey Bears (AHL), South Carolina Stingrays (ECHL)

Stanley Cups: none

Hosted All-Star Game: 1982

1st Overall Draft Choices: 1974 (Greg Joly), 1976 (Rick Green), (2005) Alexander Ovechkin

FINAL STANDINGS, REGULAR SEASON, 2008–09

EASTERN CONFERENCE

Northeast Division	GP	W	L	OT	GF	GA	Pts
Boston	82	53	19	10	274	196	116
Montreal	82	41	30	11	249	247	93
Buffalo	82	41	32	9	250	234	91
Ottawa	82	36	35	11	217	237	83
Toronto	82	34	35	13	250	293	81

Southeast Division							
Washington	82	50	24	8	272	245	108
Carolina	82	45	30	7	239	226	97
Florida	82	41	30	11	234	231	93
Atlanta	82	35	41	6	257	280	76
Tampa Bay	82	24	40	18	210	279	66

Atlantic Division							
New Jersey	82	51	27	4	244	209	106
Pittsburgh	82	45	28	9	264	239	99
Philadelphia	82	44	27	11	264	238	99
NY Rangers	82	43	30	9	210	218	95
NY Islanders	82	26	47	9	201	279	61

WESTERN CONFERENCE

Central Division							
Detroit	82	51	21	10	295	244	112
Chicago	82	46	24	12	264	216	104
St. Louis	82	41	31	10	233	233	92
Columbus	82	41	31	10	226	230	92
Nashville	82	40	34	8	213	233	88

Northwest Division	GP	W	L	OT	GF	GA	P
Vancouver	82	45	27	10	246	220	100
Calgary	82	46	30	6	254	248	98
Minnesota	82	40	33	9	219	200	89
Edmonton	82	38	35	9	234	248	85
Colorado	82	32	45	5	199	257	69
Pacific Division							
San Jose	82	53	18	11	257	204	117
Anaheim	82	42	33	7	245	238	91
Dallas	82	36	35	11	230	257	83
Phoenix	82	36	39	7	208	252	79
Los Angeles	82	34	37	11	207	234	79

SCORING LEADERS & GOALIE LEADERS, 2008–09

(Nationality and NHL affiliation in parentheses)

Points

Evgeni Malkin (RUS–PIT)	113
Alexander Ovechkin (RUS–WAS)	110
Sidney Crosby (CAN–PIT)	103
Pavel Datsyuk (RUS–DET)	97
Zach Parise (USA–NJ)	94
Ryan Getzlaf (CAN–ANA)	91
Ilya Kovalchuk (RUS–ATL)	91
Jarome Iginla (CAN–CAL)	89
Nicklas Backstrom (SWE–WAS)	88
Marc Savard (CAN–BOS)	88

Goals

Alexander Ovechkin (RUS–WAS)	56
Jeff Carter (CAN–PHI)	46
Zach Parise (USA–NJ)	45
Ilya Kovalchuk (RUS–ATL)	43
Marian Hossa (SVK–DET)	40
Rick Nash (CAN–CBJ)	40
Eric Staal (CAN–CAR)	40
Thomas Vanek (AUT–BUF)	40
Mike Cammalleri (CAN–CAL)	39
Dany Heatley (CAN–OTT)	39

Assists

Evgeni Malkin (RUS–PIT)	78
Sidney Crosby (CAN–PIT)	70
Nicklas Backstrom (SWE–WAS)	66
Ryan Getzlaf (CAN–ANA)	66

Pavel Datsyuk (RUS–DET)	65
Marc Savard (CAN–BOS)	63
Joe Thornton (CAN–SJ)	61
Henrik Sedin (SWE–VAN)	60
Mike Ribeiro (CAN–DAL)	56
Jarome Iginla (CAN–CAL)	54
Alexander Ovechkin (RUS–WAS)	54

Penalty Minutes

Daniel Carcillo (CAN–PHO)	254
Shane O'Brien (CAN–VAN)	196
Colton Orr (CAN–NYR)	193
Zach Stortini (CAN–EDM)	181
Jared Boll (USA–CBJ)	180
Eric Boulton (CAN–ATL)	176
Riley Cote (CAN–PHI)	174
Eric Godard (CAN–PIT)	171
David Backes (USA–STL)	165
David Clarkson (CAN–NJ)	165

Most Wins, Goalie

Miikka Kiprusoff (FIN–CAL)	45
Evgeni Nabokov (RUS–SJ)	41
Cam Ward (CAN–CAR)	39
Henrik Lundqvist (SWE–NYR)	38
Niklas Backstrom (FIN–MIN)	37
Tim Thomas (USA–BOS)	36
Marc-Andre Fleury (CAN–PIT)	35
Ryan Miller (USA–BUF)	34
Roberto Luongo (CAN–VAN)	33
Steve Mason (CAN–CBJ)	33
Marty Turco (CAN–DAL)	33

Most Losses, Goalie

Ilya Bryzgalov (RUS–PHO)	31
Marty Turco (CAN–DAL)	31
Peter Budaj (SVK–COL)	29
Joey MacDonald (CAN–NYI)	26
Henrik Lundqvist (SWE–NYR)	25
Niklas Backstrom (FIN–MIN)	24
Miikka Kiprusoff (FIN–CAL)	24
Dwayne Roloson (CAN–EDM)	24
Tomas Vokoun (CZE–FLO)	23
Cam Ward (CAN–CAR)	23

Most Minutes Played

Miikka Kiprusoff (FIN–CAL)	4,417:59
Marty Turco (CAN–DAL)	4,327:15
Henrik Lundqvist (SWE–NYR)	4,152:46
Niklas Backstrom (FIN–MIN)	4,088:03
Cam Ward (CAN–CAR)	3,928:03
Ilya Bryzgalov (RUS–PHO)	3,759:48
Evgeni Nabokov (RUS–SJ)	3,686:26
Steve Mason (CAN–CBJ)	3,663:37
Marc–Andre Fleury (CAN–PIT)	3,640:59
Dwayne Roloson (CAN–EDM)	3,596:51

Most Shutouts

Steve Mason (CAN–CBJ)	10
Roberto Luongo (CAN–VAN)	9
Niklas Backstrom (FIN–MIN)	8
Evgeni Nabokov (RUS–SJ)	7
Pekka Rinne (FIN–NAS)	7
Cam Ward (CAN–CAR)	6
Chris Mason (CAN–STL)	6
Tomas Vokoun (CZE–FLO)	6
Ty Conklin (USA–DET)	6

Tim Thomas (USA–BOS)　　　　6
Ryan Miller (USA–BUF)　　　　5
Martin Brodeur (CAN–NJ)　　　5

Best GAA

Tim Thomas (USA–BOS)　　　　2.10
Steve Mason (CAN–CBJ)　　　　2.20
Niklas Backstrom (FIN–MIN)　　2.33
Nikolai Khabibulin (RUS–CHI)　2.33
Roberto Luongo (CAN–VAN)　　2.34
Pekka Rinne (FIN–NAS)　　　　2.38
Jonas Hiller (SUI–ANA)　　　　2.38
Scott Clemmensen (USA–NJ)　　2.39
Chris Mason (CAN–STL)　　　　2.40
Martin Brodeur (CAN–NJ)　　　2.41

PLAYERS WHO PLAYED IN 2007–08, BUT NOT IN 2008–09

PLAYER	2008–09 STATUS
Adams, Kevyn	retired
Aebischer, David	played for Lugano (Switzerland)
Allen, Bobby	did not play
Aubin, Jean-Sebastien	played for Philadelphia (AHL)
Baranka, Ivan	played for Spartak Moscow (KHL)
Barnes, Stu	retired
Bates, Shawn	played for Helsinki (Finland)
Battaglia, Bates	played for Toronto (AHL)
Beckford-Tseu, Chris	played in AHL & ECHL
Beech, Kris	played for Jonkoping (Sweden)
Bell, Mark	played for Toronto & Hartford (AHL)
Berard, Bryan	played for Chekhov Vityaz (KHL)
Bernier, Jonathan	played for Manchester (AHL)
Berti, Adam	played in AHL & ECHL
Bickell, Bryan	played for Rockford (AHL)
Blunden, Michael	played for Rockford & Syracuse (AHL)
Bootland, Darryl	played in AHL & Austria
Bourdon, Luc	deceased
Boyce, Darryl	played for Toronto (AHL)
Brennan, Kip	played in AHL, ECHL, and Finland
Brine, David	played for Rochester (AHL)
Brown, Curtis	played for Kloten (Switzerland)
Brylin, Sergei	played for St. Petersburg (KHL)
Byers, Dane	played for Hartford (AHL)
Caldwell, Ryan	played for DEG Metro Stars (Germany)
Carney, Keith	played for Bern (Switzerland)
Clarke, Noah	played in Switzerland & Finland
Cloutier, Dan	did not play

Cowan, Jeff	played for Peoria (AHL)
Crawford, Corey	played for Rockford (AHL)
Dallman, Kevin	played for Astana Barys (KHL)
Darche, Mathieu	played for Portland (AHL)
DiPenta, Joe	played for Frolunda (Sweden)
Doell, Kevin	played for Leksand (Sweden)
Dowd, Jim	retired
Drake, Dallas	retired
Dupont, Micki	played for Zug (Switzerland)
Earl, Robbie	played for Houston (AHL)
Emery, Ray	played for Mytishi (KHL)
Eriksson, Anders	played for Quad City (AHL)
Fata, Drew	played for San Antonio & Binghamton (AHL)
Filewich, Jonathan	played for Peoria (AHL)
Fitzgerald, Zach	played for Manitoba (AHL)
Fitzpatrick, Rory	played for Rochester (AHL)
Forsberg, Peter	did not play—injured
Foy, Matt	played for Peoria (AHL)
Funk, Michael	played for Portland (AHL)
Gamache, Simon	played for Bern (Switzerland)
Gauthier, Gabe	played for Manchester (AHL)
Gelinas, Martin	played for Bern (Switzerland)
Giuliano, Jeff	played for Minsk (KHL)
Globke, Rob	played for Frederikshavn (Denmark)
Glumac, Mike	played for Hamilton (KHL)
Grahame, John	played for Avangard Omsk (KHL)
Greiss, Thomas	played for Worcester (AHL)
Hartigan, Mark	played for Dynamo Riga (KHL)
Hasek, Dominik	retired
Hatcher, Derian	retired
Haydar, Darren	played for Grand Rapids (AHL)
Hill, Sean	played for Biel (Switzerland)

Hlavac, Jan	played for Linkoping (Sweden)
Hlinka, Jaroslav	played for Linkoping (Sweden)
Holmqvist, Johan	played for Frolunda (Sweden)
Hossa, Marcel	played for Dynamo Riga (KHL)
Isbister, Brad	played for Zug (Switzerland)
Jagr, Jaromir	played for Avangard Omsk (KHL)
Johansson, Magnus	played for Mytishi (KHL)
Johnson, Erik	played in AHL & ECHL
Johnson, Mike	played for Cologne (Germany)
Jones, Blair	played for Norfolk (AHL)
Jones, Matt	played for San Antonio (AHL)
Kapanen, Niko	played for Ak Bars Kazan (KHL)
Kapanen, Sami	played for Kuopio (Finland)
Karlsson, Andreas	played for Frolunda (Sweden)
Keetley, Matt	played in AHL & ECHL
Keith, Matt	played for Ingolstadt (Germany)
Kelly, Steve	played for Syracuse (AHL)
Kilger, Chad	did not play
King, Jason	played for Mannheim (Germany)
Klemm, Jon	played for Straubing (Germany)
Kondratiev, Maxim	played for CSKA Moscow (KHL)
Kontiola, Petri	played for Iowa (AHL)
Kwiatkowski, Joel	played for Cherepovets (KHL)
Langfeld, Josh	played for Frankfurt (Germany)
Lapointe, Martin	did not play
Larman, Drew	played for Rochester (AHL)
Larsen, Brad	did not play—injured
Lessard, Junior	played for Chicago & Bridgeport (AHL)
Letowski, Trevor	played for Astana Barys (KHL)
Linden, Trevor	retired
Locke, Corey	played for Houston (AHL)
Lojek, Martin	played in Czech Republic
MacIntyre, Drew	played for Milwaukee (AHL)
Malmivaara, Olli	played for Jyvaskyla (Finland)

McCarthy, Steve	played for Ufa (KHL)
McLaren, Kyle	played for Worcester (AHL)
Meyer, Stefan	played for Rochester (AHL)
Mezei, Branislav	played for Astana Barys (KHL)
Miller, Aaron	retired
Modry, Jaroslav	played for Liberec (Czech Republic)
Moore, Greg	played for Hartford (AHL)
Mormina, Joey	played for Wilkes-Barre (AHL)
Mowers, Mark	played for Fribourg (Switzerland)
Murley, Matt	played for Khabarovsk (KHL)
Murray, Brady	played for Lugano (Switzerland)
Murray, Glen	did not play
Nagy, Ladislav	played for Cherepovets (KHL)
Nasreddine, Alain	played for Nuremburg (Germany)
Nilson, Marcus	played for Yaroslavl (KHL)
Nolan, Brandon	did not play—injured
Norstrom, Mattias	retired
Nummelin, Petteri	played for Lugano (Switzerland)
Ozolinsh, Sandis	did not play
Parker, Scott	did not play
Patzold, Dmitri	played for Hanover (Germany)
Pelley, Rod	played for Lowell (AHL)
Perreault, Yanic	did not play
Pineault, Adam	played for Rockford (AHL)
Platt, Geoff	played in Finland & Russia
Pohl, John	played in Switzerland & Sweden
Popovic, Mark	played in St. Petersburg (KHL)
Pratt, Nolan	played for Khabarovsk (KHL)
Rachunek, Karel	played for Dynamo Moscow (KHL)
Radivojevic, Branko	played for Spartak Moscow (KHL)
Radulov, Alexander	played for Ufa (KHL)
Ramholt, Tim	played for Philadelphia & Milwaukee (AHL)
Reich, Jeremy	played for Providence (AHL)
Richmond, Danny	played for Wilkes-Barre & Peoria (AHL)

Ritchie, Byron	played for Servette (Switzerland)
Ritola, Theo	played for Grand Rapids (AHL)
Robitaille, Randy	played for Lugano (Switzerland)
Rourke, Allan	played in Germany & Austria
Roy, Mathieu	played for Springfield (AHL)
Rucinsky, Martin	played for Sparta Prague (Czech Republic)
Ruzicka, Stefan	played for Spartak Moscow (KHL)
Sanderson, Geoff	did not play—injured
Schaefer, Peter	played for Providence (AHL)
Sestito, Tommy	played for Syracuse (AHL)
Simon, Chris	played for Chekhov Vityaz (KHL)
Smith, Mark	did not play
Smith, Nathan	played for Lake Erie (AHL)
Smith, Wyatt	played in AHL
Smolinski, Bryan	played for Port Huron (IHL)
Spiller, Matthew	played for Lowell (AHL)
Stewart, Karl	played for Rochester (AHL)
Straka, Martin	played for Plzen (Czech Republic)
Stumpel, Jozef	played for Astana Barys (KHL)
Tanabe, David	retired
Tarnstrom, Dick	played in Sweden
Taylor, Daniel	played in AHL & ECHL
Thibault, Jocelyn	did not play
Thoresen, Patrick	played for Lugano (Switzerland)
Thornton, Scott	retired
Tjarnqvist, Mathias	played for Rogle (Sweden)
Toivonen, Hannu	played for Tampere (Finland)
Tolpeko, Denis	played for Dynamo Moscow (KHL)
Tukonen, Lauri	played in Finland
Vandermeer, Pete	played for Quad City (AHL)
Vasicek, Josef	played for Yaroslavl (KHL)
Vishnevski, Vitali	played for Yaroslavl (KHL)

Vyborny, David	played for Sparta Prague (Czech Republic)
Walz, Wes	retired
Wanvig, Kyle	played in Sweden & Russia
Warrener, Rhett	did not play—injured
Weiman, Tyler	played for Lake Erie (AHL)
Wesley, Glen	retired
Westcott, Duvie	played for Dynamo Riga (KHL)
Wirtanen, Petteri	played for Iowa (AHL)
Young, Bryan	played for Springfield (AHL)
Zhitnik, Alexei	played for Dynamo Moscow (KHL)
Zyuzin, Andrei	played for St. Petersburg (KHL)

2009 PLAYOFF RESULTS

Eastern Conference Quarter-finals

Boston (1) vs. Montreal (8)

April 16   Montreal 2 at Boston 4
April 18   Montreal 1 at Boston 5
April 20   Boston 4 at Montreal 2
April 22   Boston 4 at Montreal 1
Boston wins best-of-seven 4–0

Washington (2) vs. NY Rangers (7)

April 15   NY Rangers 4 at Washington 3
April 18   NY Rangers 1 at Washington 0 [Lundqvist]
April 20   Washington 4 at NY Rangers 0 [Varlamov]
April 22   Washington 1 at NY Rangers 2
April 24   NY Rangers 0 at Washington 4 [Varlamov]
April 26   Washington 5 at NY Rangers 3
April 28   NY Rangers 1 at Washington 2
Washington wins best-of-seven 4–3

New Jersey (3) vs. Carolina (6)

April 15   Carolina 1 at New Jersey 4
April 17   Carolina 2 at New Jersey 1 (Gleason 2:40 OT)
April 19   New Jersey 3 at Carolina 2 (Zajac 4:58 OT)
April 21   New Jersey 3 at Carolina 4
April 23   Carolina 0 at New Jersey 1 [Brodeur]
April 26   New Jersey 0 at Carolina 4 [Ward]
April 28   Carolina 4 at New Jersey 3
Carolina wins best-of-seven 4–3

Pittsburgh (4) vs. Philadelphia (5)

April 15   Philadelphia 1 at Pittsburgh 4
April 17   Philadelphia 2 at Pittsburgh 3 (Guerin 18:29 OT)
April 19   Pittsburgh 3 at Philadelphia 6

April 21   Pittsburgh 3 at Philadelphia 1
April 23   Philadelphia 3 at Pittsburgh 0 [Biron]
April 25   Pittsburgh 5 at Philadelphia 3
Pittsburgh wins best-of-seven 4–2

Western Conference Quarter-finals

San Jose (1) vs. Anaheim (8)
April 16   Anaheim 2 at San Jose 0 [Hiller]
April 19   Anaheim 3 at San Jose 2
April 21   San Jose 4 at Anaheim 3
April 23   San Jose 0 at Anaheim 4 [Hiller]
April 25   Anaheim 2 at San Jose 3 (Marleau 6:02 OT)
April 27   San Jose 1 at Anaheim 4
Anaheim wins best-of-seven 4–2

Detroit (2) vs. Columbus (7)
April 16   Columbus 1 at Detroit 4
April 18   Columbus 0 at Detroit 4 [Osgood]
April 21   Detroit 4 at Columbus 1
April 23   Detroit 6 at Columbus 5
Detroit wins best-of-seven 4–0

Vancouver (3) vs. St. Louis (6)
April 15   St. Louis 1 at Vancouver 2
April 17   St. Louis 0 at Vancouver 3 [Luongo]
April 19   Vancouver 3 at St. Louis 2
April 21   Vancouver 3 at St. Louis 2 (Burrows 19:41 OT)
Vancouver wins best-of-seven 4–0

Chicago (4) vs. Calgary (5)
April 16   Calgary 2 at Chicago 3 (Havlat 0:12 OT)
April 18   Calgary 2 at Chicago 3

April 20   Chicago 2 at Calgary 4
April 22   Chicago 4 at Calgary 6
April 25   Calgary 1 at Chicago 5
April 27   Chicago 4 at Calgary 1
Chicago wins best-of-seven 4–2

Eastern Conference Semifinals

Boston (1) vs. Carolina (6)
May 1   Carolina 1 at Boston 4
May 3   Carolina 3 at Boston 0 [Ward]
May 6   Boston 2 at Carolina 3 (J. Jokinen 2:48 OT)
May 8   Boston 1 at Carolina 4
May 10   Carolina 0 at Boston 4 [Thomas]
May 12   Boston 4 at Carolina 2
May 14   Carolina 3 at Boston 2 (18:46 OT)
Carolina wins best-of-seven 4–3

Washington (2) vs. Pittsburgh (4)
May 2   Pittsburgh 2 at Washington 3
May 4   Pittsburgh 3 at Washington 4
May 6   Washington 2 at Pittsburgh 3 (Letang 11:23 OT)
May 8   Washington 3 at Pittsburgh 5
May 9   Pittsburgh 4 at Washington 3 (Malkin 3:28 OT)
May 11   Washington 5 at Pittsburgh 4 (Steckel 6:22 OT)
May 13   Pittsburgh 6 at Washington 2
Pittsburgh wins best-of-seven 4–3

Western Conference Semifinals

Detroit (2) vs. Anaheim (8)
May 1   Anaheim 2 at Detroit 3
May 3   Anaheim 4 at Detroit 3 (Marchant 41:15 OT)
May 5   Detroit 1 at Anaheim 2
May 7   Detroit 6 at Anaheim 3
May 10   Anaheim 1 at Detroit 4

May 12   Detroit 1 at Anaheim 2
May 14   Anaheim 3 at Detroit 4
Detroit wins best-of-seven 4–3

Vancouver (3) vs. Chicago (4)

May 1   Chicago 3 at Vancouver 5
May 3   Chicago 6 at Vancouver 3
May 6   Vancouver 3 at Chicago 1
May 8   Vancouver 1 at Chicago 2 (Ladd 2:52 OT)
May 10   Chicago 4 at Vancouver 2
May 12   Vancouver 5 at Chicago 7
Chicago wins best-of-seven 4–2

Eastern Conference Final

Pittsburgh (4) vs. Carolina (6)

May 18   Carolina 2 at Pittsburgh 3
May 21   Carolina 4 at Pittsburgh 7
May 23   Pittsburgh 6 at Carolina 2
May 26   Pittsburgh 4 at Carolina 1
Pittsburgh wins best-of-seven 4–0

Western Conference Final

Detroit (2) vs. Chicago (4)

May 17   Chicago 2 at Detroit 5
May 19   Chicago 2 at Detroit 3 (Samuelsson 5:14 OT)
May 22   Detroit 3 at Chicago 4 (Sharp 1:52 OT)
May 24   Detroit 6 at Chicago 1
May 27   Chicago 1 at Detroit 2 (Helm 3:58 OT)
Detroit wins best-of-seven 4–1

Stanley Cup Final
Pittsburgh (4) vs. Detroit (2)

May 30	Pittsburgh 1 at Detroit 3
May 31	Pittsburgh 1 at Detroit 3
June 2	Detroit 2 at Pittsburgh 4
June 4	Detroit 2 at Pittsburgh 4
June 6	Pittsburgh 0 at Detroit 5 [Osgood]
June 9	Detroit 1 at Pittsburgh 2
June 12	Pittsburgh 2 at Detroit 1

Pittsburgh wins best-of-seven 4–3

PLAYER STATISTICS BY TEAM, 2009 PLAYOFFS

Anaheim Ducks

	GP	G	A	P	Pim
Ryan Getzlaf	13	4	14	18	25
Corey Perry	13	8	6	14	36
Scott Niedermayer	13	3	7	10	11
Chris Pronger	13	2	8	10	12
Bobby Ryan	13	5	2	7	0
Teemu Selanne	13	4	2	6	4
Ryan Whitney	13	1	5	6	9
Ryan Carter	10	2	3	5	0
Drew Miller	13	2	1	3	2
James Wisniewski	12	1	2	3	10
Andrew Ebbett	13	1	2	3	8
Rob Niedermayer	13	0	3	3	12
Todd Marchant	13	1	1	2	16
Mike Brown	13	0	2	2	25
Erik Christensen	8	0	2	2	0
Francois Beauchemin	13	1	0	1	15
Sheldon Brookbank	13	0	0	0	18
George Parros	7	0	0	0	9
Petteri Nokelainen	9	0	0	0	2
Jonas Hiller	13	0	0	0	0
Josh Green	5	0	0	0	0
Brett Festerling	1	0	0	0	0
J-S Giguere	1	0	0	0	0

In Goal	GP	W-L	Mins	GA	SO	GAA
Jonas Hiller	13	7–6	806:43	30	2	2.23
J-S Giguere	1	0–0	16:49	0	0	0.00

Boston Bruins

	GP	G	A	P	Pim
Marc Savard	11	6	7	13	4
Michael Ryder	11	5	8	13	8
Phil Kessel	11	6	5	11	4
Milan Lucic	10	3	6	9	43
David Krejci	11	2	6	8	2
Dennis Wideman	11	0	7	7	4
Chuck Kobasew	11	3	3	6	14
Mark Recchi	11	3	3	6	2
Patrice Bergeron	11	0	5	5	11
Zdeno Chara	11	1	3	4	12
Steve Montador	11	1	2	3	18
Byron Bitz	5	1	1	2	2
Shawn Thornton	10	1	0	1	6
Aaron Ward	11	1	0	1	2
Shane Hnidy	7	1	0	1	0
Mark Stuart	11	0	1	1	7
P.J. Axelsson	11	0	1	1	2
Stepahne Yelle	11	0	1	1	2
Tim Thomas	11	0	1	1	0
Andrew Ference	3	0	0	0	4
Blake Wheeler	8	0	0	0	0
Matt Hunwick	1	0	0	0	0

In Goal	GP	W-L	Mins	GA	SO	GAA
Tim Thomas	11	7–4	679:44	21	1	1.85

Calgary Flames

	GP	G	A	P	Pim
Olli Jokinen	6	2	3	5	4
Jarome Iginla	6	3	1	4	0
Eric Nystrom	6	2	2	4	0
David Moss	6	3	0	3	0
Adrian Aucoin	6	2	1	3	2
Mike Cammalleri	6	1	2	3	2
Curtis Glencross	6	0	3	3	12
Daymond Langkow	6	0	3	3	2
Dion Phaneuf	5	0	3	3	4
Todd Bertuzzi	6	1	1	2	8
Adam Pardy	6	0	2	2	5
Rene Bourque	5	1	0	1	22
Dustin Boyd	5	1	0	1	0
Jordan Leopold	6	0	1	1	8
James Vandermeer	6	0	1	1	4
Cory Sarich	5	0	1	1	4
Craig Conroy	6	0	1	1	0
Miikka Kiprusoff	6	0	0	0	2
Warren Peters	4	0	0	0	0
Anders Eriksson	2	0	0	0	0
Jamie Lundmark	2	0	0	0	0
Andre Roy	2	0	0	0	0
Curtis McElhinney	1	0	0	0	0

In Goal	GP	W-L	Mins	GA	SO	GAA
Miikka Kiprusoff	6	2–4	323:49	19	0	3.52
Curtis McElhinney	1	0–0	33:46	1	0	1.76

Carolina Hurricanes

	GP	G	A	P	Pim
Eric Staal	18	10	5	15	4
Jussi Jokinen	18	7	4	11	2
Chad LaRose	18	4	7	11	16
Ray Whitney	18	3	8	11	4
Sergei Samsonov	17	5	3	8	6
Joni Pitkanen	18	0	8	8	16
Joe Corvo	18	2	5	7	4
Scott Walker	18	1	6	7	19
Matt Cullen	18	3	3	6	14
Dennis Seidenberg	16	1	5	6	16
Tim Gleason	18	1	4	5	32
Erik Cole	18	0	5	5	22
Ryan Bayda	15	2	2	4	18
Rod Brind'Amour	18	1	3	4	8
Tuomo Ruutu	16	1	3	4	8
Patrick Eaves	18	1	2	3	13
Anton Babchuk	13	0	1	1	10
Frantisek Kaberle	7	0	1	1	2
Patrick Dwyer	2	0	1	1	0
Tim Conboy	3	0	0	0	9
Niclas Wallin	18	0	0	0	4
Cam Ward	18	0	0	0	0
Dwight Helminen	1	0	0	0	0

In Goal	GP	W-L	Mins	GA	SO	GAA
Cam Ward	18	8–10	1,101:26	49	2	2.67

Chicago Blackhawks

	GP	G	A	P	Pim
Martin Havlat	16	5	10	15	8
Patrick Kane	16	9	5	14	12
Jonathan Toews	17	7	6	13	26
Dave Bolland	17	4	8	12	24
Kris Versteeg	17	4	8	12	22
Brent Seabrook	17	1	11	12	14
Patrick Sharp	17	7	4	11	6
Brian Campbell	17	2	8	10	0
Dustin Byfuglien	17	3	6	9	26
Cam Barker	17	3	6	9	2
Duncan Keith	17	0	6	6	10
Adam Birish	17	3	2	5	30
Samuel Pahlsson	17	2	3	5	4
Andrew Ladd	17	3	1	4	12
Ben Eager	17	1	1	2	61
Matt Walker	17	0	2	2	14
Troy Brower	17	0	2	2	12
Niklas Hjalmarsson	17	0	1	1	6
Colin Fraser	2	0	0	0	2
Nikolai Khabibulin	15	0	0	0	0
Cristobal Huet	3	0	0	0	0
Corey Crawford	1	0	0	0	0

In Goal	GP	W-L	Mins	GA	SO	GAA
Nikolai Khabibulin	15	8–6	880:58	43	0	2.93
Cristobal Huet	3	1–2	129:50	7	0	3.23
Corey Crawford	1	0–0	15:55	1	0	3.75

Columbus Blue Jackets

	GP	G	A	P	Pim
R.J. Umberger	4	3	0	3	0
Rick Nash	4	1	2	3	2
Kristian Huselius	4	1	1	2	4
Kris Russell	4	1	1	2	2
Raffi Torres	4	0	2	2	2
Fredrik Modin	4	1	0	1	0
Jakub Voracek	4	0	1	1	8
Jason Chimera	4	0	1	1	2
Jason Williams	4	0	1	1	2
Rostislav Klesla	4	0	1	1	0
Steve Mason	4	0	1	1	0
Aaron Rome	1	0	1	1	0
Mike Commodore	4	0	0	0	18
Antoine Vermette	4	0	0	0	10
Marc Methot	4	0	0	0	2
Michael Peca	4	0	0	0	2
Derek Dorsett	3	0	0	0	2
Jan Hejda	3	0	0	0	2
Manny Malhotra	4	0	0	0	0
Fedor Tyutin	4	0	0	0	0
Jared Boll	1	0	0	0	0

In Goal	GP	W-L	Mins	GA	SO	GAA
Steve Mason	4	0–4	239:20	17	0	4.27

Detroit Red Wings

	GP	G	A	P	Pim
Henrik Zetterberg	23	11	13	24	13
Johan Franzen	23	12	11	23	12
Nicklas Lidstrom	21	4	12	16	6
Valtteri Filppula	23	3	13	16	8
Dan Cleary	23	9	6	15	12
Marian Hossa	23	6	9	15	10
Jiri Hudler	23	4	8	12	6
Brian Rafalski	18	3	9	12	11
Mikael Samuelsson	23	5	5	10	6
Brad Stuart	23	3	6	9	12
Niklas Kronwall	23	2	7	9	33
Pavel Datsyuk	16	1	8	9	9
Jonathan Ericsson	22	4	4	8	25
Tomas Holmstrom	23	2	5	7	22
Brett Lebda	23	0	6	6	22
Darren Helm	23	4	1	5	4
Justin Abdelkader	10	2	1	3	0
Ville Leino	7	0	2	2	0
Chris Osgood	23	0	2	2	2
Kris Draper	8	1	0	1	0
Tomas Kopecky	8	0	1	1	7
Kirk Maltby	20	0	1	1	2
Derek Meech	2	0	0	0	0
Chris Chelios	6	0	0	0	2
Ty Conklin	1	0	0	0	0

In Goal	GP	W-L	Mins	GA	SO	GAA
Chris Osgood	23	15–8	1,405:51	47	2	2.01
Ty Conklin	1	0–0	19:36	0	0	0.00

Montreal Canadiens

	GP	G	A	P	Pim
Alexei Kovalev	4	2	1	3	2
Saku Koivu	4	0	3	3	2
Chris Higgins	4	2	0	2	2
Yannick Weber	3	1	1	2	0
Glen Metropolit	4	0	2	2	2
Andrei Kostitsyn	4	1	0	1	2
Josh Gorges	4	0	1	1	7
Tom Kostopoulos	4	0	1	1	4
Alex Tanguay	2	0	1	1	2
Maxim Lapierre	4	0	0	0	26
Mike Komisarek	4	0	0	0	20
Guillaume Latendresse	4	0	0	0	12
Georges Laraque	4	0	0	0	4
Tomas Plekanec	3	0	0	0	4
Mathieu Schneider	2	0	0	0	4
Roman Hamrlik	4	0	0	0	2
Ryan O'Byrne	2	0	0	0	2
Gregory Stewart	2	0	0	0	2
Sergei Kostitsyn	1	0	0	0	2
Mathieu Dandenault	4	0	0	0	0
Carey Price	4	0	0	0	0
Matt D'Agostini	3	0	0	0	0
Francis Bouillon	1	0	0	0	0
Patrice Brisebois	1	0	0	0	0
Jaroslav Halak	1	0	0	0	0

In Goal	GP	W-L	Mins	GA	SO	GAA
Jaroslav Halak	1	0–0	20:00	0	0	0.00
Carey Price	4	0–4	219:10	15	0	4.11

New Jersey Devils

	GP	G	A	P	Pim
Zach Parise	7	3	3	6	2
Brian Gionta	7	2	3	5	4
Travis Zajac	7	1	3	4	6
Paul Martin	7	0	4	4	2
Jamie Langenbrunner	4	2	1	3	2
Patrik Elias	7	1	2	3	2
Brendan Shanahan	7	1	2	3	2
David Clarkson	7	2	0	2	19
Brian Rolston	7	1	1	2	4
Mike Mottau	7	1	1	2	0
Jay Pandolfo	7	1	0	1	0
Dainius Zubrus	7	0	1	1	10
Colin White	7	0	1	1	6
John Madden	7	0	1	1	4
Niclas Havelid	7	0	1	1	2
Bobby Holik	3	0	1	1	2
Andy Greene	3	0	1	1	0
Michael Rupp	7	0	0	0	14
Martin Brodeur	7	0	0	0	4
Bryce Salvador	4	0	0	0	4
Johnny Oduya	7	0	0	0	2

In Goal	GP	W-L	Mins	GA	SO	GAA
Martin Brodeur	7	3–4	426:41	17	1	2.39

New York Rangers

	GP	G	A	P	Pim
Scott Gomez	7	2	3	5	4
Brandon Dubinsky	7	1	3	4	18
Nik Antropov	7	2	1	3	6
Marcus Naslund	7	1	2	3	10
Ryan Callahan	7	2	0	2	4
Paul Mara	7	1	1	2	8
Sean Avery	6	0	2	2	24
Lauri Korpikoski	7	0	2	2	0
Derek Morris	7	0	2	2	0
Wade Redden	7	0	2	2	0
Chris Drury	6	1	0	1	2
Marc Staal	7	1	0	1	0
Fredrik Sjostrom	7	0	1	1	0
Colton Orr	5	0	0	0	16
Aaron Voros	4	0	0	0	14
Daniel Girardi	7	0	0	0	6
Michal Rozsival	7	0	0	0	4
Nikolai Zherdev	7	0	0	0	2
Henrik Lundqvist	7	0	0	0	0
Blair Betts	6	0	0	0	0
Stephen Valiquette	2	0	0	0	0
Artem Anisimov	1	0	0	0	0

In Goal	GP	W-L	Mins	GA	SO	GAA
Henrik Lundqvist	7	3–4	379:44	19	1	3.00
Stephen Valiquette	2	0–0	40:00	0	0	0.00

Philadelphia Flyers

	GP	G	A	P	Pim
Claude Giroux	6	2	3	5	6
Mike Richards	6	1	4	5	6
Simon Gagne	6	3	1	4	2
Daniel Briere	6	1	3	4	8
Mike Knuble	6	2	1	3	2
Darroll Powe	6	1	2	3	7
Braydon Coburn	6	0	3	3	7
Matt Carle	6	0	3	3	4
Scott Hartnell	6	1	1	2	23
Aaron Asham	6	1	1	2	6
Daniel Carcillo	5	1	1	2	5
Joffrey Lupul	6	1	1	2	2
Jeff Carter	6	1	0	1	8
Jared Ross	6	1	0	1	0
Kimmo Timonen	6	0	1	1	12
Andrew Alberts	6	0	1	1	10
Randy Jones	6	0	1	1	0
Ryan Parent	6	0	0	0	6
Luca Sbisa	1	0	0	0	2
Martin Biron	6	0	0	0	0

In Goal	GP	W-L	Mins	GA	SO	GAA
Martin Biron	6	2–4	374:44	16	1	2.56

Pittsburgh Penguins

	GP	G	A	P	Pim
Evgeni Malkin	24	14	22	36	51
Sidney Crosby	24	15	16	31	14
Bill Guerin	24	7	8	15	15
Ruslan Fedotenko	24	7	7	14	4
Sergei Gonchar	22	3	11	14	12
Chris Kunitz	24	1	13	14	19
Maxime Talbot	24	8	5	13	19
Kris Letang	23	4	9	13	26
Tyler Kennedy	24	5	4	9	4
Jordan Staal	24	4	5	9	8
Mark Eaton	24	4	3	7	10
Matt Cooke	24	1	6	7	22
Miroslav Satan	17	1	5	6	11
Craig Adams	24	3	2	5	16
Rob Scuderi	24	1	4	5	6
Philippe Boucher	9	1	3	4	4
Brooks Orpik	24	0	4	4	22
Hal Gill	24	0	2	2	6
Petr Sykora	7	0	1	1	0
Alex Goligoski	2	0	1	1	0
Pascal Dupuis	16	0	0	0	8
Marc-Andre Fleury	24	0	0	0	2
Mathieu Garon	1	0	0	0	0

In Goal	GP	W-L	Mins	GA	SO	GAA
Marc-Andre Fleury	24	16–8	1,447:18	63	0	2.61
Mathieu Garon	1	0–0	24:20	0	0	0.00

San Jose Sharks

	GP	G	A	P	Pim
Joe Thornton	6	1	4	5	5
Dan Boyle	6	2	2	4	8
Rob Blake	6	1	3	4	4
Patrick Marleau	6	2	1	3	8
Devin Setoguchi	6	1	2	3	2
Ryane Clowe	6	1	1	2	8
Jonathan Cheechoo	6	1	1	2	4
Milan Michalek	6	1	0	1	2
Jeremy Roenick	6	0	1	1	12
Joe Pavelski	6	0	1	1	9
Marc-Edouard Vlasic	6	0	1	1	0
Douglas Murray	6	0	0	0	9
Mike Grier	6	0	0	0	6
Christian Ehrhoff	6	0	0	0	2
Marcel Goc	6	0	0	0	2
Travis Moen	6	0	0	0	2
Torrey Mitchell	4	0	0	0	2
Brad Lukowich	6	0	0	0	0
Evgeni Nabokov	6	0	0	0	0
Claude Lemieux	1	0	0	0	0
Jody Shelley	1	0	0	0	0

In Goal	GP	W-L	Mins	GA	SO	GAA
Evgeni Nabokov	6	2–4	361:35	17	0	2.82

St. Louis Blues

	GP	G	A	P	Pim
Andy McDonald	4	1	3	4	0
Brad Boyes	4	2	1	3	0
David Backes	4	1	2	3	10
David Perron	4	1	1	2	4
Barret Jackman	4	0	1	1	5
Alexander Steen	4	0	1	1	0
Brandon Crombeen	4	0	0	0	12
Brad Winchester	4	0	0	0	10
Jay McClement	4	0	0	0	4
Jay McKee	4	0	0	0	4
Dan Hinote	3	0	0	0	4
Patrik Berglund	4	0	0	0	2
Carlo Colaiacovo	4	0	0	0	2
T.J. Oshie	4	0	0	0	2
Keith Tkachuk	4	0	0	0	2
Chris Mason	4	0	0	0	0
Roman Polak	4	0	0	0	0
Mike Weaver	4	0	0	0	0
Jeff Woywitka	4	0	0	0	0
Cam Janssen	1	0	0	0	0

In Goal	GP	W-L	Mins	GA	SO	GAA
Chris Mason	4	0–4	256:17	10	0	2.34

Vancouver Canucks

	GP	G	A	P	Pim
Daniel Sedin	10	4	6	10	8
Henrik Sedin	10	4	6	10	2
Mats Sundin	8	3	5	8	2
Alexander Edler	10	1	7	8	6
Sami Salo	7	3	4	7	2
Kyle Wellwood	10	1	5	6	0
Kevin Bieksa	10	0	5	5	14
Alex Burrows	10	3	1	4	20
Ryan Kesler	10	2	2	4	14
Steve Bernier	10	2	2	4	7
Mason Raymond	10	2	1	3	2
Mattias Ohlund	10	1	2	3	6
Pavol Demitra	6	1	2	3	2
Shane O'Brien	10	1	1	2	24
Ryan Johnson	10	1	1	2	2
Rick Rypien	10	0	2	2	40
Willie Mitchell	10	0	2	2	22
Darcy Hordichuk	10	1	0	1	14
Taylor Pyatt	4	0	0	0	2
Ossi Vaananen	3	0	0	0	2
Roberto Luongo	10	0	0	0	0
Jannik Hansen	2	0	0	0	0

In Goal	GP	W-L	Mins	GA	SO	GAA
Roberto Luongo	10	6–4	617:57	26	1	2.52

Washington Capitals

	GP	G	A	P	Pim
Alexander Ovechkin	14	11	10	21	8
Nicklas Backstrom	14	3	12	15	8
Alexander Semin	14	5	9	14	16
Mike Green	14	1	8	9	12
Sergei Fedorov	14	1	7	8	12
Brooks Laich	14	3	4	7	10
Tom Poti	14	2	5	7	4
Viktor Kozlov	14	4	2	6	6
Matt Bradley	14	2	4	6	0
David Steckel	14	3	2	5	4
Tomas Fleischmann	14	3	1	4	4
Boyd Gordon	14	0	3	3	4
Milan Jurcina	14	2	0	2	12
Brian Pothier	13	0	2	2	8
Chris Clarke	8	1	0	1	8
John Erskine	12	0	1	1	16
Shaone Morrisonn	14	0	1	1	8
Tyler Sloane	2	0	1	1	0
Donald Brashear	4	0	0	0	18
Simeon Varlamov	13	0	0	0	2
Michael Nylander	3	0	0	0	2
Eric Fehr	9	0	0	0	0
Jay Beagle	4	0	0	0	0
Jose Theodore	2	0	0	0	0
Jeff Schultz	1	0	0	0	0

In Goal	GP	W-L	Mins	GA	SO	GAA
Simeon Varlamov	13	7–6	758:52	32	2	2.53
Jose Theodore	2	0–1	96:45	6	0	3.71

ALL REGULAR-SEASON SCORES, 2008–09

October 4, 2008
NY Rangers 2 at Tampa Bay 1 (played in Prague)
Pittsburgh 4 at Ottawa 3 (Kennedy 4:35 OT—played in Stockholm)

October 5, 2008
Tampa Bay 1 at NY Rangers 2 (played in Prague)
Ottawa 3 at Pittsburgh 1 (played in Stockholm)

October 9, 2008
Toronto 3 at Detroit 2 (Leafs scored in each period)
Boston 5 at Colorado 4 (Krejci broke 4–4 tie at 17:24 of 3rd)
Calgary 0 at Vancouver 6 [Luongo]
Anaheim 1 at San Jose 4 (no goals in 1st)

October 10, 2008
NY Islanders 1 at New Jersey 2 (no scoring in 3rd)
Chicago 2 at NY Rangers 4 (game tied 1–1 after 1st)
Florida 4 at Carolina 6 (Hurricanes scored two goals in each
    period)
Montreal 1 at Buffalo 2 (SO)
Washington 4 at Atlanta 7 (game tied 4–4 after 2nd)
Nashville 2 at St. Louis 5 (no scoring in 3rd)
Columbus 5 at Dallas 4 (Nash 4:39 OT)

October 11, 2008
Montreal 6 at Toronto 1 (Canadiens scored four goals in 2nd)
Detroit 3 at Ottawa 2 (Senators led 2–1 after 2nd)
St. Louis 2 at NY Islanders 5 (Islanders led 4–1 after 1st)
NY Rangers 4 at Philadelphia 3 (seven different scorers)
Chicago 2 at Washington 4 (Ovechkin (WAS) two goals)
Atlanta 2 at Florida 3 (Booth 3:54 OT)

New Jersey 2 at Pittsburgh 1 (Parise 4:22 OT)
Carolina 4 at Tampa Bay 3 (E. Staal 4:36 OT)
Dallas 1 at Nashville 3 (Arnott two goals)
Boston 3 at Minnesota 4 (Wild led 4–1 after 2nd)
Vancouver 5 at Calgary 4 (Demitra 3:54 OT)
Columbus 1 at Phoenix 3 (no scoring in 3rd)
Los Angeles 1 at San Jose 3 (Kings led 1–0 after 1st)

October 12, 2008
Colorado 2 at Edmonton 3 (Penner broke 2–2 tie at 19:54 of 3rd)
Phoenix 4 at Anaheim 2 (Doan (PHO) two goals)
San Jose 1 at Los Angeles 0 (Kaspar 9:56 2nd) {Boucher}

October 13, 2008
St. Louis 5 at Toronto 4 (SO)
Buffalo 7 at NY Islanders 1 (Sabres led 6–0 early in 3rd)
New Jersey 1 at NY Rangers 4 (Voros two goals)
Montreal 5 at Philadelphia 3 (Flyers led 2–1 after 2nd)
Vancouver 1 at Washington 5 (game tied 1–1 early in 1st)
Detroit 3 at Carolina 1 (game tied 1–1 early in 2nd)
Nashville 3 at Chicago 2 (SO)

October 14, 2008
Philadelphia 2 at Pittsburgh 3 (Dupuis 4:49 OT)
Minnesota 4 at Atlanta 2 (game tied 1–1 after 2nd)
Colorado 4 at Calgary 5 (game tied 3–3 after 2nd)
Anaheim 3 at Los Angeles 6 (nine different scorers)
Columbus 2 at San Jose 5 (game tied 2–2 midway through 2nd)

October 15, 2008
Buffalo 3 at NY Rangers 1 (Rangers led 1–0 early in 2nd)
Boston 3 at Montreal 4 (SO)
Phoenix 1 at Chicago 4 (Coyotes led 1–0 midway through 2nd)
Nashville 4 at Dallas 6 (Brunnstrom (DAL) hat trick in NHL
    debut)

Edmonton 3 at Anaheim 2 (Oilers scored only goal of 3rd)

October 16, 2008
New Jersey 1 at Atlanta 0 (Rolston 18:57 2nd) [Brodeur—97th
    career shutout]
Washington 4 at Pittsburgh 3 (Penguins led 3–1 after 2nd)
NY Islanders 4 at Tampa Bay 5 (Hunter 0:51 OT)
Minnesota 6 at Florida 2 (Wild led 2–1 early in 2nd)
Vancouver 4 at Detroit 3 (Burrows 0:27 OT)
Dallas 1 at St. Louis 6 (seven different scorers)
Philadelphia 2 at Colorado 5 (Avs led 3–0 early in 2nd)

October 17, 2008
Phoenix 3 at Ottawa 6 (Senators led 4–0 after 2nd)
Toronto 0 at NY Rangers 1 (SO) [Toskala/Valiquette]
Nashville 5 at Columbus 5 (Jackets led 4–0 early in 2nd)
Vancouver 2 at Buffalo 5 (Kotalik (BUF) two goals)
Edmonton 4 at Calgary 3 (Oilers scored three goals in 2nd)
San Jose 0 at Anaheim 4 [Giguere]
Carolina 3 at Los Angeles 4 (Handzus 3:21 OT)

October 18, 2008
Colorado 5 at Dallas 4 (Avs led 5–2 after 2nd)
Phoenix 1 at Montreal 4 (Canadiens led 4–0 midway through 3rd)
Boston 4 at Ottawa 2 (game tied 1–1 early in 2nd)
Toronto 1 at Pittsburgh 4 (Crosby one goal, three assists)
New Jersey 4 at Washington 3 (SO)
Buffalo 2 at Atlanta 3 (SO)
NY Islanders 0 at Florida 1 [Vokoun]
NY Rangers 4 at Detroit 5 (Hossa 0:23 OT)
Minnesota 1 at Tampa Bay 0 (SO) [Backstrom/Smith]
Columbus 3 at Nashville 6 (Predators led 4–0 early in 2nd)
Chicago 3 at St. Louis 4 (SO)
Calgary 2 at Edmonton 3 (Flames scored both goals in 1st; Oilers
    scored all three goals in 2nd)

Philadelphia 4 at San Jose 5 (Boyle 1:25 OT)

October 19, 2008
Vancouver 2 at Chicago 4 (Canucks led 1–0 midway through 1st)
Carolina 3 at Anaheim 1 (Hurricanes scored in each period)

October 20, 2008
Pittsburgh 2 at Boston 1 (SO)
Dallas 2 at NY Rangers 1 (Stars scored only goal of 3rd)
Florida 1 at Montreal 3 (game tied 1–1 early in 3rd)
Colorado 4 at Los Angeles 3 (Smyth (Avs) two goals)

October 21, 2008
Boston 2 at Buffalo 3 (SO)
Anaheim 3 at Toronto 2 (SO) (Leafs changed goalies prior to
    shootout)
Vancouver 2 at Columbus 4 (Blue Jackets scored in each period)
Atlanta 2 at Tampa Bay 3 (Lecavalier 1:41 OT)
Washington 1 at Calgary 2 (Capitals scored in 1st; Flames scored
    both goals in 2nd)

October 22, 2008
Florida 3 at Ottawa 1 (no scoring in 3rd)
Dallas 0 at New Jersey 5 [Brodeur—98th career shutout]
San Jose 7 at Philadelphia 6 (SO)
Detroit 4 at St. Louis 3 (all Detroit goals scored by Swedes)
Edmonton 0 at Chicago 3 [Khabibulin]

October 23, 2008
Toronto 4 at Boston 2 (Leafs trailed 2–0 after 1st)
Dallas 5 at NY Islanders 3 (Stars led 3–0 midway through game)
Carolina 1 at Pittsburgh 4 (Hurricanes led 1–0 early in 3rd)
Calgary 5 at Nashville 3 (Iginla (CAL) hat trick)

Buffalo 4 at Minnesota 3 (Roy 0:44 OT)
Edmonton 1 at Colorado 4 (Oilers led 1–0 early in 2nd)
Washington 1 at Phoenix 2 (Coyotes scored only two goals of 3rd)

October 24, 2008

Anaheim 4 at Ottawa 3 (Ducks led 4–0 after 2nd)
Philadelphia 6 at New Jersey 3 (Devils led 3–2 after 1st)
NY Rangers 3 at Columbus 1 (Blue Jackets led 1–0 after 1st)
San Jose 3 at Florida 4 (no scoring in 3rd)
Atlanta 3 at Detroit 5 (game tied 1–1 late in 1st)
Los Angeles 4 at St. Louis 0 [LaBarbera]

October 25, 2008

Atlanta 4 at Boston 5 (Lucic (BOS) hat trick)
Ottawa 2 at Toronto 3 (Leafs scored in each period)
Anaheim 6 at Montreal 4 (Canadiens led 3–2 early in 2nd)
Carolina 4 at NY Islanders 3 (seven different scorers)
Pittsburgh 2 at NY Rangers 3 (SO)
New Jersey 2 at Philadelphia 3 (Carter 3:44 OT)
San Jose 3 at Tampa Bay 0 [Boucher]
Los Angeles 4 at Nashville 5 (Predators led 3–0 after 1st; 3–2 after 2nd)
Columbus 1 at Minnesota 2 (Wild led 1–0 after 1st and 2nd)
Washington 6 at Dallas 5 (Semin 2:17 OT)
Detroit 6 at Chicago 5 (SO)
Florida 0 at St. Louis 4 [Schwarz/Bishop]
Buffalo 1 at Colorado 2 (SO)
Edmonton 3 at Vancouver 6 (game tied 3–3 after 2nd)
Calgary 4 at Phoenix 1 (Flames led 2–1 after 1st)

October 26, 2008

No Games Scheduled

October 27, 2008
Ottawa 5 at Buffalo 2 (Senators led 4–0 after 2nd)
NY Rangers 4 at NY Islanders 2 (Rangers led 4–1 late in 3rd)
Anaheim 3 at Columbus 2 (Blue Jackets led 2–1 after 2nd)
Chicago 2 at Minnesota 3 (Blackhawks led 1–0 late in 1st)
Boston 1 at Edmonton 0 (Wideman 3:18 OT) [Thomas]
Detroit 4 at Los Angeles 3 (SO)

October 28, 2008
Nashville 3 at Washington 4 (SO)
Philadelphia 7 at Atlanta 0 [Niittymaki]
Tampa Bay 3 at Toronto 2 (no scoring in 3rd)
Carolina 2 at Montreal 3 (SO)
Colorado 0 at Calgary 3 [Kiprusoff]
Boston 1 at Vancouver 0 (Ryder 10:16 1st) [Thomas]
Pittsburgh 1 at San Jose 2 (Sharks led 1–0 after 1st and 2nd)

October 29, 2008
Toronto 6 at New Jersey 5 (SO)
Minnesota 2 at Dallas 4 (game tied 1–1 early in 1st)
Detroit 4 at Anaheim 5 (Beauchemin 1:39 OT)

October 30, 2008
Tampa Bay 5 at Buffalo 2 (Lightning led 5–1 late in 2nd)
Atlanta 2 at NY Rangers 3 (game tied 2–2 midway through 3rd)
NY Islanders 2 at Philadelphia 3 (Carter 4:37 OT)
Ottawa 2 at Florida 1 (Panthers led 1–0 after 1st and 2nd)
Edmonton 1 at Nashville 3 (Predators scored in each period)
Montreal 2 at Minnesota 1 (no goals in final 37 minutes)
Carolina 1 at St. Louis 0 (Ruutu 10:19 3rd) [Ward]
Columbus 4 at Colorado 2 (Blue Jackets led 4–0 late in 2nd)
Boston 2 at Calgary 3 (Bruins led 1–0 early in 2nd)
Pittsburgh 1 at Phoenix 4 (game tied 1–1 midway through 2nd)

Vancouver 4 at Los Angeles 0 [Luongo]
Detroit 2 at San Jose 4 (Red Wings led 1–0 early in 2nd)

October 31, 2008
Dallas 2 at Chicago 5 (game tied 2–2 midway through 2nd)
Vancouver 7 at Anaheim 6 (SO—13 shots)

November 1, 2008
Edmonton 3 at Carolina 1 (game tied 1–1 after 2nd)
Dallas 1 at Boston 5 (game tied 1–1 after 1st)
Washington 0 at Buffalo 5 [Miller]
NY Rangers 2 at Toronto 5 (Rangers led 2–0 after 2nd)
Atlanta 1 at New Jersey 6 (NJ goalie Brodeur sidelined for four
    months)
Montreal 5 at NY Islanders 4 (Canadiens scored only four goals
    of 3rd)
Chicago 4 at Columbus 3 (SO)
Ottawa 2 at Tampa Bay 3 (SO)
Florida 2 at Nashville 3 (SO)
Pittsburgh 6 at St. Louis 3 (nine different scorers)
Minnesota 3 at Phoenix 2 (Wild scored only goal of 3rd)
Calgary 3 at Los Angeles 2 (Langkow broke 2–2 tie at 16:23 of 3rd)

November 2, 2008
Edmonton 5 at Philadelphia 4 (Hemsky (EDM) two goals)
Toronto 4 at Carolina 6 (Hurricanes scored four goals in 2nd)
Florida 3 at Atlanta 5 (Kovalchuk (ATL) two goals)
San Jose 5 at Colorado 3 (Setoguchi (SJ) two goals)
Calgary 2 at Anaheim 3 (Ducks led 3–0 midway through game)
Detroit 3 at Vancouver 2 (Red Wings led 2–0 midway through
    2nd)

November 3, 2008
Buffalo 2 at New Jersey 0 [Miller]
Columbus 3 at NY Islanders 4 (Campoli 3:13 OT)
Colorado 2 at Chicago 6 (Blackhawks scored three goals in last half of 3rd)

November 4, 2008
NY Islanders 2 at NY Rangers 1 (game tied 0–0 after 2nd)
Carolina 5 at Toronto 4 (Wallin 1:52 OT)
Washington 1 at Ottawa 2 (Fisher 4:20 OT)
Phoenix 4 at Calgary 2 (game tied 2–2 after 1st)
Nashville 0 at Vancouver 4 [Luongo]
Anaheim 1 at Los Angeles 0 (Pronger 0:40 OT) [Giguere]
Minnesota 1 at San Jose 3 (game tied 1–1 after 1st and 2nd)

November 5, 2008
Tampa Bay 3 at New Jersey 4 (SO)
Edmonton 4 at Columbus 5 (Malhotra broke 4–4 tie at 18:51 of 3rd)
St. Louis 2 at Anaheim 5 (game tied 2–2 early in 2nd)

November 6, 2008
Toronto 2 at Boston 5 (Wheeler hat trick)
Tampa Bay 2 at NY Rangers 5 (Drury hat trick)
Carolina 2 at Washington 3 (Hurricanes led 2–1 after 2nd)
NY Islanders 3 at Atlanta 4 (Thrashers scored only three goals of 3rd)
Philadelphia 1 at Ottawa 4 (Senators led 2–0 after 1st)
Edmonton 4 at Pittsburgh 5 (Penguins led 5–0 late in 2nd)
Minnesota 2 at Colorado 1 (no scoring in 3rd)
Nashville 6 at Calgary 7 (Flames led 4–0 after 1st)
Phoenix 0 at Vancouver 1 (Bieksa 11:56 1st) [Luongo]
Florida 2 at Los Angeles 3 (Kings led 2–0 after 1st and 2nd)
St. Louis 4 at San Jose 5 (SO)

November 7, 2008

Ottawa 1 at Carolina 2 (Senators led 1–0 after 2nd)
Montreal 3 at Columbus 4 (SO)
Atlanta 5 at Buffalo 4 (J. Williams 0:48 OT)
Dallas 5 at Anaheim 2 (Parrish hat trick)

November 8, 2008

Buffalo 1 at Boston 3 (game tied 1–1 after 1st)
Montreal 3 at Toronto 6 (game tied 3–3 midway through 2nd)
Pittsburgh 4 at NY Islanders 3 (SO)
Tampa Bay 2 at Philadelphia 1 (Flyers led 1–0 after 1st)
NY Rangers 1 at Washington 3 (Capitals led 2–0 after 1st and 2nd)
New Jersey 1 at Detroit 3 (Red Wings scored in each period)
Calgary 1 at Columbus 3 (game tied 1–1 early in 2nd)
Nashville 0 at Colorado 1 (Tucker 15:39 2nd) [Budaj]
Florida 1 at Phoenix 4 (Panthers led 1–0 after 1st)
Minnesota 0 at Vancouver 2 [Luongo]
Dallas 1 at San Jose 2 (Marleau broke 1–1 tie at 19:31 of 3rd)
St. Louis 3 at Los Angeles 5 (Kings led 4–1 midway through 3rd)

November 9, 2008

Atlanta 5 at Carolina 2 (Thrashers scored four goals in 2nd)
Edmonton 2 at New Jersey 1 (Oilers scored both goals in 2nd)
Calgary 1 at Chicago 6 (Blackhawks scored only three goals of 3rd)
San Jose 2 at Phoenix 4 (Sharks led 2–0 late in 1st)
Florida 3 at Anaheim 1 (Ducks led 1–0 early in 1st)

November 10, 2008

Edmonton 3 at NY Rangers 2 (SO)
Tampa Bay 2 at Washington 4 (Capitals led 3–0 after 1st)

November 11, 2008

Philadelphia 3 at NY Islanders 1 (all goals in 2nd half of game)
Pittsburgh 7 at Detroit 6 (Fedotenko 3:49 OT)

Ottawa 0 at Montreal 4 [Price]
Toronto 3 at Calgary 4 (Flames led 4–1 midway through 3rd)
Dallas 2 at Los Angeles 3 (SO)
Nashville 4 at San Jose 3 (Koistinen 2:28 OT)

November 12, 2008

St. Louis 3 at Buffalo 4 (Sabres led 3–0 early in 1st)
NY Rangers 5 at New Jersey 2 (Rangers scored four goals in 2nd)
Washington 5 at Carolina 1 (Capitals led 3–1 after 1st)
Phoenix 5 at Columbus 2 (Coyotes led 4–0 midway through 3rd)
Tampa Bay 0 at Florida 4 [Anderson]
Boston 2 at Chicago 1 (SO)
Colorado 2 at Vancouver 1 (SO)

November 13, 2008

Montreal 1 at Boston 6 (Bruins led 4–0 midway through game)
NY Islanders 3 at Ottawa 1 (Senators led 1–0 early in 1st)
Philadelphia 4 at Pittsburgh 5 (SO)
Detroit 4 at Tampa Bay 3 (Lightning led 2–0 after 1st)
Phoenix 0 at Minnesota 4 [Backstrom]
Los Angeles 3 at Dallas 2 (no scoring in 3rd)
Toronto 5 at Edmonton 2 (game tied 1–1 early in 2nd)
Calgary 1 at San Jose 6 (Sharks led 6–0 midway through 3rd)

November 14, 2008

New Jersey 1 at Washington 3 (Capitals scored in each period)
Columbus 6 at Buffalo 1 (seven different scorers)
Carolina 2 at Atlanta 3 (Thrashers led 2–0 early in 2nd)
Detroit 3 at Florida 2 (Red Wings scored only goal of 3rd)
St. Louis 4 at Chicago 3 (McDonald 2:15 OT)
Nashville 4 at Anaheim 3 (Hamhuis 2:17 OT)

November 15, 2008
Philadelphia 2 at Montreal 1 (Flyers led 2–0 after 2nd)
Washington 5 at New Jersey 6 (SO)
Ottawa 2 at NY Islanders 3 (Islanders led 3–0 early in 3rd)
Boston 2 at NY Rangers 3 (SO)
Toronto 2 at Vancouver 4 (Canucks led 4–0 after 2nd)
Buffalo 2 at Pittsburgh 5 (Penguins scored only four goals of 3rd)
Columbus 2 at Minnesota 3 (SO)
Dallas 3 at Phoenix 2 (no scoring in 3rd)
Colorado 3 at Edmonton 2 (SO)
Nashville 3 at Los Angeles 1 (Predators scored only two goals of 3rd)

November 16, 2008
Tampa Bay 2 at Carolina 3 (SO)
Montreal 3 at St. Louis 2 (SO)
Atlanta 3 at Philadelphia 4 (game tied 3–3 midway through 3rd)
San Jose 6 at Chicago 5 (Sharks led 1–0, 2–1, 4–2, trailed 5–4)
Los Angeles 0 at Anaheim 2 [Hiller]

November 17, 2008
Vancouver 1 at NY Islanders 2 (SO)
Ottawa 1 at NY Rangers 2 (SO)
Boston 3 at Toronto 2 (Bruins led 3–1 after 2nd)
Edmonton 0 at Detroit 4 [Conklin]
San Jose 4 at Nashville 1 (Sharks led 4–0 after 2nd)

November 18, 2008
Minnesota 2 at Pittsburgh 1 (SO)
Montreal 1 at Carolina 2 (Canadiens led 1–0 after 2nd)
Edmonton 7 at Columbus 2 (Oilers scored four goals in 3rd)
Florida 4 at Tampa Bay 3 (SO)
Chicago 3 at Phoenix 2 (SO)
Colorado 1 at Calgary 4 (Flames scored only three goals of 3rd)

November 19, 2008

Buffalo 4 at Boston 7 (Sabres led 4–3 after 1st)
Vancouver 6 at NY Rangers 3 (Canucks led 4–0 early in 2nd)
Washington 6 at Anaheim 4 (Capitals led 5–2 after 2nd)

November 20, 2008

Florida 1 at New Jersey 3 (Devils led 1–0 after 2nd)
Pittsburgh 3 at Atlanta 2 (Penguins scored only goal of 3rd)
Montreal 3 at Ottawa 2 (SO)
Vancouver 3 at Minnesota 2 (Canucks scored only goal of 3rd)
Chicago 6 at Dallas 3 (game tied 2–2 late in 2nd)
Calgary 1 at Colorado 0 (Langkow 10:16 2nd) [Kiprusoff]
Detroit 4 at Edmonton 3 (Red Wings led 3–0 midway through
  2nd)
Washington 2 at Los Angeles 5 (Kings led 2–1 after 2nd)

November 21, 2008

Florida 2 at Boston 4 (game tied 1–1 midway through 1st)
NY Islanders 2 at New Jersey 5 (Devils led 2–1 early in 2nd)
Phoenix 2 at Carolina 5 (Coyotes led 2–1 after 1st)
Philadelphia 3 at Buffalo 0 [Biron]
Nashville 1 at Tampa Bay 4 (no scoring in 3rd)
Anaheim 2 at St. Louis 3 (Stempniak 2:39 OT)

November 22, 2008

Vancouver 3 at Pittsburgh 1 (Demitra two goals)
NY Rangers 1 at Ottawa 4 (Senators led 3–0 after 2nd)
NY Islanders 4 at Buffalo 2 (Islanders led 2–1 after 2nd)
Chicago 5 at Toronto 4 (Bolland 0:49 OT)
Boston 3 at Montreal 2 (SO)
Phoenix 3 at Philadelphia 4 (Richards 1:35 OT)
Columbus 2 at Atlanta 0 [Mason]
St. Louis 2 at Minnesota 1 (all goals in 2nd)
Anaheim 2 at Dallas 1 (SO)

Detroit 5 at Calgary 2 (game tied 2–2 early in 3rd)
Colorado 4 at Los Angeles 3 (SO)
Washington 2 at San Jose 7 (Sharks led 3–0 early in 2nd)

November 23, 2008

Nashville 5 at Carolina 2 (Arnott & Weber (both CAR) two goals
    each)
New Jersey 7 at Tampa Bay 3 (Zubrus four goals)

November 24, 2008

Phoenix 1 at NY Rangers 4 (game tied 1–1 after 1st)
Dallas 3 at Philadelphia 4 (Flyers scored only goal of 3rd)
NY Islanders 4 at Montreal 3 (SO)
Carolina 2 at Florida 3 (game tied 2–2 late in 2nd)
Washington 3 at Minnesota 4 (Wild led 3–0 early in 3rd)
Detroit 2 at Vancouver 3 (Salo 2:33 OT)
Colorado 1 at Anaheim 4 (Ducks led 3–0 after 2nd)

November 25, 2008

St. Louis 1 at Nashville 0 (SO) [Mason/Ellis]
Atlanta 6 at Toronto 3 (Thrashers led 3–0 early in 2nd)
Los Angeles 2 at Calgary 6 (Flames scored two goals in each
    period)

November 26, 2008

Boston 2 at Buffalo 3 (Sabres led 2–0 after 1st)
Pittsburgh 5 at NY Islanders 3 (Penguins scored only four goals
    of 3rd)
Atlanta 3 at Washington 5 (Ovechkin (WAS) hat trick)
Philadelphia 3 at Carolina 1 (Flyers scored only two goals of 3rd)
Phoenix 3 at Columbus 2 (Tikhonov broke 2–2 tie at 17:28 of 3rd)
NY Rangers 3 at Tampa Bay 2 (SO)
New Jersey 3 at Florida 2 (Oduya 4:04 OT)
Montreal 3 at Detroit 1 (Canadiens scored all goals in 2nd)

Dallas 4 at Minnesota 3 (Stars trailed 3–2 after 2nd)
St. Louis 1 at Colorado 3 (Avs scored in each period)
Los Angeles 2 at Edmonton 1 (game tied 1–1 late in 2nd)
Chicago 2 at San Jose 3 (Thornton 0:45 OT)

November 27, 2008

Toronto 1 at Ottawa 2 (SO)
Calgary 4 at Vancouver 3 (Cammalleri (CAL) hat trick)

November 28, 2008

NY Islanders 2 at Boston 7 (Bruins scored five goals in 3rd)
Carolina 3 at Philadelphia 2 (Samsonov 3:53 OT)
Tampa Bay 2 at Minnesota 4 (Wild scored only three goals of 3rd)
Colorado 1 at Phoenix 2 (Coyotes scored in 1st and 2nd; Avs in
     3rd)
Chicago 0 at Anaheim 1 (Getzlaf 15:19 2nd) [Hiller]
Montreal 0 at Washington 3 [Theodore]
Pittsburgh 3 at Buffalo 4 (Pens led 3–2 after 2nd)
Nashville 4 at Atlanta 3 (Suter 1:44 OT)
NY Rangers 4 at Florida 3 (SO)
Columbus 3 at Detroit 5 (Hossa (DET) and Tyutin (CBJ) two
     goals each)
San Jose 6 at Dallas 2 (game tied 1–1 midway through 1st)

November 29, 2008

Edmonton 4 at St. Louis 2 (Oilers scored only two goals of 3rd)
Chicago 2 at Los Angeles 5 (game tied 2–2 after 2nd)
Detroit 1 at Boston 4 (Bruins led 3–0 late in 2nd)
Philadelphia 2 at Toronto 4 (first game with new Leafs GM,
     Brian Burke)
Buffalo 2 at Montreal 3 (Canadiens scored all goals in 2nd)
Ottawa 2 at NY Islanders 4 (game tied 1–1 late in 2nd)
Washington 0 at Columbus 3 [Mason]

New Jersey 1 at Pittsburgh 4 (Crosby hat trick and assist)

Minnesota 6 at Nashville 2 (Wild scored two goals in each period)

Tampa Bay 3 at Colorado 4 (Avs led 3–0 after 1st)

San Jose 3 at Phoenix 2 (game tied 2–2 after 1st and 2nd)

Vancouver 1 at Calgary 3 (Flames led 1–0 after 2nd)

November 30, 2008

Florida 4 at NY Rangers 0 [C. Anderson]

St. Louis 4 at Atlanta 2 (game tied 1–1 late in 1st)

Edmonton 3 at Dallas 4 (Modano broke 3–3 tie at 17:39 of 3rd)

Anaheim 4 at Carolina 1 (game tied 1–1 after 1st & 2nd)

December 1, 2008

Nashville 2 at Buffalo 0 [Rinne]

Vancouver 2 at Columbus 3 (game tied 0–0 after 1st, 1–1 after 2nd)

Anaheim 1 at Detroit 2 (Ducks led 1–0 after 1st)

Colorado 6 at Minnesota 5 (Wild led 1–0, 3–2)

Toronto 3 at Los Angeles 1 (Kings led 1–0 after 1st & 2nd)

December 2, 2008

Tampa Bay 3 at Philadelphia 4 (Richards 2:05 OT)

Florida 5 at Washington 3 (Capitals led 3–0 after 1st)

Atlanta 4 at Montreal 5 (Habs led 3–0 after 2nd)

Dallas 3 at Calgary 1 (game tied 1–1 early in 2nd)

Los Angeles 2 at Phoenix 4 (Kings led 2–1 after 2nd)

Toronto 2 at San Jose 5 (Sharks led 4–0 after 1st)

December 3, 2008

Atlanta 1 at Ottawa 5 (game tied 1–1 early in 1st)

Pittsburgh 2 at NY Rangers 3 (SO)

St. Louis 0 at Minnesota 4 (Backstrom)

Anaheim 2 at Chicago 4 (game tied 1–1 after 2nd)
Dallas 2 at Edmonton 5 (Oilers led 3–0 after 2nd)

December 4, 2008
NY Rangers 2 at Montreal 6 (Habs led 4–0 midway through game)
New Jersey 3 at Philadelphia 2 (Elias 2:46 OT)
NY Islanders 2 at Washington 5 (seven different scorers)
Pittsburgh 5 at Carolina 2 (no scoring in 3rd)
Boston 3 at Tampa Bay 1 (Bruins scored only two goals of 3rd)
Buffalo 1 at Florida 2 (Panthers led 2–0 after 2nd)
Vancouver 5 at Detroit 6 (Red Wings trailed 1–0, led 2–1, trailed 3–2, led 6–3)
Colorado 2 at Nashville 3 (all goals in 1st)
Toronto 3 at Phoenix 6 (Hanzal (PHO) hat trick)
Columbus 2 at San Jose 3 (game tied 1–1 after 2nd)

December 5, 2008
Vancouver 2 at Minnesota 1 (no scoring in 3rd)
Calgary 4 at St. Louis 3 (Cammalleri 2:21 OT)
Colorado 1 at Dallas 2 (SO)
Edmonton 5 at Los Angeles 4 (SO)

December 6, 2008
Washington 2 at Toronto 1 (game tied 1–1 early in 3rd)
New Jersey 2 at Montreal 1 (Parise 0:31 OT)
Pittsburgh 2 at Ottawa 3 (Senators scored all goals in 2nd)
Atlanta 5 at NY Islanders 1 (Islanders led 1–0 at 0:51 of 1st)
Philadelphia 2 at Carolina 1 (Carter 3:34 OT)
Boston 4 at Florida 0 [Fernandez]
Chicago 4 at Detroit 5 (SO)
Buffalo 4 at Tampa Bay 3 (Sabres scored only goal of 3rd)
Minnesota 0 at Nashville 1 (Dumont 10:48 3rd) [Rinne]
Phoenix 3 at St. Louis 4 (no scoring in 3rd)

Edmonton 3 at San Jose 2 (Brodziak 2:40 OT)

Columbus 0 at Los Angeles 3 [LaBarbera]

December 7, 2008

Washington 1 at Carolina 3 (Hurricanes scored two late goals in 3rd)

Calgary 3 at NY Rangers 0 [Kiprusoff]

Phoenix 1 at Chicago 7 (no scoring in 3rd)

Vancouver 4 at Colorado 5 (SO)

Columbus 3 at Anaheim 5 (Getzlaf (ANA) two goals)

December 8, 2008

Tampa Bay 3 at Boston 5 (eight different scorers)

NY Islanders 2 at Toronto 4 (game tied 1–1 after 1st)

Florida 4 at Ottawa 3 (Weiss 4:50 OT)

Buffalo 4 at Pittsburgh 3 (Sabres scored only goal of 3rd)

Nashville 3 at St. Louis 6 (Blues scored only three goals of 3rd)

December 9, 2008

NY Islanders 3 at Philadelphia 4 (Islanders led 2–1 after 1st)

Calgary 1 at Montreal 4 (Lang two goals)

Vancouver 3 at Nashville 1 (game tied 1–1 after 1st & 2nd)

Los Angeles 1 at Colorado 6 (no scoring in 3rd)

December 10, 2008

Tampa Bay 2 at Buffalo 4 (Lightning led 2–0 late in 1st)

Pittsburgh 1 at New Jersey 4 (Devils led 1–0 after 2nd)

Boston 1 at Washington 3 (Capitals scored in each period)

NY Rangers 3 at Atlanta 2 (Gomez 0:18 OT)

Calgary 3 at Detroit 4 (Lidstrom 3:50 OT)

Ottawa 0 at Chicago 2 [Huet]

Phoenix 5 at Dallas 3 (O. Jokinen & Hanzal (PHO) two goals each)

St. Louis 2 at Anaheim 4 (game tied 1–1 after 1st)

December 11, 2008

Carolina 5 at Philadelphia 6 (SO)
Nashville 1 at Columbus 2 (SO)
Tampa Bay 3 at Montreal 1 (no scoring in final 31 minutes)
NY Islanders 2 at Pittsburgh 9 (Sykora & Dupuis both hat tricks)
Florida 2 at Edmonton 0 [C. Anderson]
Minnesota 1 at Phoenix 3 Coyotes led 3–0 early in 3rd)
St. Louis 2 at Los Angeles 6 (D. Brown hat trick)
Anaheim 0 at San Jose 2 [Nabokov]

December 12, 2008

NY Rangers 5 at New Jersey 8 (Rangers rallied from 5–1 to tie 5–5
    in 3rd)
Ottawa 1 at Washington 5 (Ovechkin two goals)
Toronto 2 at Buffalo 1 (Leafs scored only goal of 3rd)
Boston 7 at Atlanta 3 (Bruins led 4–0 in 1st)
Detroit 1 at Dallas 3 (Red Wings led 1–0 after 1st)
Chicago 4 at Colorado 3 (Byfuglien (CHI) two goals)
Florida 3 at Calgary 2 (SO)

December 13, 2008

Pittsburgh 3 at Philadelphia 6 (Flyers led 5–1 after 2nd)
Minnesota 1 at Los Angeles 3 (Kings led 1–0 after 1st & 2nd)
Atlanta 2 at Boston 4 (Ryder (BOS) two goals)
Washington 2 at Montreal 1 (Nylander broke 1–1 tie at 17:28
    of 3rd)
Tampa Bay 0 at Ottawa 2 [Gerber]
Buffalo 4 at New Jersey 2 (Vanek (BUF) two goals)
Carolina 2 at NY Rangers 3 (SO)
NY Islanders 1 at Columbus 3 (no scoring in 1st)
Dallas 0 at Nashville 3 [Ellis]
Detroit 5 at Phoenix 4 (SO)
Vancouver 0 at Edmonton 3 (Roloson)
St. Louis 4 at San Jose 5 (Blues led 1–0, 3–2)

December 14, 2008

Columbus 1 at Chicago 3 (Blue Jackets led 1–0 after 1st)

Minnesota 2 at Anaheim 4 (no scoring in 3rd)

Florida 3 at Vancouver 5 (Canucks scored only four goals of 2nd)

December 15, 2008

Colorado 3 at Detroit 2 (Avs led 2–0 after 1st)

San Jose 3 at Los Angeles 2 (SO)

December 16, 2008

Washington 5 at NY Islanders 4 (Ovechkin 4:49 OT)

Colorado 2 at Philadelphia 5 (Avs led 1–0 midway through 1st)

Montreal 2 at Carolina 3 (no scoring in 3rd)

New Jersey 2 at Toronto 3 (SO)

Atlanta 4 at Ottawa 1 (Thrashers led 1–0 after 1st & 2nd)

Calgary 6 at St. Louis 3 (Iginla (CAL) two goals)

Phoenix 1 at Dallas 2 (Eriksson 3:39 OT)

Chicago 9 at Edmonton 2 (eleven different scorers)

NY Rangers 3 at Anaheim 1 (Rangers scored only two goals of 3rd)

December 17, 2008

New Jersey 5 at Buffalo 3 (both teams scored in all periods)

San Jose 1 at Columbus 2 (Umberger 2:55 OT)

Calgary 3 at Minnesota 2 (Bertuzzi 3:48 OT)

Edmonton 2 at Vancouver 4 (Canucks scored only three goals of 2nd)

NY Rangers 3 at Los Angeles 2 (Rozsival 3:41 OT)

December 18, 2008

Toronto 5 at Boston 8 (teams combined for eight goals in 2nd)

St. Louis 2 at Washington 4 (Kozlov (WAS) two goals)

Florida 1 at Carolina 2 (Corvo 4:16 OT)

Pittsburgh 6 at Atlanta 3 (Malkin (PIT) two goals)

Philadelphia 2 at Montreal 5 (Habs led 3–0 late in 1st)
Colorado 2 at Tampa Bay 1 (SO)
San Jose 0 at Detroit 6 [Conklin]
Columbus 5 at Dallas 6 (SO)
Nashville 1 at Phoenix 2 (Coyotes scored only goal of 3rd)

December 19, 2008

Ottawa 1 at New Jersey 5 (Elias two goals)
Los Angeles 0 at Buffalo 5 [Miller]
NY Islanders 1 at Minnesota 4 (Wild scored only three goals of 3rd)
Chicago 3 at Calgary 2 (Keith 0:23 OT)
Anaheim 3 at Edmonton 2 (SO)

December 20, 2008

Carolina 2 at Boston 4 (Hurricanes led 1–0 after 1st)
Washington 1 at Philadelphia 7 (Hartnell hat trick)
Buffalo 3 at Montreal 4 (Kovalev 4:35 OT)
Dallas 4 at Ottawa 5 (J. Smith 3:30 OT)
Toronto 7 at Pittsburgh 3 (seven different scorers for Leafs)
Tampa Bay 3 at Atlanta 4 (St. Louis (TB) two goals)
Los Angeles 4 at Detroit 6 (ten different scorers)
NY Islanders 0 at Nashville 1 (Fiddler 6:48 1st) [Rinne]
Minnesota 2 at St. Louis 4 (game tied 2–2 early in 3rd)
Columbus 0 at Phoenix 2 [Bryzgalov]
Chicago 3 at Vancouver 1 (Canucks led 1–0 after 1st)
NY Rangers 2 at San Jose 3 (no scoring in 3rd)

December 21, 2008

Colorado 0 at Florida 3 [Vokoun]
Boston 6 at St. Louis 3 (Wheeler (BOS) two goals)
Carolina 3 at Montreal 2 (T. Ruutu 1:43 OT)
Philadelphia 2 at New Jersey 3 (SO)

December 22, 2008

Pittsburgh 4 at Buffalo 3 (Crosby 0:43 OT)
Toronto 6 at Atlanta 2 (Leafs led 3–0 late in 2nd)
Phoenix 2 at Edmonton 4 (Oilers scored only two goals of 3rd)
Anaheim 3 at Vancouver 4 (Ducks led 1–0 midway through 1st)

December 23, 2008

Boston 2 at New Jersey 0 [Thomas]
Atlanta 4 at NY Islanders 2 (Little (ATL) two goals)
Washington 5 at NY Rangers 4 (Morrisonn 0:59 OT)
Ottawa 4 at Philadelphia 6 (Flyers scored two goals in each period)
Los Angeles 3 at Columbus 0 [Quick]
Dallas 8 at Toronto 2 (Stars led 7–0 midway through game)
Tampa Bay 2 at Pittsburgh 0 [M. Smith]
Nashville 0 at Florida 3 [Vokoun]
St. Louis 1 at Detroit 4 (Red Wings led 2–0 after 1st)
Carolina 2 at Minnesota 3 (no scoring in 3rd)
Phoenix 4 at Colorado 5 (Clark 1:48 OT)
Anaheim 3 at Calgary 4 (game tied 1–1 after 2nd)
Vancouver 0 at San Jose 5 [Nabokov]

December 24, 2008

No Games Scheduled

December 25, 2008

No Games Scheduled

December 26, 2008

Pittsburgh 1 at New Jersey 0 (Fedotenko 12:51 2nd) [Fleury]
Toronto 1 at NY Islanders 4 (game tied 1–1 late in 1st)
Buffalo 2 at Washington 3 (Capitals led 1–0 after 2nd)
Carolina 5 at Atlanta 4 (E. Staal (CAR) & Little (ATL) hat tricks)
Tampa Bay 4 at Florida 3 (SO)

Detroit 2 at Nashville 3 (game tied 1–1 midway through 1st)
Philadelphia 1 at Chicago 5 (Hawks led 2–1 after 1st)
Edmonton 3 at Vancouver 2 (Oilers led 3–0 late in 2nd)
Phoenix 2 at Los Angeles 1 (Kings scored only goal of 3rd)

December 27, 2008

NY Islanders 3 at Buffalo 4 (SO)
Montreal 3 at Pittsburgh 2 (Habs scored only goal of 3rd)
Boston 4 at Carolina 2 (Bruins scored only two goals of 3rd)
Philadelphia 0 at Columbus 3 [Mason]
New Jersey 4 at NY Rangers 2 (Devils scored in each period)
Florida 4 at Tampa Bay 6 (Lecavalier (TB) two goals)
Anaheim 3 at Dallas 4 (Modano 3:34 OT)
San Jose 2 at St. Louis 3 (SO)
Detroit 3 at Colorado 4 (SO)
Los Angeles 4 at Phoenix 0 [Quick]
Ottawa 3 at Calgary 6 (Flames scored three goals in 2nd & 3rd)

December 28, 2008

Boston 2 at Atlanta 1 (Thrashers led 1–0 after 1st)
Anaheim 4 at St. Louis 3 (both Niedermayers scored for Ducks)
Chicago 4 at Minnesota 1 (Hawks led 3–0 after 2nd)
Toronto 1 at Washington 4 (Leafs led 1–0 after 1st)
Nashville 2 at Edmonton 5 (Predators led 1–0 midway through
   1st)
Ottawa 0 at Vancouver 3 [Sanford]

December 29, 2008

NY Islanders 4 at NY Rangers 5 (Rangers scored four goals in 3rd)
Montreal 5 at Florida 2 (Lapierre hat trick)
San Jose 3 at Dallas 1 (Sharks led 1–0 after 1st & 2nd)
Nashville 1 at Colorado 5 (McLeod two goals)
Minnesota 1 at Calgary 2 (Flames scored only goal of 3rd)
Columbus 2 at Los Angeles 0 [Mason]

December 30, 2008

Washington 4 at Buffalo 2 (Capitals led 3–0 early in 3rd)
Atlanta 3 at Toronto 4 (Kubina 0:33 OT)
Boston 5 at Pittsburgh 2 (game tied 2–2 late in 2nd)
Montreal 2 at Tampa Bay 1 (SO)
Chicago 0 at Detroit 4 [Conklin]
New Jersey 4 at St. Louis 3 (Blues led 2–1 after 1st)
Ottawa 3 at Edmonton 2 (Senators scored only goal of 3rd)
Philadelphia 3 at Vancouver 2 (no scoring in 3rd)

December 31, 2008

Florida 2 at NY Islanders 4 (Islanders scored only three goals of 2nd)
San Jose 2 at Minnesota 3 (Burns 1:38 OT)
Atlanta 1 at Carolina 3 (Thrashers led 1–0 late in 1st)
Colorado 1 at Phoenix 3 (Avs led 1–0 after 1st)
New Jersey 2 at Dallas 4 (Devils led 2–1 after 1st)
Columbus 2 at Anaheim 0 [Mason]
Edmonton 4 at Calgary 6 (Flames broke 3–3 tie with three goals in 3rd)

January 1, 2009

Detroit 6 at Chicago 4 (game played outdoors at Wrigley Field—attendance 40,818)
Pittsburgh 2 at Boston 4 (Penguins led 1–0 early in 1st)
Buffalo 4 at Toronto 1 (Sabres led 4–0 early in 3rd)
Tampa Bay 4 at Washington 7 (Capitals led 3–0 after 1st)
Vancouver 2 at Nashville 1 (Canucks scored only goal of 3rd)

January 2, 2009

Montreal 1 at New Jersey 4 (game tied 1–1 late in 1st)
St. Louis 1 at Carolina 2 (Hurricanes led 1–0 after 1st & 2nd)
Vancouver 3 at Atlanta 4 (SO)
Columbus 6 at Colorado 1 (Avs led 1–0 after 1st)

NY Islanders 4 at Phoenix 5 (Park (NYI) two goals)
Philadelphia 5 at Anaheim 4 (SO)

January 3, 2009
Buffalo 4 at Boston 2 (Ellis (BUF) two goals)
Florida 6 at Pittsburgh 1 (Panthers led 2–1 early in 2nd)
Calgary 3 at Nashville 2 (Flames scored only two goals of 3rd)
Ottawa 1 at Toronto 3 (game tied 1–1 after 2nd)
NY Rangers 1 at Washington 2 (all goals in 2nd)
Carolina 3 at Tampa Bay 2 (game tied 2–2 after 1st)
Detroit 3 at Minnesota 2 (SO)
Columbus 2 at St. Louis 5 (game tied 2–2 after 1st)
Dallas 1 at Edmonton 4 (Oilers led 3–0 midway through game)
Philadelphia 1 at Los Angeles 2 (SO)
NY Islanders 3 at San Jose 5 (Grier (SJ) two goals)

January 4, 2009
Florida 5 at Montreal 6 (SO)
Tampa Bay 4 at Atlanta 1 (St. Louis two goals)
Ottawa 3 at New Jersey 4 (Rolston 1:43 OT)
Calgary 2 at Chicago 5 (score tied 1–1 midway through game)
Minnesota 2 at Colorado 0 [N. Backstrom]
Phoenix 0 at Anaheim 2 [Hiller]
Dallas 3 at Vancouver 2 (SO)

January 5, 2009
Pittsburgh 0 at NY Rangers 4 [H. Lundqvist]
NY Islanders 2 at Edmonton 3 (Islanders led 2–0 after 1st)

January 6, 2009
Minnesota 1 at Boston 0 (Zidlicky 7:29 2nd) [N. Backstrom]
Ottawa 2 at Buffalo 4 (Sabres led 3–0 early in 2nd)
Philadelphia 1 at Washington 2 (SO)

New Jersey 2 at Carolina 3 (Hurricanes scored in each period)
Florida 4 at Toronto 2 (Panthers led 3–0 after 2nd)
Atlanta 1 at Pittsburgh 3 (Thrashers scored only goal of 3rd)
Columbus 0 at Detroit 3 [Conklin]
Colorado 2 at Nashville 1 (no scoring in 3rd)
San Jose 2 at Calgary 5 (Langkow & Moss (CAL) two goals each)
Chicago 6 at Phoenix 0 [Huet]
Los Angeles 1 at Anaheim 3 (score tied 1–1 after 2nd)

January 7, 2009

Montreal 6 at NY Rangers 3 (Habs scored four goals in 3rd)
Vancouver 4 at Edmonton 2 (game tied 1–1 late in 2nd)

January 8, 2009

Ottawa 4 at Boston 6 (ten different scorers)
Atlanta 4 at New Jersey 0 [Lehtonen]
Minnesota 1 at Philadelphia 3 (Flyers scored only two goals
     of 3rd)
Toronto 2 at Montreal 6 (A. Kostitsyn (MON) two goals)
Carolina 2 at Florida 4 (game tied 1–1 after 1st & 2nd)
Dallas 1 at Detroit 6 (Red Wings scored two goals in each period)
Pittsburgh 3 at Nashville 5 (Penguins led 3–0 early in 2nd)
Chicago 1 at Colorado 2 (Avs scored only goal of 3rd)
NY Islanders 2 at Calgary 5 (game tied 2–2 late in 2nd)
Tampa Bay 2 at Phoenix 3 (game tied 2–2 after 2nd)
Anaheim 3 at Los Angeles 4 (Frolov broke 3–3 tie at 7:43 of 3rd)

January 9, 2009

Columbus 3 at Washington 0 [Mason]
NY Rangers 1 at Buffalo 2 (SO)
San Jose 4 at Edmonton 1 (Sharks led 3–1 after 1st)
St. Louis 6 at Vancouver 4 (game tied 3–3 early in 3rd)
Tampa Bay 4 at Anaheim 3 (Lightning scored only goal of 3rd)

January 10, 2009

Carolina 1 at Boston 5 (Bruins led 5–0 after 2nd)
Pittsburgh 3 at Colorado 5 (Avs scored three goals in 2nd)
Washington 4 at Montreal 5 (S. Kostitsyn broke 4–4 tie at 19:38 of 3rd)
NY Rangers 2 at Ottawa 0 [Lundqvist]
Toronto 1 at Philadelphia 4 (Carter two goals)
Atlanta 4 at Florida 8 (game tied 3–3 after 2nd)
Buffalo 1 at Detroit 3 (Sabres led 1–0 after 1st)
Minnesota 2 at Columbus 4 (game tied 1–1 after 1st & 2nd)
Chicago 1 at Nashville 4 (Predators led 2–0 after 2nd)
Dallas 0 at Phoenix 1 (SO) [Turco/Bryzgalov]
San Jose 4 at Vancouver 2 (game tied 2–2 after 2nd)
New Jersey 5 at Los Angeles 1 (Devils led 3–0 after 2nd)

January 11, 2009

Nashville 1 at Chicago 3 (game tied 1–1 midway through 1st)
St. Louis 1 at Edmonton 2 (Oilers scored only goal of 3rd)
New Jersey 3 at Anaheim 4 (game tied 2–2 after 2nd)

January 12, 2009

Detroit 4 at Dallas 5 (Daley 1:51 OT)
Tampa Bay 3 at Los Angeles 1 (no scoring in 3rd)

January 13, 2009

Montreal 1 at Boston 3 (no scoring in 1st)
NY Rangers 2 at NY Islanders 1 (Islanders led 1–0 after 1st)
Pittsburgh 4 at Philadelphia 2 (game tied 1–1 after 1st)
Edmonton 5 at Washington 2 (hat trick)
Colorado 3 at Columbus 4 (game tied 1–1 after 2nd)
Nashville 2 at Toronto 0 [Rinne]
Carolina 1 at Ottawa 5 (Senators led 2–1 midway through game)
Phoenix 3 at Minnesota 6 (nine different scorers)

St. Louis 1 at Calgary 3 (Cammalleri two goals)
New Jersey 5 at Vancouver 3 (Devils led 3–0 after 1st)
Tampa Bay 1 at San Jose 7 (Thornton two goals)

January 14, 2009

Washington 6 at Pittsburgh 3 (game tied 3–3 early in 3rd)
Ottawa 3 at Atlanta 2 (no scoring in last half of game)
Buffalo 1 at Chicago 4 (Sabres led 1–0 midway through 1st)
Detroit 4 at Anaheim 3 (Red Wings scored only two goals of 3rd)

January 15, 2009

Boston 2 at NY Islanders 1 (Bruins led 2–0 early in 3rd)
Toronto 6 at Carolina 4 (Blake (TOR) hat trick & two assists)
Nashville 2 at Montreal 3 (Habs scored in each period)
Philadelphia 1 at Tampa Bay 4 (Flyers led 1–0 midway through 2nd)
Edmonton 1 at Minnesota 5 (game tied 1–1 late in 1st)
Colorado 2 at St. Louis 5 (Blues led 3–0 early in 3rd)
Buffalo 5 at Dallas 4 (SO)
Phoenix 4 at Vancouver 1 (Coyotes led 4–0 after 2nd)
Detroit 4 at Los Angeles 0 [Conklin]
Calgary 3 at San Jose 2 (Phaneuf broke 2–2 tie at 16:03 of 3rd)

January 16, 2009

New Jersey 2 at Columbus 1 (Blue Jackets led 1–0 after 2nd)
Anaheim 1 at Pittsburgh 3 (Penguins scored in each period)
Toronto 3 at Atlanta 4 (Peverley 3:51 OT)
Philadelphia 3 at Florida 2 (SO)
NY Rangers 3 at Chicago 2 (Drury 2:23 OT)
Edmonton 3 at Colorado 2 (Oilers scored only goal of 3rd)

January 17, 2009
Los Angeles 2 at Dallas 3 (SO)
Carolina 1 at Buffalo 3 (Connolly two goals)
Montreal 5 at Ottawa 4 (SO)
New Jersey 3 at NY Islanders 1 (Devils led 3–0 after 2nd)
Boston 1 at Washington 2 (Capitals scored only goal of 3rd)
Florida 4 at Tampa Bay 3 (Lightning led 3–1 after 1st)
Atlanta 7 at Nashville 2 (nine different scorers)
Chicago 2 at St. Louis 1 (Havlat 1:23 OT)
Anaheim 3 at Minnesota 0 [Hiller]
Phoenix 4 at Calgary 3 (Coyotes led 3–1 after 2nd)
Detroit 5 at San Jose 6 (Sharks scored two goals in each period)

January 18, 2009
NY Rangers 0 at Pittsburgh 3 [Fleury]
Calgary 2 at Colorado 6 (Avs scored two goals in each period)
Phoenix 3 at Edmonton 6 (Coyotes led 1–0 midway through 1st)
Columbus 6 at Vancouver 5 (SO)

January 19, 2009
St. Louis 5 at Boston 4 (SO)
Washington 2 at NY Islanders 1 (Ovechkin 1:46 OT)
Carolina 2 at Toronto 0 [Ward]
Dallas 2 at Tampa Bay 4 (Lightning scored only three goals
     of 3rd)
Buffalo 3 at Florida 2 (SO)
Minnesota 4 at Chicago 1 (Zidlicky two goals)
New Jersey 3 at Nashville 1 (Devils led 2–0 after 2nd)

January 20, 2009
Anaheim 2 at NY Rangers 4 (Rangers scored only two goals of
     3rd)
Montreal 2 at Atlanta 4 (Thrashers led 2–0 early in 2nd)
Washington 2 at Ottawa 3 (Bell broke 2–2 tie at 18:38 of 3rd)

Carolina 2 at Pittsburgh 1 (no scoring final 32 minutes of game)

Los Angeles 5 at Minnesota 2 (Kings led 3–1 midway through 2nd)

Columbus 3 at Edmonton 4 (Oilers scored only two goals of 3rd)

Detroit 3 at Phoenix 6 (game tied 3–3 after 2nd)

Vancouver 1 at San Jose 2 (Marleau 3:08 OT)

January 21, 2009

Montreal 2 at New Jersey 5 (Devils led 4–1 early in 3rd)

Anaheim 1 at NY Islanders 2 (Islanders led 2–0 after 1st)

Atlanta 3 at Philadelphia 5 (Flyers led 3–0 after 2nd)

Boston 4 at Toronto 3 (SO)

Buffalo 3 at Tampa Bay 5 (no scoring in 3rd)

Dallas 4 at Florida 1 (Panthers led 1–0 after 1st)

St. Louis 2 at Chicago 0 [Mason]

Los Angeles 6 at Colorado 5 (Kings scored five goals in 2nd)

Columbus 4 at Calgary 5 (SO)

January 22–26, 2009

All-Star Game break

January 27, 2009

Washington 2 at Boston 3 (Krejci 1:55 OT)

Carolina 2 at NY Rangers 3 (Rangers led 2–1 after 1st & 2nd)

Detroit 2 at Columbus 3 (Nash 3:27 OT to complete hat trick)

New Jersey 4 at Ottawa 1 (game tied 1–1 midway through game)

Montreal 3 at Tampa Bay 5 (Habs led 2–1 after 1st)

Philadelphia 2 at Florida 3 (Panthers led 3–1 after 2nd)

Toronto 1 at Minnesota 6 (game tied 1–1 early in 2nd)

Atlanta 0 at Dallas 2 [Turco]

San Jose 3 at Colorado 0 [Nabokov]

Buffalo 10 at Edmonton 2 (worst home loss in Oilers' history)

Anaheim 7 at Phoenix 3 (game tied 2–2 early in 2nd)

January 28, 2009

NY Rangers 2 at Pittsburgh 6 (Penguins scored five goals in 3rd)
Buffalo 2 at Calgary 5 (Flames scored only three goals of 3rd)
Chicago 3 at Anaheim 2 (no scoring in 3rd)
Nashville 5 at Vancouver 3 (game tied 3–3 after 2nd)

January 29, 2009

New Jersey 4 at Boston 3 (Langenbrunner 1:11 OT)
Tampa Bay 2 at Carolina 3 (E. Staal broke 2–2 tie at 18:24 of 3rd)
NY Islanders 5 at Atlanta 4 (Thrashers scored all four goals in 3rd)
Montreal 1 at Florida 5 Panthers led 2–1 early in 2nd)
Dallas 4 at Detroit 2 (Stars led 4–0 early in 2nd)
Ottawa 3 at St. Louis 1 (game tied 1–1 after 1st & 2nd)
Toronto 7 at Colorado 4 (game tied 4–4 early in 3rd)
Chicago 2 at Los Angeles 5 (Kings led 3–0 after 2nd)
Phoenix 0 at San Jose 2 [Nabokov]

January 30, 2009

Pittsburgh 3 at New Jersey 4 (Langenbrunner 4:00 OT)
Ottawa 0 at Columbus 1 (Voracek 3:55 2nd) [Mason]
Philadelphia 6 at Tampa Bay 1 (game tied 1–1 after 1st)
Nashville 1 at Calgary 3 (Flames led 2–0 after 2nd)
Minnesota 1 at Edmonton 3 (Wild scored only goal of 3rd)

January 31, 2009

Detroit 2 at Washington 4 (Ovechkin (WAS) scored only two goals of 3rd)
NY Rangers 0 at Boston 1 (Savard 19:37 2nd) [Rask]
Los Angeles 3 at Montreal 2 (Kings led 3–2 after 2nd)
Anaheim 4 at Colorado 3 (Selanne (ANA) scored only goal of 3rd)
Pittsburgh 4 at Toronto 5 (nine different scorers)
Florida 1 at NY Islanders 3 (Islanders led 1–0 after 1st & 2nd)

Dallas 7 at Columbus 3 (Stars led 3–2 midway through 2nd)
Atlanta 0 at Carolina 2 [Ward]
Philadelphia 0 at St. Louis 4 [Mason]
Buffalo 2 at Phoenix 0 [Miller]
Minnesota 4 at Vancouver 3 (Bergeron 1:52 OT)
Chicago 4 at San Jose 2 (game tied 1–1 early in 2nd)

February 1, 2009
Ottawa 4 at Washington 7 (Ovechkin (WAS) hat trick)
Boston 3 at Montreal 1 (Habs led 1–0 late in 1st)
Nashville 2 at Edmonton 1 (Predators led 2–0 midway through
     3rd)

February 2, 2009
St. Louis 3 at Detroit 4 (SO)
Calgary 3 at Colorado 4 (no scoring in 3rd)
Buffalo 2 at Anaheim 3 (Sabres led 1–0 midway through game)

February 3, 2009
Washington 5 at New Jersey 2 (Capitals led 3–0 early in 2nd)
Tampa Bay 1 at NY Islanders 3 (Islanders scored all goals in 2nd)
Atlanta 2 at NY Rangers 1 (SO)
St. Louis 4 at Columbus 2 (game tied 2–2 late in 2nd)
Florida 4 at Toronto 3 (McCabe 3:30 OT)
Pittsburgh 2 at Montreal 4 (game tied 1–1 after 1st)
Los Angeles 1 at Ottawa 0 (Handzus 17:21 3rd) [Quick]
Phoenix 1 at Nashville 2 (Predators led 2–0 after 2nd)
Calgary 1 at Dallas 3 (Flames led 1–0 late in 1st)
Chicago 3 at Edmonton 1 (Oilers led 1–0 early in 2nd)
Carolina 3 at Vancouver 4 (game tied 2–2 midway through 2nd)

February 4, 2009

Boston 3 at Philadelphia 1 (Bruins scored only two goals of 3rd)
Toronto 0 at Buffalo 5 (Vanek hat trick) [Miller]
Tampa Bay 3 at Pittsburgh 4 (Malkin 4:44 OT)
Phoenix 4 at Detroit 5 (Lidstrom broke 4–4 tie at 19:21 of 3rd)
Anaheim 0 at Minnesota 3 [Backstrom]

February 5, 2009

Los Angeles 5 at Washington 4 (Kopitar (LA) two goals)
Boston 4 at Ottawa 3 (SO)
NY Islanders 2 at Florida 3 (no scoring in 3rd)
Anaheim 2 at Nashville 4 (Perry both Ducks goals)
Edmonton 2 at St. Louis 1 (SO)
Dallas 2 at Colorado 3 (McLeod broke 2–2 tie at 12:49 of 3rd)
Chicago 5 at Calgary 2 (game tied 1–1 early in 1st)
Carolina 4 at San Jose 3 (SO)

February 6, 2009

Montreal 2 at Buffalo 3 (game tied 1–1 midway through 2nd)
Columbus 1 at Pittsburgh 4 (Letang two goals)
New Jersey 5 at Atlanta 1 (no scoring in final 32 minutes)
Nashville 2 at Minnesota 0 [Ellis]
NY Rangers 2 at Dallas 10 (Stars scored only six goals of 3rd)

February 7, 2009

Philadelphia 4 at Boston 3 (R. Jones 3:00 OT)
Edmonton 3 at Detroit 8 (Wings led 5–0 after 1st)
Anaheim 2 at Calgary 1 (Ducke led 1–0 after 1st, 2–0 after 2nd)
Toronto 5 at Montreal 2 (game tied 1–1 early in 2nd)
Buffalo 2 at Ottawa 1 (SO)
Los Angeles 3 at New Jersey 1 (Kings scored all goals in 2nd)
Florida 1 at Washington 3 (game tied 1–1 after 1st & 2nd)
San Jose 2 at Columbus 3 (C. Backman 1:33 OT)

NY Islanders 0 at Tampa Bay 1 (Roberts 13:34 3rd) [McKenna]
Colorado 1 at St. Louis 4 (Avs led 1–0 after 1st)
Carolina 7 at Phoenix 2 (game tied 1–1 early in 2nd)
Chicago 3 at Vancouver 7 (Canucks led 5–0 late in 2nd)

February 8, 2009

Detroit 3 at Pittsburgh 0 [Conklin]
Philadelphia 3 at Atlanta 2 (Carter (PHI) two goals)
Edmonton 2 at Minnesota 3 (SO)
Nashville 1 at Dallas 4 (Stars scored only two goals of 3rd)

February 9, 2009

NY Rangers 0 at New Jersey 3 [Clemmensen]
Montreal 2 at Calgary 6 (Habs led 1–0 midway through 1st)

February 10, 2009

San Jose 5 at Boston 2 (Bruins led 2–1 after 1st & 2nd)
Los Angeles 4 at NY Islanders 3 (SO)
Colorado 0 at Columbus 3 [Lacosta]
Atlanta 3 at Tampa Bay 1 (Thrashers scored in each period)
Toronto 4 at Florida 5 (Zednik 1:08 OT)
Detroit 5 at Nashville 3 (Zetterberg & Datsyuk (DET) two goals each)
Vancouver 6 at St. Louis 4 (Sundin (VAN) two goals)

February 11, 2009

NY Islanders 2 at New Jersey 4 (Devils scored only two goals of 3rd)
Washington 4 at NY Rangers 5 (SO)
Chicago 3 at Atlanta 1 (game tied 1–1 late in 2nd)
Ottawa 3 at Buffalo 1 (Sabres scored only goal of 3rd)
San Jose 1 at Pittsburgh 2 (SO)

Colorado 2 at Minnesota 3 (Miettinen broke 2–2 tie at 18:49 of 3rd)

Phoenix 1 at Dallas 0 (Lisin 2:19 2nd) [Bryzgalov]

Montreal 2 at Edmonton 7 (nine different scorers)

Calgary 2 at Anaheim 3 (S. Niedermayer 0:55 OT)

February 12, 2009

Ottawa 5 at Philadelphia 2 (Sens led 3–0 early in 3rd)

Florida 5 at Carolina 0 [Vokoun]

Toronto 4 at Tampa Bay 6 (Leafs led 1–0 midway through 1st)

Minnesota 2 at Detroit 4 (game tied 1–1 midway through 2nd)

St. Louis 2 at Nashville 3 (SO)

Vancouver 4 at Phoenix 3 (Canucks scored only three goals of 3rd)

Calgary 2 at Los Angeles 0 [Kiprusoff]

February 13, 2009

Boston 0 at New Jersey 1 (Salvador 10:54 2nd) [Clemmensen]

Detroit 2 at Columbus 3 (J. Williams broke 2–2 tie at 13:05 of 3rd)

San Jose 5 at Buffalo 6 (SO)

NY Rangers 1 at Florida 2 (SO)

Chicago 0 at St. Louis 1 (Boyes 0:57 3rd) [C. Mason]

Vancouver 1 at Dallas 2 (no scoring in 3rd)

Montreal 4 at Colorado 2 (game tied 2–2 midway through 3rd)

February 14, 2009

NY Islanders 1 at Philadelphia 5 (Flyers scored last three goals of 3rd)

Edmonton 3 at Los Angeles 2 (SO)

Pittsburgh 2 at Toronto 6 (Penguins led 2–0 after 1st)

Columbus 5 at Carolina 1 (Blue Jackets led 3–0 early in 3rd)

Washington 5 at Tampa Bay 1 (Capitals led 4–0 early in 2nd)

Boston 2 at Nashville 3 (SO)

Ottawa 5 at Minnesota 3 (Senators scored only two goals of 3rd)
Dallas 2 at Chicago 6 ('Hawks led 5–0 early in 3rd)
Calgary 7 at Phoenix 5 (Flames led 6–2 early in 3rd)

February 15, 2009

San Jose 5 at New Jersey 6 (Clarkson broke 5–5 tie at 16:28 of 3rd)
Philadelphia 5 at NY Rangers 2 (Flyers scored four goals in 2nd)
Washington 4 at Florida 2 (Ovechkin hat trick)
Colorado 6 at Detroit 5 (SO)
Carolina 3 at Buffalo 0 [Ward]
Atlanta 8 at Anaheim 4 (Kovalchuk (ATL) hat trick
Montreal 2 at Vancouver 4 (Canucks led 3–1 after 2nd)

February 16, 2009

Pittsburgh 2 at NY Islanders 3 (SO)
Dallas 3 at Columbus 2 (SO)
NY Rangers 1 at St. Louis 2 (Blues scored only goal of 3rd)
Ottawa 2 at Nashville 0 (both goals in 1st) [Auld]
Edmonton 3 at Phoenix 1 (game tied 1–1 after 2nd)
Atlanta 7 at Los Angeles 6 (SO)

February 17, 2009

Boston 5 at Carolina 1 (Bruins scored only three goals of 3rd)
Buffalo 4 at Toronto 1 (Bruins scored three goals on first seven
    shots)
Chicago 5 at Tampa Bay 3 (Stamkos scored all Lightning goals)
New Jersey 0 at Florida 4 [Vokoun]
Ottawa 2 at Colorado 3 (Wolski 1:20 OT)
Vancouver 4 at Calgary 3 (SO)
Edmonton 2 at San Jose 4 (Oilers led 2–1 after 1st)

February 18, 2009

NY Islanders 1 at NY Rangers 3 (game tied 1–1 midway through
    1st)
St. Louis 3 at Columbus 4 (Blue Jackets led 3–1 early in 2nd)

Montreal 3 at Washington 4 (SO)

Nashville 2 at Detroit 6 (Red Wings scored two goals in each
period)

Los Angeles 4 at Anaheim 3 (game tied 2–2 early in 3rd)

February 19, 2009

Carolina 6 at NY Islanders 2 (game tied 1–1 late in 1st)

Buffalo 3 at Philadelphia 6 (Flyers scored only three goals of 3rd)

Montreal 4 at Pittsburgh 5 (Penguins led 1–0, 2–1, 4–2, Habs tied
game 4–4 early in 3rd)

Columbus 4 at Toronto 3 (SO)

Vancouver 5 at Ottawa 2 (Canucks led 4–0 midway through 2nd)

New Jersey 3 at Tampa Bay 2 (SO)

Chicago 4 at Florida 0 [Huet]

St. Louis 2 at Nashville 1 (Tkachuk 2:52 OT)

Calgary 3 at Minnesota 2 (Aucoin 3:50 OT)

Edmonton 2 at Dallas 4 (game tied 2–2 early in 2nd)

Atlanta 3 at Phoenix 4 (SO)

Los Angeles 2 at San Jose 4 (no scoring in 3rd)

February 20, 2009

Colorado 4 at Washington 1 (game tied 1–1 after 1st)

Tampa Bay 1 at Carolina 4 (Corvo two goals)

Anaheim 2 at Detroit 5 (seven different scorers)

February 21, 2009

Pittsburgh 5 at Philadelphia 4 (Crosby & Fedotenko (PIT) two
goals each)

Ottawa 3 at Montreal 5 (Habs led 4–0 midway through 2nd)

Chicago 3 at Dallas 1 (Stars scored only goal of 3rd)

Phoenix 6 at Los Angeles 3 (O. Jokinen (PHO) hat trick)

Atlanta 1 at San Jose 3 (all goals in 3rd)

NY Rangers 2 at Buffalo 4 (Sabres led 3–0 after 2nd)
Vancouver 3 at Toronto 2 (SO)
New Jersey 0 at NY Islanders 4 [Danis]
Boston 0 at Florida 2 [Vokoun]
Anaheim 5 at Columbus 2 (Ducks led 2–1 late in 2nd)
Detroit 2 at Minnesota 5 (Nolan (MIN) two goals)
Nashville 1 at St. Louis 0 (Weber 2:36 OT) [Rinne]
Calgary 3 at Edmonton 2 (SO)

February 22, 2009

Pittsburgh 2 at Washington 5 (game tied 1–1 midway through 1st)
Colorado 2 at Carolina 5 (game tied 2–2 early in 2nd)
Boston 3 at Tampa Bay 4 (Prospal broke 3–3 tie at 18:27 of 3rd)
Toronto 3 at NY Rangers 2 (Hagman 3:00 OT)
Minnesota 2 at Chicago 1 (Wild scored only goal of 3rd)

February 23, 2009

San Jose 1 at Dallas 0 (Setoguchi 7:55 3rd) [Nabokov]

February 24, 2009

Florida 1 at Boston 6 (Bitz two goals)
Anaheim 3 at Buffalo 2 (Sabres scored only goal of 3rd)
Philadelphia 4 at Washington 2 (Capitals led 2–1 after 2nd)
Colorado 3 at Atlanta 4 (Thrashers led 3–0 late in 1st)
Vancouver 0 at Montreal 3 [Halak]
Carolina 2 at Ottawa 4 (teams combined for three goals in 46
    seconds in 1st)
Chicago 3 at Nashville 5 (Predators scored only four goals of 3rd)
Los Angeles 2 at Minnesota 1 (SO)
Phoenix 1 at St. Louis 2 (no scoring in 3rd)
Columbus 1 at Calgary 4 (game tied 1–1 early in 1st)
Tampa Bay 3 at Edmonton 5 (Souray (EDM) two goals)

February 25, 2009
Los Angeles 0 at Philadelphia 2 [Biron]
NY Rangers 1 at Toronto 2 (SO)
NY Islanders 0 at Pittsburgh 1 (Sykora 17:32 3rd) [Fleury]
San Jose 1 at Detroit 4 (Red Wings led 3–0 early in 2nd)

February 26, 2009
Anaheim 0 at Boston 6 [Thomas]
Colorado 0 at New Jersey 4 [Brodeur]
Toronto 5 at NY Islanders 4 (SO)
Florida 2 at NY Rangers 1 (Rangers led 1–0 after 1st & 2nd)
Atlanta 3 at Washington 4 (both teams scored in all periods)
Buffalo 1 at Carolina 2 (SO)
San Jose 2 at Ottawa 1 (no scoring in 3rd)
Phoenix 1 at Nashville 4 (game tied 1–1 midway through 2nd)
St. Louis 3 at Dallas 1 (game tied 1–1 after 1st & 2nd)
Columbus 1 at Edmonton 0 (Torres 7:45 3rd) [Mason]

February 27, 2009
Montreal 4 at Philadelphia 3 (Schneider 3:21 OT)
Los Angeles 1 at Detroit 2 (Red Wings led 1–0 after 2nd)
Pittsburgh 5 at Chicago 4 (Malkin 1:36 OT)
Minnesota 1 at Calgary 4 (Flames led 3–0 after 2nd)
Tampa Bay 1 at Vancouver 2 (Canucks scored only goal of 3rd)

February 28, 2009
Washington 4 at Boston 3 (Semin 0:22 OT)
Florida 2 at New Jersey 7 (Parise (NJ) two goals)
Anaheim 4 at Dallas 3 (game tied 2–2 after 2nd)
San Jose 2 at Montreal 3 (Habs scored all goals in 1st; Sharks
    scored all goals in 2nd)
Toronto 4 at Ottawa 3 (Kubina 0:33 OT)
Buffalo 0 at NY Islanders 2 [Danis]
Colorado 1 at NY Rangers 6 (Rangers led 5–0 midway through 2nd)

Carolina 3 at Atlanta 5 (Peverley & Kovalchuk (ATL) two goals each)
Detroit 0 at Nashville 8 [Rinne]
St. Louis 3 at Phoenix 1 (Blues led 1–0 after 2nd)
Minnesota 2 at Edmonton 3 (Wild led 1–0 midway through 1st)

March 1, 2009
Philadelphia 0 at New Jersey 3 [Brodeur—100th career shutout]
Florida 6 at Washington 2 (Capitals led 1–0 early in 1st)
Los Angeles 2 at Chicago 4 (Hawks led 3–2 after 1st)
Pittsburgh 4 at Dallas 1 (Stars scored only goal of 3rd)
Tampa Bay 8 at Calgary 6 (Lightning led 1–0, 2–1, trailed 4–2, led 5–4, Flames tied game 5–5)
Columbus 1 at Vancouver 3 (Canucks scored in each period)

March 2, 2009
Colorado 2 at NY Islanders 4 (game tied 1–1 early in 2nd)

March 3, 2009
Philadelphia 4 at Boston 2 (Flyers scored three goals in 3rd)
Carolina 5 at Washington 2 (Hurricanes scored four goals in 2nd)
Florida 4 at Atlanta 3 (Frolik (FLO) two goals)
Los Angeles 4 at Columbus 5 (Blue Jackets scored only goal of 3rd)
New Jersey 3 at Toronto 2 (Oduya 4:48 OT)
Calgary 6 at Ottawa 3 (Senators led 2–1 midway through 1st)
Pittsburgh 3 at Tampa Bay 1 (game tied 1–1 late in 1st)
Edmonton 5 at Nashville 6 (Arnott 2:31 OT)
Anaheim 2 at Chicago 3 (Havlat 1:40 OT)
Detroit 5 at St. Louis 0 [Osgood]
Minnesota 2 at Vancouver 4 (Wild led 2–0 midway through 1st)
Dallas 4 at San Jose 1 (game tied 1–1 midway through 1st)

March 4, 2009
Montreal 1 at Buffalo 5 (Buffalo led 5–0 late in 3rd)
Detroit 3 at Colorado 2 (Avs led 1–0 late in 1st)

March 5, 2009
Phoenix 2 at Boston 1 (Bruins led 1–0 midway through 1st)
NY Rangers 4 at NY Islanders 2 (game tied 1–1 early in 2nd)
Calgary 5 at Philadelphia 1 (Flames led 4–0 after 1st & 2nd)
Toronto 2 at Washington 1 (all goals in 3rd)
Edmonton 2 at Ottawa 4 (Spezza (OTT) scored at 0:12 of 1st)
Pittsburgh 4 at Florida 1 (game tied 1–1 after 2nd)
Columbus 2 at Nashville 4 (Blue Jackets led 2–1 late in 2nd)
Dallas 4 at Los Angeles 5 (Handzus 1:31 OT)
Minnesota 4 at San Jose 3 (M. Koivu 4:46 OT)

March 6, 2009
Calgary 1 at Carolina 6 (Hurricanes led 6–0 late in 3rd)
Phoenix 1 at Buffalo 5 (Connolly two goals)
Montreal 0 at Atlanta 2 [Lehtonen]
St. Louis 4 at Tampa Bay 3 (Boyes 0:27 OT)
Dallas 3 at Anaheim 2 (Stars led 2–0 after 2nd)

March 7, 2009
Chicago 3 at Boston 5 (game tied 1–1 late in 2nd)
New Jersey 3 at NY Islanders 7 (Bergenheim (NYI) hat trick)
Minnesota 3 at Los Angeles 4 (Wild scored only goal of 3rd)
Edmonton 4 at Toronto 1 (Leafs led 1–0 early in 2nd)
Buffalo 3 at Ottawa 6 (Alfredsson & Foligno (BUF) two goals
    each)
Nashville 1 at Philadelphia 4 (Lupul two goals)
St. Louis 3 at Florida 5 (Booth (FLO) hat trick)
Columbus 8 at Detroit 2 (Nash hat trick)
Carolina 9 at Tampa Bay 3 (E. Staal four goals, two assists)
San Jose 1 at Vancouver 3 (Canucks scored in 1st & 3rd; Sharks
    scored in 2nd)

March 8, 2009

Phoenix 2 at NY Islanders 3 (Islanders scored all goals in 2nd)

Boston 3 at NY Rangers 4 (Rangers led 3–1; Bruins tied game early in 3rd)

Pittsburgh 4 at Washington 3 (SO)

Calgary 2 at Atlanta 5 (Little [ATL] two goals)

Colorado 5 at Chicago 1 (Avs led 2–1 early in 2nd)

Montreal 3 at Dallas 1 (Stars led 1–0 after 1st)

Minnesota 3 at Anaheim 2 (Wild scored in each period)

March 9, 2009

NY Rangers 0 at Carolina 3 [Ward]

Toronto 1 at Ottawa 2 (Leafs scored in 1st; Senators scored both goals in 2nd)

Vancouver 2 at Los Angeles 3 (Kings led 2–0 after 1st)

March 10, 2009

Calgary 2 at New Jersey 3 (Flames led 1–0 early in 2nd)

Buffalo 2 at Philadelphia 5 (Flyers scored four goals in 3rd)

Boston 0 at Columbus 2 [Mason]

NY Islanders 2 at Toronto 3 (Grabovski 0:50 OT)

Edmonton 3 at Montreal 4 (Koivu 1:40 OT)

Florida 3 at Pittsburgh 4 (SO)

Phoenix 2 at Detroit 3 (Franzen 3:35 OT)

Washington 2 at Nashville 1 (Fedorov 2:20 OT)

San Jose 5 at Minnesota 4 (Ehrhoff 3:34 OT)

Dallas 2 at St. Louis 5 (Blues led 3–0 early in 2nd)

Atlanta 3 at Colorado 0 [Lehtonen]

March 11, 2009

Tampa Bay 2 at Ottawa 3 (Fisher 2:38 OT)

Carolina 2 at Chicago 3 (SO)

Vancouver 3 at Anaheim 4 (S. Niedermayer 3:37 OT)

March 12, 2009

Ottawa 3 at Boston 5 (Bruins led 3–1 early in 3rd)
Florida 1 at Buffalo 3 (game tied 1–1 midway through 1st)
Phoenix 2 at New Jersey 5 (Parise (NJ) scored at 0:18 of 1st)
Washington 2 at Philadelphia 1 (no scoring in 3rd)
Pittsburgh 3 at Columbus 4 (SO)
Tampa Bay 4 at Toronto 1 (Leafs led 1–0 early in 2nd)
NY Islanders 3 at Montreal 2 (Okposo 0:26 OT)
Calgary 6 at Detroit 5 (SO)
NY Rangers 4 at Nashville 2 (Predators led 2–1 after 1st)
San Jose 1 at St. Louis 3 (Blues scored in each period)
Carolina 2 at Dallas 3 (Stars scored all goals in 2nd)
Minnesota 1 at Colorado 2 (SO)
Atlanta 4 at Edmonton 3 (Reasoner 4:10 OT)

March 13, 2009

Columbus 5 at Chicago 3 (game tied 2–2 late in 2nd)
Los Angeles 2 at Vancouver 4 (game tied 2–2 early in 3rd)

March 14, 2009

NY Islanders 1 at Boston 2 (no scoring in 3rd)
NY Rangers 2 at Philadelphia 4 (Rangers led 1–0 late in 1st)
Detroit 5 at St. Louis 2 (Red Wings scored four goals in 2nd)
Ottawa 4 at Pittsburgh 3 (SO)
Atlanta 4 at Buffalo 3 (SO)
Calgary 6 at Toronto 8 (Leafs led 3–0 early in 1st; game tied 3–3 after 1st)
New Jersey 3 at Montreal 1 (Martin Brodeur (NJ) won 551st career game to tie all-time record)
Carolina 4 at Washington 5 (SO)
Tampa Bay 4 at Florida 3 (SO)
Minnesota 2 at Dallas 3 (Grossman 2:23 OT)
Colorado 3 at Edmonton 2 (Liles 0:42 OT)

Nashville 2 at Phoenix 0 [Rinne]
Los Angeles 1 at San Jose 2 (SO)

March 15, 2009

Philadelphia 1 at NY Rangers 4 (Avery two goals)
Boston 4 at Pittsburgh 6 (Bruins led 4–3 early in 3rd)
NY Islanders 4 at Chicago 2 (game tied 1–1 late in 2nd)
Detroit 4 at Columbus 0 [Osgood]
Minnesota 3 at St. Louis 5 (eight different scorers)
San Jose 1 at Anaheim 0 (Moen 18:58 2nd) [Nabokov]
Colorado 2 at Vancouver 4 (Canucks led 3–0 after 1st)

March 16, 2009

Washington 1 at Atlanta 5 (Capitals scored final goal of game)
Nashville 4 at Los Angeles 3 (Jones broke 3–3 tie at 17:42 of 3rd)

March 17, 2009

Chicago 2 at New Jersey 3 (Martin Brodeur (NJ) established all-
    time wins mark for a goalie with 552nd victory)
NY Rangers 4 at Montreal 1
Buffalo 2 at Ottawa 4 (game tied 2–2 after 2nd)
Atlanta 2 at Pittsburgh 6 (Thrashers led 1–0 early in 1st)
Toronto 4 at Tampa Bay 3 (SO)
Washington 3 at Florida 0 [Theodore]
Philadelphia 2 at Detroit 3 (Flyers led 2–0 late in 2nd)
Colorado 2 at Minnesota 3 (SO)
St. Louis 1 at Edmonton 2 (SO)
Dallas 2 at Vancouver 4 (game tied 1–1 after 1st)
San Jose 3 at Phoenix 4 (Coyotes led 3–0 after 1st)

March 18, 2009

New Jersey 2 at Carolina 4 (Hurricanes led 2–0 early in 2nd)
Chicago 3 at Columbus 4 (Vermette 2:38 OT)

Dallas 1 at Calgary 2 (Flames scored only goal of 3rd)
Nashville 3 at Anaheim 4 (Selanne 0:34 OT)

March 19, 2009

Los Angeles 3 at Boston 2 (D. Brown 4:25 OT)
Montreal 4 at Ottawa 1 (no scoring in 3rd)
Washington 5 at Tampa Bay 2 (Capitals scored only three goals
    of 3rd)
Toronto 1 at Florida 3 (game tied 1–1 after 1st)
Edmonton 8 at Colorado 1 (game tied 1–1 early in 1st)
St. Louis 0 at Vancouver 3 [Luongo]
Anaheim 3 at Phoenix 2 (SO)
Nashville 2 at San Jose 3 (SO)

March 20, 2009

Minnesota 0 at New Jersey 4 [Brodeur]
NY Islanders 4 at Carolina 5 (Islanders led 4–3 after 2nd)
Philadelphia 6 at Buffalo 4 (Briere (PHI) two goals)
Los Angeles 1 at Pittsburgh 4 (Kings scored only goal of 3rd)
Detroit 6 at Atlanta 3 (both teams scored three goals in 3rd)
Edmonton 2 at Chicago 3 (SO)
St. Louis 3 at Calgary 2 (Flames led 2–1 after 2nd)

March 21, 2009

Dallas 2 at San Jose 5 (Stars led 1–0 early in 1st)
Toronto 5 at Montreal 2 (Leafs led 4–0 midway through 2nd)
NY Islanders 2 at Ottawa 5 (Senators scored four goals in 2nd)
Buffalo 3 at NY Rangers 5 (Callahan (NYR) two goals)
Washington 1 at Carolina 4 (game tied 1–1 after 2nd)
Columbus 3 at Florida 1 (Panthers led 1–0 after 1st & 2nd)
Atlanta 4 at Tampa Bay 3 (SO)
Vancouver 1 at Phoenix 5 (Canucks scored last goal of game)

March 22, 2009

New Jersey 1 at Boston 4 (Bruins scored three goals in 2nd)
Philadelphia 3 at Pittsburgh 1 (Flyers scored in each period)
Los Angeles 1 at Chicago 4 (Havlat two goals)
Edmonton 0 at Minnesota 3 [N. Backstrom]
Ottawa 2 at NY Rangers 1 (Senators scored only goal of 3rd)
Phoenix 2 at Anaheim 6 (Getzlaf (ANA) two goals)
Colorado 1 at San Jose 3 (game tied 1–1 midway through 2nd)

March 23, 2009

New Jersey 2 at Philadelphia 4 (game tied 2–2 after 2nd)
Carolina 3 at Florida 2 (Whitney 1:37 OT)
Detroit 3 at Calgary 5 (Flames led 3–0 early in 2nd)

March 24, 2009

Washington 2 at Toronto 3 (SO)
Minnesota 1 at NY Rangers 2 (no scoring in 3rd)
Atlanta 3 at Montreal 6 (Canadiens scored four goals in 2nd)
Columbus 1 at Tampa Bay 2 (St. Louis 3:04 OT)
Anaheim 2 at Nashville 1 (SO)
Los Angeles 0 at St. Louis 2 [C. Mason]
Vancouver 5 at Dallas 2 (H. Sedin two goals, D. Sedin one goal)
Detroit 3 at Edmonton 2 (Oilers led 1–0 midway through 3rd)

March 25, 2009

Florida 3 at Buffalo 5 (Sabres scored four goals in 3rd)
Minnesota 6 at NY Islanders 2 (Gaborik (MIN) two goals)
Ottawa 1 at Carolina 2 (all goals in 3rd)
Calgary 0 at Pittsburgh 2 [Fleury]
San Jose 5 at Chicago 6 (SO)
Anaheim 7 at Colorado 2 (Avs scored only goal of 3rd)

March 26, 2009

Florida 4 at Philadelphia 2 (game tied 2–2 after 2nd)
NY Rangers 4 at Atlanta 5 (SO)
Calgary 0 at Columbus 5 [S. Mason]
Tampa Bay 2 at Montreal 3 (Koivu 1:45 OT)
San Jose 2 at Nashville 3 (no scoring in 3rd)
Vancouver 2 at St. Louis 4 (game tied 2–2 midway through 2nd)
Los Angeles 1 at Dallas 0 (SO) [Quick/Turco]
Edmonton 2 at Phoenix 3 (Coyotes led 3–0 after 2nd)

March 27, 2009

Tampa Bay 3 at Washington 5 (Backstrom & Ovechkin (WAS) two
    goals each)
Toronto 3 at Buffalo 5 (Connolly (BUF) two goals)
NY Islanders 2 at Detroit 0 [MacDonald]
New Jersey 2 at Chicago 3 (Seabrook 3:36 OT)
Vancouver 4 at Colorado 1 (Avs led 1–0 midway through game)
Edmonton 5 at Anaheim 3 (Oilers led 2–0 at 1:48 of 1st)

March 28, 2009

NY Rangers 3 at Pittsburgh 4 (Penguins scored only goal of 3rd)
Boston 7 at Toronto 5 (Bruins outscored Leafs 4–1 in 2nd)
Buffalo 4 at Montreal 3 (SO)
Carolina 2 at New Jersey 1 (Devils led 1–0 after 1st & 2nd)
Philadelphia 4 at NY Islanders 3 (SO)
Ottawa 3 at Atlanta 6 (game tied 2–2 after 1st)
Los Angeles 3 at Nashville 4 (Sullivan 3:41 OT)
Florida 6 at Dallas 3 (Stars led 2–1 midway through game)
Columbus 3 at St. Louis 4 (SO)
Minnesota 2 at Calgary 3 (no scoring in 3rd)
Phoenix 2 at San Jose 3 (Sharks scored only goal of 3rd)

March 29, 2009
Nashville 4 at Detroit 3 (Red Wings led 2–1 after 2nd)
St. Louis 5 at Columbus 2 (game tied 1–1 early in 2nd)
Ottawa 3 at Tampa Bay 0 [Elliott]
Boston 4 at Philadelphia 3 (Flyers led 1–0 early in 3rd)
Vancouver 4 at Chicago 0 [Luongo]
Minnesota 3 at Edmonton 2 (Wild led 2–0 after 1st & 2nd)
Colorado 1 at Anaheim 4 (game tied 1–1 early in 2nd)

March 30, 2009
New Jersey 0 at NY Rangers 3 [Lundqvist]
San Jose 2 at Calgary 1 (game tied 1–1 midway through 2nd)
Dallas 5 at Phoenix 6 (Prucha 0:53 OT)

March 31, 2009
Tampa Bay 1 at Boston 3 (Lightning scored only goal of 3rd)
Nashville 1 at Columbus 2 (game tied 1–1 after 1st & 2nd)
Chicago 1 at Montreal 4 (Canadiens led 3–0 after 2nd)
Ottawa 2 at Florida 5 (no scoring in 1st)
Vancouver 2 at Minnesota 1 (H. Sedin 4:00 OT)
Anaheim 5 at Edmonton 3 (R. Niedermayer (ANA) two goals;
    S. Niedermayer (ANA) one goal)
Dallas 3 at Los Angeles 2 (Morrison (DAL) two goals)

April 1, 2009
NY Islanders 3 at Washington 5 (Green (WAS) two goals)
Buffalo 2 at Atlanta 3 (Kovalchuk 4:30 OT)
Philadelphia 2 at Toronto 3 (Flyers scored only goal of 3rd)
New Jersey 1 at Pittsburgh 6 (seven different scorers)
St. Louis 1 at Chicago 3 (Hawks led 2–0 after 1st & 2nd)
Phoenix 3 at Colorado 0 [Montoya—first NHL game]

April 2, 2009
Ottawa 1 at Boston 2 (Senators led 1–0 after 1st)
Montreal 5 at NY Islanders 1 (Canadiens led 4–0 midway through game)
NY Rangers 2 at Carolina 4 (Hurricanes scored only two goals of 3rd)
St. Louis 5 at Detroit 4 (both teams scored three goals in 3rd)
Calgary 2 at Dallas 1 (Stars led 1–0 midway through 1st)
San Jose 2 at Edmonton 1 (no scoring in 3rd)
Anaheim 6 at Vancouver 5 (SO)
Los Angeles 1 at Phoenix 2 (Kings led 1–0 after 1st & 2nd)

April 3, 2009
Tampa Bay 4 at New Jersey 5 (Parise 1:21 OT)
Toronto 5 at Philadelphia 8 (Flyers led 6–0 midway through 2nd)
Buffalo 5 at Washington 4 (Pominville 1:51 OT)
Atlanta 3 at Florida 1 (Thrashers scored only two goals of 3rd)
Calgary 0 at Minnesota 4 [N. Backstrom]
Nashville 1 at Chicago 3 (Hawks scored in each period)

April 4, 2009
NY Rangers 0 at Boston 1 (Wheeler 9:04 1st) [Thomas]
New Jersey 3 at Buffalo 2 (Devils led 3–0 after 2nd)
Montreal 6 at Toronto 2 (Canadiens scored two goals in each period)
Philadelphia 3 at Ottawa 4 (SO)
Tampa Bay 1 at NY Islanders 3 (Islanders scored in each period)
Pittsburgh 2 at Carolina 3 (Babchuk 1:11 OT)
Columbus 4 at Nashville 5 (SO)
St. Louis 4 at Dallas 5 (Daley 0:16 OT)
Vancouver 3 at Edmonton 5 (Oilers led 2–0 after 2nd)
Anaheim 5 at San Jose 2 (Ryan (ANA) two goals)
Phoenix 1 at Los Angeles 6 (Kings scored three goals in 3rd)

April 5, 2009

Atlanta 4 at Washington 6 (ten different scorers)
Pittsburgh 2 at Florida 4 (game tied 1–1 late in 1st)
Minnesota 2 at Detroit 3 (Red Wings scored only goal of 3rd)
Chicago 1 at Columbus 0 (Versteeg 3:10 OT) [Khabibulin]
San Jose 3 at Anaheim 2 (game tied 2–2 after 2nd)
Colorado 4 at Vancouver 1 (Canucks scored final goal of game)

April 6, 2009

Detroit 4 at Buffalo 1 (Red Wings scored three goals in 3rd)
Ottawa 3 at Montreal 2 (Senators trailed 2–1 after 2nd)
Los Angeles 1 at Calgary 1 (game tied 1–1 midway through 2nd)

April 7, 2009

Toronto 4 at New Jersey 1 (Leafs led 3–0 after 1st)
Montreal 1 at NY Rangers 3 (game tied 1–1 after 1st)
Florida 1 at Philadelphia 2 (Flyers scored only goal of 3rd)
NY Islanders 0 at Carolina 9 (worst loss in Islanders history)
   [Ward]
Washington 4 at Atlanta 2 (game tied 1–1 midway through 1st)
Boston 2 at Ottawa 3 (no scoring in 3rd)
Pittsburgh 6 at Tampa Bay 4 (Crosby (PIT) two goals)
Chicago 4 at Nashville 2 (Hawks scored only three goals of 2nd)
Dallas 1 at Minnesota 3 (Wild led 3–0 after 2nd)
Los Angeles 2 at Edmonton 1 (Kings led 2–0 after 1st)
Calgary 1 at Vancouver 4 (game tied 1–1 midway through 2nd)
St. Louis 5 at Phoenix 1 (Coyotes led 1–0 early in 1st)
Colorado 0 at San Jose 1 (SO) [Budaj/Nabokov]

April 8, 2009

Buffalo 3 at Toronto 1 (Sabres scored only two goals of 3rd)
Columbus 4 at Chicago 3 (SO)

April 9, 2009
Montreal 4 at Boston 5 (Recchi 2:42 OT)
Philadelphia 1 at NY Rangers 2 (Rangers scored both goals in 1st)
Buffalo 5 at Carolina 1 (Hurricanes scored in final minute)
Florida 3 at Atlanta 2 (Booth broke 2–2 tie at 15:35 of 3rd)
New Jersey 3 at Ottawa 2 (SO)
NY Islanders 1 at Pittsburgh 6 (game tied 1–1 early in 1st)
Washington 4 at Tampa Bay 2 (Laich (WAS) two goals)
Nashville 4 at Detroit 3 (SO)
Dallas 3 at Colorado 2 (SO)
Los Angeles 0 at Vancouver 1 (Kessler 5:49 2nd) [Luongo]
Phoenix 4 at San Jose 1 (Coyotes led 3–0 early in 2nd)

April 10, 2009
Nashville 4 at Minnesota 8 (game tied 1–1 late in 1st)
Columbus 1 at St. Louis 3 (Tkachuk two goals)
Calgary 1 at Edmonton 5 (no scoring in 1st)
Dallas 3 at Anaheim 4 (SO)

April 11, 2009
Carolina 2 at New Jersey 3 (Zubrus broke 2–2 tie at 15:34 of 3rd)
Philadelphia 3 at NY Islanders 2 (Flyers scored all goals in 2nd)
Chicago 4 at Detroit 2 (Red Wings led 2–1 after 2nd)
Vancouver 1 at Colorado 0 (H. Sedin 0:40 OT) [Luongo]
Boston 1 at Buffalo 6 (Sabres led 5–0 early in 2nd)
San Jose 3 at Los Angeles 4 (seven different scorers)
Ottawa 2 at Toronto 5 (game tied 2–2 after 1st)
Pittsburgh 3 at Montreal 1 (game tied 1–1 after 1st & 2nd)
Tampa Bay 2 at Atlanta 6 (Thrashers scored three goals in 2nd)
Washington 4 at Florida 7 (Booth (FLO) and Semin (WAS) two goals each)
Minnesota 6 at Columbus 3 (Gaborik (MIN) two goals)
Anaheim 4 at Phoenix 5 (SO)
Edmonton 1 at Calgary 4 (Oilers led 1–0 early in 2nd)

April 12, 2009

St. Louis 1 at Colorado 0 (Boyes 6:00 1st) [C. Mason]
Boston 6 at NY Islanders 2 (Kessel hat trick)
NY Rangers 4 at Philadelphia 3 (Flyers led 3–2 after 2nd)
Detroit 0 at Chicago 3 [Khabibulin]

IN THE NEWS

September 11, 2008—Eric Staal signs a seven-year, $57.75-million contract extension with Carolina.

September 17, 2008—Mike Richards is named captain of Philadelphia.

September 18, 2008—Vincent Lecavalier is named captain of Tampa Bay for the second time in his career.

September 20, 2008—Former player and coach Ned Harkness dies in Rochester, New York, at age 89.

September 23, 2008—Los Angeles and St. Louis play an exhibition game in Kansas City.

September 23, 2008—Montreal and Buffalo play a pre-season game in Roberval, Quebec, the town that won the "Hockeyville" contest.

September 26, 2008—NY Rangers cut Petr Nedved from training camp.

September 27, 2008—Los Angeles and Colorado play an exhibition game at the MGM Grand Garden Arena in Las Vegas.

September 30, 2008—Vancouver names goalie Roberto Luongo captain even though NHL rules prohibit him from wearing the C.

September 30, 2008—NY Rangers beat SC Bern 8–1 in Bern, Switzerland, in a tune-up for the Victoria Cup the next night.

October 1, 2008—NY Rangers beat Metallurg 4–3 to win the inaugural Victoria Cup.

October 1, 2008—Tampa Bay beats Slovan Bratislava 3–2 in a shootout, in an exhibition game played in Slovakia.

October 2, 2008—Ottawa defeats Frolunda 4–1 in an exhibition game in Sweden. Pittsburgh defeats Jokerit 4–1 in an exhibition game in Finland.

October 3, 2008—Chris Drury is named captain of NY Rangers.

October 4, 2008—The NHL season begins with two games in Europe as Pittsburgh beats Ottawa 4–3 in overtime in Stockholm, Sweden, and the Rangers beat Tampa Bay 2–1 in Prague, Czech Republic.

October 10, 2008—The U.S. Hockey Hall of Fame inducts Mike Richter, Brian Leetch, Brett Hull and Cammi Granato.

October 11, 2008—Los Angeles signs Anze Kopitar to a seven-year contract extension.

October 13, 2008—Top Russian prospect Alexei Cherepanov dies after suffering a heart attack while playing a game with his club team, Avangard Omsk.

October 17, 2008—Michael Peca of Columbus is suspended five games for making contact with an official during a game.

October 18, 2008—Steve Yzerman is named executive director of Team Canada for the 2010 Olympics.

October 25, 2008—For only the second time in league history, all 30 teams play on the same night.

November 1, 2008—NY Islanders goalie Rick DiPietro undergoes knee surgery and is lost for 4–6 weeks.

November 5, 2008—Canada's Sports Hall of Fame inducts Steve Yzerman.

November 7, 2008—The Hockey Hall of Fame in Toronto unveils a special exhibit to honour the 100th-anniversary season of the Montreal Canadiens.

November 8, 2008—The Rangers ask to be awarded the 17th selection in the second round of the 2009 Entry Draft as compensation for the death of Alexei Cherepanov. In explaining its request, the team notes Article 8.3 (b) of the Collective Bargaining Agreement, which refers to compensation for an unsigned first-round draft pick who is "again eligible for the Entry Draft or becomes an Unrestricted Free Agent." Rangers assistant GM Cam Hope says, "We understand that this is a sensitive issue, but with all due respect to Alexei's family and his memory, he is technically eligible to be drafted again next year."

November 10, 2008—The Hockey Hall of Fame induction ceremony honours Glenn Anderson, Igor Larionov, Ray Scapinello and Ed Chynoweth.

November 12, 2008—Chicago retires number 3 in honour of Keith Magnuson and Pierre Pilote.

November 17, 2008—Doug Gilmour is named coach of Kingston Frontenacs of the OHL.

November 28, 2008—Brian Burke is named general manager of the Toronto Maple Leafs.

November 30, 2008—Pit Martin, a member of the Chicago Blackhawks during the 1960s and '70s, perishes when his snowmobile falls through thin ice into freezing waters near his home in Rouyn-Noranda, Quebec. He was 64.

December 2, 2008—Sean Avery's lewd and odious remarks about Dion Phaneuf's girlfriend land him a six-game suspension and prompt the Dallas Stars to release him.

December 18, 2008—Mats Sundin ends months of speculation about his future by signing a contract with the Vancouver Canucks.

January 1, 2009—The outdoor game between Detroit and Chicago draws the largest U.S. TV audience for an NHL game since 1975.

January 3, 2009—Don Sanderson, a 21-year-old defenceman with the Whitby Dunlops, dies as a result of a head injury sustained when his head struck the ice at the end of a fight during a Senior AAA game on December 12.

January 8, 2009—Just days after leading Canada to its fifth straight gold medal at the World Junior Championship, John Tavares is traded by Oshawa to London of the OHL.

January 12, 2009—Daryl "Doc" Seaman, one of the original owners of the Calgary Flames, passes away at age 86.

January 15, 2009—In the most important rule change in major junior hockey history, OHL commissioner David Branch announces that, effective at the beginning of the 2009–10 season, any player who removes his or an opponent's helmet during a fight will be given an automatic game misconduct plus a one-game suspension. The rule is implemented in reaction to the death of Don Sanderson (see January 3).

January 16, 2009—NY Islanders announce that they will play a pre-season game in Kansas City in September, a move many consider a warning sign that the team will be moved if a massive Long Island real-estate development—which includes a renovated arena—is not approved in a timely fashion.

January 21, 2009—Claude Lemieux plays his first NHL game in five and a half years, coming out of retirement at age 43 to play for San Jose.

January 21, 2009—Former NHL coach Pat Burns reveals he has lung cancer, the recent of a series of health issues for the popular bench boss.

January 23, 2009—The NHLPA declines to exercise its option to open the Collective Bargaining Agreement.

January 24, 2009—Boston's Zdeno Chara unleashes a slapshot clocked at 105.4 m.p.h. in the skills competition at the 2009 All-Star Game Weekend in Montreal, setting a new record for the hardest shot.

January 28, 2009—Detroit signs Henrik Zetterberg to a 12-year, $73-million contract extension.

February 3, 2009—Eric Lindros resigns as NHLPA ombudsman.

February 5, 2009—Alexander Ovechkin scores his 200th career goal.

February 10, 2009—Sean Avery clears waivers and is assigned to Hartford of the AHL.

February 14, 2009—Washington defenceman Mike Green sets an all-time NHL record by scoring a goal in his eighth successive game.

February 16, 2009—By firing head coach Michel Therrien, the Pittsburgh Penguins complete an unusual grand slam. All four teams that started the season in Europe had now fired their head coach.

February 20, 2009—After police in Montreal arrest Pasquale Mangiola on weapons and drug charges, it is learned that three members of the Canadiens were friends of the criminal—Andrei and Sergei Kostitsyn and Roman Hamrlik.

February 27, 2009—In one of the stranger transactions of recent times, the Montreal Canadiens claim Glen Metropolit off waivers from Philadelphia in the early afternoon. He practises in the morning with the Flyers, but dresses for the game as a Canadiens forward and plays against his old club.

March 1, 2009—Alf Pike dies in Calgary at age 91. He was a member of the Rangers' 1940 Stanley Cup team.

March 4, 2009—Trade Deadline Day sees some 21 deals involving 45 players and 22 draft choices. One player not involved in a deal is 42-year-old Gary Roberts, who is put on waivers by Tampa Bay. Roberts announces his retirement six days later.

March 8, 2009—John Tavares of the London Knights records a hat trick and breaks Peter Lee's OHL career goal-scoring record of 213 goals, set in 1976.

March 11, 2009—Colleen Howe, wife of Gordie, passes away after a lengthy battle with Pick's disease.

March 11, 2009—In California, former Edmonton owner Peter Pocklington is arrested for making false statements in bankruptcy. Glen Sather provides the $1-million bail.

March 11, 2009—At the general managers' meeting, it is agreed to assess a 10-minute misconduct to players involved in "staged" fights immediately after a faceoff.

March 13, 2009—The NHL announces that its annual awards ceremony, held in June, will move from its usual location in Toronto to Las Vegas.

March 25, 2009—Former Toronto forward Walt Poddubny dies in Thunder Bay, Ontario, at age 49.

March 31, 2009—The Hockey Hall of Fame announces that, starting next year, two women players will be eligible for induction.

April 6, 2009—Toronto GM Brian Burke, also GM of the USA team for the 2010 Olympics, announces that Leafs coach Ron Wilson will coach Team USA at both the 2009 World Championship in Zurich and the 2010 Olympics.

April 15, 2009—The 30th-place NY Islanders win the NHL's draft lottery, giving them the first-overall selection in June.

April 26, 2009—NY Rangers coach John Tortorella is suspended for one game after tossing a water bottle at a fan in Washington.

April 28, 2009—Washington's Donald Brashear is suspended for six games, five for a vicious blind-side hit on the Rangers' Blair Betts, and one more for making contact with Colton Orr during the pre-game skate.

May 5, 2009—Vancouver's Markus Naslund announces his retirement after 15 years in the NHL.

May 6, 2009—Jim Balsillie puts in an offer to buy and relocate the Phoenix Coyotes moments after owner Jerry Moyes files for bankruptcy protection. The moves trigger a lengthy and public court battle.

May 26, 2009—Former NHLer Peter Zezel passes away after a lengthy battle with a rare blood disorder.

June 2, 2009—As part of the ongoing process to bring the Coyotes to Hamilton, Ontario, Jim Balsillie formally files a request with the NHL for permission to relocate.

June 6, 2009—The former home of the Buffalo Sabres, Memorial Auditorium (affectionately known as "The Aud"), is razed.

June 10, 2009—Ottawa forward Dany Heatley publicly demands to be traded.

June 16, 2009—Judge Redfield T. Baum rejects Jim Balsillie's bid to move the Phoenix Coyotes to Hamilton on such short notice, giving the NHL more time to find a buyer willing to keep the team in Arizona but leaving the door open to bids from buyers seeking to move the team later in the year should the NHL fail.

June 17, 2009—Guy Lafleur is given a one-year suspended sentence, fined $100 and ordered to contribute $10,000 to charity for giving false evidence at his son's bail hearing in 2007.

June 20, 2009—Montreal Canadiens majority owner George Gillett agrees to sell his share in the team and the Bell Centre to the Molson family for $540 million.

June 25, 2009—Mike Babcock is named Canada's coach for the 2010 Olympics. His assistants are Ken Hitchcock, Lindy Ruff and Jacques Lemaire.

June 27, 2009—Jerry Reinsdorf, owner of the Chicago Bulls and Chicago White Sox, submits a bid of $148 million for the Phoenix Coyotes, promising to keep the team in Arizona. He withdraws the bid in late August.

SHOOTOUT LEADERS, 2008–09

SKATERS

Most Shots

Nikolai Zherdev (NYR)	14
Ales Kotalik (EDM)	13
Milan Hejduk (COL)	13
Brad Boyes (STL)	12
Jussi Jokinen (CAR)	12
Markus Naslund (NYR)	12
Wojtek Wolski (COL)	12
Vincent Lecavalier (TB)	11
Rick Nash (CBJ)	11
Patrick O'Sullivan (EDM)	11
Mike Ribeiro (DAL)	11
Drew Stafford (BUF)	11

Most Goals

Wojtek Wolski (COL)	10
Ales Kotalik (EDM)	8
Brad Boyes (STL)	6
Milan Hejduk (COL)	6
Vyacheslav Kozlov (ATL)	6
Mike Ribeiro (DAL)	6
Jonathan Toews (CHI)	6

Best % (minimum 5 shots)

Wojtek Wolski (COL)	83.3%	(10/12)
Vyacheslav Kozlov (ATL)	75.0%	(6/8)
James Neal (DAL)	71.4%	(5/7)
Ales Kotalik (EDM)	61.5%	(8/13)
Jonathan Toews (CHI)	60.0%	(6/10)

Ryane Clowe (SJ)	60.0% (3/5)
Antti Miettinen (MIN)	60.0% (3/5)
Marek Zidlicky (MIN)	60.0% (3/5)
Frans Nielsen (NYI)	60.0% (3/5)
Blake Wheeler (BOS)	57.1% (4/7)

GOALIES

Most Wins

Henrik Lundqvist (NYR)	9
Ryan Miller (BUF)	8
Peter Budaj (COL)	7
Steve Mason (CBJ)	6
Niklas Backstrom (MIN)	5
Jonas Hiller (ANA)	5
Evgeni Nabokov (SJ)	5
Carey Price (MON)	5
Pekka Rinne (NAS)	5
Marty Turco (DAL)	5

Most Losses

Mike Smith (TB)	7
Carey Price (MON)	6
Marty Turco (DAL)	6
Nikolai Khabibulin (CHI)	5
Jason LaBarbera (VAN)	5
Steve Mason (CBJ)	5
Vesa Toskala (TOR)	5

Most Shots Faced

Marty Turco (DAL)	43
Henrik Lundqvist (NYR)	40
Ryan Miller (BUF)	40
Peter Budaj (COL)	35
Carey Price (MON)	35
Evgeni Nabokov (SJ)	32

Jonas Hiller (ANA)	31
Steve Mason (CBJ)	31
Roberto Luongo (VAN)	29
Vesa Toskala (TOR)	29

Best Save % (minimum 10 shots faced)

Johan Hedberg (ATL)	.923 (12/13)
J-S Giguere (ANA)	.667 (8/12)
Evgeni Nabokov (SJ)	.656 (21/32)
Alex Auld (OTT)	.640 (16/25)
Cam Ward (CAR)	.632 (12/19)
Peter Budaj (COL)	.629 (22/35)
Carey Price (MON)	.629 (22/35)
Marty Turco (DAL)	.628 (27/43)
Brian Elliott (OTT)	.625 (10/16)
Karri Ramo (TB)	.615 (8/13)

Team Records

	SO	W	L
NY Rangers	16	10	6
Montreal	14	7	7
Colorado	13	9	4
Buffalo	13	8	5
Columbus	13	6	7
Toronto	13	6	7
Los Angeles	13	5	8
Tampa Bay	13	3	10
Dallas	12	6	6
Pittsburgh	12	6	6
St. Louis	12	6	6
Nashville	11	6	5
San Jose	11	6	5
Chicago	11	4	7

Florida	11	3	8
Anaheim	10	7	3
Detroit	10	6	4
Edmonton	10	6	4
Boston	10	4	6
Ottawa	10	4	6
Philadelphia	10	4	6
Vancouver	10	3	7
Washington	9	4	5
Atlanta	8	7	1
New Jersey	8	6	2
Minnesota	8	5	3
Carolina	8	3	5
NY Islanders	8	3	5
Phoenix	6	3	3
Calgary	5	3	2

NATIONALITY OF ALL PLAYERS, 2008–09

SUMMARY
(figures in parentheses show league-wide representation as a percentage)

TOTAL	979
CANADA	512 (52.3%)
Alberta	87
British Columbia	55
Manitoba	26
New Brunswick	1
Newfoundland	7
Nova Scotia	10
Ontario	206
Prince Edward Island	3
Quebec	68
Saskatchewan	49
UNITED STATES	216 (22.1%)
CZECH REPUBLIC	58 (5.9%)
SWEDEN	54 (5.5%)
FINLAND	42 (4.3%)
RUSSIA	33 (3.4%)
SLOVAKIA	17 (1.7%)
GERMANY	9 (0.9%)
LATVIA	5 (0.5%)
SWITZERLAND	5 (0.5%)
DENMARK	4 (0.4%)
AUSTRIA	3 (0.3%)
BELARUS	3 (0.3%)
UKRAINE	3 (0.3%)
KAZAKHSTAN	2 (0.2%)
BAHAMAS	1 (0.1%)

BRAZIL	1 (0.1%)
FRANCE	1 (0.1%)
ITALY	1 (0.1%)
LITHUANIA	1 (0.1%)
MALAYSIA	1 (0.1%)
NORWAY	1 (0.1%)
POLAND	1 (0.1%)
SLOVENIA	1 (0.1%)
SOUTH AFRICA	1 (0.1%)
SOUTH KOREA	1 (0.1%)
UNITED KINGDOM	1 (0.1%)

NOTE: Owen Nolan was born in Belfast, which is not in Ireland (i.e., Eire), but Northern Ireland, which is part of the U.K.

NATIONALITY BREAKDOWN

CANADA	**512**	
Alberta	**87**	
Airdrie	1	Zach Boychuk
Banff	1	Ryan Smyth
Beaverlodge	1	Matt Walker
Blackie	1	Jeremy Colliton
Bonnyville	1	Jon Kalinski
Calgary	17	Jay Beagle, Braydon Coburn, Patrick Eaves, T.J. Galiardi, Mike Green, Connor James, Krys Kolanos, Robert Nilsson, Lawrence Nycholat, Chris Phillips, Jeff Schultz, Tyler Sloan, Jason Smith, Brent Sopel, Ryan Stone, Jeff Tambellini, Craig Weller
Caroline	2	Kris Russell, Jim Vandermeer
Castor	1	Darcy Tucker

Cochrane	1	Mason Raymond
Cold Lake	1	Alexander Auld
Coleman	1	Rick Rypien
Daysland	1	Richard Petiot
Edmonton	27	Blair Betts, Jay Bouwmeester, Johnny Boychuk, Gilbert Brule, Jason Chimera, Erik Christensen, Mike Comrie, Andrew Ference, Vernon Fiddler, Mark Fistric, Jarome Iginla, Daymond Langkow, Bryan Little, Jamie Lundmark, Joffrey Lupul, Derek Morris, Scott Nichol, Scott Niedermayer, Matt Pettinger, Dion Phaneuf, Fernando Pisani, Steve Regier, Steve Reinprecht, David Schlemko, Jason Strudwick, Brian Sutherby, Darryl Sydor
Elk Point	1	Sheldon Souray
Fort McMurray	3	Scott Lehman, Justin Pogge, Scottie Upshall
Fort Saskatchewan	2	Mike Commodore, Ray Whitney
Grand Cache	1	Dean McAmmond
Halkirk	1	Shane Doan
Lac La Biche	1	Rene Bourque
Leduc	1	Matt Climie
Lethbridge	2	Spencer Machacek, Kris Versteeg
Lloydminster	1	Clarke MacArthur
Mannville	1	Kyle Calder
Medicine Hat	2	Brooks Laich, Zach Smith
Peace River	1	Chris Osgood
Red Deer	2	Trent Hunter, Chris Mason
Redwater	1	Todd Fedoruk
Rimbey	1	Jason Jaffray
Rocky Mountain House	2	Brad Stuart, Nick Tarnasky
St. Paul	1	Kyle Brodziak

Sherwood Park	2	Ben Ondrus, Cam Ward
Stony Plain	1	Steve Goertzen
Taber	1	Devin Setoguchi
Vermilion	1	Jeff Woywitka
Viking	1	Brett Sutter
Westlock	1	Kyle Chipchura

British Columbia	**55**	
Abbotsford	3	Ryan Craig, Kyle Cumiskey, David van der Gulik
Burnaby	6	Karl Alzner, Kris Chucko, Jason LaBarbera, Darren McCarty, Joe Sakic, Greg Zanon
Cassiar	1	Rob Niedermayer
Comox	1	Brett McLean
Cranbrook	1	Brad Lukowich
Fernie	1	Jason Krog
Hope	1	Jeff Hoggan
Invermere	1	Wade Dubielewicz
Kamloops	1	Mark Recchi
Kelowna	1	Josh Gorges
Maple Ridge	1	Andrew Ladd
Nelson	1	Jeff Kinrade
New Westminster	1	Kyle Turris
North Vancouver	2	Ben Maxwell, Trevor Smith
Osoyoos	2	Mitch Fritz, Chuck Kobasew
Pitt Meadows	1	Brendan Morrison
Port McNeill	1	Willie Mitchell
Quesnel	1	Brett Festerling
Richmond	4	Scott Hannan, Raymond Sawada, Brent Seabrook, Brandon Segal
Sicamous	2	Colin Fraser, Shea Weber
Smithers	1	Dan Hamhuis
Trail	2	Shawn Horcoff, Barret Jackman

Vancouver	10	Troy Brouwer, Chris Holt, Paul Kariya, Milan Lucic, Steve Montador, Shaone Morrisonn, Cam Paddock, Carey Price, Mike Santorelli, Aaron Voros
Vernon	4	Eric Brewer, Andrew Ebbett, Eric Godard, Jerred Smithson
Victoria	2	Kyle Greentree, Ryan O'Byrne
West Vancouver	1	John Negrin
White Rock	2	Jason Garrison, Colton Gillies

Manitoba	**26**	
Binscarth	1	Cody McLeod
Brandon	2	Bryce Salvador, Brett Skinner
Churchill	1	Jordin Tootoo
Neepawa	1	Shane Hnidy
Nesbitt	1	Aaron Rome
Portage La Prairie	2	Arron Asham, Troy Bodie
Selkirk	1	Andrew Murray
Thompson	2	Chris Minard, Jody Shelley
Winkler	2	Eric Fehr, Dustin Penner
Winnipeg	13	Cam Barker, Dustin Boyd, Riley Cote, Nigel Dawes, Darren Helm, Duncan Keith, Brent Krahn, Derek Meech, Colton Orr, Alexander Steen, Jonathan Toews, Ian White, Travis Zajac

Ontario	**206**	
Ajax	1	Brent Burns
Alfred	1	Benoit Pouliot
Almonte	1	Kent Huskins
Amherstburg	1	Kevin Westgarth
Barrie	1	John Madden
Beaconsfield	1	Ben Walter
Belleville	4	Matt Cooke, Andrew Raycroft, Brad

		Richardson, Ty Wishart
Bramalea	1	Mike Weaver
Brampton	2	Rick Nash, Kris Newbury
Brantford	2	Chris Gratton, Paul Szczechura
Brights Grove	1	Brad Staubitz
Cambridge	2	Tim Brent, Scott Walker
Carp	1	Kurtis Foster
Chapleau	1	Jason Ward
Chatham	1	Ryan Jones
Cobourg	1	Justin Williams
Collingwood	1	Jason Arnott
Dryden	1	Chris Pronger
Elliot Lake	2	Alex Henry, Zachery Stortini
Fergus	1	Jamie McGinn
Grimsby	1	Kevin Bieksa
Guelph	4	Krys Barch, David Jones, Kirk Maltby, Rich Peverley
Hamilton	3	Adam Mair, Brian McGratton, Steve Staios
Hearst	1	Claude Giroux
Huntsville	1	Ethan Moreau
Kanata	2	Cory Murphy, Todd White
Kenora	1	Mike Richards
Keswick	1	Curtis Joseph
King City	2	Daniel Carcillo, Alex Pietrangelo
Kingston	6	Bryan Allen, John Erskine, Jay McClement, Jay McKee, Mike Smith, Andy Sutton
Kirkland Lake	2	Kurtis McLean, Andy Sutton
Kitchener	4	Kevin Klein, Kyle Quincey, Gregory Stewart, Dennis Wideman
London	13	Gregory Campbell, Jeff Carter, Drew Doughty, Sam Gagner, Mark Mancari, Cody McCormick, Curtis McElhinney, Brandon Prust, Bryan Rodney, Joe

		Thornton, Mike Van Ryn, Jason Williams, Brian Willsie
Long Sault	1	Jesse Winchester
Markdale	1	Chris Neil
Markham	1	Steve Stamkos
Millgrove	1	Danny Syvret
Mimico	1	Brendan Shanahan
Mississauga	6	Brad Boyes, Tom Kostopoulos, Manny Malhotra, Shawn Matthias, Jason Spezza, Matt Stajan
Moose Factory	1	Jonathan Cheechoo
Newmarket	2	Steve Downie, Brian Elliott
Niagara-on-the-Lake	1	Zenon Konopka
Nobleton	1	Nick Boynton
North Bay	1	Craig Rivet
Oakville	1	Steve Mason
Oshawa	4	Josh Bailey, Jay Harrison, James Neal, Shawn Thornton
Ottawa	13	Derek Armstrong, Adrian Aucoin, Brendan Bell, Dan Boyle, Rod Brind'Amour, Ben Eager, Marc Methot, Sean O'Donnell, Luke Richardson, Derek Roy, Marc Savard, Martin St. Pierre, Stephane Yelle
Owen Sound	2	Cody Bass, Curtis Sanford
Peterborough	3	Mike Fisher, Corey Perry, Cory Stillman
Petrolia	1	Michael Leighton
Pickering	1	Sean Avery
Port Hope	1	Shane O'Brien
Richmond Hill	3	Mike Cammalleri, Derek Joslin, Theo Peckham
Sarnia	2	Jamie Fraser, Dustin Jeffrey

Sault Ste. Marie	5	Matt D'Agostini, Bryan Helmer, Tyler Kennedy, Chris Thorburn, Marty Turco
Seaforth	1	Boyd Devereaux
Shelburne	1	Aaron Downey
Simcoe	3	Rob Blake, Jassen Cullimore, Dwayne Roloson
St. Catharines	5	Rob Davison, Mike Iggulden, Bryan McCabe, Andrew Peters, John Scott
Stittsville	1	Matt Bradley
Strathroy	2	Brian Campbell, Andy McDonald
Sudbury	3	Todd Bertuzzi, Andrew Brunette, Derek MacKenzie
Sundridge	1	Greg de Vries
Terrace Bay	1	Aaron MacKenzie
Thorold	1	Sean Bentivoglio
Thornhill	1	Dominic Moore
Thunder Bay	7	Taylor Chorney, Ryan Johnson, Taylor Pyatt, Patrick Sharp, Eric Staal, Jordan Staal, Marc Staal
Timmins	2	Shean Donovan, Steve Sullivan
Toronto	40	Dave Bolland, Chris Campoli, Luca Caputi, David Clarkson, Andrew Cogliano, Carlo Colaiacovo, Trevor Daley, Kris Draper, Chris Durno, Manny Fernandez, Adam Foote, Mark Giordano, Josh Gratton, Matt Halischuk, Chris Kelly, Mike Knuble, Manny Legace, Brad May, Jamal Mayers, Kenndal McArdle, Glen Metropolit, Matt Moulson, Cal O'Reilly, Phil Oreskovic, Michael Peca, Matt Pelech, Chris Porter, Wayne Primeau, Liam Reddox, Gary Roberts, Wayne Simmonds, Chris Stewart, Raffi

		Torres, Stephen Valiquette, Mike Vernace, Joel Ward, Kevin Weekes, Stephen Weiss, Daniel Winnick, Mike Zigomanis
Waterloo	1	John Mitchell
Welland	6	Paul Bissonnette, Cal Clutterbuck, Matt Ellis, Daniel Girardi, Nathan Horton, Daniel Paille
Winchester	1	Matt Carkner
Whitby	1	Paul Ranger
Windsor	6	Matt Beleskey, Dan Jancevski, Ed Jovanovski, Wes O'Neill, Aaron Ward, Kyle Wellwood
Woodbridge	1	Steve Eminger

Quebec	**68**	
L'Ancienne Lorette	1	Patrice Bergeron
Beauceville	1	Stephane Veilleux
Buckingham	1	Claude Lemieux
Chandler	1	Mathieu Garon
Gatineau	2	Daniel Briere, Alexandre Picard (b. Jul '85)
Hull	1	Derick Brassard
Ile Bizard	1	Vincent Lecavalier
Lac St. Charles	1	Martin Biron
Lafontaine	1	Yann Danis
LaSalle	1	Anthony Stewart
Laval	5	Pascal Dupuis, Philippe Dupuis, Eric Perrin, Martin St. Louis, Jose Theodore
Lemoyne	1	Maxime Talbot
Les Saules	1	Alexandre Picard (b. Oct '85)
Levis	1	Pierre-Luc Letourneau-Leblond
Longueuil	1	Bruno Gervais
Montreal	20	Alexandre Bolduc, Patrice Brisebois,

		Martin Brodeur, Corey Crawford, Marc Denis, J-P Dumont, Denis Gauthier, J-S Giguere, Marc-Andre Gragnani, Ben Guite, Ian Laperriere, Georges Laraque, Kris Letang, Matt Lombardi, Roberto Luongo, Torrey Mitchell, Joel Perrault, Mike Ribeiro, Josh Tordjman, Marc-Edouard Vlasic
Pointe-Claire	1	Alex Burrows
Quebec City	5	Steve Bernier, Alexandre Giroux, Marc-Antoine Pouliot, Paul Stastny, Yan Stastny
Repentigny	2	Pascal Leclaire, Jason Pominville
Rimouski	1	Michel Ouellet
Sherbrooke	5	Eric Belanger, Pierre-Marc Bouchard, Mathieu Dandenault, David Perron, Stephane Robidas
Sorel	2	Francois Beauchemin, Marc-Andre Fleury
St. Agapit	1	Antoine Vermette
St. Bonaventure	1	Patrick Lalime
Ste. Apollinaire	1	Philippe Boucher
Ste. Catherine	1	Guillaume Latendresse
Ste. Foy	1	Simon Gagne
Ste. Justine	1	Alex Tanguay
St. Jean-sur-Richelieu	1	Jeff Drouin-Deslauriers
St. Leonard	1	Maxim Lapierre
St. Louis de France	1	Marc-Andre Bergeron
Terrebonne	1	J-F Jacques
Trois Rivieres	1	Steve Begin
Val d'Or	1	Dany Sabourin
New Brunswick	**1**	
Quispamsis	1	Randy Jones

Newfoundland	7	
Bonavista	1	Adam Pardy
Carbonear	1	Daniel Cleary
Labrador City	2	Daniel LaCosta, Pascal Pelletier
St. John's	3	Ryane Clowe, Teddy Purcell, Michael Ryder
Nova Scotia	10	
Antigonish	1	Craig MacDonald
Halifax	4	Eric Boulton, Sidney Crosby, Andrew Gordon, James Sheppard
Judique	1	Andrew MacDonald
New Glasgow	2	Jon Sim, Colin White
Pictou	1	Joey MacDonald
Port Hawkesbury	1	Aaron Johnson
Prince Edward Island	3	
Kinkora	1	Nathan McIver
Murray Harbour	1	Brad Richards
Summerside	1	Steve Ott
Saskatchewan	49	
Alameda	1	Trent Whitfield
Aneroid	1	Patrick Marleau
Brock	1	Steve MacIntyre
Carlyle	1	Brenden Morrow
Craik	1	Garnet Exelby
Humboldt	1	Brendan Witt
Kamsack	1	Darcy Hordichuk
Kindersley	2	Derek Dorsett, Curtis Glencross
Lanigan	2	Sheldon Brookbank, Wade Brookbank
Leroy	1	Nathan Paetsch
Lloydminster	2	Colby Armstrong, Wade Redden
Meadow Lake	2	Blake Comeau, Dwayne King

Melfort	1	Tyson Strachan
Melville	1	Jarret Stoll
Nokomis	1	Jordan Henry
Prince Albert	1	Ryan Parent
Regina	12	Brett Carson, Ryan Getzlaf, Tanner Glass, Josh Harding, Scott Hartnell, Jamie Heward, Chris Kunitz, Brendan Mikkelson, Garth Murray, Nathan Oystrick, Mike Sillinger, Jeremy Williams
Rosetown	1	Quintin Laing
Saskatoon	11	Riley Armstrong, Ryan Bayda, Wade Belak, Byron Bitz, Derek Boogaard, Sean Collins, Dan Ellis, Warren Peters, Darroll Powe, Cory Sarich, Luke Schenn
Stewart Valley	1	Travis Moen
Strasbourg	1	Nick Schultz
Swift Current	1	Boyd Kane
Unity	1	Boyd Gordon
Wapella	1	Brett Clark
USA	**217**	
Alabama	1	Jared Ross
Alaska	7	Matt Carle, Ty Conklin, Joey Crabb, Brandon Dubinsky, Scott Gomez, Nate Thompson, Tim Wallace
California	6	Ryan Hollweg, Ray Macias, Brooks Orpik, Brian Salcido, Garrett Stafford, Brett Sterling
Colorado	3	Ben Bishop, Brandon Crombeen, David Hale
Connecticut	7	Chris Clark, Chris Drury, Ron Hainsey,

		Max Pacioretty, Jonathan Quick, Ryan Shannon, Jamie Sifers
Delaware	1	Mark Eaton
Florida	1	Dan Hinote
Illinois	10	Craig Anderson, Jarred Boll, Mike Brown, Chris Chelios, Joe Corvo, Andrew Hutchinson, Brett Lebda, Al Montoya, Tim Stapleton, Andy Wozniewski
Indiana	4	Donald Brashear, Jack Johnson, Ken Klee, John-Michael Liles
Iowa	1	Scott Clemmensen
Maryland	2	Jamie Fritsch, Jeff Halpern
Massachusetts	22	Keith Aucoin, Chris Bourque, Brian Boyle, Joe Callahan, Rick DiPietro, Hal Gill, Bill Guerin, Josh Hennessy, Doug Janik, Dan Lacouture, Mike Mottau, Jay Pandolfo, Brian Pothier, Tom Poti, Pat Rismiller, Jeremy Roenick, Michael Ryan, Cory Schneider, Keith Tkachuk, Noah Welch, Ryan Whitney, Keith Yandle
Michigan	34	Justin Abdelkader, David Booth, Chris Conner, Patrick Davis, Jeff Finger, Alex Foster, Nathan Gerbe, Tim Gleason, Andy Greene, Matt Greene, Mike Grier, Adam Hall, Dwight Helminen, T.J. Hensick, Andy Hilbert, Matt Hunwick, Brent Johnson, Ryan Kesler, Chad LaRose, David Legwand, Peter Mannino, Ryan Miller, Mike Modano, David Moss, Kevin Porter, Corey Potter, Brian Rafalski, Erik Reitz, Brian

		Rolston, Jim Slater, Tim Thomas, Doug Weight, James Wisniewski, Mike York
Minnesota	39	Andrew Alberts, David Backes, Keith Ballard, Jason Blake, Brandon Bochenski, Casey Borer, Dustin Byfuglien, Ryan Carter, Tim Conboy, Matt Cullen, John Curry, Tom Gilbert, Alex Goligoski, Bret Hedican, Matt Hendricks, Jamie Langenbrunner, Brian Lee, Jordan Leopold, Mike Lundin, Paul Martin, Joe Motzko, Peter Mueller, Matt Niskanen, Kyle Okposo, Zach Parise, Mark Parrish, Derek Peltier, Toby Petersen, Tom Preissing, Nate Raduns, Kurt Sauer, Mike Sauer, Matt Smaby, Colin Stuart, Mark Stuart, Jeff Taffe, Steve Wagner, Blake Wheeler, Clay Wilson
Missouri	4	Chris Butler, Cam Janssen, Mike McKenna, Landon Wilson
Nebraska	1	Jed Ortmeyer
New Hampshire	2	Ben Lovejoy, Freddy Meyer
New Jersey	3	Paul Mara, Drew Miller, Bobby Ryan
New York	30	Zach Bogosian, Francis Bouillon, Jesse Boulerice, Dustin Brown, Ryan Callahan, Erik Cole, Tim Connolly, Craig Conroy, Nick Foligno, Brian Gionta, Chris Higgins, Jimmy Howard, Patrick Kaleta, Patrick Kane, Tim Kennedy, Mike Komisarek, Matt Lashoff, Jay Leach, Todd Marchant, Eric Nystrom, Kevin Quick, Marty Reasoner, Andre Roy, Mathieu

		Schneider, Rob Schremp, Rob Scuderi, Tim Sestito, Lee Stempniak, Brandon Sutter, Ryan Vesce
North Carolina	1	Patrick O'Sullivan
North Dakota	4	Paul Gaustad, Tim Jackman, Ryan Potulny, Barry Tallackson
Ohio	4	Dan Fritsche, Jeff Hamilton, Peter Harrold, Mike Rupp
Oklahoma	1	Tyler Arnason
Oregon	2	Jack Hillen, Jordan Lavallee-Smotherman
Pennsylvania	10	Nathan Guenin, Christian Hanson, Grant Lewis, Ryan Malone, George Parros, David Sloane, Bill Thomas, R.J. Umberger, Mike Weber, John Zeiler
Rhode Island	2	Brian Boucher, Tom Cavanagh
Utah	1	Trevor Lewis
Vermont	1	Graham Mink
Washington	2	Pat Dwyer, T.J. Oshie
Wisconsin	11	Adam Burish, Jacob Dowell, Davis Drewiske, Phil Kessel, Joe Pavelski, Joel Rechlicz, Jack Skille, Drew Stafford, David Steckel, Ryan Suter, Brad Winchester
CZECH REPUBLIC	58	Radek Bonk, Radek Dvorak, Patrik Elias, Martin Erat, Tomas Fleischmann, Michael Frolik, Roman Hamrlik, Martin Hanzal, Martin Havlat, Jan Hejda, Milan Hejduk, Ales Hemsky, Bobby Holik, Jiri Hudler, Frantisek Kaberle, Tomas Kaberle, Lukas Kaspar, Rostislav Klesla, David

Koci, Ales Kotalik, Lukas Krajicek,
David Krejci, Kamil Kreps, Filip Kuba,
Pavel Kubina, Robert Lang, Marek
Malik, Radek Martinek, Josef Melichar,
Milan Michalek, Zbynek Michalek,
Vladimir Mihalek, Tomas Mojzis,
Michal Neuvirth, Jiri Novotny,
Rostislav Olesz, Ondrej Pavelec, Jakub
Petruzalek, Tomas Plekanec, Tomas
Plihal, Roman Polak, Vaclav Prospal,
Petr Prucha, Michal Repik, Michal
Rozsival, Marek Schwarz, Martin
Skoula, Ladislav Smid, Radek
Smolenak, Vladimir Sobotka, Jaroslav
Spacek, Petr Sykora, Jiri Tlusty, Tomas
Vokoun, Jakub Voracek, Petr Vrana,
Radim Vrbata, Marek Zidlicky

SWEDEN   54   Daniel Alfredsson, P-J Axelsson,
Mikael Backlund, Christian Backman,
Nicklas Backstrom, Niklas Bergfors,
Patrik Berglund, Fabian Brunnstrom,
Alexander Edler, Tobias Enstrom,
Jonathan Ericsson, Anders Eriksson,
Loui Eriksson, Erik Ersberg, Johan
Franzen, Jonas Frogren, Nicklas
Grossman, Niclas Havelid, Johan
Hedberg, Niklas Hjalmarsson, Tomas
Holmstrom, Patrik Hornqvist, Kristian
Huselius, Kim Johnsson, Jonas
Junland, Niklas Kronwall, Staffan
Kronwall, Per Ledin, Nicklas Lidstrom,
Andreas Lilja, Joakim Lindstrom,
Henrik Lundqvist, Joel Lundqvist,
Fredrik Modin, Oscar Moller, Doug

Murray, Markus Naslund, Janne Niskala, Michael Nylander, John Oduya, Mattias Ohlund, Samuel Pahlsson, Mikael Samuelsson, Daniel Sedin, Henrik Sedin, Fredrik Sjostrom, Anton Stralman, Mats Sundin, Henrik Tallinder, Mikael Tellqvist, Daniel Tjarnqvist, Niclas Wallin, Tom Wandell, Henrik Zetterberg

FINLAND   42   Niklas Backstrom, Sean Bergenheim, Valtteri Filppula, Niklas Hagman, Riku Helenius, Jesse Joensuu, Jussi Jokinen, Olli Jokinen, Miikka Kiprusoff, Ville Koistinen, Mikko Koivu, Saku Koivu, Lauri Korpikoski, Lasse Kukkonen, Jere Lehtinen, Kari Lehtonen, Mikko Lehtonen, Ville Leino, Sami Lepisto, Toni Lydman, Antti Miettinen, Antti Niemi, Antero Niittymaki, Petteri Nokelainen, Fredrik Norrena, Teppo Numminen, Oskar Osala, Ville Peltonen, Janne Pesonen, Antti Pihlstrom, Joni Pitkanen, Karri Ramo, Tuuka Rask, Pekka Rinne, Jarkko Ruutu, Tuomo Ruutu, Anssi Salmela, Sami Salo, Teemu Selanne, Kimmo Timonen, Vesa Toskala, Ossi Vaananen

RUSSIA   33   Maxim Afinogenov, Artem Anisimov, Evgeni Artyukin, Anton Babchuk, Ilya Bryzgalov, Pavel Datsyuk, Sergei Fedorov, Nikita Filatov, Alexander Frolov, Sergei Gonchar, Denis Grebeshkov, Dmitri Kalinin, Nikolai Khabibulin, Ilya Kovalchuk, Alexei

Kovalev, Viktor Kozlov, Vyacheslav Kozlov, Nikolai Kulemin, Enver Lisin, Evgeni Malkin, Andrei Markov, Maxim Mayorov, Alexander Nikulin, Alexander Ovechkin, Sergei Samsonov, Alexei Semenov, Alexander Semin, Fedor Tyutin, Simeon Varlamov, Ivan Vishnevskiy, Anton Volchenkov, Ilja Zubov, Sergei Zubov

SLOVAKIA	17	Peter Budaj, Zdeno Chara, Pavol Demitra, Marian Gaborik, Jaroslav Halak, Michal Handzus, Marian Hossa, Milan Jurcina, Tomas Kopecky, Andrei Meszaros, Peter Olvecky, Miroslav Satan, Andrej Sekera, Marek Svatos, Boris Valabik, Lubomir Visnovsky, Richard Zednik
GERMANY	9	Christian Ehrhoff, Marcel Goc, Mikhail Grabovski, Dany Heatley, Jochen Hecht, Christoph Schubert, Dennis Seidenberg, Marco Sturm, Alexander Sulzer
LATVIA	5	Raitis Ivanins, Martins Karsums, Karlis Skrastins, Janis Sprukts, Viktor Tikhonov
SWITZERLAND	5	Martin Gerber, Jonas Hiller, Tobias Stephan, Mark Streit, Yannick Weber
DENMARK	4	Mikkel Boedker, Jannik Hansen, Frans Nielsen, Peter Regin
AUSTRIA	3	Andreas Nodl, Thomas Pock, Thomas Vanek
BELARUS	3	Andrei Kostitsyn, Sergei Kostitsyn, Ruslan Salei
UKRAINE	3	Ruslan Fedotenko, Alexei Ponikarovsky, Nikolai Zherdev

KAZAKHSTAN	2	Nik Antropov, Evgeny Nabokov
BAHAMAS	1	Andre Deveaux
BRAZIL	1	Robyn Regehr
FRANCE	1	Cristobal Huet
ITALY	1	Luca Sbisa
LITHUANIA	1	Dainius Zubrus
MALAYSIA	1	Craig Adams
NORWAY	1	Ole-Kristian Tollefsen
POLAND	1	Wojtek Wolski
SLOVENIA	1	Anze Kopitar
SOUTH AFRICA	1	Olaf Kolzig
SOUTH KOREA	1	Richard Park
UNITED KINGDOM	1	Owen Nolan

FIRST GAMES PLAYED, 2008–09

Skater (NAT)	Team (date)	G	A	P	Pim
Goalie (NAT)	Team (date)		Mins	W-L	GA
Karl Alzner (CAN)	WAS (Nov. 26)	0	0	0	0
Artem Anisimov (RUS)	NYR (Feb. 3)	0	0	0	0
Riley Armstrong (CAN)	SJ (Nov. 29)	0	0	0	0
Mikael Backlund (SWE)	CAL (Jan. 8)	0	0	0	0
Joshua Bailey (CAN)	NYI (Nov. 11)	0	0	0	4
Jay Beagle (CAN)	WAS (Feb. 11)	0	0	0	0
Matt Beleskey (CAN)	ANA (Jan. 9)	0	0	0	0
Sean Bentivoglio (CAN)	NYI (Apr. 2)	0	0	0	2
Patrik Berglund (SWE)	STL (Oct. 10)	0	1	1	0
Ben Bishop (USA)	STL (Oct. 24)		40:00	ND	2
Paul Bissonnette (CAN)	PIT (Oct. 4)	0	0	0	0
Byron Bitz (CAN)	BOS (Jan. 10)	0	1	1	0
Troy Bodie (CAN)	ANA (Jan. 16)	0	0	0	0
Mikkel Boedker (DEN)	PHO (Oct. 11)	0	0	0	0
Zach Bogosian (USA)	ATL (Oct. 10)	0	0	0	9
Alexandre Bolduc (CAN)	VAN (Nov. 27)	0	0	0	0
Zach Boychuk (CAN)	CAR (Oct. 17)	0	0	0	0
Fabian Brunnstrom (SWE)	DAL (Oct. 15)	3	0	3	0
Chris Butler (USA)	BUF (Dec. 19)	0	1	1	0
Joe Callahan (USA)	NYI (Dec. 9)	0	0	0	0
Luca Caputi (CAN)	PIT (Feb. 3)	1	0	1	2
Brett Carson (CAN)	CAR (Dec. 7)	0	0	0	0
Taylor Chorney (CAN)	EDM (Apr. 10)	0	0	0	0
Kris Chucko (CAN)	CAL (Mar. 5)	0	0	0	2
Matt Climie (CAN)	DAL (Apr. 4)		60:16	W	4
Sean Collins (USA)	WAS (Dec. 6)	0	0	0	0
Joey Crabb (USA)	ATL (Nov. 28)	0	0	0	0
John Curry (USA)	PIT (Nov. 26)		30:33	W	0

Patrick Davis (USA)	NJ (Nov. 9)	0	0	0	0
Andre Deveaux (BAH)	TOR (Nov. 27)	0	0	0	0
Derek Dorsett (CAN)	CBJ (Oct. 11)	0	0	0	9
Drew Doughty (CAN)	LA (Oct. 11)	0	0	0	0
Davis Drewiske (USA)	LA (Feb. 3)	0	0	0	0
J. Drouin-Deslauriers (CAN)	EDM (Oct. 17)		59:35	W	3
Philippe Dupuis (CAN)	COL (Oct. 17)	0	0	0	2
Chris Durno (CAN)	COL (Jan. 18)	0	0	0	0
Pat Dwyer (USA)	CAR (Nov. 2)	0	0	0	0
Brett Festerling (CAN)	ANA (Nov. 16)	0	0	0	0
Nikita Filatov (RUS)	CBJ (Oct. 11)	1	0	1	0
Jamie Fraser (CAN)	NYI (Apr. 4)	0	0	0	0
Jamie Fritsch (USA)	PHI (Apr. 12)	0	0	0	0
Mitch Fritz (CAN)	NYI (Oct. 30)	0	0	0	2
Jonas Frogren (SWE)	TOR (Oct. 9)	0	1	1	0
Michael Frolik (CZE)	FLO (Oct. 11)	0	0	0	0
T.J. Galiardi (CAN)	COL (Mar. 19)	0	0	0	0
Jason Garrison (CAN)	FLO (Oct. 25)	0	0	0	0
Nathan Gerbe (USA)	BUF (Dec. 6)	0	0	0	2
Colton Gillies (CAN)	MIN (Oct. 11)	0	1	1	0
Andrew Gordon (CAN)	WAS (Dec. 23)	0	0	0	0
Matt Halischuk (CAN)	NJ (Oct. 29)	0	1	1	0
Christian Hanson (USA)	TOR (Apr. 3)	0	0	0	0
Riku Helenius (FIN)	TB (Jan. 30)		6:52	ND	2
Dwight Helminen (USA)	CAR (Oct. 28)	0	0	0	0
Matt Hendricks (USA)	COL (Mar. 10)	0	0	0	2
Patric Hornqvist (SWE)	NAS (Oct. 10)	0	0	0	0
Dustin Jeffrey (CAN)	PIT (Dec. 26)	0	0	0	0
Jesse Joensuu (FIN)	NYI (Mar. 2)	1	0	1	0
Ryan Jones (CAN)	NAS (Oct. 10)	0	0	0	0
Derek Joslin (CAN)	SJ (Jan. 3)	0	0	0	2
Jonas Junland (SWE)	STL (Dec. 18)	0	0	0	2
Jon Kalinski (CAN)	PHI (Nov. 21)	0	0	0	0

Martins Karsums (LAT)	BOS (Dec. 13)	0	0	0	0
Tim Kennedy (USA)	BUF (Dec. 27)	0	0	0	0
Jeff Kinrade (CAN)	TB (Apr. 9)	0	0	0	0
Lauri Korpikoski (FIN)	NYR (Oct. 4)	0	0	0	0
Nikolai Kulemin (RUS)	TOR (Oct. 9)	1	0	1	0
Per Ledin (SWE)	COL (Apr. 9)	0	0	0	0
Scott Lehman (CAN)	ATL (Dec. 18)	0	0	0	0
Mikko Lehtonen (FIN)	BOS (Apr. 11)	0	0	0	0
Ville Leino (FIN)	DET (Jan. 31)	1	0	1	0
P-L Letourneau-Leblond (CAN)	NJ (Oct. 22)	0	1	1	0
Grant Lewis (USA)	ATL (Mar. 3)	0	0	0	0
Trevor Lewis (USA)	LA (Dec. 19)	0	0	0	0
Ben Lovejoy (USA)	PIT (Dec. 8)	0	0	0	0
Andrew MacDonald (CAN)	NYI (Feb. 28)	0	0	0	0
Spencer Machacek (CAN)	ATL (Mar. 16)	0	0	0	0
Ray Macias (USA)	COL (Apr. 1)	0	0	0	0
Steve MacIntyre (CAN)	EDM (Oct. 15)	0	0	0	0
Aaron MacKenzie (CAN)	COL (Apr. 5)	0	0	0	0
Peter Mannino (USA)	NYI (Nov. 28)		13:03	ND	3
Steve Mason (CAN)	CBJ (Nov. 5)		59:46	W	4
Ben Maxwell (CAN)	MON (Dec. 13)	0	0	0	0
Maxim Mayorov (RUS)	CBJ (Jan. 3)	0	0	0	0
Kenndal McArdle (CAN)	FLO (Dec. 2)	0	0	0	0
Jamie McGinn (CAN)	SJ (Oct. 28)	0	0	0	0
Mike McKenna (USA)	TB (Feb. 3)		28:26	ND	0
Kurtis McLean (CAN)	NYI (Jan. 19)	0	0	0	0
Vladimir Mihalik (SVK)	TB (Oct. 4)	0	0	0	0
Brendan Mikkelson (CAN)	ANA (Jan. 2)	0	0	0	0
John Mitchell (CAN)	TOR (Oct. 9)	0	0	0	0
Oscar Moller (SWE)	LA (Oct. 11)	0	0	0	0
Al Montoya (USA)	PHO (Apr. 1)		59:48	W	0
James Neal (CAN)	DAL (Oct. 10)	1	0	1	0
John Negrin (CAN)	CAL (Apr. 3)	0	0	0	2

Michal Neuvirth (CZE)	WAS (Feb. 14)		59:52	W	1
Antti Niemi (FIN)	CHI (Feb. 27)		21:36	OTL	1
Janne Niskala (SWE)	TB (Oct. 4)	0	0	0	0
Andreas Nodl (AUT)	PHI (Oct. 22)	0	1	1	0
Peter Olvecky (SVK)	MIN (Jan. 30)	0	0	0	0
Wes O'Neill (CAN)	COL (Mar. 27)	0	0	0	2
Cal O'Reilly (CAN)	NAS (Feb. 28)	0	1	1	0
Phil Oreskovic (CAN)	TOR (Mar. 9)	0	0	0	0
Oskar Osala (FIN)	WAS (Dec. 10)	0	0	0	0
T.J. Oshie (USA)	STL (Oct. 10)	0	0	0	0
Nathan Oystrick (CAN)	ATL (Oct. 14)	0	0	0	0
Max Pacioretty (USA)	MON (Jan. 2)	1	0	1	0
Cam Paddock (CAN)	STL (Nov. 14)	1	0	1	0
Adam Pardy (CAN)	CAL (Oct. 9)	0	0	0	0
Matt Pelech (CAN)	CAL (Apr. 3)	0	0	0	0
Derek Peltier (USA)	COL (Mar. 17)	0	0	0	0
Janne Pesonen (FIN)	PIT (Nov. 1)	0	0	0	0
Jakub Petruzalek (CZE)	CAR (Feb. 5)	0	1	1	0
Alex Pietrangelo (CAN)	STL (Oct. 10)	0	0	0	0
Justin Pogge (CAN)	TOR (Dec. 22)		59:53	W	2
Chris Porter (CAN)	STL (Oct. 10)	0	1	1	0
Kevin Porter (USA)	PHO (Oct. 11)	0	1	1	0
Corey Potter (USA)	NYR (Dec. 7)	0	0	0	0
Darroll Powe (CAN)	PHI (Oct. 24)	0	0	0	0
Kevin Quick (USA)	TB (Jan. 13)	0	0	0	0
Nate Raduns (USA)	PHI (Nov. 6)	0	0	0	0
Joel Rechlicz (USA)	NYI (Mar. 5)	0	1	1	0
Peter Regin (DEN)	OTT (Jan. 20)	0	0	0	0
Michal Repik (CZE)	FLO (Dec. 8)	1	0	1	0
Bryan Rodney (CAN)	CAR (Dec. 11)	0	0	0	2
Jared Ross (USA)	PHI (Oct. 11)	0	0	0	2
Brian Salcido (USA)	ANA (Feb. 20)	0	0	0	0
Anssi Salmela (FIN)	NJ (Oct. 10)	0	0	0	0
Mike Santorelli (CAN)	NAS (Jan. 8)	0	0	0	0
Mike Sauer (USA)	NYR (Mar. 24)	0	0	0	0

Raymond Sawada (CAN)	DAL (Feb. 19)	1	0	1	0
Luca Sbisa (ITA)	PHI (Oct. 11)	0	0	0	2
Luke Schenn (CAN)	TOR (Oct. 9)	0	0	0	0
David Schlemko (CAN)	PHO (Feb. 3)	0	0	0	0
Cory Schneider (USA)	VAN (Nov. 29)		59:45	L	3
John Scott (CAN)	MIN (Jan. 3)	0	0	0	0
Brandon Segal (CAN)	TB (Mar. 3)	0	0	0	0
Tim Sestito (USA)	EDM (Nov. 26)	0	0	0	0
Jamie Sifers (USA)	TOR (Dec. 8)	0	0	0	0
Wayne Simmonds (CAN)	LA (Oct. 11)	0	0	0	0
Brett Skinner (CAN)	NYI (Oct. 27)	0	0	0	0
Tyler Sloan (CAN)	WAS (Oct. 21)	0	0	0	2
David Sloane (USA)	PHI (Apr. 9)	0	0	0	0
Trevor Smith (CAN)	NYI (Dec. 31)	0	0	0	0
Zack Smith (CAN)	OTT (Nov. 29)	0	0	0	0
Radek Smolenak (CZE)	TB (Dec. 2)	0	1	1	5
Steve Stamkos (CAN)	TB (Oct. 4)	0	0	0	0
Brad Staubitz (CAN)	SJ (Oct. 17)	0	0	0	5
Chris Stewart (CAN)	COL (Dec. 5)	0	0	0	0
Tyson Strachan (CAN)	STL (Dec. 18)	0	0	0	2
Alexander Sulzer (GER)	NAS (Jan. 15)	0	0	0	0
Brandon Sutter (USA)	CAR (Oct. 10)	0	1	1	0
Brett Sutter (CAN)	CAL (Dec. 23)	1	0	1	0
Paul Szczechura (CAN)	TB (Dec. 2)	0	0	0	0
Viktor Tikhonov (LAT)	PHO (Oct. 11)	0	0	0	0
Josh Tordjman (CAN)	PHO (Mar. 8)		57:42	L	3
David van der Gulik (CAN)	CAL (Feb. 27)	0	0	0	0
Simeon Varlamov (RUS)	WAS (Dec. 13)		60:00	W	1
Mike Vernace (CAN)	COL (Mar. 17)	0	0	0	0
Ryan Vesce (USA)	SJ (Feb. 11)	0	0	0	0
Ivan Vishnevskiy (RUS)	DAL (Apr. 7)	0	0	0	2
Jakub Voracek (CZE)	CBJ (Oct. 10)	1	1	2	0
Petr Vrana (CZE)	NJ (Oct. 18)	1	0	1	0
Tim Wallace (USA)	PIT (Dec. 10)	0	0	0	2
Tom Wandell (SWE)	DAL (Dec. 10)	0	0	0	0

Yannick Weber (SUI)	MON (Jan. 8)	0	0	0	2
Kevin Westgarth (CAN)	LA (Jan. 20)	0	0	0	0
Blake Wheeler (USA)	BOS (Oct. 9)	1	0	1	2
Ty Wishart (CAN)	TB (Jan. 3)	0	0	0	0

BY NATION

Canada	83
United States	42
Sweden	10
Finland	9
Czech Republic	7
Russia	6
Denmark	2
Latvia	2
Slovakia	2
Austria	1
Bahamas	1
Germany	1
Italy	1
Switzerland	1
TOTAL	**168**

BY NHL TEAM

Anaheim	5
Atlanta	6
Boston	4
Buffalo	3
Calgary	7
Carolina	7
Chicago	1
Colorado	11

Columbus	5
Dallas	6
Detroit	1
Edmonton	4
Florida	4
Los Angeles	6
Minnesota	3
Montreal	3
Nashville	5
New Jersey	5
NY Islanders	12
NY Rangers	4
Ottawa	2
Philadelphia	8
Phoenix	6
Pittsburgh	7
San Jose	5
St. Louis	8
Tampa Bay	11
Toronto	9
Vancouver	2
Washington	8
TOTAL	**168**

PLAYER REGISTER, 2008–09

Player YEAR	GP	G	A	P	Pim		
Goalie YEAR	GP	W-L-OTL-T	Mins	GA	SO	GAA	

Abdelkader, Justin b. Muskegon, Michigan, February 25, 1987

	GP	G	A	P	Pim
2008–09 DET	2	0	0	0	0
NHL Totals	4	0	0	0	2

Adams, Craig b. Seria, Brunei (Malaysia), April 26, 1977

	GP	G	A	P	Pim
2008–09 CHI/PIT	45	2	5	7	22
NHL Totals	507	37	53	90	383

• claimed off waivers by Pittsburgh from Chicago on March 4, 2009

Afinogenov, Maxim b. Moscow, Soviet Union (Russia), September 4, 1979

	GP	G	A	P	Pim
2008–09 BUF	48	6	14	20	20
NHL Totals	569	134	200	334	440

Alberts, Andrew b. Minneapolis, Minnesota, June 30, 1981

	GP	G	A	P	Pim
2008–09 PHI	79	1	12	13	61
NHL Totals	263	2	30	32	292

Alfredsson, Daniel b. Gothenburg, Sweden, December 11, 1972

	GP	G	A	P	Pim
2008–09 OTT	79	24	50	74	24
NHL Totals	932	355	566	921	409

Allen, Bryan b. Kingston, Ontario, August 21, 1980

	GP	G	A	P	Pim
2008–09 FLO	2	0	1	1	0
NHL Totals	373	20	54	74	467

Alzner, Karl b. Burnaby, British Columbia, September 24, 1988

2008–09 WAS	30	1	4	5	2
NHL Totals	30	1	4	5	2

Anderson, Craig b. Park Ridge, Illinois, May 21, 1981

2008–09 FLO	31	15–7–5–0	1,635	74	3	2.71
NHL Totals	109	36–43–11–2	5,816	278	7	2.87

Anisimov, Artem b. Yaroslavl, Soviet Union (Russia), May 24, 1988

2008–09 NYR	1	0	0	0	0
NHL Totals	1	0	0	0	0

Antropov, Nik b. Vost, Soviet Union (Kazakhstan), February 18, 1980

2008–09 TOR/NYR	81	28	31	59	30
NHL Totals	527	132	172	304	483

• traded March 4, 2009, by Toronto to NY Rangers for a 2nd-round draft choice in 2009 and a conditional draft choice

Armstrong, Colby b. Lloydminster, Saskatchewan, November 23, 1982

2008–09 ATL	82	22	18	40	75
NHL Totals	281	63	86	149	256

Armstrong, Derek b. Ottawa, Ontario, April 23, 1973

2008–09 LA	56	5	4	9	63
NHL Totals	471	72	149	221	353

Armstrong, Riley b. Saskatoon, Saskatchewan, November 8, 1984

2008–09 SJ	2	0	0	0	2
NHL Totals	2	0	0	0	2

Arnason, Tyler b. Oklahoma City, Oklahoma, March 16, 1979

2008–09 COL	71	5	17	22	14
NHL Totals	487	88	157	245	140

Arnott, Jason b. Collingwood, Ontario, October 11, 1974

| 2008–09 NAS | 65 | 33 | 24 | 57 | 49 |
| NHL Totals | 1,036 | 364 | 463 | 827 | 1,150 |

Artyukin, Evgeni b. Moscow, Soviet Union (Russia), April 4, 1983

| 2008–09 TB | 73 | 6 | 10 | 16 | 151 |
| NHL Totals | 145 | 10 | 23 | 33 | 241 |

Asham, Arron b. Portage La Prairie, Manitoba, April 13, 1978

| 2008–09 PHI | 78 | 8 | 12 | 20 | 155 |
| NHL Totals | 576 | 72 | 83 | 155 | 692 |

Aucoin, Adrian b. Ottawa, Ontario, July 3, 1973

| 2008–09 CAL | 81 | 10 | 24 | 34 | 46 |
| NHL Totals | 851 | 108 | 228 | 336 | 627 |

Aucoin, Keith b. Waltham, Massachusetts, November 6, 1978

| 2008–09 WAS | 12 | 2 | 4 | 6 | 4 |
| NHL Totals | 65 | 7 | 14 | 21 | 18 |

Auld, Alexander b. Cold Lake, Alberta, January 7, 1981

| 2008–09 OTT | 43 | 16–18–7–0 | 2,449 | 101 | 1 | 2.47 |
| NHL Totals | 183 | 74–75–23–2 | 10,292 | 473 | 6 | 2.76 |

Avery, Sean b. Pickering, Ontario, April 10, 1980

| 2008–09 DAL/NYR | 41 | 8 | 14 | 22 | 111 |
| NHL Totals | 420 | 73 | 116 | 189 | 1,178 |

• claimed off waivers by NY Rangers from Dallas on March 3, 2009

Axelsson, P-J b. Kungalv, Sweden, February 26, 1975

| 2008–09 BOS | 75 | 6 | 24 | 30 | 16 |
| NHL Totals | 797 | 103 | 184 | 287 | 276 |

Babchuk, Anton b. Kiev, Soviet Union (Russia), May 6, 1984

2008–09 CAR	72	16	19	35	16
NHL Totals	168	23	38	61	70

Backes, David b. Blaine, Minnesota, May 1, 1984

2008–09 STL	82	31	23	54	165
NHL Totals	203	54	54	108	301

Backlund, Mikael b. Vasteras, Sweden, March 17, 1989

2008–09 CAL	1	0	0	0	0
NHL Totals	1	0	0	0	0

Backman, Christian b. Alingsas, Sweden, April 28, 1980

2008–09 CBJ	56	2	5	7	32
NHL Totals	302	23	56	79	182

Backstrom, Nicklas b. Gavle, Sweden, November 23, 1987

2008–09 WAS	82	22	66	88	46
NHL Totals	164	36	121	157	70

Backstrom, Niklas b. Helsinki, Finland, February 13, 1978

2008–09 MIN	71	37–24–8–0	4,088	159	9	2.33
NHL Totals	170	93–45–22–0	9,723	363	17	2.24

Bailey, Josh b. Oshawa, Ontario, October 2, 1989

2008–09 NYI	68	7	18	25	16
NHL Totals	68	7	18	25	16

Ballard, Keith b. Baudette, Minnesota, November 26, 1982

2008–09 FLO	82	6	28	34	72
NHL Totals	315	25	96	121	315

Barch, Krys b. Guelph, Ontario, March 26, 1980

2008–09 DAL	72	4	5	9	133
NHL Totals	146	8	9	17	345

Barker, Cam b. Winnipeg, Manitoba, April 4, 1986

2008–09 CHI	68	6	34	40	65
NHL Totals	149	13	53	66	161

Bass, Cody b. Owen Sound, Ontario, January 7, 1987

2008–09 OTT	12	0	0	0	15
NHL Totals	33	2	2	4	34

Bayda, Ryan b. Saskatoon, Saskatchewan, December 9, 1980

2008–09 CAR	70	5	7	12	26
NHL Totals	179	16	24	40	94

Beagle, Jay b. Calgary, Alberta, October 16, 1985

2008–09 WAS	3	0	0	0	2
NHL Totals	3	0	0	0	2

Beauchemin, Francois b. Sorel, Quebec, June 4, 1980

2008–09 ANA	20	4	1	5	12
NHL Totals	246	21	69	90	172

Begin, Steve b. Trois Rivieres, Quebec, June 14, 1978

2008–09 MON/DAL	62	7	5	12	42
NHL Totals	409	47	39	86	482

• traded February 26, 2009, by Montreal to Dallas for Doug Janik

Belak, Wade b. Saskatoon, Saskatchewan, July 3, 1976

2008–09 FLO/NAS	53	0	2	2	79
NHL Totals	495	8	23	31	1,187

• traded November 27, 2008, by Florida to Nashville for Nick Tarnasky

Belanger, Eric   b. Sherbrooke, Quebec, December 16, 1977

2008–09 MIN	79	13	23	36	26
NHL Totals	557	106	152	258	251

Beleskey, Matt   b. Windsor, Ontario, June 7, 1988

2008–09 ANA	2	0	0	0	0
NHL Totals	2	0	0	0	0

Bell, Brendan   b. Ottawa, Ontario, March 31, 1983

2008–09 OTT	53	6	15	21	24
NHL Totals	101	7	21	28	51

Bentivoglio, Sean   b. Thorold, Ontario, October 16, 1985

2008–09 NYI	1	0	0	0	2
NHL Totals	1	0	0	0	2

Bergenheim, Sean   b. Helsinki, Finland, February 8, 1984

2008–09 NYI	59	15	9	24	64
NHL Totals	183	30	27	57	150

Bergeron, Marc-Andre   b. St. Louis de France, Quebec, October 13, 1980

2008–09 MIN	72	14	18	32	30
NHL Totals	339	62	98	160	161

Bergeron, Patrice   b. L'Ancienne Lorette, Quebec, July 24, 1985

2008–09 BOS	64	8	31	39	16
NHL Totals	303	80	148	228	88

Bergfors, Niklas   b. Sodertalje, Sweden, March 7, 1987

2008–09 NJ	8	1	0	1	0
NHL Totals	9	1	0	1	0

Berglund, Patrik   b. Vasteras, Sweden, June 2, 1988

2008–09 STL	76	21	26	47	16
NHL Totals	76	21	26	47	16

Bernier, Steve b. Quebec City, Quebec, March 31, 1985

2008–09 VAN	81	15	17	32	27
NHL Totals	258	60	62	122	155

Bertuzzi, Todd b. Sudbury, Ontario, February 2, 1975

2008–09 CAL	66	15	29	44	74
NHL Totals	859	255	369	624	1,221

Betts, Blair b. Edmonton, Alberta, February 16, 1980

2008–09 NYR	81	6	4	10	16
NHL Totals	339	28	20	48	96

Bieksa, Kevin b. Grimsby, Ontario, June 16, 1981

2008–09 VAN	72	11	32	43	97
NHL Totals	226	25	78	103	398

Biron, Martin b. Lac St. Charles, Quebec, August 15, 1977

2008–09 PHI	55	29–19–5–0	3,176	146	2	2.76
NHL Totals	433	199–162–20–25	24,424	1,053	25	2.59

Bishop, Ben b. Denver, Colorado, November 21, 1986

2008–09 STL	6	1–1–1–0	244	12	0	2.94
NHL Totals	6	1–1–1–0	244	12	0	2.94

Bissonnette, Paul b. Welland, Ontario, March 11, 1985

2008–09 PIT	15	0	1	1	22
NHL Totals	15	0	1	1	22

Bitz, Byron b. Saskatoon, Saskatchewan, July 21, 1984

2008–09 BOS	35	4	3	7	18
NHL Totals	35	4	3	7	18

Blake, Jason b. Moorhead, Minnesota, September 2, 1973

2008–09 TOR	78	25	38	63	40
NHL Totals	668	174	227	401	372

Blake, Rob b. Simcoe, Ontario, December 10, 1969

2008–09 SJ	73	10	35	45	110
NHL Totals	1,200	233	514	747	1,619

Bochenski, Brandon b. Blaine, Minnesota, April 4, 1982

2008–09 TB	7	0	1	1	2
NHL Totals	128	24	31	55	52

Bodie, Troy b. Portage La Prairie, Manitoba, January 25, 1985

2008–09 ANA	4	0	0	0	0
NHL Totals	4	0	0	0	0

Boedker, Mikkel b. Brondby, Denmark, December 16, 1989

2008–09 PHO	78	11	17	28	18
NHL Totals	78	11	17	28	18

Bogosian, Zach b. Massena, New York, July 15, 1990

2008–09 ATL	47	9	10	19	47
NHL Totals	47	9	10	19	47

Bolduc, Alexandre b. Montreal, Quebec, June 26, 1985

2008–09 VAN	7	0	1	1	4
NHL Totals	7	0	1	1	4

Boll, Jarred b. Crystal Lake, Illinois, May 13, 1986

2008–09 CBJ	75	4	10	14	180
NHL Totals	150	9	15	24	406

Bolland, Dave b. Toronto, Ontario, June 5, 1986

2008–09 CHI	81	19	28	47	52
NHL Totals	121	23	41	64	80

Bonk, Radek   b. Krnov, Czechoslovakia (Czech Republic),
January 9, 1976

2008–09 NAS	66	9	16	25	34
NHL Totals	969	194	303	497	581

Boogaard, Derek   b. Saskatoon, Saskatchewan, June 23, 1982

2008–09 MIN	51	0	3	3	87
NHL Totals	198	2	8	10	439

Booth, David   b. Detroit, Michigan, November 24, 1984

2008–09 FLO	72	31	29	60	38
NHL Totals	193	56	54	110	76

Borer, Casey   b. Minneapolis, Minnesota, July 28, 1985

2008–09 CAR	3	0	0	0	5
NHL Totals	14	1	2	3	9

Bouchard, Pierre-Marc   b. Sherbrooke, Quebec, April 27, 1984

2008–09 MIN	71	16	30	46	20
NHL Totals	425	77	190	267	136

Boucher, Brian   b. Woonsocket, Rhode Island, January 2, 1977

2008–09 SJ	22	12–6–3–0	1,291	47	2	2.18
NHL Totals	247	92–103–7–30	13,901	629	16	2.71

Boucher, Philippe   b. Ste. Apollinaire, Quebec, March 24, 1973

2008–09 DAL/PIT	41	3	6	9	39
NHL Totals	748	94	206	300	702

• traded November 16, 2008, by Dallas to Pittsburgh for Daryl Sydor

Bouillon, Francis   b. New York, New York, October 17, 1975

2008–09 MON	54	5	4	9	53
NHL Totals	485	21	81	102	371

Boulerice, Jesse b. Plattsburgh, New York, August 10, 1978

2008–09 EDM	2	0	0	0	0
NHL Totals	172	8	2	10	333

Boulton, Eric b. Halifax, Nova Scotia, August 17, 1976

2008–09 ATL	76	3	10	13	176
NHL Totals	418	19	36	55	950

Bourque, Chris b. Boston, Massachusetts, January 29, 1986

2008–09 WAS	8	1	0	1	0
NHL Totals	12	1	0	1	2

Bourque, Rene b. Lac La Biche, Alberta, December 10, 1981

2008–09 CAL	58	21	19	40	70
NHL Totals	241	54	61	115	206

Bouwmeester, Jay b. Edmonton, Alberta, September 27, 1983

2008–09 FLO	82	15	27	42	68
NHL Totals	471	53	150	203	329

Boychuk, Johnny b. Edmonton, Alberta, January 19, 1984

2008–09 BOS	1	0	0	0	0
NHL Totals	5	0	0	0	0

Boychuk, Zach b. Airdrie, Alberta, October 4, 1989

2008–09 CAR	2	0	0	0	0
NHL Totals	2	0	0	0	0

Boyd, Dustin b. Winnipeg, Manitoba, July 16, 1986

2008–09 CAL	71	11	11	22	10
NHL Totals	132	20	18	38	20

Boyes, Brad b. Mississauga, Ontario, April 17, 1982

2008–09 STL	82	33	39	72	26
NHL Totals	328	119	133	252	107

Boyle, Brian b. Dorchester, Massachusetts, December 18, 1984

2008–09 LA	28	4	1	5	42
NHL Totals	36	8	2	10	46

Boyle, Dan b. Ottawa, Ontario, July 12, 1976

2008–09 SJ	77	16	41	57	52
NHL Totals	600	92	257	349	390

Boynton, Nick b. Nobleton, Ontario, January 14, 1979

2008–09 FLO	68	5	16	21	91
NHL Totals	505	32	96	128	751

Bradley, Matt b. Stittsville, Ontario, June 13, 1978

2008–09 WAS	81	5	6	11	59
NHL Totals	492	42	64	106	416

Brashear, Donald b. Bedford, Indiana, January 7, 1972

2008–09 WAS	63	1	3	4	121
NHL Totals	989	85	119	204	2,561

Brassard, Derick b. Hull, Quebec, September 22, 1987

2008–09 CBJ	31	10	15	25	17
NHL Totals	48	11	16	27	23

Brent, Tim b. Cambridge, Ontario, March 10, 1984

2008–09 CHI	2	0	0	0	2
NHL Totals	18	1	0	1	8

Brewer, Eric b. Vernon, British Columbia, April 17, 1979

2008–09 STL	28	1	5	6	24
NHL Totals	623	48	131	179	491

Briere, Daniel b. Gatineau, Quebec, October 6, 1977

2008–09 PHI	29	11	14	25	26
NHL Totals	591	204	269	473	459

Brind'Amour, Rod   b. Ottawa, Ontario, August 9, 1970

2008–09 CAR	80	16	35	51	36
NHL Totals	1,404	443	722	1,165	1,064

Brisebois, Patrice   b. Montreal, Quebec, January 27, 1971

2008–09 MON	62	5	13	18	19
NHL Totals	1,009	98	322	420	623

Brodeur, Martin   b. Montreal, Quebec, May 6, 1972

2008–09 NJ	31	19–9–3–0	1,813	73	5	2.41
NHL Totals	999	557–299–23–105	59,021	2,172	101	2.21

Brodziak, Kyle   b. St. Paul, Alberta, May 25, 1984

2008–09 EDM	79	11	16	27	21
NHL Totals	175	26	33	59	60

Brookbank, Sheldon   b. Lanigan, Saskatchewan, October 3, 1980

2008–09 NJ/ANA	44	1	3	4	76
NHL Totals	91	1	12	13	151

• traded February 3, 2009, by New Jersey to Anaheim for David McIntyre

Brookbank, Wade   b. Lanigan, Saskatchewan, September 29, 1977

2008–09 CAR	27	1	0	1	40
NHL Totals	127	6	3	9	345

Brouwer, Troy   b. Vancouver, British Columbia, August 17, 1985

2008–09 CHI	69	10	16	26	50
NHL Totals	81	10	17	27	57

Brown, Dustin   b. Ithaca, New York, November 4, 1984

2008–09 LA	80	24	29	53	64
NHL Totals	349	89	103	192	269

Brown, Mike   b. Northbrook, Illinois, June 24, 1985

2008–09 VAN/ANA	48	2	2	4	145
NHL Totals	67	3	2	5	200

• traded February 4, 2009, by Vancouver to Anaheim for Nathan McIver

Brule, Gilbert   b. Edmonton, Alberta, January 1, 1987

2008–09 EDM	11	2	1	3	12
NHL Totals	157	14	21	35	64

Brunette, Andrew   b. Sudbury, Ontario, August 24, 1973

2008–09 MIN	80	22	28	50	18
NHL Totals	868	213	386	599	282

Brunnstrom, Fabian   b. Jonstorp, Sweden, February 6, 1985

2008–09 DAL	55	17	12	29	8
NHL Totals	55	17	12	29	8

Bryzgalov, Ilya   b. Togliatti, Soviet Union (Russia), June 22, 1980

2008–09 PHO	65	26–31–6–0	3,759	187	3	2.98
NHL Totals	189	78–76–19–0	10,550	465	8	2.64

Budaj, Peter   b. Banska Bystrica, Czechoslovakia (Slovakia), September 18, 1982

2008–09 COL	56	20–29–5–0	3,231	154	2	2.86
NHL Totals	182	81–65–21–0	10,144	465	7	2.75

Burish, Adam   b. Madison, Wisconsin, January 6, 1983

2008–09 CHI	66	6	3	9	93
NHL Totals	156	10	7	17	309

Burns, Brent   b. Ajax, Ontario, March 9, 1985

2008–09 MIN	59	8	19	27	45
NHL Totals	326	35	82	117	195

Burrows, Alex b. Pointe-Claire, Quebec, April 11, 1981

2008–09 VAN	82	28	23	51	150
NHL Totals	288	50	53	103	483

Butler, Chris b. St. Louis, Missouri, October 27, 1986

2008–09 BUF	47	2	4	6	18
NHL Totals	47	2	4	6	18

Byfuglien, Dustin b. Minneapolis, Minnesota, March 27, 1985

2008–09 CHI	77	15	16	31	81
NHL Totals	178	38	37	75	174

Calder, Kyle b. Mannville, Alberta, January 5, 1979

2008–09 LA	74	8	19	27	41
NHL Totals	576	114	178	292	301

Callahan, Joe b. Brockton, Massachusetts, December 20, 1982

2008–09 NYI	18	0	2	2	4
NHL Totals	18	0	2	2	4

Callahan, Ryan b. Rochester, New York, March 21, 1985

2008–09 NYR	81	22	18	40	45
NHL Totals	147	34	25	59	85

Cammalleri, Mike b. Richmond Hill, Ontario, June 8, 1982

2008–09 CAL	81	39	43	82	44
NHL Totals	364	132	155	287	214

Campbell, Brian b. Strathroy, Ontario, May 23, 1979

2008–09 CHI	82	7	45	52	22
NHL Totals	493	42	205	247	143

Campbell, Gregory b. London, Ontario, December 17, 1983

2008–09 FLO	77	13	19	32	76
NHL Totals	303	27	41	68	259

Campoli, Chris b. North York (Toronto), Ontario, July 9, 1984

2008–09 NYI/OTT	76	11	19	30	55
NHL Totals	253	25	71	96	140

• traded February 20, 2009, by NY Islanders to Ottawa with Mike Comrie for Dean McAmmond and a 1st-round draft choice in 2009

Caputi, Luca b. Toronto, Ontario, October 1, 1988

2008–09 PIT	5	1	0	1	4
NHL Totals	5	1	0	1	4

Carcillo, Daniel b. King City, Ontario, January 28, 1985

2008–09 PHO/PHI	74	3	11	14	254
NHL Totals	149	20	25	45	652

• traded March 4, 2009, by Phoenix to Philadelphia for Scottie Upshall and a 2nd-round draft choice in 2011

Carkner, Matt b. Winchester, Ontario, November 3, 1980

2008–09 OTT	1	0	0	0	0
NHL Totals	2	0	1	1	2

Carle, Matt b. Anchorage, Alaska, September 25, 1984

2008–09 TB/PHI	76	5	21	26	22
NHL Totals	227	21	68	89	92

• traded November 7, 2008, by Tampa Bay to Philadelphia with a 3rd-round draft choice in 2009, for Steve Eminger, Steve Downie, and a 4th-round draft choice in 2009

Carson, Brett b. Regina, Saskatchewan, November 29, 1985

2008–09 CAR	5	0	0	0	4
NHL Totals	5	0	0	0	4

Carter, Jeff b. London, Ontario, January 1, 1985

2008–09 PHI	82	46	38	84	68
NHL Totals	307	112	104	216	211

Carter, Ryan b. White Bear Lake, Minnesota, August 3, 1983

2008–09 ANA	48	3	6	9	52
NHL Totals	82	7	10	17	88

Cavanagh, Tom b. Warwick, Rhode Island, March 24, 1982

2008–09 SJ	17	1	1	2	4
NHL Totals	18	1	2	3	4

Chara, Zdeno b. Trencin, Czechoslovakia (Slovakia), March 18, 1977

2008–09 BOS	80	19	31	50	95
NHL Totals	767	104	215	319	1,210

Cheechoo, Jonathan b. Moose Factory, Ontario, July 15, 1980

2008–09 SJ	66	12	17	29	59
NHL Totals	440	165	126	291	304

Chelios, Chris b. Chicago, Illinois, January 25, 1962

2008–09 DET	28	0	0	0	18
NHL Totals	1,644	185	763	948	2,891

Chimera, Jason b. Edmonton, Alberta, May 2, 1979

2008–09 CBJ	49	8	14	22	41
NHL Totals	422	73	82	155	418

Chipchura, Kyle b. Westlock, Alberta, February 19, 1986

2008–09 MON	13	0	3	3	5
NHL Totals	49	4	10	14	15

Chorney, Taylor b. Thunder Bay, Ontario, April 27, 1987

2008–09 EDM	2	0	0	0	0
NHL Totals	2	0	0	0	0

Christensen, Erik b. Edmonton, Alberta, December 17, 1983

2008–09 ATL/ANA	64	7	21	28	20
NHL Totals	217	42	56	98	110

• traded March 4, 2009, by Atlanta to Anaheim for Eric O'Dell

Chucko, Kris b. Burnaby, British Columbia, March 13, 1986

2008–09 CAL	2	0	0	0	2
NHL Totals	2	0	0	0	2

Clark, Brett b. Wapella, Saskatchewan, December 23, 1976

2008–09 COL	76	2	10	12	32
NHL Totals	453	31	88	119	231

Clark, Chris b. South Windsor, Connecticut, March 8, 1976

2008–09 WAS	32	1	5	6	32
NHL Totals	480	91	88	179	614

Clarkson, David b. Toronto, Ontario, March 31, 1984

2008–09 NJ	82	17	15	32	164
NHL Totals	170	29	29	58	353

Cleary, Daniel b. Carbonear, Newfoundland, December 18, 1978

2008–09 DET	74	14	26	40	46
NHL Totals	614	98	151	249	336

Clemmensen, Scott b. Des Moines, Iowa, July 23, 1977

2008–09 NJ	40	25–13–1–0	2,355	94	2	2.39
NHL Totals	68	33–20–5–0	3,700	160	4	2.59

Climie, Matt b. Leduc, Alberta, February 11, 1983

2008–09 DAL	3	2–1–0–0	185	9	0	2.92
NHL Totals	3	2–1–0–0	185	9	0	2.92

Clowe, Ryane b. St. John's, Newfoundland, September 30, 1982

2008–09 SJ	71	22	30	52	51
NHL Totals	162	41	55	96	160

Clutterbuck, Cal b. Welland, Ontario, November 18, 1987

2008–09 MIN	78	11	7	18	76
NHL Totals	80	11	7	18	76

Coburn, Braydon b. Calgary, Alberta, February 27, 1985

2008–09 PHI	80	7	21	28	97
NHL Totals	216	19	57	76	221

Cogliano, Andrew b. Toronto, Ontario, June 14, 1987

2008–09 EDM	82	18	20	38	22
NHL Totals	164	36	47	83	42

Colaiacovo, Carlo b. Toronto, Ontario, January 27, 1983

2008–09 TOR/STL	73	3	27	30	35
NHL Totals	174	15	47	62	86

• traded November 24, 2008, by Toronto to St. Louis with Alexander Steen for Lee Stempniak

Cole, Erik b. Oswego, New York, November 6, 1978

2008–09 EDM/CAR	80	18	24	42	73
NHL Totals	498	147	175	322	479

• traded March 4, 2009, by Edmonton to Carolina with a 5th-round draft choice in 2009 for Patrick O'Sullivan and a 2nd-round draft choice in 2009

Collins, Sean b. Saskatoon, Saskatchewan, December 29, 1988

2008–09 WAS	15	1	1	2	12
NHL Totals	15	1	1	2	12

Colliton, Jeremy b. Blackie, Alberta, January 13, 1985

2008–09 NYI	6	0	1	1	2
NHL Totals	42	1	2	3	16

Comeau, Blake b. Meadow Lake, Saskatchewan, February 18, 1986

2008–09 NYI	53	7	18	25	32
NHL Totals	107	15	25	40	54

Commodore, Mike b. Fort Saskatchewan, Alberta, November 7, 1979

2008–09 CBJ	81	5	19	24	100
NHL Totals	377	19	68	87539	

Comrie, Mike b. Edmonton, Alberta, September 11, 1980

2008–09 NYI/OTT	63	10	17	27	32
NHL Totals	525	154	184	338	395

• traded February 20, 2009, by NY Islanders to Ottawa with Chris Campoli for Dean McAmmond and a 1st-round draft choice in 2009

Conboy, Tim b. Farmington, Minnesota, March 22, 1981

2008–09 CAR	28	0	1	1	37
NHL Totals	47	0	6	6	97

Conklin, Ty b. Anchorage, Alaska, March 30, 1976

2008–09 DET	40	25–11–2–0	2,246	94	6	2.51
NHL Totals	149	73–43–10–4	7,985	343	10	2.58

Conner, Chris b. Westland, Michigan, December 23, 1983

2008–09 DAL	38	3	10	13	10
NHL Totals	71	7	14	21	20

Connolly, Tim b. Syracuse, New York, May 7, 1981

2008–09 BUF	48	18	29	47	22
NHL Totals	486	88	200	288	212

Conroy, Craig b. Potsdam, New York, September 4, 1971

2008–09 CAL	82	12	36	48	28
NHL Totals	928	177	348	525	570

Cooke, Matt b. Belleville, Ontario, September 7, 1978

| 2008–09 PIT | 76 | 13 | 18 | 31 | 101 |
| NHL Totals | 659 | 99 | 142 | 241 | 753 |

Corvo, Joe b. Oak Park, Illinois, June 20, 1977

| 2008–09 CAR | 81 | 14 | 24 | 38 | 18 |
| NHL Totals | 434 | 62 | 138 | 200 | 174 |

Cote, Riley b. Winnipeg, Manitoba, March 16, 1982

| 2008–09 PHI | 63 | 0 | 3 | 3 | 174 |
| NHL Totals | 141 | 1 | 6 | 7 | 387 |

Crabb, Joey b. Anchorage, Alaska, April 3, 1983

| 2008–09 ATL | 29 | 4 | 5 | 9 | 28 |
| NHL Totals | 29 | 4 | 5 | 9 | 28 |

Craig, Ryan b. Abbotsford, British Columbia, January 6, 1982

| 2008–09 TB | 54 | 2 | 4 | 6 | 60 |
| NHL Totals | 181 | 32 | 31 | 63 | 121 |

Crawford, Corey b. Montreal, Quebec, December 31, 1984
• appeared only in the playoffs for Chicago

Crombeen, Brandon b. Denver, Colorado, July 10, 1985

| 2008–09 DAL/STL | 81 | 12 | 10 | 22 | 148 |
| NHL Totals | 89 | 12 | 12 | 24 | 187 |
• claimed off waivers by St. Louis from Dallas on November 18, 2008

Crosby, Sidney b. Halifax, Nova Scotia, August 7, 1987

| 2008–09 PIT | 77 | 33 | 70 | 103 | 76 |
| NHL Totals | 290 | 132 | 265 | 397 | 285 |

Cullen, Matt b. Virginia, Minnesota, November 2, 1976

| 2008–09 CAR | 69 | 22 | 21 | 43 | 20 |
| NHL Totals | 799 | 153 | 260 | 413 | 358 |

Cullimore, Jassen b. Simcoe, Ontario, December 4, 1972

2008–09 FLO	68	2	8	10	37
NHL Totals	776	26	77	103	696

Cumiskey, Kyle b. Abbotsford, British Columbia, December 2, 1986

2008–09 COL	6	0	0	0	0
NHL Totals	53	1	6	7	18

Curry, John b. Shorewood, Minnesota, February 27, 1984

2008–09 PIT	3	2–1–0–0	149	6	0	2.40
NHL Totals	3	2–1–0–0	149	6	0	2.40

D'Agostini, Matt b. Sault Ste. Marie, Ontario, October 23, 1986

2008–09 MON	53	12	9	21	18
NHL Totals	54	12	9	21	18

Daley, Trevor b. Toronto, Ontario, October 9, 1983

2008–09 DAL	75	7	18	25	73
NHL Totals	339	20	61	81	322

Dandenault, Mathieu b. Sherbrooke, Quebec, February 3, 1976

2008–09 MON	41	4	8	12	17
NHL Totals	868	68	135	203	516

Danis, Yann b. Lafontaine, Quebec, June 21, 1981

2008–09 NYI	31	10–17–3–0	1,760	84	2	2.86
NHL Totals	37	13–19–3–0	2,072	98	3	2.84

Datsyuk, Pavel b. Sverdlovsk, Soviet Union (Russia), July 20, 1978

2008–09 DET	81	32	65	97	22
NHL Totals	526	171	351	522	139

Davis, Patrick b. Sterling, Michigan, December 28, 1986

2008–09 NJ	1	0	0	0	0
NHL Totals	1	0	0	0	0

Davison, Rob b. St. Catharines, Ontario, May 1, 1980

2008–09 VAN	23	0	2	2	51
NHL Totals	218	3	15	18	321

Dawes, Nigel b. Winnipeg, Manitoba, February 9, 1985

2008–09 NYR/PHO	64	10	11	21	15
NHL Totals	133	25	26	51	25

• traded March 4, 2009, by NY Rangers to Phoenix with Dmitri Kalinin and Petr Prucha for Derek Morris

Demitra, Pavol b. Dubnica, Czechoslovakia (Slovakia), November 29, 1974

2008–09 VAN	69	20	33	53	20
NHL Totals	819	301	451	752	284

Denis, Marc b. Montreal, Quebec, August 1, 1977

2008–09 MON	1	0–0–0–0	20	1	0	3.00
NHL Totals	349	112–179–3–28	19,525	982	16	3.02

Deveaux, Andre b. Freeport, Bahamas, February 23, 1984

2008–09 TOR	21	0	1	1	75
NHL Totals	21	0	1	1	75

Devereaux, Boyd b. Seaforth, Ontario, April 16, 1978

2008–09 TOR	23	6	5	11	2
NHL Totals	627	67	112	179	205

de Vries, Greg b. Sundridge, Ontario, January 4, 1973

2008–09 NAS	71	1	4	5	65
NHL Totals	878	48	146	194	780

DiPietro, Rick b. Winthrop, Massachusetts, September 19, 1981

2008–09 NYI	5	1–3–0–0	255	15	0	3.52
NHL Totals	273	117–112–21–8	15,673	729	14	2.79

Doan, Shane b. Halkirk, Alberta, October 10, 1976

| 2008–09 PHO | 82 | 31 | 42 | 73 | 72 |
| NHL Totals | 965 | 258 | 365 | 623 | 915 |

Donovan, Shean b. Timmins, Ontario, January 22, 1975

| 2008–09 OTT | 65 | 5 | 5 | 10 | 34 |
| NHL Totals | 921 | 110 | 126 | 236 | 665 |

Dorsett, Derek b. Kindersley, Saskatchewan, December 20, 1986

| 2008–09 CBJ | 52 | 4 | 1 | 5 | 150 |
| NHL Totals | 52 | 4 | 1 | 5 | 150 |

Doughty, Drew b. London, Ontario, December 8, 1989

| 2008–09 LA | 81 | 6 | 21 | 27 | 56 |
| NHL Totals | 81 | 6 | 21 | 27 | 56 |

Dowell, Jacob b. Eau Claire, Wisconsin, March 4, 1985

| 2008–09 CHI | 1 | 0 | 0 | 0 | 2 |
| NHL Totals | 20 | 2 | 1 | 3 | 12 |

Downey, Aaron b. Shelburne, Ontario, August 27, 1974

| 2008–09 DET | 4 | 1 | 1 | 2 | 7 |
| NHL Totals | 243 | 8 | 10 | 18 | 494 |

Downie, Steve b. Newmarket, Ontario, April 3, 1987

| 2008–09 PHI/TB | 29 | 3 | 3 | 6 | 65 |
| NHL Totals | 61 | 9 | 9 | 18 | 138 |

• traded November 7, 2008, by Philadelphia to Tampa Bay with Steve Eminger and a 4th-round draft choice in 2009, for Matt Carle and a 3rd-round draft choice in 2009

Draper, Kris b. Toronto, Ontario, May 24, 1971

| 2008–09 DET | 79 | 7 | 10 | 17 | 40 |
| NHL Totals | 1,029 | 148 | 183 | 331 | 750 |

Drewiske, Davis b. Hudson, Wisconsin, November 22, 1984

2008–09 LA	17	0	3	3	18
NHL Totals	17	0	3	3	18

Drouin-Deslauriers, Jeff b. St. Jean sur Richelieu, Quebec, May 15, 1984

2008–09 EDM	10	4–3–0–0	539	30	0	3.33
NHL Totals	10	4–3–0–0	539	30	0	3.33

Drury, Chris b. Trumbull, Connecticut, August 20, 1976

2008–09 NYR	81	22	34	56	32
NHL Totals	791	240	338	578	429

Dubielewicz, Wade b. Invermere, British Columbia, January 30, 1978

2008–09 CBJ	3	1–2–0–0	168	10	0	3.55
NHL Totals	40	17–15–1–1	2,094	92	0	2.63

Dubinsky, Brandon b. Anchorage, Alaska, April 29, 1986

2008–09 NYR	82	13	28	41	112
NHL Totals	170	27	54	81	193

Dumont, J-P b. Montreal, Quebec, April 1, 1978

2008–09 NAS	82	16	49	65	20
NHL Totals	678	187	272	459	328

Dupuis, Pascal b. Laval, Quebec, April 7, 1979

2008–09 PIT	71	12	16	28	30
NHL Totals	506	95	107	202	228

Dupuis, Philippe b. Laval, Quebec, April 24, 1985

2008–09 COL	8	0	0	0	4
NHL Totals	8	0	0	0	4

Durno, Chris b. Scarborough (Toronto), Ontario, October 31, 1980

| 2008–09 COL | 2 | 0 | 0 | 0 | 0 |
| NHL Totals | 2 | 0 | 0 | 0 | 0 |

Dvorak, Radek b. Tabor, Czechoslovakia (Czech Republic),
   March 9, 1977

| 2008–09 FLO | 81 | 15 | 21 | 36 | 42 |
| NHL Totals | 976 | 194 | 308 | 502 | 350 |

Dwyer, Pat b. Spokane, Washington, June 22, 1983

| 2008–09 CAR | 13 | 1 | 0 | 1 | 0 |
| NHL Totals | 13 | 1 | 0 | 1 | 0 |

Eager, Ben b. Ottawa, Ontario, January 22, 1984

| 2008–09 CHI | 75 | 11 | 4 | 15 | 161 |
| NHL Totals | 195 | 20 | 16 | 36 | 501 |

Eaton, Mark b. Wilmington, Delaware, May 6, 1977

| 2008–09 PIT | 68 | 4 | 5 | 9 | 36 |
| NHL Totals | 452 | 20 | 42 | 62 | 194 |

Eaves, Patrick b. Calgary, Alberta, May 1, 1984

| 2008–09 CAR | 74 | 6 | 8 | 14 | 31 |
| NHL Totals | 242 | 45 | 45 | 90 | 99 |

Ebbett, Andrew b. Vernon, British Columbia, January 2, 1983

| 2008–09 ANA | 48 | 8 | 24 | 32 | 24 |
| NHL Totals | 51 | 8 | 24 | 32 | 26 |

Edler, Alexander b. Stockholm, Sweden, April 21, 1986

| 2008–09 VAN | 80 | 10 | 27 | 37 | 54 |
| NHL Totals | 177 | 19 | 41 | 60 | 102 |

Ehrhoff, Christian b. Moers, West Germany (Germany), July 6, 1982

| 2008–09 SJ | 77 | 8 | 34 | 42 | 63 |
| NHL Totals | 341 | 25 | 107 | 132 | 244 |

Elias, Patrik b. Trebic, Czechoslovakia (Czech Republic), April 13, 1976

| 2008–09 NJ | 77 | 31 | 47 | 78 | 32 |
| NHL Totals | 822 | 295 | 411 | 706 | 403 |

Elliott, Brian b. Newmarket, Ontario, April 9, 1985

| 2008–09 OTT | 31 | 16–8–3–0 | 1,667 | 77 | 1 | 2.77 |
| NHL Totals | 32 | 17–8–3–0 | 1,726 | 78 | 1 | 2.71 |

Ellis, Dan b. Saskatoon, Saskatchewan, June 19, 1980

| 2008–09 NAS | 35 | 11–19–4–0 | 1,964 | 96 | 3 | 2.93 |
| NHL Totals | 80 | 35–29–7–0 | 4,523 | 186 | 9 | 2.62 |

Ellis, Matt b. Welland, Ontario, August 31, 1981

| 2008–09 BUF | 45 | 7 | 5 | 12 | 12 |
| NHL Totals | 115 | 10 | 10 | 20 | 44 |

Eminger, Steve b. Woodbridge, Ontario, October 31, 1983

| 2008–09 PHI/TB/FLO | 71 | 5 | 21 | 26 | 50 |
| NHL Totals | 283 | 11 | 58 | 69 | 271 |

- traded November 7, 2008, by Philadelphia to Tampa Bay with Steve Downie and a 4th-round draft choice in 2009, for Matt Carle and a 3rd-round draft choice in 2009,
- traded March 4, 2009, by Tampa Bay to Florida for Noah Welch and a future 3rd-round draft choice

Enstrom, Tobias b. Nordringra, Sweden, November 5, 1984

| 2008–09 ATL | 82 | 5 | 27 | 32 | 52 |
| NHL Totals | 164 | 10 | 60 | 70 | 94 |

Erat, Martin   b. Trebic, Czechoslovakia (Czech Republic), August 28, 1981

2008–09 NAS	71	17	33	50	48
NHL Totals	478	102	201	303	298

Ericsson, Jonathan   b. Karlskrona, Sweden, March 2, 1984

2008–09 DET	19	1	3	4	15
NHL Totals	27	2	3	5	19

Eriksson, Anders   b. Bollnas, Sweden, January 9, 1975
• appeared only in the playoffs with Calgary

Eriksson, Loui   b. Gothenburg, Sweden, July 17, 1985

2008–09 DAL	82	36	27	63	14
NHL Totals	210	56	57	113	60

Ersberg, Erik   b. Sala, Sweden, March 8, 1982

2008–09 LA	28	8–11–5–0	1,477	65	0	2.64
NHL Totals	42	14–16–8–0	2,275	98	2	2.56

Erskine, John   b. Kingston, Ontario, June 26, 1980

2008–09 WAS	52	0	4	4	63
NHL Totals	273	6	19	25	564

Exelby, Garnet   b. Craik, Saskatchewan, August 16, 1981

2008–09 ATL	59	0	7	7	120
NHL Totals	357	6	40	46	511

Fedorov, Sergei   b. Pskov, Soviet Union (Russia), December 13, 1969

2008–09 WAS	52	11	22	33	50
NHL Totals	1,248	483	696	1,179	839

Fedoruk, Todd   b. Redwater, Alberta, February 13, 1979

2008–09 PHO	72	6	7	13	72
NHL Totals	495	29	62	91	996

Fedotenko, Ruslan b. Kiev, Soviet Union (Ukraine), January 18, 1979

2008–09 PIT	65	16	23	39	44
NHL Totals	597	139	139	278	369

Fehr, Eric b. Winkler, Manitoba, September 7, 1985

2008–09 WAS	61	12	13	25	22
NHL Totals	109	15	19	34	38

Ference, Andrew b. Edmonton, Alberta, March 17, 1979

2008–09 BOS	47	1	15	16	40
NHL Totals	519	24	109	133	488

Fernandez, Manny b. Etobicoke (Toronto), Ontario, August 26, 1974

2008–09 BOS	28	16–8–3–0	1,644	71	1	2.59
NHL Totals	325	143–123–11–24	18,580	775	15	2.50

Festerling, Brett b. Quesnel, British Columbia, March 3, 1986

2008–09 ANA	40	0	5	5	18
NHL Totals	40	0	5	5	18

Fiddler, Vernon b. Edmonton, Alberta, May 9, 1980

2008–09 NAS	78	11	6	17	24
NHL Totals	305	45	48	93	190

Filatov, Nikita b. Moscow, Soviet Union (Russia), May 25, 1990

2008–09 CBJ	8	4	0	4	0
NHL Totals	8	4	0	4	0

Filppula, Valtteri b. Vantaa, Finland, March 20, 1984

2008–09 DET	80	12	28	40	42
NHL Totals	235	41	53	94	92

Finger, Jeff b. Houghton, Michigan, December 18, 1979

2008–09 TOR	66	6	17	23	43
NHL Totals	160	15	32	47	94

Fisher, Mike b. Peterborough, Ontario, June 5, 1980

2008–09 OTT	78	13	19	32	66
NHL Totals	541	128	143	271	462

Fistric, Mark b. Edmonton, Alberta, June 1, 1986

2008–09 DAL	36	0	4	4	42
NHL Totals	73	0	6	6	66

Fleischmann, Tomas b. Koprivnice, Czechoslovakia (Czech Republic), May 16, 1984

2008–09 WAS	73	19	18	37	20
NHL Totals	191	33	44	77	46

Fleury, Marc-Andre b. Sorel, Quebec, November 28, 1984

2008–09 PIT	62	35–18–7–0	3,640	162	4	2.67
NHL Totals	235	111–85–24–2	13,367	640	15	2.87

Foligno, Nick b. Buffalo, New York, October 31, 1987

2008–09 OTT	81	17	15	32	59
NHL Totals	126	23	18	41	79

Foote, Adam b. Toronto, Ontario, July 10, 1971

2008–09 COL	42	1	6	7	30
NHL Totals	1,040	66	225	291	1,437

Foster, Alex b. Canton, Michigan, August 26, 1984

2008–09 TOR	3	0	0	0	0
NHL Totals	3	0	0	0	0

Foster, Kurtis b. Carp, Ontario, November 24, 1981

2008–09 MIN	10	1	5	6	6
NHL Totals	186	21	56	77	155

Franzen, Johan b. Landsbro, Sweden, December 23, 1979

2008–09 DET	71	34	25	59	44
NHL Totals	292	83	60	143	168

Fraser, Colin b. Sicamous, British Columbia, January 28, 1985

2008–09 CHI	81	6	11	17	55
NHL Totals	87	6	11	17	64

Fraser, Jamie b. Sarnia, Ontario, November 17, 1985

2008–09 NYI	1	0	0	0	0
NHL Totals	1	0	0	0	0

Fritsch, Jamie b. Odenton, Maryland, February 25, 1985

2008–09 PHI	1	0	0	0	0
NHL Totals	1	0	0	0	0

Fritsche, Dan b. Cleveland, Ohio, July 13, 1985

2008–09 NYR/MIN	50	5	8	13	12
NHL Totals	256	34	42	76	103

• traded January 29, 2009, by NY Rangers to Minnesota for Erik Reitz

Fritz, Mitch b. Osoyoos, British Columbia, November 24, 1980

2008–09 NYI	20	0	0	0	42
NHL Totals	20	0	0	0	42

Frogren, Jonas b. Falun, Sweden, August 28, 1980

2008–09 TOR	41	1	6	7	28
NHL Totals	41	1	6	7	28

Frolik, Michael b. Kladno, Czechoslovakia (Czech Republic), February 17, 1988

2008–09 FLO	79	21	24	45	22
NHL Totals	79	21	24	45	22

Frolov, Alexander b. Moscow, Soviet Union (Russia), June 19, 1982

2008–09 LA	77	32	27	59	30
NHL Totals	455	149	181	330	184

Gaborik, Marian b. Trencin, Czechoslovakia (Slovakia), February 14, 1982

2008–09 MIN	17	13	10	23	2
NHL Totals	502	219	218	437	301

Gagne, Simon b. Ste. Foy, Quebec, February 29, 1980

2008–09 PHI	79	34	40	74	42
NHL Totals	606	242	242	484	231

Gagner, Sam b. London, Ontario, August 10, 1989

2008–09 EDM	76	16	25	41	51
NHL Totals	155	29	61	90	74

Galiardi, T.J. b. Calgary, Alberta, April 22, 1988

2008–09 COL	11	3	1	4	6
NHL Totals	11	3	1	4	6

Garon, Mathieu b. Chandler, Quebec, January 9, 1978

2008–09 EDM/PIT	19	8–9–0–0	1,020	53	0	3.11
NHL Totals	204	94–83–10–3	11,238	532	14	2.84

• traded January 17, 2009, by Edmonton to Pittsburgh for Dany Sabourin, Ryan Stone and a 4th-round draft choice in 2011

Garrison, Jason b. White Rock, British Columbia, November 13, 1984

2008–09 FLO	1	0	0	0	0
NHL Totals	1	0	0	0	0

Gaustad, Paul b. Fargo, North Dakota, February 3, 1982

2008–09 BUF	62	12	17	29	108
NHL Totals	277	40	71	111	332

Gauthier, Denis b. Montreal, Quebec, October 1, 1975

2008–09 LA	65	2	2	4	90
NHL Totals	554	17	60	77	748

Gerbe, Nathan b. Oxford, Michigan, July 24, 1987

2008–09 BUF	10	0	1	1	4
NHL Totals	10	0	1	1	4

Gerber, Martin b. Burgdorf, Switzerland, September 3, 1974

2008–09 TOR	26	10–14–1–0	1,544	78	1	3.03
NHL Totals	226	110–78–14–7	12,735	562	10	2.65

Gervais, Bruno b. Longueuil, Quebec, October 3, 1984

2008–09 NYI	69	3	16	19	33
NHL Totals	207	6	39	45	103

Getzlaf, Ryan b. Regina, Saskatchewan, May 10, 1985

2008–09 ANA	81	25	66	91	121
NHL Totals	297	88	182	270	303

Giguere, Jean-Sebastien b. Montreal, Quebec, May 16, 1977

2008–09 ANA	46	19–18–6–0	2,458	127	2	3.10
NHL Totals	457	210–169–31–25	26,122	1,084	31	2.49

Gilbert, Tom b. Minneapolis, Minnesota, January 10, 1983

2008–09 EDM	82	5	40	45	26
NHL Totals	176	19	65	84	46

Gill, Hal b. Concord, Massachusetts, April 6, 1975

2008–09 PIT	62	2	8	10	53
NHL Totals	851	31	120	151	800

Gillies, Colton b. White Rock, British Columbia, February 12, 1989

2008–09 MIN	45	2	5	7	18
NHL Totals	45	2	5	7	18

Gionta, Brian b. Rochester, New York, January 18, 1979

2008–09 NJ	81	20	40	60	32
NHL Totals	473	152	160	312	227

Giordano, Mark b. Toronto, Ontario, March 10, 1983

2008–09 CAL	58	2	17	19	59
NHL Totals	113	9	26	35	103

Girardi, Daniel b. Welland, Ontario, April 29, 1984

2008–09 NYR	82	4	18	22	53
NHL Totals	198	14	42	56	75

Giroux, Alexandre b. Quebec City, Quebec, June 16, 1981

2008–09 WAS	12	1	1	2	10
NHL Totals	22	3	3	6	12

Giroux, Claude b. Hearst, Ontario, January 12, 1988

2008–09 PHI	42	9	18	27	14
NHL Totals	44	9	18	27	14

Glass, Tanner b. Regina, Saskatchewan, November 29, 1983

2008–09 FLO	3	0	0	0	7
NHL Totals	44	1	1	2	46

Gleason, Tim b. Southfield, Michigan, January 29, 1983

2008–09 CAR	70	0	12	12	68
NHL Totals	332	7	58	65	307

Glencross, Curtis b. Kindersley, Saskatchewan, December 28, 1982

2008–09 CAL	74	13	27	40	42
NHL Totals	145	29	37	66	97

Goc, Marcel b. Calw, West Germany (Germany), August 24, 1983

2008–09 SJ	55	2	9	11	18
NHL Totals	265	20	34	54	76

Godard, Eric b. Vernon, British Columbia, March 7, 1980

2008–09 PIT	71	2	2	4	171
NHL Totals	271	5	7	12	652

Goertzen, Steve b. Stony Plain, Alberta, May 26, 1984

2008–09 PHO	16	2	2	4	24
NHL Totals	62	2	2	4	78

Goligoski, Alex b. Grand Rapids, Minnesota, July 30, 1985

2008–09 PIT	45	6	14	20	16
NHL Totals	48	6	16	22	18

Gomez, Scott b. Anchorage, Alaska, December 23, 1979

2008–09 NYR	77	16	42	58	60
NHL Totals	706	148	430	578	458

Gonchar, Sergei b. Chelyabinsk, Soviet Union (Russia), April 13, 1974

2008–09 PIT	25	6	13	19	26
NHL Totals	929	191	443	634	793

Gordon, Andrew b. Halifax, Nova Scotia, December 13, 1985

2008–09 WAS	1	0	0	0	0
NHL Totals	1	0	0	0	0

Gordon, Boyd b. Unity, Saskatchewan, October 19, 1983

2008–09 WAS	63	5	9	14	16
NHL Totals	267	20	46	66	54

Gorges, Josh b. Kelowna, British Columbia, August 14, 1984

2008–09 MON	81	4	19	23	37
NHL Totals	246	5	37	42	126

Grabovski, Mikhail b. Potsdam, East Germany (Germany), January 31, 1984

2008–09 TOR	78	20	28	48	92
NHL Totals	105	23	34	57	100

Gragnani, Marc-Andre b. Montreal, Quebec, March 11, 1987

2008–09 BUF	4	0	0	0	2
NHL Totals	6	0	0	0	6

Gratton, Chris b. Brantford, Ontario, July 5, 1975

2008–09 TB/CBJ	24	0	3	3	12
NHL Totals	1,092	214	354	568	1,638

• claimed off waivers by Columbus from Tampa Bay on February 21, 2009

Gratton, Josh b. Scarborough (Toronto), Ontario, September 9, 1982

2008–09 PHI	19	1	2	3	57
NHL Totals	86	3	3	6	294

Grebeshkov, Denis b. Yaroslavl, Soviet Union (Russia), October 11, 1983

2008–09 EDM	72	7	32	39	38
NHL Totals	176	10	53	63	80

Green, Mike b. Calgary, Alberta, October 12, 1985

2008–09 WAS	68	31	42	73	68
NHL Totals	242	52	92	144	184

Greene, Andy b. Trenton, Michigan, October 30, 1982

2008–09 NJ	49	2	7	9	22
NHL Totals	131	5	20	25	50

Greene, Matt b. Grand Ledge, Michigan, May 13, 1983

2008–09 LA	82	2	12	14	111
NHL Totals	233	3	24	27	316

Greentree, Kyle b. Victoria, British Columbia, November 15, 1983

2008–09 CAL	2	0	0	0	0
NHL Totals	4	0	0	0	0

Grier, Mike b. Detroit, Michigan, January 5, 1975

2008–09 SJ	62	10	13	23	25
NHL Totals	914	147	198	345	484

Grossman, Nicklas b. Stockholm, Sweden, January 22, 1985

2008–09 DAL	81	2	10	12	51
NHL Totals	151	2	17	19	77

Guenin, Nathan b. Sewickley, Pennsylvania, December 10, 1982

2008–09 PHI	1	0	0	0	0
NHL Totals	12	0	2	2	6

Guerin, Bill b. Worcester, Massachusetts, November 9, 1970

2008–09 NYI/PIT	78	21	27	48	81
NHL Totals	1,185	408	403	811	1,585

• traded March 4, 2009, by NY Islanders to Pittsburgh for a conditional draft choice in 2009

Guite, Ben b. Montreal, Quebec, July 17, 1978

2008–09 COL	50	5	7	12	30
NHL Totals	169	19	26	45	93

Hagman, Niklas b. Espoo, Finland, December 5, 1979

2008–09 TOR	65	22	20	42	4
NHL Totals	546	102	105	207	157

Hainsey, Ron b. Bolton, Connecticut, March 24, 1981

2008–09 ATL	81	6	33	39	32
NHL Totals	326	26	98	124	175

Halak, Jaroslav b. Bratislava, Czechoslovakia (Slovakia), May 13, 1985

2008–09 MON	34	18–14–1–0	1,930	92	1	2.86
NHL Totals	56	30–21–2–0	3,127	146	4	2.80

Hale, David b. Colorado Springs, Colorado, June 18, 1981

2008–09 PHO	48	3	6	9	36
NHL Totals	263	3	17	20	211

Halischuk, Matt b. Toronto, Ontario, June 1, 1988

2008–09 NJ	1	0	1	1	0
NHL Totals	1	0	1	1	0

Hall, Adam b. Kalamazoo, Michigan, August 14, 1980

2008–09 TB	74	5	5	10	29
NHL Totals	426	56	62	118	187

Halpern, Jeff b. Potomac, Maryland, May 3, 1976

2008–09 TB	52	7	9	16	32
NHL Totals	649	122	175	297	515

Hamhuis, Dan b. Smithers, British Columbia, December 13, 1982

2008–09 NAS	82	3	23	26	67
NHL Totals	405	27	110	137	326

Hamilton, Jeff b. Englewood, Ohio, September 4, 1977

2008–09 TOR	15	3	3	6	4
NHL Totals	157	32	45	77	44

Hamrlik, Roman b. Zlin, Czechoslovakia (Czech Republic), April 12, 1974

2008–09 MON	81	6	27	33	62
NHL Totals	1,157	142	422	564	1,229

Handzus, Michal b. Banska Bystrica, Czechoslovakia (Slovakia),
  March 11, 1977

2008–09 LA	82	18	24	42	32
NHL Totals	681	140	223	363	390

Hannan, Scott b. Richmond, British Columbia, January 23, 1979

2008–09 COL	81	1	9	10	26
NHL Totals	671	28	130	158	410

Hansen, Jannick b. Herlev, Denmark, March 15, 1986

2008–09 VAN	55	6	15	21	37
NHL Totals	60	6	15	21	39

Hanson, Christian b. Venetia, Pennsylvania, March 10, 1986

2008–09 TOR	5	1	1	2	2
NHL Totals	5	1	1	2	2

Hanzal, Martin b. Pisek, Czechoslovakia (Czech Republic),
  February 20, 1987

2008–09 PHO	74	11	20	31	40
NHL Totals	146	19	47	66	68

Harding, Josh b. Regina, Saskatchewan, June 18, 1984

2008–09 MIN	19	3–9–1–0	869	32	0	2.21
NHL Totals	58	19–27–4–0	2,986	124	3	2.49

Harrison, Jay b. Oshawa, Ontario, November 3, 1982

2008–09 TOR	7	0	1	1	10
NHL Totals	20	0	2	2	18

Harrold, Peter b. Kirtland Hills, Ohio, June 8, 1983

2008–09 LA	69	4	8	12	28
NHL Totals	106	6	13	19	38

Hartnell, Scott b. Regina, Saskatchewan, April 18, 1982

| 2008–09 PHI | 82 | 30 | 30 | 60 | 143 |
| NHL Totals | 598 | 147 | 167 | 314 | 846 |

Havelid, Niclas b. Stockholm, Sweden, April 12, 1973

| 2008–09 ATL/NJ | 78 | 2 | 17 | 19 | 48 |
| NHL Totals | 628 | 34 | 137 | 171 | 342 |

• traded March 2, 2009, by Atlanta to New Jersey with Myles Stoesz for Anssi Salmela

Havlat, Martin b. Mlada Bolslav, Czechoslovakia (Czech Republic), April 19, 1981

| 2008–09 CHI | 81 | 29 | 48 | 77 | 30 |
| NHL Totals | 470 | 169 | 227 | 396 | 246 |

Heatley, Dany b. Freiburg, West Germany (Germany), January 21, 1981

| 2008–09 OTT | 82 | 39 | 33 | 72 | 88 |
| NHL Totals | 507 | 260 | 283 | 543 | 456 |

Hecht, Jochen b. Mannheim, West Germany (Germany), June 21, 1977

| 2008–09 BUF | 70 | 12 | 15 | 27 | 33 |
| NHL Totals | 618 | 144 | 226 | 370 | 359 |

Hedberg, Johan b. Leksand, Sweden, May 3, 1973

| 2008–09 ATL | 33 | 13–12–3–0 | 1,716 | 100 | 0 | 3.49 |
| NHL Totals | 2.46 | 102–98–9–14 | 13,709 | 684 | 11 | 2.99 |

Hedican, Bret b. St. Paul, Minnesota, August 10, 1970

| 2008–09 ANA | 51 | 1 | 5 | 6 | 36 |
| NHL Totals | 1,039 | 55 | 239 | 294 | 893 |

Hejda, Jan b. Prague, Czechoslovakia (Czech Republic),
June 18, 1978

2008–09 CBJ	82	3	18	21	38
NHL Totals	202	4	39	43	119

Hejduk, Milan b. Usti-nad-Labem, Czechoslovakia (Czech
Republic), February 14, 1976

2008–09 COL	82	27	32	59	16
NHL Totals	783	312	345	657	274

Helenius, Riku b. Palkane, Finland, March 1, 1988

2008–09 TB	1	0–0–0–0	6	0	0	0.00
NHL Totals	1	0–0–0–0	6	0	0	0.00

Helm, Darren b. Winnipeg, Manitoba, January 21, 1987

2008–09 DET	16	0	1	1	4
NHL Totals	23	0	1	1	6

Helmer, Brian b. Sault Ste. Marie, Ontario, July 15, 1972

2008–09 WAS	12	0	3	3	2
NHL Totals	146	8	18	26	135

Helminen, Dwight b. Hancock, Michigan, June 22, 1983

2008–09 CAR	23	1	1	2	0
NHL Totals	23	1	1	2	0

Hemsky, Ales b. Pardubice, Czechoslovakia (Czech Republic),
August 13, 1983

2008–09 EDM	72	23	43	66	32
NHL Totals	421	93	238	331	198

Hendricks, Matt b. Blaine, Minnesota, June 17, 1981

2008–09 COL	4	0	0	0	13
NHL Totals	4	0	0	0	13

Hendry, Jordan b. Nokomis, Saskatchewan, February 23, 1984

| 2008–09 CHI | 9 | 0 | 0 | 0 | 4 |
| NHL Totals | 49 | 1 | 3 | 4 | 26 |

Hennessy, Josh b. Brockton, Massachusetts, February 7, 1985

| 2008–09 OTT | 1 | 0 | 0 | 0 | 0 |
| NHL Totals | 16 | 1 | 0 | 1 | 4 |

Henry, Alex b. Elliot Lake, Ontario, October 18, 1979

| 2008–09 MON | 2 | 0 | 0 | 0 | 10 |
| NHL Totals | 177 | 2 | 9 | 11 | 269 |

Hensick, T.J. b. Lansing, Michigan, December 10, 1985

| 2008–09 COL | 81 | 4 | 17 | 21 | 14 |
| NHL Totals | 92 | 10 | 22 | 32 | 16 |

Heward, Jamie b. Regina, Saskatchewan, March 30, 1971

| 2008–09 TB | 13 | 0 | 2 | 2 | 4 |
| NHL Totals | 394 | 38 | 86 | 124 | 221 |

Higgins, Chris b. Smithtown, New York, June 2, 1983

| 2008–09 MON | 57 | 12 | 11 | 23 | 22 |
| NHL Totals | 282 | 84 | 67 | 151 | 96 |

Hilbert, Andy b. Lansing, Michigan, February 6, 1981

| 2008–09 NYI | 67 | 11 | 16 | 27 | 22 |
| NHL Totals | 303 | 42 | 62 | 104 | 130 |

Hillen, Jack b. Portland, Oregon, January 24, 1986

| 2008–09 NYI | 40 | 1 | 5 | 6 | 16 |
| NHL Totals | 42 | 1 | 6 | 7 | 20 |

Hiller, Jonas   b. Felben Wellhausen, Switzerland, February 12, 1982

2008–09 ANA	46	23–15–1–0	2,486	99	4	2.39
NHL Totals	69	33–22–2–0	3,709	141	4	2.28

Hinote, Dan   b. Leesburg, Florida, January 30, 1977

2008–09 STL	51	1	4	5	64
NHL Totals	503	38	52	90	383

Hjalmarsson, Niklas   b. Eksjo, Sweden, June 6, 1987

2008–09 CHI	21	1	2	3	0
NHL Totals	34	1	3	4	13

Hnidy, Shane   b. Neepawa, Manitoba, November 8, 1975

2008–09 BOS	65	3	9	12	45
NHL Totals	477	14	43	57	565

Hoggan, Jeff   b. Hope, British Columbia, February 1, 1978

2008–09 PHO	4	0	1	1	7
NHL Totals	103	2	9	11	74

Holik, Bobby   b. Jihlava, Czechoslovakia (Czech Republic), January 1, 1971

2008–09 NJ	62	4	5	9	66
NHL Totals	1,314	326	421	747	1,421

Hollweg, Ryan   b. Downey, California, April 23, 1983

2008–09 TOR	25	0	2	2	38
NHL Totals	225	5	9	14	349

Holmstrom, Tomas   b. Pitea, Sweden, January 23, 1973

2008–09 DET	53	14	23	37	38
NHL Totals	811	189	235	424	607

Holt, Chris   b. Vancouver, British Columbia, June 5, 1985

| 2008–09 STL | 1 | 0–0–0–0 | 18 | 0 | 0 | 0.00 |
| NHL Totals | 2 | 0–0–0–0 | 28 | 0 | 0 | 0.00 |

Horcoff, Shawn   b. Trail, British Columbia, September 17, 1978

| 2008–09 EDM | 80 | 17 | 36 | 53 | 39 |
| NHL Totals | 560 | 120 | 218 | 338 | 366 |

Hordichuk, Darcy   b. Kamsack, Saskatchewan, August 10, 1980

| 2008–09 VAN | 73 | 4 | 1 | 5 | 109 |
| NHL Totals | 375 | 17 | 14 | 31 | 856 |

Hornqvist, Patric   b. Sollentuna, Sweden, January 1, 1987

| 2008–09 NAS | 28 | 2 | 5 | 7 | 16 |
| NHL Totals | 28 | 2 | 5 | 7 | 16 |

Horton, Nathan   b. Welland, Ontario, May 29, 1985

| 2008–09 FLO | 67 | 22 | 23 | 45 | 48 |
| NHL Totals | 357 | 122 | 116 | 238 | 340 |

Hossa, Marian   b. Stara Lubovna, Czechoslovakia (Slovakia), January 12, 1979

| 2008–09 DET | 74 | 40 | 31 | 71 | 63 |
| NHL Totals | 775 | 339 | 380 | 719 | 458 |

Howard, Jimmy   b. Syracuse, New York, March 26, 1984

| 2008–09 DET | 1 | 0–1–0–0 | 58 | 4 | 0 | 4.07 |
| NHL Totals | 9 | 1–5–0–0 | 456 | 21 | 0 | 2.76 |

Hudler, Jiri   b. Olomouc, Czechoslovakia (Czech Republic), January 4, 1984

| 2008–09 DET | 82 | 23 | 34 | 57 | 16 |
| NHL Totals | 255 | 52 | 75 | 127 | 90 |

Huet, Cristobal   b. St. Martin d'Heres, France, September 3, 1975

2008–09 CHI	41	20–15–4–0	2,350	99	3	2.53
NHL Totals	224	103–76–17–11	12,529	511	20	2.45

Hunter, Trent   b. Red Deer, Alberta, July 5, 1980

2008–09 NYI	55	14	17	31	41
NHL Totals	381	87	110	197	160

Hunwick, Matt   b. Warren, Michigan, May 21, 1985

2008–09 BOS	53	6	21	27	31
NHL Totals	66	6	22	28	35

Huselius, Kristian   b. Osterhaninge, Sweden, November 10, 1978

2008–09 CBJ	74	21	35	56	44
NHL Totals	547	153	212	365	208

Huskins, Kent   b. Almonte, Ontario, May 4, 1979

2008–09 ANA	33	2	4	6	27
NHL Totals	142	6	22	28	100

Hutchinson, Andrew   b. Evanston, Illinois, March 24, 1980

2008–09 TB/DAL	40	2	3	5	12
NHL Totals	135	12	26	38	64

• traded November 30, 2008, by Tampa Bay to Dallas for Lauri Tukonen

Iggulden, Mike   b. St. Catharines, Ontario, November 9, 1982

2008–09 NYI	11	1	4	5	4
NHL Totals	12	1	4	5	4

Iginla, Jarome   b. Edmonton, Alberta, July 1, 1977

2008–09 CAL	82	35	54	89	37
NHL Totals	942	409	442	851	668

Ivanans, Raitis b. Riga, Soviet Union (Latvia), January 1, 1979

2008–09 LA	76	2	0	2	145
NHL Totals	219	12	6	18	428

Jackman, Barret b. Trail, British Columbia, March 5, 1981

2008–09 STL	82	4	17	21	86
NHL Totals	391	17	79	96	648

Jackman, Tim b. Minot, North Dakota, November 14, 1981

2008–09 NYI	69	5	7	12	155
NHL Totals	137	7	12	19	259

Jacques, Jean-Francois b. Terrebonne, Quebec, April 29, 1985

2008–09 EDM	7	1	0	1	9
NHL Totals	60	1	0	1	44

Jaffray, Jason b. Rimbey, Alberta, June 30, 1981

2008–09 VAN	14	2	2	4	14
NHL Totals	33	4	6	10	33

James, Connor b. Calgary, Alberta, August 25, 1982

2008–09 PIT	1	0	0	0	0
NHL Totals	16	1	0	1	2

Jancevski, Dan b. Windsor, Ontario, June 15, 1981

2008–09 DAL	3	0	0	0	0
NHL Totals	9	0	0	0	2

Janik, Doug b. Agawam, Massachusetts, March 26, 1980

2008–09 DAL/MON	15	0	1	1	4
NHL Totals	161	3	13	16	123

• traded February 26, 2009, by Dallas to Montreal for Steve Begin

Janssen, Cam b. St. Louis, Missouri, April 15, 1984

2008–09 STL	56	1	3	4	131
NHL Totals	163	2	4	6	354

Jeffrey, Dustin b. Sarnia, Ontario, February 27, 1988

2008–09 PIT	14	1	2	3	0
NHL Totals	14	1	2	3	0

Joensuu, Jesse b. Pori, Finland, October 5, 1987

2008–09 NYI	7	1	2	3	4
NHL Totals	7	1	2	3	4

Johnson, Aaron b. Port Hawkesbury, Nova Scotia, April 30, 1983

2008–09 CHI	38	3	5	8	33
NHL Totals	184	10	26	36	156

Johnson, Brent b. Farmington, Michigan, March 12, 1977

2008–09 WAS	21	12–6–2–0	1,131	53	0	2.81
NHL Totals	247	111–94–12–13	13,762	604	13	2.63

Johnson, Jack b. Indianapolis, Indiana, January 13, 1987

2008–09 LA	41	6	5	11	46
NHL Totals	120	9	13	22	140

Johnson, Ryan b. Thunder Bay, Ontario, June 14, 1976

2008–09 VAN	62	2	7	9	12
NHL Totals	609	36	75	111	230

Johnsson, Kim b. Malmo, Sweden, March 16, 1976

2008–09 MIN	81	2	22	24	44
NHL Totals	679	60	207	267	376

Jokinen, Jussi b. Kalajoki, Finland, April 1, 1983

2008–09 TB/CAR	71	7	20	27	28
NHL Totals	306	54	118	172	94

• traded February 7, 2009, by Tampa Bay to Carolina for Wade Brookbank, Josef Melichar and a 4th-round draft choice in 2009

Jokinen, Olli b. Kuopio, Finland, December 5, 1978

2008–09 PHO/CAL	76	29	28	57	67
NHL Totals	799	237	281	518	794

• traded March 4, 2009, by Phoenix to Calgary with a 3rd-round draft choice in 2009 for Matthew Lombardi, Brandon Prust and a 1st-round draft choice in either 2009 or 2010

Jones, David b. Guelph, Ontario, August 10, 1984

2008–09 COL	40	8	5	13	8
NHL Totals	67	10	9	19	16

Jones, Randy b. Quispamsis, New Brunswick, July 23, 1981

2008–09 PHI	47	4	4	8	22
NHL Totals	217	13	56	69	134

Jones, Ryan b. Chatham, Ontario, June 14, 1984

2008–09 NAS	46	7	10	17	22
NHL Totals	46	7	10	17	22

Joseph, Curtis b. Keswick, Ontario, April 29, 1967

2008–09 TOR	21	5–9–1–0	840	50	0	3.57
NHL Totals	943	454–352–6–90	54,054	2,516	51	2.79

Joslin, Derek b. Richmond Hill, Ontario, March 17, 1987

2008–09 SJ	12	0	0	0	6
NHL Totals	12	0	0	0	6

Jovanovski, Ed b. Windsor, Ontario, June 26, 1976

2008–09 PHO	82	9	27	36	106
NHL Totals	903	118	315	433	1,327

Junland, Jonas b. Linkoping, Sweden, November 15, 1987

2008–09 STL	1	0	0	0	2
NHL Totals	1	0	0	0	2

Jurcina, Milan b. Liptovsky Mikulas, Czechoslovakia (Slovakia), June 7, 1983

2008–09 WAS	79	3	11	14	68
NHL Totals	275	14	32	46	196

Kaberle, Frantisek b. Kladno, Czechoslovakia (Czech Republic), November 8, 1973

2008–09 CAR	30	1	7	8	8
NHL Totals	523	29	164	193	218

Kaberle, Tomas b. Rakovnik, Czechoslovakia (Czech Republic), March 2, 1978

2008–09 TOR	57	4	27	31	8
NHL Totals	738	73	360	433	206

Kaleta, Patrick b. Buffalo, New York, June 8, 1986

2008–09 BUF	51	4	5	9	89
NHL Totals	98	7	9	16	151

Kalinin, Dmitri b. Chelyabinsk, Soviet Union (Russia), July 22, 1980

2008–09 NYR/PHO	73	2	15	17	32
NHL Totals	539	36	126	162	321

• traded March 4, 2009, by NY Rangers to Phoenix with Nigel Dawes and Petr Prucha for Derek Morris

Kalinski, Jon b. Bonnyville, Alberta, May 25, 1987

2008–09 PHI	12	1	2	3	0
NHL Totals	12	1	2	3	0

Kane, Boyd b. Swift Current, Saskatchewan, April 18, 1978

2008–09 PHI	1	0	0	0	0
NHL Totals	28	0	3	3	37

Kane, Patrick b. Buffalo, New York, November 19, 1988

2008–09 CHI	80	25	45	70	42
NHL Totals	162	46	96	142	94

Kariya, Paul b. Vancouver, British Columbia, October 16, 1974

2008–09 STL	11	2	13	15	2
NHL Totals	914	384	562	946	363

Karsums, Martins b. Riga, Soviet Union (Latvia), February 26, 1986

2008–09 BOS/TB	24	1	5	6	6
NHL Totals	24	1	5	6	6

• traded by Boston to Tampa Bay on March 4, 2009, with Matt Lashoff for Marck Recchi and a 2nd-round draft choice in 2010

Kaspar, Lukas b. Most, Czechoslovakia (Czech Republic), September 23, 1985

2008–09 SJ	13	2	2	4	8
NHL Totals	16	2	2	4	8

Keith, Duncan b. Winnipeg, Manitoba, July 16, 1983

2008–09 CHI	77	8	36	44	60
NHL Totals	322	31	97	128	271

Kelly, Chris b. Toronto, Ontario, November 11, 1980

2008–09 OTT	82	12	11	23	38
NHL Totals	325	48	73	121	184

Kennedy, Tim b. Buffalo, New York, April 30, 1986

2008–09 BUF	1	0	0	0	0
NHL Totals	1	0	0	0	0

Kennedy, Tyler b. Sault Ste. Marie, Ontario, July 15, 1986

2008–09 PIT	67	15	20	35	30
NHL Totals	122	25	29	54	65

Kesler, Ryan b. Detroit, Michigan, August 31, 1984

2008–09 VAN	82	26	33	59	61
NHL Totals	320	65	75	140	275

Kessel, Phil b. Madison, Wisconsin, October 2, 1987

2008–09 BOS	70	36	24	60	16
NHL Totals	222	66	60	126	56

Khabibulin, Nikolai b. Sverdlovsk, Soviet Union (Russia), January 13, 1973

2008–09 CHI	42	25–8–7–0	2,467	96	3	2.33
NHL Totals	678	299–267–24–58	38,705	1,720	41	2.67

King, Dwayne b. Meadow Lake, Saskatchewan, June 27, 1984

2008–09 STL	1	0	1	1	0
NHL Totals	89	4	5	9	152

Kinrade, Jeff b. Nelson, British Columbia, July 29, 1985

2008–09 TB	1	0	0	0	0
NHL Totals	1	0	0	0	0

Kiprusoff, Miikka b. Turku, Finland, October 26, 1976

2008–09 CAL	76	45–24–5–0	4,417	209	4	2.84
NHL Totals	385	204–125–35–7	22,306	916	30	2.46

Klee, Ken b. Indianapolis, Indiana, April 24, 1971

2008–09 ANA/PHO	71	1	10	11	28
NHL Totals	934	55	140	195	880

• claimed off waivers by Phoenix from Anaheim on October 28, 2008

Klein, Kevin b. Kitchener, Ontario, December 13, 1984

2008–09 NAS	63	4	8	12	19
NHL Totals	81	5	10	15	25

Klesla, Rostislav b. Novy Jicin, Czechoslovakia (Czech Republic), March 21, 1982

2008–09 CBJ	34	1	8	9	38
NHL Totals	444	36	79	115	456

Knuble, Mike b. Toronto, Ontario, July 4, 1972

2008–09 PHI	82	27	20	47	62
NHL Totals	820	215	214	429	494

Kobasew, Chuck b. Osoyoos, British Columbia, April 17, 1982

2008–09 BOS	68	21	21	42	56
NHL Totals	361	78	76	154	270

Koci, David b. Prague, Czechoslovakia (Czech Republic), May 12, 1981

2008–09 TB/STL	37	1	1	2	141
NHL Totals	64	1	1	2	297

• claimed off waivers by St. Louis from Tampa Bay on October 21, 2008

Koistinen, Ville   b. Oulu, Finland, June 17, 1981

2008–09 NAS	38	3	8	11	14
NHL Totals	86	7	21	28	32

• claimed off waivers by Tampa Bay from St. Louis on November 20, 2008

Koivu, Mikko   b. Turku, Finland, March 12, 1983

2008–09 MIN	79	20	47	67	66
NHL Totals	282	57	127	184	206

Koivu, Saku   b. Turku, Finland, November 23, 1974

2008–09 MON	65	16	34	50	44
NHL Totals	792	191	450	641	623

Kolanos, Krys   b. Calgary, Alberta, July 27, 1981

2008–09 MIN	21	3	3	6	16
NHL Totals	136	20	21	41	92

Kolzig, Olaf   b. Johannesburg, South Africa, April 9, 1970

2008–09 TB	8	2–4–1–0	410	25	0	3.66
NHL Totals	719	303–297–24–63	41,670	1,885	35	2.71

Komisarek, Mike   b. Islip Terrace, New York, January 19, 1982

2008–09 MON	66	2	9	11	121
NHL Totals	361	12	46	58	496

Konopka, Zenon   b. Niagara-on-the-Lake, Ontario, January 2, 1981

2008–09 TB	7	0	1	1	29
NHL Totals	39	4	4	8	112

Kopecky, Tomas   b. Ilava, Czechoslovakia (Slovakia), February 5, 1982

2008–09 DET	79	6	13	19	46
NHL Totals	183	12	20	32	113

Kopitar, Anze   b. Jesenice, Yugoslavia (Slovenia), August 24, 1987

2008–09 LA	82	27	39	66	32
NHL Totals	236	79	125	204	78

Korpikoski, Lauri   b. Turku, Finland, July 28, 1986

2008–09 NYR	68	6	8	14	14
NHL Totals	68	6	8	14	14

Kostitsyn, Andrei   b. Novopolosk, Soviet Union (Belarus), February 3, 1985

2008–09 MON	74	23	18	41	50
NHL Totals	186	52	56	108	87

Kostitsyn, Sergei   b. Novopolsk, Soviet Union (Belarus), March 20, 1987

2008–09 MON	56	8	15	23	64
NHL Totals	108	17	33	50	115

Kostopoulos, Tom   b. Mississauga, Ontario, January 24, 1979

2008–09 MON	78	8	14	22	106
NHL Totals	376	40	65	105	468

Kotalik, Ales   b. Jindrichuv Hradec, Czechoslovakia (Czech Republic), December 23, 1978

2008–09 BUF/EDM	75	20	23	43	34
NHL Totals	445	121	130	251	273

• traded by Buffalo to Edmonton on March 4, 2009, for a 2nd-round draft choice in 2009

Kovalchuk, Ilya   b. Tver, Soviet Union (Russia), April 15, 1983

2008–09 ATL	79	43	48	91	50
NHL Totals	545	297	260	557	384

Kovalev, Alexei   b. Togliatti, Soviet Union (Russia), February 24, 1973

2008–09 MON	78	26	39	65	74
NHL Totals	1,151	394	547	941	1,200

Kozlov, Viktor   b. Togliatti, Soviet Union (Russia), February 14, 1975

2008–09 WAS	67	13	28	41	16
NHL Totals	897	198	339	537	248

Kozlov, Vyacheslav   b. Voskresensk, Soviet Union (Russia), May 3, 1972

2008–09 ATL	82	26	50	76	44
NHL Totals	1,127	348	479	827	671

Krahn, Brent   b. Winnipeg, Manitoba, April 2, 1982

2008–09 DAL	1	0–0–0–0	20	3	0	9.00
NHL Totals	1	0–0–0–0	20	3	0	9.00

Krajicek, Lukas   b. Prostejov, Czechoslovakia (Czech Republic), March 11, 1983

2008–09 TB	71	2	17	19	48
NHL Totals	278	10	59	69	210

Krejci, David   b. Sternberk, Czechoslovakia (Czech Republic), April 28, 1986

2008–09 BOS	82	22	51	73	26
NHL Totals	144	28	72	100	48

Kreps, Kamil   b. Litomerice, Czechoslovakia (Czech Republic), November 18, 1984

2008–09 FLO	66	4	15	19	18
NHL Totals	156	13	33	46	53

Krog, Jason   b. Fernie, British Columbia, October 9, 1975

2008–09 VAN	4	1	0	1	2
NHL Totals	202	22	37	59	46

Kronwall, Niklas b. Stockholm, Sweden, January 12, 1981

2008–09 DET	80	6	45	51	50
NHL Totals	260	16	106	122	192

Kronwall, Staffan b. Jarfalla, Sweden, September 10, 1982

2008–09 WAS	3	0	0	0	0
NHL Totals	55	0	1	1	21

Kuba, Filip b. Ostrava, Czechoslovakia (Czech Republic),
  December 29, 1976

2008–09 OTT	71	3	37	40	28
NHL Totals	602	58	189	247	267

Kubina, Pavel b. Celadna, Czechoslovakia (Czech Republic),
  April 15, 1977

2008–09 TOR	82	14	26	40	94
NHL Totals	746	97	213	310	921

Kukkonen, Lasse b. Oulu, Finland, September 18, 1981

2008–09 PHI	22	0	2	2	10
NHL Totals	159	6	16	22	90

Kulemin, Nikolai b. Magnitogorsk, Soviet Union (Russia), July 14, 1986

2008–09 TOR	73	15	16	31	18
NHL Totals	73	15	16	31	18

Kunitz, Chris b. Regina, Saskatchewan, September 26, 1979

2008–09 ANA/PIT	82	23	30	53	71
NHL Totals	335	88	122	210	315

• traded February 26, 2009, by Anaheim to Pittsburgh with Eric Tangradi
for Ryan Whitney

LaBarbera, Jason b. Burnaby, British Columbia, January 18, 1980

2008–09 LA/VAN	28	8–10–6–0	1,446	67	2	2.78
NHL Totals	107	37–44–10–0	5,507	273	4	2.97

LaCosta, Daniel b. Labrador City, Newfoundland, March 28, 1986

2008–09 CBJ	3	2–0–0–0	155	4	1	1.54
NHL Totals	4	2–0–0–0	168	4	1	1.42

Lacouture, Dan b. Hyannis, Massachusetts, April 18, 1977

2008–09 CAR	11	2	0	2	10
NHL Totals	337	20	25	45	348

Ladd, Andrew b. Maple Ridge, British Columbia, December 12, 1985

2008–09 CHI	82	15	34	49	28
NHL Totals	239	46	65	111	113

Laich, Brooks b. Medicine Hat, Alberta, June 23, 1983

2008–09 WAS	82	23	30	53	31
NHL Totals	315	59	71	130	123

Laing, Quintin b. Rosetown, Saskatchewan, June 8, 1979

2008–09 WAS	1	0	0	0	0
NHL Totals	43	1	6	7	10

Lalime, Patrick b. St. Bonaventure, Quebec, July 7, 1974

2008–09 BUF	24	5–13–3–0	1,296	67	0	3.10
NHL Totals	421	196–161–14–32	24,021	1,027	35	2.57

Lang, Robert b. Teplice, Czechoslovakia (Czech Republic), December 19, 1970

2008–09 MON	50	18	21	39	36
NHL Totals	925	252	422	674	394

Langenbrunner, Jamie b. Duluth, Minnesota, July 24, 1975

2008–09 NJ	81	29	40	69	56
NHL Totals	884	209	336	545	716

Langkow, Daymond b. Edmonton, Alberta, September 27, 1976

2008–09 CAL	73	21	28	49	20
NHL Totals	941	245	359	604	503

Laperriere, Ian b. Montreal, Quebec, January 19, 1974

2008–09 COL	74	7	12	19	163
NHL Totals	1,001	118	198	316	1,794

Lapierre, Maxim b. St. Leonard, Quebec, March 29, 1985

2008–09 MON	79	15	13	28	76
NHL Totals	179	28	30	58	160

Laraque, Georges b. Montreal, Quebec, December 7, 1976

2008–09 MON	33	0	2	2	61
NHL Totals	667	52	98	150	1,098

LaRose, Chad b. Fraser, Michigan, March 27, 1982

2008–09 CAR	81	19	12	31	35
NHL Totals	268	37	48	85	126

Lashoff, Matt b. East Greenbush, New York, September 29, 1986

2008–09 BOS/TB	28	0	8	8	20
NHL Totals	58	1	14	15	32

• traded March 4, 2009, by Boston to Tampa Bay with Martins Karsums for
  Mark Recchi and a 2nd-round draft choice in 2010

Latendresse, Guillaume b. Ste. Catherine, Quebec, May 24, 1987

2008–09 MON	56	14	12	26	45
NHL Totals	209	46	36	82	133

Lavallee-Smotherman, Jordan b. Corvallis, Oregon, May 11, 1986

2008–09 ATL	2	0	0	0	0
NHL Totals	4	1	1	2	0

Leach, Jay b. Syracuse, New York, September 2, 1979

2008–09 NJ	24	0	1	1	21
NHL Totals	28	0	1	1	28

Lebda, Brett b. Buffalo Grove, Illinois, January 15, 1982

2008–09 DET	65	6	10	16	48
NHL Totals	163	17	43	60	177

Lecavalier, Vincent b. Ile Bizard, Quebec, April 21, 1980

2008–09 TB	77	29	38	67	54
NHL Totals	787	302	367	669	561

Leclaire, Pascal b. Repentigny, Quebec, November 7, 1982

2008–09 CBJ	12	4–6–1–0	673	43	0	3.83
NHL Totals	125	45–55–12–0	6,898	324	10	2.82

Ledin, Per b. Lulea, Sweden, September 14, 1978

2008–09 COL	3	0	0	0	2
NHL Totals	3	0	0	0	2

Lee, Brian b. Moorehead, Minnesota, March 26, 1987

2008–09 OTT	53	2	11	13	33
NHL Totals	59	2	12	14	37

Legace, Manny b. Toronto, Ontario, February 4, 1973

2008–09 STL	29	13–9–2–0	1,452	77	0	3.18
NHL Totals	337	177–92–18–18	18,667	740	23	2.38

Legwand, David b. Detroit, Michigan, August 17, 1980

2008–09 NAS	73	20	22	42	32
NHL Totals	622	141	228	369	350

Lehman, Scott b. Fort McMurray, Alberta, January 6, 1986

2008–09 ATL	1	0	0	0	0
NHL Totals	1	0	0	0	0

Lehtinen, Jere   b. Espoo, Finland, June 24, 1973

2008–09 DAL	48	8	16	24	8
NHL Totals	817	239	258	497	202

Lehtonen, Kari   b. Helsinki, Finland, November 16, 1983

2008–09 ATL	46	19–22–3–0	2,624	134	3	3.06
NHL Totals	204	94–83–17–0	11,670	559	14	2.87

Lehtonen, Mikko   b. Espoo, Finland, April 1, 1987

2008–09 BOS	1	0	0	0	0
NHL Totals	1	0	0	0	0

Leighton, Michael   b. Petrolia, Ontario, May 19, 1981

2008–09 CAR	19	8–7–2–0	1,028	50	0	2.92
NHL Totals	69	17–31–2–10	3,835	191	3	2.99

Leino, Ville   b. Savonlinna, Finland, October 6, 1983

2008–09 DET	13	5	4	9	6
NHL Totals	13	5	4	9	6

Lemieux, Claude   b. Buckingham, Quebec, July 16, 1965

2008–09 SJ	18	0	1	1	21
NHL Totals	1,215	379	407	786	1,777

Leopold, Jordan   b. Golden Valley, Minnesota, August 3, 1980

2008–09 COL/CAL	83	7	17	24	24
NHL Totals	355	29	80	109	162

• traded March 4, 2009, by Colorado to Calgary for Lawrence Nycholat, Ryan Wilson and a 2nd-round draft choice in 2009

Lepisto, Sami   b. Espoo, Finland, October 17, 1984

2008–09 WAS	7	0	4	4	6
NHL Totals	14	0	5	5	18

Letang, Kris b. Montreal, Quebec, April 24, 1987

2008–09 PIT	74	10	23	33	24
NHL Totals	144	18	34	52	51

Letourneau-Leblond, Pierre-Luc b. Levis, Quebec, June 4, 1985

2008–09 NJ	8	0	1	1	22
NHL Totals	8	0	1	1	22

Lewis, Grant b. Pittsburgh, Pennsylvania, January 20, 1985

2008–09 ATL	1	0	0	0	0
NHL Totals	1	0	0	0	0

Lewis, Trevor b. Salt Lake City, Utah, January 8, 1987

2008–09 LA	6	1	2	3	0
NHL Totals	6	1	2	3	0

Lidstrom, Nicklas b. Vasteras, Sweden, April 28, 1970

2008–09 DET	78	16	43	59	30
NHL Totals	1,330	228	769	997	442

Liles, John-Michael b. Zionsville, Indiana, November 25, 1980

2008–09 COL	75	12	27	39	31
NHL Totals	388	56	142	198	153

Lilja, Andreas b. Helsingborg, Sweden, July 13, 1975

2008–09 DET	60	2	11	13	66
NHL Totals	458	14	58	72	497

Lindstrom, Joakim b. Skelleftea, Sweden, December 5, 1983

2008–09 PHO	44	9	11	20	28
NHL Totals	81	13	15	28	46

Lisin, Enver b. Moscow, Soviet Union (Russia), April 22, 1986

2008–09 PHO	48	13	8	21	24
NHL Totals	78	18	10	28	46

Little, Bryan   b. Edmonton, Alberta, November 12, 1987

2008–09 ATL	79	31	20	51	24
NHL Totals	127	37	30	67	42

Lombardi, Matt   b. Montreal, Quebec, March 18, 1982

2008–09 CAL/PHO	69	14	32	46	44
NHL Totals	366	70	113	183	239

• traded March 4, 2009, by Calgary to Phoenix with Brandon Prust and a
1st-round draft choice in either 2009 or 2010 for Olli Jokinen and a 3rd-
round draft choice in 2009

Lovejoy, Ben   b. Concord, New Hampshire, February 20, 1984

2008–09 PIT	2	0	0	0	0
NHL Totals	2	0	0	0	0

Lucic, Milan   b. Vancouver, British Columbia, June 7, 1988

2008–09 BOS	72	17	25	42	136
NHL Totals	149	25	44	69	225

Lukowich, Brad   b. Cranbrook, British Columbia, August 12, 1976

2008–09 SJ	58	0	8	8	12
NHL Totals	640	22	89	111	365

Lundin, Mike   b. Burnsville, Minnesota, September 24, 1984

2008–09 TB	25	0	2	2	4
NHL Totals	106	0	8	8	20

Lundmark, Jamie   b. Edmonton, Alberta, January 16, 1981

2008–09 CAL	27	8	8	16	17
NHL Totals	259	35	52	87	184

Lundqvist, Henrik   b. Are, Sweden, March 2, 1982

2008–09 NYR	70	38–25–7–0	4,152	168	3	2.43
NHL Totals	265	142–83–34–0	15,678	604	20	2.31

Lundqvist, Joel b. Are, Sweden, March 2, 1982

2008–09 DAL	43	1	5	6	20	
NHL Totals	134	7	19	26	56	

Luongo, Roberto b. Montreal, Quebec, April 4, 1979

2008–09 VAN	54	33–13–7	3,181	124	9	2.34
NHL Totals	544	230–232–31–33	31,037	1,329	47	2.57

Lupul, Joffrey b. Edmonton, Alberta, September 23, 1983

2008–09 PHI	79	25	25	50	58	
NHL Totals	372	102	109	211	214	

Lydman, Toni b. Lahti, Finland, September 25, 1977

2008–09 BUF	80	3	20	23	70	
NHL Totals	593	29	149	178	421	

MacArthur, Clarke b. Lloydminster, Alberta, April 6, 1985

2008–09 BUF	71	17	14	31	56	
NHL Totals	127	28	25	53	80	

MacDonald, Andrew b. Judique, Nova Scotia, September 7, 1986

2008–09 NYI	3	0	0	0	2	
NHL Totals	3	0	0	0	2	

MacDonald, Craig b. Antigonish, Nova Scotia, April 7, 1977

2008–09 CBJ	8	1	1	2	0	
NHL Totals	233	11	24	35	91	

MacDonald, Joey b. Pictou, Nova Scotia, February 7, 1980

2008–09 NYI	49	14–26–6–0	2,792	157	1	3.37
NHL Totals	66	17–34–9–0	3,739	206	1	3.31

Machacek, Spencer   b. Lethbridge, Alberta, October 14, 1988

2008–09 ATL	2	0	0	0	0
NHL Totals	2	0	0	0	0

Macias, Ray   b. Long Beach, California, September 18, 1986

2008–09 COL	6	0	1	1	0
NHL Totals	6	0	1	1	0

MacIntyre, Steve   b. Brock, Saskatchewan, August 8, 1980

2008–09 EDM	22	2	0	2	40
NHL Totals	22	2	0	2	40

MacKenzie, Aaron   b. Terrace Bay, Ontario, March 7, 1981

2008–09 COL	5	0	0	0	0
NHL Totals	5	0	0	0	0

MacKenzie, Derek   b. Sudbury, Ontario, June 11, 1981

2008–09 CBJ	1	0	0	0	2
NHL Totals	46	2	2	4	30

Madden, John   b. Barrie, Ontario, May 4, 1973

2008–09 NJ	76	7	16	23	26
NHL Totals	712	140	157	297	193

Mair, Adam   b. Hamilton, Ontario, February 15, 1979

2008–09 BUF	75	8	11	19	95
NHL Totals	481	31	65	96	711

Malhotra, Manny   b. Mississauga, Ontario, May 18, 1980

2008–09 CBJ	77	11	24	35	28
NHL Totals	634	76	121	197	344

Malik, Marek b. Ostrava, Czechoslovakia (Czech Republic),
  June 24, 1975

2008–09 TB	42	0	5	5	36
NHL Totals	691	33	135	168	620

Malkin, Evgeni b. Magnitogorsk, Soviet Union (Russia), July 31, 1986

2008–09 PIT	82	35	78	113	80
NHL Totals	242	115	189	304	238

Malone, Ryan b. Pittsburgh, Pennsylvania, December 1, 1979

2008–09 TB	70	26	19	45	98
NHL Totals	369	113	101	214	399

Maltby, Kirk b. Guelph, Ontario, December 22, 1972

2008–09 DET	78	5	6	11	28
NHL Totals	1,020	124	130	254	835

Mancari, Mark b. London, Ontario, July 11, 1985

2008–09 BUF	7	1	1	2	4
NHL Totals	10	1	2	3	6

Mannino, Peter b. Farmington Hills, Michigan, March 17, 1984

2008–09 NYI	3	1–1–0–0	132	10	0	4.51
NHL Totals	3	1–1–0–0	132	10	0	4.51

Mara, Paul b. Ridgewood, New Jersey, September 7, 1979

2008–09 NYR	76	5	16	21	94
NHL Totals	639	63	176	239	640

Marchant, Todd b. Buffalo, New York, August 12, 1973

2008–09 ANA	72	5	13	18	34
NHL Totals	1,038	176	292	468	716

Markov, Andrei   b. Voskresensk, Soviet Union (Russia), December 20, 1978

2008–09 MON	78	12	52	64	36
NHL Totals	571	74	255	329	325

Marleau, Patrick   b. Aneroid, Saskatchewan, September 15, 1979

2008–09 SJ	76	38	33	71	18
NHL Totals	871	276	334	610	303

Martin, Paul   b. Minneapolis, Minnesota, March 5, 1981

2008–09 NJ	73	5	28	33	36
NHL Totals	378	24	128	152	112

Martinek, Radek   b. Havlickuv Brod, Czechoslovakia (Czech Republic), August 31, 1976

2008–09 NYI	51	6	4	10	28
NHL Totals	373	16	68	84	225

Mason, Chris   b. Red Deer, Alberta, April 20, 1976

2008–09 STL	57	27–21–7–0	3,214	129	6	2.41
NHL Totals	192	85–64–18–1	10,346	439	18	2.55

Mason, Steve   b. Oakville, Ontario, May 29, 1988

2008–09 CBJ	61	33–20–7–0	3,663	140	10	2.29
NHL Totals	61	33–20–7–0	3,663	140	10	2.29

Matthias, Shawn   b. Mississauga, Ontario, February 19, 1988

2008–09 FLO	16	0	2	2	2
NHL Totals	20	2	2	4	4

Maxwell, Ben   b. North Vancouver, British Columbia, March 30, 1988

2008–09 MON	7	0	0	0	2
NHL Totals	7	0	0	0	2

May, Brad b. Toronto, Ontario, November 29, 1971

2008–09 ANA/TOR	58	1	6	7	89
NHL Totals	1,001	127	160	287	2,182

• traded January 7, 2009, by Anaheim to Toronto for a conditional 6th-round draft choice in 2010

Mayers, Jamal b. Toronto, Ontario, October 24, 1974

2008–09 TOR	71	7	9	16	82
NHL Totals	666	78	96	174	838

Mayorov, Maxim b. Andizhan, Soviet Union (Russia), March 26, 1989

2008–09 CBJ	3	0	0	0	0
NHL Totals	3	0	0	0	0

McAmmond, Dean b. Grand Cache, Alberta, June 15, 1973

2008–09 OTT/NYI	82	5	11	16	24
NHL Totals	934	178	253	431	450

• traded February 20, 2009, by Ottawa to NY Islanders with a 1st-round draft choice for Chris Campoli and Mike Comrie

McArdle, Kenndal b. Toronto, Ontario, January 4, 1987

2008–09 FLO	3	0	0	0	2
NHL Totals	3	0	0	0	2

McCabe, Bryan b. St. Catharines, Ontario, June 8, 1975

2008–09 FLO	69	15	24	39	41
NHL Totals	986	130	327	457	1,615

McCarty, Darren b. Burnaby, British Columbia, April 1, 1972

2008–09 DET	13	1	0	1	25
NHL Totals	758	127	161	288	1,477

McClement, Jay b. Kingston, Ontario, March 2, 1983

2008–09 STL	82	12	14	26	29
NHL Totals	311	35	76	111	140

McCormick, Cody b. London, Ontario, April 18, 1983

2008–09 COL	55	1	11	12	92
NHL Totals	190	9	21	30	250

McDonald, Andy b. Strathroy, Ontario, August 25, 1977

2008–09 STL	46	15	29	44	24
NHL Totals	486	121	218	339	218

McElhinney, Curtis b. London, Ontario, May 23, 1983

2008–09 CAL	14	1–6–1–0	517	31	0	3.59
NHL Totals	19	1–8–1–0	667	36	0	3.23

McGinn, Jamie b. Fergus, Ontario, August 5, 1988

2008–09 SJ	35	4	2	6	2
NHL Totals	35	4	2	6	2

McGratton, Brian b. Hamilton, Ontario, September 2, 1981

2008–09 PHO	5	0	0	0	22
NHL Totals	148	2	8	10	309

McIver, Nathan b. Kinkora, Prince Edward Island, January 6, 1985

2008–09 ANA	18	0	1	1	36
NHL Totals	36	0	1	1	95

McKee, Jay b. Kingston, Ontario, September 8, 1977

2008–09 STL	69	1	7	8	44
NHL Totals	740	20	95	115	568

McKenna, Mike b. St. Louis, Missouri, April 11, 1983

2008–09 TB	15	4–8–1–0	775	46	1	3.56
NHL Totals	15	4–8–1–0	775	46	1	3.56

McLean, Brett b. Comox, British Columbia, August 14, 1978

| 2008–09 FLO | 80 | 7 | 12 | 19 | 29 |
| NHL Totals | 385 | 56 | 106 | 162 | 204 |

McLean, Kurtis b. Kirkland Lake, Ontario, November 2, 1980

| 2008–09 NYI | 4 | 1 | 0 | 1 | 0 |
| NHL Totals | 4 | 1 | 0 | 1 | 0 |

McLeod, Cody b. Binscarth, Manitoba, June 26, 1984

| 2008–09 COL | 79 | 15 | 5 | 20 | 162 |
| NHL Totals | 128 | 19 | 10 | 29 | 282 |

Meech, Derek b. Winnipeg, Manitoba, April 21, 1984

| 2008–09 DET | 41 | 2 | 5 | 7 | 12 |
| NHL Totals | 77 | 2 | 8 | 10 | 20 |

Melichar, Josef b. Ceske Budejovice, Czechoslovakia (Czech Republic), January 20, 1979

| 2008–09 CAR/TB | 39 | 0 | 9 | 9 | 37 |
| NHL Totals | 349 | 7 | 42 | 49 | 300 |

• traded February 7, 2009, by Carolina to Tampa Bay with Wade Brookbank and a 4th-round draft choice in 2009 for Jussi Jokinen

Meszaros, Andrei b. Povazska Bystrica, Czechoslovakia (Slovakia), October 13, 1985

| 2008–09 TB | 52 | 2 | 14 | 16 | 36 |
| NHL Totals | 298 | 28 | 98 | 126 | 249 |

Methot, Marc b. Ottawa, Ontario, June 21, 1985

| 2008–09 CBJ | 66 | 4 | 13 | 17 | 55 |
| NHL Totals | 95 | 4 | 17 | 21 | 75 |

Metropolit, Glen b. Toronto, Ontario, June 25, 1974

2008–09 PHI/MON	76	6	11	17	28
NHL Totals	338	41	89	130	124

• claimed off waivers by Montreal from Philadelphia on February 27, 2009

Meyer, Freddy b. Sanbornville, New Hampshire, January 4, 1981

2008–09 NYI	27	4	5	9	14
NHL Totals	202	15	41	56	107

Michalek, Milan b. Jindrichuv Hradec, Czechoslovakia (Czech Republic), December 7, 1984

2008–09 SJ	77	23	34	57	52
NHL Totals	317	91	123	214	184

Michalek, Zbynek b. Jindrichuv Hradec, Czechoslovakia (Czech Republic), December 23, 1982

2008–09 PHO	82	6	21	27	28
NHL Totals	343	24	74	98	162

Miettinen, Antti b. Hameenlinna, Finland, July 3, 1980

2008–09 MIN	82	15	29	44	32
NHL Totals	320	53	82	135	150

Mihalik, Vladimir b. Presov, Czechoslovakia (Czech Republic), January 29, 1987

2008–09 TB	11	0	3	3	6
NHL Totals	11	0	3	3	6

Mikkelson, Brendan b. Regina, Saskatchewan, June 22, 1987

2008–09 ANA	34	0	2	2	17
NHL Totals	34	0	2	2	17

Miller, Drew b. Dover, New Jersey, February 17, 1984

2008–09 ANA	27	4	6	10	17
NHL Totals	53	6	9	15	23

Miller, Ryan b. East Lansing, Michigan, July 17, 1980

| 2008–09 BUF | 59 | 34–18–6–0 | 3,443 | 145 | 5 | 2.53 |
| NHL Totals | 264 | 146–86–25–1 | 15,561 | 689 | 12 | 2.66 |

Minard, Chris b. Thompson, Manitoba, November 18, 1981

| 2008–09 PIT | 20 | 1 | 2 | 3 | 4 |
| NHL Totals | 35 | 2 | 3 | 5 | 14 |

Mink, Graham b. Stowe, Vermont, May 21, 1979

| 2008–09 WAS | 2 | 0 | 0 | 0 | 0 |
| NHL Totals | 7 | 0 | 0 | 0 | 2 |

Mitchell, John b. Waterloo, Ontario, January 22, 1985

| 2008–09 TOR | 76 | 12 | 17 | 29 | 33 |
| NHL Totals | 76 | 12 | 17 | 29 | 33 |

Mitchell, Torrey b. Montreal, Quebec, January 30, 1985
• appeared only in the playoffs for San Jose

Mitchell, Willie b. Port McNeill, British Columbia, April 23, 1977

| 2008–09 VAN | 82 | 3 | 20 | 23 | 59 |
| NHL Totals | 538 | 15 | 92 | 107 | 573 |

Modano, Mike b. Livonia, Michigan, June 7, 1970

| 2008–09 DAL | 80 | 15 | 31 | 46 | 46 |
| NHL Totals | 1,400 | 543 | 786 | 1,329 | 900 |

Modin, Fredrik b. Sundsvall, Sweden, October 8, 1974

| 2008–09 CBJ | 50 | 9 | 16 | 25 | 28 |
| NHL Totals | 814 | 220 | 221 | 441 | 413 |

Moen, Travis b. Stewart Valley, Saskatchewan, April 6, 1982

| 2008–09 ANA/SJ | 82 | 7 | 9 | 16 | 91 |
| NHL Totals | 362 | 29 | 27 | 56 | 487 |

• traded March 4, 2009, by Anaheim to San Jose with Kent Huskins for Nick Bonino, Timo Pielmeier and a conditional draft choice in 2009

Mojzis, Tomas b. Kolin, Czechoslovakia (Czech Republic), May 2, 1982

2008–09 MIN	4	0	1	1	2
NHL Totals	17	1	2	3	14

Moller, Oscar b. Stockholm, Sweden, January 22, 1989

2008–09 LA	40	7	8	15	16
NHL Totals	40	7	8	15	16

Montador, Steve b. Vancouver, British Columbia, December 21, 1979

2008–09 ANA/BOS	78	4	17	21	143
NHL Totals	368	18	50	68	604

• traded March 4, 2009, by Anaheim to Boston for Petteri Nokelainen

Montoya, Al b. Chicago, Illinois, February 13, 1985

2008–09 PHO	5	3–1–0–0	259	9	1	2.08
NHL Totals	5	3–1–0–0	259	9	1	2.08

Moore, Dominic b. Thornhill, Ontario, August 3, 1980

2008–09 TOR/BUF	81	13	32	45	92
NHL Totals	305	35	65	100	200

• traded March 4, 2009, by Toronto to Buffalo for a 2nd-round draft choice in 2009

Moreau, Ethan b. Huntsville, Ontario, September 22, 1975

2008–09 EDM	77	14	12	26	133
NHL Totals	787	136	123	259	1,004

Morris, Derek b. Edmonton, Alberta, August 24, 1978

2008–09 PHO/NYR	75	5	15	20	40
NHL Totals	793	76	264	340	794

• traded March 4, 2009, by Phoenix to NY Rangers for Nigel Dawes, Petr Prucha and Dmitri Kalinin

Morrison, Brendan b. Pitt Meadows, British Columbia, August 15, 1975

2008–09 ANA/DAL	81	16	15	31	32
NHL Totals	755	175	330	505	384

• claimed off waivers by Dallas from Anaheim on March 4, 2009

Morrisonn, Shaone b. Vancouver, British Columbia, December 23, 1982

2008–09 WAS	72	3	10	13	77
NHL Totals	350	9	49	58	355

Morrow, Brenden b. Carlyle, Saskatchewan, January 16, 1979

2008–09 DAL	18	5	10	15	49
NHL Totals	591	173	216	389	943

Moss, David b. Dearborn, Michigan, December 28, 1981

2008–09 CAL	81	20	19	39	22
NHL Totals	163	34	34	68	44

Mottau, Mike b. Quincey, Massachusetts, March 19, 1978

2008–09 NJ	80	1	14	15	35
NHL Totals	179	5	30	35	96

Motzko, Joe b. Bemidji, Minnesota, March 14, 1980

2008–09 ATL	6	1	0	1	0
NHL Totals	25	4	2	6	0

Moulson, Matt b. North York (Toronto), Ontario, November 1, 1983

2008–09 LA	7	1	0	1	2
NHL Totals	29	6	4	10	6

Mueller, Peter b. Bloomington, Minnesota, April 14, 1988

2008–09 PHO	72	13	23	36	24
NHL Totals	153	35	55	90	56

Murphy, Cory b. Kanata, Ontario, February 13, 1978

2008–09 FLO/TB	32	5	11	16	14
NHL Totals	79	7	26	33	36

• claimed off waivers by Tampa Bay from Florida on January 19, 2009

Murray, Andrew b. Selkirk, Manitoba, November 6, 1981

2008–09 CBJ	67	8	3	11	10
NHL Totals	106	14	7	21	22

Murray, Doug b. Bromma, Sweden, March 12, 1980

2008–09 SJ	75	0	7	7	38
NHL Totals	210	1	20	21	194

Murray, Garth b. Regina, Saskatchewan, September 17, 1982

2008–09 PHO	10	0	0	0	12
NHL Totals	116	8	2	10	131

Nabokov, Evgeni b. Ust-Kamenogorsk, Soviet Union
  (Kazakhstan), July 25, 1975

2008–09 SJ	62	41–12–8–0	3,686	150	7	2.44
NHL Totals	492	249–162–27–29	28,297	1,124	47	2.38

Nash, Rick b. Brampton, Ontario, June 16, 1984

2008–09 CBJ	78	40	39	79	52
NHL Totals	441	194	161	355	436

Naslund, Markus b. Ornskoldsvik, Sweden, July 30, 1973

2008–09 NYR	82	24	22	46	57
NHL Totals	1,117	395	474	869	736

Neal, James b. Oshawa, Ontario, September 3, 1987

2008–09 DAL	77	24	13	37	51
NHL Totals	77	24	13	37	51

Negrin, John b. West Vancouver, British Columbia, March 25, 1989

2008–09 CAL	3	0	1	1	2
NHL Totals	3	0	1	1	2

Neil, Chris b. Markdale, Ontario, June 18, 1979

2008–09 OTT	60	3	7	10	146
NHL Totals	511	61	73	134	1,298

Neuvirth, Michal b. Usti nad Labem, Czechoslovakia (Czech Republic), March 23, 1988

2008–09 WAS	5	2–1–0–0	219	11	0	3.00
NHL Totals	5	2–1–0–0	219	11	0	3.00

Newbury, Kris b. Brampton, Ontario, February 19, 1982

2008–09 TOR	1	0	0	0	2
NHL Totals	44	3	3	6	60

Nichol, Scott b. Edmonton, Alberta, December 31, 1974

2008–09 NAS	43	4	6	10	41
NHL Totals	417	44	48	92	

Niedermayer, Rob b. Cassiar, British Columbia, December 28, 1974

2008–09 ANA	79	14	7	21	42
NHL Totals	1,011	171	257	428	837

Niedermayer, Scott b. Edmonton, Alberta, August 31, 1973

2008–09 ANA	82	14	45	59	70
NHL Totals	1,183	162	530	692	746

Nielsen, Frans b. Herning, Denmark, April 24, 1984

2008–09 NYI	59	9	24	33	18
NHL Totals	90	12	26	38	18

Niemi, Antti   b. Vantaa, Finland, August 29, 1983

2008–09 CHI	3	1–1–1–0	141	8	0	3.40
NHL Totals	3	1–1–1–0	141	8	0	3.40

Niittymaki, Antero   b. Turku, Finland, June 18, 1980

2008–09 PHI	32	15–8–6–0	1,804	83	1	2.76
NHL Totals	161	62–61–23–0	9,041	454	4	3.01

Nikulin, Alexander   b. Moscow, Soviet Union (Russia), August 25, 1985

2008–09 PHO	1	0	0	0	0
NHL Totals	3	0	0	0	0

Nilsson, Robert   b. Calgary, Alberta, January 10, 1985

2008–09 EDM	64	9	20	29	26
NHL Totals	192	26	65	91	78

Niskala, Janne   b. Vasteras, Sweden, September 22, 1981

2008–09 TB	6	1	2	3	6
NHL Totals	6	1	2	3	6

Niskanen, Matt   b. Virginia, Minnesota, December 6, 1986

2008–09 DAL	80	6	29	35	52
NHL Totals	158	13	48	61	88

Nodl, Andreas   b. Vienna, Austria, February 28, 1987

2008–09 PHI	38	1	3	4	2
NHL Totals	38	1	3	4	2

Nokelainen, Petteri   b. Imatra, Finland, January 16, 1986

2008–09 BOS/ANA	50	4	5	9	16
NHL Totals	122	12	9	21	39

• traded March 4, 2009, by Boston to Anaheim for Steve Montador

Nolan, Owen b. Belfast, Northern Ireland, February 12, 1972

2008–09 MIN	59	25	20	45	26
NHL Totals	1,127	406	446	852	1,753

Norrena, Fredrik b. Pietarsaari, Finland, November 29, 1973

2008–09 CBJ	8	1–3–2–0	323	17	0	3.16
NHL Totals	100	35–45–11–0	5,234	243	5	2.79

Novotny, Jiri b. Pelhrimov, Czechoslovakia (Czech Republic), August 12, 1983

2008–09 CBJ	42	4	3	7	14
NHL Totals	189	20	31	51	66

Numminen, Teppo b. Tampere, Finland, July 3, 1968

2008–09 BUF	57	2	15	17	22
NHL Totals	1,372	117	520	637	513

Nycholat, Lawrence b. Calgary, Alberta, May 7, 1979

2008–09 VAN/COL	19	0	1	1	6
NHL Totals	50	2	7	9	24

• claimed off waivers by Calgary from Vancouver on March 3, 2009; traded March 4, 2009, by Calgary to Colorado with Ryan Wilson and a 2nd-round draft choice in 2009 for Jordan Leopold

Nylander, Michael b. Stockholm, Sweden, October 3, 1972

2008–09 WAS	72	9	24	33	32
NHL Totals	920	209	470	679	468

Nystrom, Eric b. Syosset, New York, February 14, 1983

2008–09 CAL	76	5	5	10	89
NHL Totals	122	8	12	20	137

O'Brien, Shane   b. Port Hope, Ontario, August 9, 1983

| 2008–09 TB/VAN | 77 | 0 | 10 | 10 | 196 |
| NHL Totals | 234 | 6 | 41 | 47 | 526 |

• traded October 6, 2008, by Tampa Bay to Vancouver with Michel Ouellet
  for Lukas Krajicek and Juraj Simek

O'Byrne, Ryan   b. Victoria, British Columbia, July 19, 1984

| 2008–09 MON | 37 | 0 | 5 | 5 | 58 |
| NHL Totals | 70 | 1 | 11 | 12 | 103 |

O'Donnell, Sean   b. Ottawa, Ontario, October 13, 1971

| 2008–09 LA | 82 | 0 | 12 | 12 | 71 |
| NHL Totals | 1,014 | 27 | 162 | 189 | 1,629 |

Oduya, John   b. Stockholm, Sweden, October 1, 1981

| 2008–09 NJ | 82 | 7 | 22 | 29 | 30 |
| NHL Totals | 233 | 15 | 51 | 66 | 137 |

Ohlund, Mattias   b. Pitea, Sweden, September 9, 1976

| 2008–09 VAN | 82 | 6 | 19 | 25 | 105 |
| NHL Totals | 770 | 93 | 232 | 325 | 756 |

Okposo, Kyle   b. St. Paul, Minnesota, April 16, 1988

| 2008–09 NYI | 65 | 18 | 21 | 39 | 36 |
| NHL Totals | 74 | 20 | 24 | 44 | 38 |

Olesz, Rostislav   b. Bilovec, Czechoslovakia (Czech Republic),
  October 10, 1985

| 2008–09 FLO | 37 | 4 | 5 | 9 | 8 |
| NHL Totals | 227 | 37 | 49 | 86 | 76 |

Olvecky, Peter   b. Trencin, Czechoslovakia (Slovakia), October 11, 1985

| 2008–09 MIN | 31 | 2 | 5 | 7 | 12 |
| NHL Totals | 31 | 2 | 5 | 7 | 12 |

Ondrus, Ben b. Sherwood Park, Alberta, June 25, 1982

2008–09 TOR	11	0	0	0	34
NHL Totals	52	0	2	2	77

O'Neill, Wes b. Windsor, Ontario, March 3, 1986

2008–09 COL	3	0	0	0	4
NHL Totals	3	0	0	0	4

O'Reilly, Cal b. Toronto, Ontario, September 30, 1986

2008–09 NAS	11	3	2	5	2
NHL Totals	11	3	2	5	2

Oreskovic, Phil b. North York (Toronto), Ontario, January 26, 1987

2008–09 TOR	10	1	1	2	21
NHL Totals	10	1	1	2	21

Orpik, Brooks b. San Francisco, California, September 26, 1980

2008–09 PIT	79	2	17	19	73
NHL Totals	376	6	49	55	465

Orr, Colton b. Winnipeg, Manitoba, March 3, 1982

2008–09 NYR	82	1	4	5	193
NHL Totals	245	4	7	11	549

Ortmeyer, Jed b. Omaha, Nebraska, September 3, 1978

2008–09 NAS	2	0	0	0	0
NHL Totals	230	13	19	32	108

Osala, Oskar b. Vaasa, Finland, December 26, 1987

2008–09 WAS	2	0	0	0	0
NHL Totals	2	0	0	0	0

Osgood, Chris b. Peace River, Alberta, November 26, 1972

2008–09 DET	46	26–9–8–0	2,662	137	2	3.09
NHL Totals	710	389–204–23–66	40,682	1,676	49	2.47

Oshie, T.J. b. Mt. Vernon, Washington, December 23, 1986

2008–09 STL	57	14	25	39	30
NHL Totals	57	14	25	39	30

O'Sullivan, Patrick b. Winston-Salem, North Carolina, February 1, 1985

2008–09 LA/EDM	81	16	27	43	28
NHL Totals	207	43	72	115	78

• traded March 4, 2009, by Los Angeles to Carolina with a 2nd-round draft choice in 2009, for Justin Williams; traded immediately after to Edmonton with a 2nd-round draft choice in 2009 for Erik Cole and a 5th-round draft choice in 2009

Ott, Steve b. Summerside, Prince Edward Island, August 19, 1982

2008–09 DAL	64	19	27	46	135
NHL Totals	337	40	73	113	678

Ouellet, Michel b. Rimouski, Quebec, March 5, 1982

2008–09 VAN	3	0	0	0	0
NHL Totals	190	52	64	116	58

Ovechkin, Alexander b. Moscow, Soviet Union (Russia), September 17, 1985

2008–09 WAS	79	56	54	110	72
NHL Totals	324	219	201	420	216

Oystrick, Nathan b. Regina, Saskatchewan, December 17, 1982

2008–09 ATL	53	4	8	12	50
NHL Totals	53	4	8	12	50

Pacioretty, Max b. New Canaan, Connecticut, November 20, 1988

2008–09 MON	34	3	8	11	27
NHL Totals	34	3	8	11	27

Paddock, Cam b. Vancouver, British Columbia, March 22, 1983

2008–09 STL	16	2	1	3	0
NHL Totals	16	2	1	3	0

Paetsch, Nathan b. Leroy, Saskatchewan, March 30, 1983

2008–09 BUF	23	2	4	6	25
NHL Totals	146	6	34	40	102

Pahlsson, Samuel b. Ornskoldsvik, Sweden, December 17, 1977

2008–09 ANA/CHI	65	7	11	18	35
NHL Totals	557	54	92	146	260

• traded March 4, 2009, by Anaheim to Chicago with Logan Stephenson and a conditional 4th-round draft choice in 2009, for James Wisniewski and Petri Kontiola

Paille, Daniel b. Welland, Ontario, April 15, 1984

2008–09 BUF	73	12	15	27	20
NHL Totals	193	35	41	76	54

Pandolfo, Jay b. Winchester, Massachusetts, December 27, 1974

2008–09 NJ	61	5	5	10	10
NHL Totals	767	95	119	214	148

Pardy, Adam b. Bonavista, Newfoundland, March 29, 1984

2008–09 CAL	60	1	9	10	69
NHL Totals	60	1	9	10	69

Parent, Ryan b. Prince Albert, Saskatchewan, March 17, 1987

2008–09 PHI	31	0	4	4	10
NHL Totals	54	0	4	4	16

Parise, Zach b. Minneapolis, Minnesota, July 28, 1984

2008–09 NJ	82	45	49	94	24
NHL Totals	326	122	131	253	107

Park, Richard b. Seoul, South Korea, May 27, 1976

2008–09 NYI	71	14	17	31	34
NHL Totals	603	86	110	196	226

Parrish, Mark b. Edina, Minnesota, February 2, 1977

2008–09 DAL	44	8	5	13	18
NHL Totals	704	216	169	385	242

Parros, George b. Washington, Pennsylvania, December 29, 1979

2008–09 ANA	74	5	5	10	135
NHL Totals	232	9	12	21	558

Pavelec, Ondrej b. Kladno, Czechoslovakia (Czech Republic), August 31, 1987

2008–09 ATL	12	3–7–0–0	599	36	0	3.61
NHL Totals	19	6–10–0–0	946	54	0	3.42

Pavelski, Joe b. Plover, Wisconsin, July 11, 1984

2008–09 SJ	80	25	34	59	46
NHL Totals	208	58	69	127	92

Peca, Michael b. Toronto, Ontario, March 26, 1974

2008–09 CBJ	71	4	18	22	58
NHL Totals	864	176	289	465	798

Peckham, Theo b. Richmond Hill, Ontario, November 10, 1987

2008–09 EDM	15	0	0	0	59
NHL Totals	16	0	0	0	61

Pelech, Matt b. Toronto, Ontario, September 4, 1987

2008–09 CAL	5	0	3	3	9
NHL Totals	5	0	3	3	9

Pelletier, Pascal b. Labrador City, Newfoundland, June 16, 1983

2008–09 CHI	7	0	0	0	0
NHL Totals	13	0	0	0	0

Peltier, Derek b. Plymouth, Minnesota, March 14, 1985

2008–09 COL	11	0	0	0	2
NHL Totals	11	0	0	0	2

Peltonen, Ville b. Vantaa, Finland, May 24, 1973

2008–09 FLO	79	12	19	31	31
NHL Totals	382	52	96	148	119

Penner, Dustin b. Winkler, Manitoba, September 28, 1982

2008–09 EDM	78	17	20	37	61
NHL Totals	261	73	63	136	178

Perrault, Joel b. Montreal, Quebec, April 6, 1983

2008–09 PHO	7	2	1	3	4
NHL Totals	87	11	14	25	68

Perrin, Eric b. Laval, Quebec, November 1, 1975

2008–09 ATL	78	7	16	23	36
NHL Totals	245	32	72	104	92

Perron, David b. Sherbrooke, Quebec, May 28, 1988

2008–09 STL	81	15	35	50	50
NHL Totals	143	28	49	77	88

Perry, Corey b. Peterborough, Ontario, May 16, 1985

2008–09 ANA	78	32	40	72	109
NHL Totals	286	91	104	195	322

Pesonen, Janne b. Suomussalmi, Finland, May 11, 1982

2008–09 PIT	7	0	0	0	0
NHL Totals	7	0	0	0	0

Peters, Andrew b. St. Catharines, Ontario, May 5, 1980

2008–09 BUF	28	0	1	1	81
NHL Totals	200	4	3	7	557

Peters, Warren b. Saskatoon, Saskatchewan, July 10, 1982

2008–09 CAL	16	1	0	1	12
NHL Totals	16	1	0	1	12

Petersen, Toby b. Minneapolis, Minnesota, October 27, 1978

2008–09 DAL	57	4	7	11	14
NHL Totals	220	20	35	55	30

Petiot, Richard b. Daysland, Alberta, August 20, 1982

2008–09 TB	11	0	3	3	21
NHL Totals	13	0	3	3	23

Petruzalek, Jakub b. Most, Czechoslovakia (Czech Republic), April 24, 1985

2008–09 CAR	2	0	1	1	0
NHL Totals	2	0	1	1	0

Pettinger, Matt b. Edmonton, Alberta, October 22, 1980

2008–09 TB	59	8	7	15	24
NHL Totals	413	64	56	120	204

Peverley, Rich b. Guelph, Ontario, July 8, 1982

2008–09 NAS/ATL	66	15	29	44	33
NHL Totals	112	20	35	55	41

• claimed off waivers by Atlanta from Nashville on January 10, 2009

Phaneuf, Dion b. Edmonton, Alberta, April 10, 1985

2008–09 CAL	80	11	36	47	100
NHL Totals	323	65	141	206	473

Phillips, Chris b. Calgary, Alberta, March 9, 1978

2008–09 OTT	82	6	16	22	66
NHL Totals	781	51	153	204	578

Picard, Alexandre b. Les Saules, Quebec, October 9, 1985

2008–09 CBJ	15	0	1	1	26
NHL Totals	58	0	2	2	48

Picard, Alexandre b. Gatineau, Quebec, July 5, 1985

2008–09 OTT	47	6	8	14	8
NHL Totals	139	12	30	42	39

Pietrangelo, Alex b. King City, Ontario, January 18, 1990

2008–09 STL	8	0	1	1	2
NHL Totals	8	0	1	1	2

Pihlstrom, Antti b. Vantaa, Finland, October 22, 1984

2008–09 NAS	53	2	5	7	10
NHL Totals	53	2	5	7	10

Pisani, Fernando b. Edmonton, Alberta, December 27, 1976

2008–09 EDM	38	7	8	15	14
NHL Totals	362	76	69	145	180

Pitkanen, Joni b. Oulu, Finland, September 19, 1983

2008–09 CAR	71	7	26	33	58
NHL Totals	340	40	135	175	324

Plekanec, Tomas b. Kladno, Czechoslovakia (Czech Republic), October 31, 1982

2008–09 MON	80	20	19	39	54
NHL Totals	311	78	106	184	164

Plihal, Tomas b. Frydlant, Czechoslovakia (Czech Republic), March 28, 1983

| 2008–09 SJ | 64 | 5 | 8 | 13 | 22 |
| NHL Totals | 89 | 7 | 9 | 16 | 26 |

Pock, Thomas b. Klagenfurt, Austria, December 2, 1981

| 2008–09 NYI | 59 | 1 | 2 | 3 | 35 |
| NHL Totals | 118 | 8 | 9 | 17 | 55 |

Pogge, Justin b. Fort McMurray, Alberta, April 22, 1986

| 2008–09 TOR | 7 | 1–4–1–0 | 371 | 27 | 0 | 4.35 |
| NHL Totals | 7 | 1–4–1–0 | 371 | 27 | 0 | 4.35 |

Polak, Roman b. Ostrava, Czechoslovakia (Czech Republic), April 28, 1986

| 2008–09 STL | 69 | 1 | 14 | 15 | 45 |
| NHL Totals | 94 | 1 | 15 | 16 | 51 |

Pominville, Jason b. Repentigny, Quebec, November 30, 1982

| 2008–09 BUF | 82 | 20 | 46 | 66 | 18 |
| NHL Totals | 304 | 99 | 145 | 244 | 90 |

Ponikarovsky, Alexei b. Kiev, Soviet Union (Ukraine), April 9, 1980

| 2008–09 TOR | 82 | 23 | 38 | 61 | 38 |
| NHL Totals | 416 | 95 | 121 | 216 | 274 |

Porter, Chris b. Toronto, Ontario, May 29, 1984

| 2008–09 STL | 6 | 1 | 1 | 2 | 0 |
| NHL Totals | 6 | 1 | 1 | 2 | 0 |

Porter, Kevin b. Detroit, Michigan, March 12, 1986

| 2008–09 PHO | 34 | 5 | 5 | 10 | 4 |
| NHL Totals | 34 | 5 | 5 | 10 | 4 |

Pothier, Brian b. New Bedford, Massachusetts, April 15, 1977

2008–09 WAS	9	1	2	3	4
NHL Totals	301	21	82	103	181

Poti, Tom b. Worcester, Massachusetts, March 22, 1977

2008–09 WAS	52	3	10	13	28
NHL Totals	717	63	231	294	536

Potter, Corey b. Lansing, Michigan, January 5, 1984

2008–09 NYR	5	1	1	2	0
NHL Totals	5	1	1	2	0

Potulny, Ryan b. Grand Forks, North Dakota, September 5, 1984

2008–09 EDM	8	0	3	3	0
NHL Totals	52	7	10	17	26

Pouliot, Benoit b. Alfred, Ontario, September 29, 1986

2008–09 MIN	37	5	6	11	18
NHL Totals	51	7	7	14	18

Pouliot, Marc-Antoine b. Quebec City, Quebec, May 22, 1985

2008–09 EDM	63	8	12	20	23
NHL Totals	141	14	25	39	53

Powe, Darroll b. Saskatoon, Saskatchewan, June 22, 1985

2008–09 PHI	60	6	5	11	35
NHL Totals	60	6	5	11	35

Preissing, Tom b. Rosemount, Minnesota, December 3, 1978

2008–09 LA	22	3	4	7	6
NHL Totals	322	31	100	131	78

Price, Carey b. Vancouver, British Columbia, August 16, 1987

2008–09 MON	52	23–16–10–0	3,035	143	1	2.83
NHL Totals	93	47–28–13–0	5,448	246	4	2.71

Primeau, Wayne   b. Scarborough (Toronto), Ontario, June 4, 1976

2008–09 CAL	24	0	4	4	14
NHL Totals	715	66	120	186	754

Pronger, Chris   b. Dryden, Ontario, October 10, 1974

2008–09 ANA	82	11	37	48	88
NHL Totals	1,022	142	464	606	1,457

Prospal, Vaclav   b. Ceske Budejovice, Czechoslovakia (Czech Republic), February 17, 1975

2008–09 TB	82	19	26	45	52
NHL Totals	874	198	401	599	473

Prucha, Petr   b. Chrudim, Czechoslovakia (Czech Republic), September 14, 1982

2008–09 NYR/PHO	47	6	13	19	22
NHL Totals	256	65	58	123	106

• traded March 4, 2009, by NY Rangers to Phoenix with Nigel Dawes and Dmitri Kalinin for Derek Morris

Prust, Brandon   b. London, Ontario, March 16, 1984

2008–09 CAL/PHO	36	1	2	3	108
NHL Totals	46	1	2	3	133

• traded March 4, 2009, by Calgary to Phoenix with Matthew Lombardi and a 1st-round draft choice in either 2009 or 2010 for Olli Jokinen and a 3rd-round draft choice in 2009

Purcell, Teddy   b. St. John's, Newfoundland, September 8, 1985

2008–09 LA	40	4	12	16	4
NHL Totals	50	5	14	19	4

Pyatt, Taylor   b. Thunder Bay, Ontario, August 19, 1981

2008–09 VAN	69	10	9	19	43
NHL Totals	532	91	100	191	315

Quick, Jon b. Milford, Connecticut, January 21, 1986

2008–09 LA	44	21–18–2–0	2,494	103	4	2.48
NHL Totals	47	22–20–2–0	2,635	112	4	2.55

Quick, Kevin b. Buffalo, New York, March 29, 1988

2008–09 TB	6	0	1	1	0
NHL Totals	6	0	1	1	0

Quincey, Kyle b. Kitchener, Ontario, August 12, 1985

2008–09 LA	72	4	34	38	63
NHL Totals	85	5	34	39	67

Raduns, Nate b. Sauk Rapids, Minnesota, May 17, 1984

2008–09 PHI	1	0	0	0	0
NHL Totals	1	0	0	0	0

Rafalski, Brian b. Dearborn, Michigan, September 28, 1973

2008–09 DET	78	10	49	59	20
NHL Totals	692	67	358	425	234

Ramo, Karri b. Asikkala, Finland, July 1, 1986

2008–09 TB	24	4–10–7–0	1,311	80	0	3.66
NHL Totals	48	11–21–10–0	2,650	148	0	3.35

Ranger, Paul b. Whitby, Ontario, September 12, 1984

2008–09 TB	42	2	11	13	56
NHL Totals	262	17	73	90	212

Rask, Tuukka b. Savonlinna, Finland, March 10, 1987

2008–09 BOS	1	1–0–0–0	59	0	1	0.00
NHL Totals	5	3–1–1–0	244	10	1	2.46

Raycroft, Andrew b. Belleville, Ontario, May 4, 1980

2008–09 COL	31	12–16–0–0	1,722	90	0	3.14
NHL Totals	230	94–96–16–10	12,847	622	6	2.90

Raymond, Mason b. Cochrane, Alberta, September 17, 1985

2008–09 VAN	72	11	12	23	24
NHL Totals	121	20	24	44	26

Reasoner, Marty b. Honeoye Falls, New York, February 26, 1977

2008–09 ATL	79	14	16	30	36
NHL Totals	544	78	128	206	295

Recchi, Mark b. Kamloops, British Columbia, February 1, 1968

2008–09 TB/BOS	80	23	38	61	22
NHL Totals	1,490	545	897	1,442	964

• traded March 4, 2009, by Tampa Bay to Boston with a 2nd-round draft choice in 2010 for Matt Lashoff and Martins Karsums

Rechlicz, Joel b. Brookfield, Wisconsin, June 14, 1987

2008–09 NYI	17	0	1	1	68
NHL Totals	17	0	1	1	68

Redden, Wade b. Lloydminster, Saskatchewan, June 12, 1977

2008–09 NYR	81	3	23	26	51
NHL Totals	919	104	332	436	627

Reddox, Liam b. East York (Toronto), Ontario, January 27, 1986

2008–09 EDM	46	5	7	12	10
NHL Totals	47	5	7	12	10

Regehr, Robyn b. Recife, Brazil, April 19, 1980

2008–09 CAL	75	0	8	8	73
NHL Totals	666	25	104	129	664

Regier, Steve b. Edmonton, Alberta, August 31, 1984

2008–09 STL	8	3	1	4	4
NHL Totals	26	3	1	4	8

Regin, Peter b. Herning, Denmark, April 16, 1986

2008–09 OTT	11	1	1	2	2
NHL Totals	11	1	1	2	2

Reinprecht, Steve b. Edmonton, Alberta, May 7, 1976

2008–09 PHO	73	14	27	41	20
NHL Totals	552	120	214	334	162

Reitz, Eric b. Detroit, Michigan, July 29, 1982

2008–09 MIN/NYR	42	1	1	2	65
NHL Totals	48	1	1	2	69

• traded January 29, 2009, by Minnesota to NY Rangers for Dan Fritsche

Repik, Michal b. Vlasim, Czechoslovakia (Czech Republic), December 31, 1988

2008–09 FLO	5	2	0	2	2
NHL Totals	5	2	0	2	2

Ribeiro, Mike b. Montreal, Quebec, February 10, 1980

2008–09 DAL	82	22	56	78	52
NHL Totals	515	117	256	373	212

Richards, Brad b. Murray Harbour, Prince Edward Island, May 2, 1980

2008–09 DAL	56	16	32	48	6
NHL Totals	620	168	380	548	139

Richards, Mike b. Kenora, Ontario, February 11, 1985

2008–09 PHI	79	30	50	80	63
NHL Totals	290	79	142	221	256

Richardson, Brad b. Belleville, Ontario, February 4, 1985

2008–09 LA	31	0	5	5	11
NHL Totals	167	19	26	45	59

Richardson, Luke b. Ottawa, Ontario, March 26, 1969

2008–09 OTT	2	0	0	0	2
NHL Totals	1,417	35	166	201	2,055

Rinne, Pekka b. Kempele, Finland, November 3, 1982

2008–09 NAS	52	29–15–4–0	2,999	119	7	2.38
NHL Totals	55	30–16–4–0	3,091	123	7	2.39

Rissmiller, Pat b. Belmont, Massachusetts, October 26, 1978

2008–09 NYR	2	0	0	0	0
NHL Totals	182	18	27	45	60

Rivet, Craig b. North Bay, Ontario, September 13, 1974

2008–09 BUF	64	2	22	24	125
NHL Totals	808	47	171	218	1,036

Roberts, Gary b. North York (Toronto), Ontario, May 23, 1966

2008–09 TB	30	4	3	7	27
NHL Totals	1,224	438	472	910	2,560

Robidas, Stephane b. Sherbrooke, Quebec, March 3, 1977

2008–09 DAL	72	3	23	26	76
NHL Totals	561	30	105	135	418

Rodney, Bryan b. London, Ontario, April 22, 1984

2008–09 CAR	8	0	2	2	2
NHL Totals	8	0	2	2	2

Roenick, Jeremy b. Boston, Massachusetts, January 17, 1970

2008–09 SJ	42	4	9	13	24
NHL Totals	1,363	513	703	1,216	1,463

Roloson, Dwayne b. Simcoe, Ontario, October 12, 1969

2008–09 EDM	63	28–24–9–0	3,596	166	1	2.77
NHL Totals	462	167–198–25–42	26,101	1,141	23	2.62

Rolston, Brian b. Flint, Michigan, February 21, 1973

2008–09 NJ	64	15	17	32	30
NHL Totals	1,041	301	365	666	402

Rome, Aaron b. Nesbitt, Manitoba, September 27, 1983

2008–09 CBJ	8	0	1	1	0
NHL Totals	26	1	2	3	33

Ross, Jared b. Huntsville, Alabama, September 18, 1982

2008–09 PHI	10	0	0	0	2
NHL Totals	10	0	0	0	2

Roy, Andre b. Port Chester, New York, February 8, 1975

2008–09 CAL	44	3	0	3	83
NHL Totals	515	35	33	68	1,169

Roy, Derek b. Ottawa, Ontario, May 4, 1983

2008–09 BUF	82	28	42	70	38
NHL Totals	354	108	171	279	213

Rozsival, Michal b. Vlasim, Czechoslovakia (Czech Republic),
   September 3, 1978

2008–09 NYR	76	8	22	30	52
NHL Totals	555	54	149	203	435

Rupp, Mike b. Cleveland, Ohio, January 13, 1980

2008–09 NJ	72	3	6	9	136
NHL Totals	335	27	26	53	412

Russell, Kris b. Caroline, Alberta, May 2, 1987

2008–09 CBJ	66	2	19	21	28
NHL Totals	133	4	27	31	42

Ruutu, Jarkko b. Vantaa, Finland, August 23, 1975

2008–09 OTT	78	7	14	21	144
NHL Totals	497	43	61	104	860

Ruutu, Tuomo b. Vantaa, Finland, February 16, 1983

2008–09 CAR	79	26	28	54	79
NHL Totals	324	78	95	173	354

Ryan, Bobby b. Cherry Hill, New Jersey, March 17, 1987

2008–09 ANA	64	31	26	57	33
NHL Totals	87	36	31	67	39

Ryan, Michael b. Boston, Massachusetts, May 16, 1980

2008–09 CAR	18	0	2	2	2
NHL Totals	83	7	8	15	34

Ryder, Michael b. St. John's, Newfoundland, March 31, 1980

2008–09 BOS	74	27	26	53	26
NHL Totals	388	126	134	260	182

Rypien, Rick b. Coleman, Alberta, May 16, 1984

2008–09 VAN	12	3	0	3	19
NHL Totals	41	5	2	7	69

Sabourin, Dany b. Val d'Or, Quebec, September 2, 1980

2008–09 PIT	19	6–8–2–0	989	47	0	2.85
NHL Totals	57	18–25–4–0	2,899	139	2	2.87

Sakic, Joe b. Burnaby, British Columbia, July 7, 1969

2008–09 COL	15	2	10	12	6
NHL Totals	1,378	625	1,016	1,641	614

Salcido, Brian b. Los Angeles, California, April 14, 1985

2008–09 ANA	2	0	1	1	0
NHL Totals	2	0	1	1	0

Salei, Ruslan b. Minsk, Soviet Union (Belarus), November 2, 1974

2008–09 COL	70	4	17	21	72
NHL Totals	828	42	146	188	1,007

Salmela, Anssi b. Tampere, Finland, August 13, 1984

2008–09 NJ/ATL	26	1	5	6	8
NHL Totals	26	1	5	6	8

• traded March 2, 2009, by New Jersey to Atlanta for Niclas Havelid and Myles Stoesz

Salo, Sami b. Turku, Finland, September 2, 1974

2008–09 VAN	60	5	20	25	26
NHL Totals	597	72	173	245	210

Salvador, Bryce b. Brandon, Manitoba, February 11, 1976

2008–09 NJ	76	3	13	16	78
NHL Totals	531	19	60	79	502

Samsonov, Sergei b. Moscow, Soviet Union (Russia), October 27, 1978

2008–09 CAR	81	16	32	48	28
NHL Totals	738	208	294	502	163

Samuelsson, Mikael b. Mariefred, Sweden, December 23, 1976

2008–09 DET	81	19	21	40	50
NHL Totals	466	86	122	208	244

Sanford, Curtis b. Owen Sound, Ontario, October 5, 1979

2008–09 VAN	19	7–8–0–0	972	42	1	2.59
NHL Totals	108	37–37–11–0	5,370	247	5	2.76

Santorelli, Mike   b. Vancouver, British Columbia, December 14, 1985

2008–09 NAS	7	0	0	0	2
NHL Totals	7	0	0	0	2

Sarich, Cory   b. Saskatoon, Saskatchewan, August 16, 1978

2008–09 CAL	76	2	18	20	112
NHL Totals	692	14	102	116	836

Satan, Miroslav   b. Topolcany, Czechoslovakia (Slovakia), October 22, 1974

2008–09 PIT	65	17	19	36	36
NHL Totals	1,012	354	367	721	452

Sauer, Kurt   b. St. Cloud, Minnesota, January 16, 1981

2008–09 PHO	68	1	6	7	36
NHL Totals	356	5	28	33	250

Sauer, Mike   b. St. Cloud, Minnesota, August 7, 1987

2008–09 NYR	3	0	0	0	0
NHL Totals	3	0	0	0	0

Savard, Marc   b. Ottawa, Ontario, July 17, 1977

2008–09 BOS	82	25	63	88	70
NHL Totals	741	195	468	663	694

Sawada, Raymond   b. Richmond, British Columbia, February 19, 1985

2008–09 DAL	5	1	0	1	0
NHL Totals	5	1	0	1	0

Sbisa, Luca   b. Ozieri, Italy, January 30, 1990

2008–09 PHI	39	0	7	7	36
NHL Totals	39	0	7	7	36

Schenn, Luke   b. Saskatoon, Saskatchewan, November 2, 1989

2008–09 TOR	70	2	12	14	71
NHL Totals	70	2	12	14	71

Schlemko, David   b. Edmonton, Alberta, May 7, 1987

2008–09 PHO	3	0	1	1	0
NHL Totals	3	0	1	1	0

Schneider, Cory   b. Marblehead, Massachusetts, March 18, 1986

2008–09 VAN	8	2–4–1–0	355	20	0	3.38
NHL Totals	8	2–4–1–0	355	20	0	3.39

Schneider, Mathieu   b. New York, New York, June 12, 1969

2008–09 ATL/MON	67	9	23	32	64
NHL Totals	1,264	221	513	734	1,229

• traded February 16, 2009, by Atlanta to Montreal for a 2nd-round draft
  choice in 2009 and a 3rd-round draft choice in 2010

Schremp, Rob   b. Syracuse, New York, July 1, 1986

2008–09 EDM	4	0	3	3	2
NHL Totals	7	0	3	3	2

Schubert, Christoph   b. Munich, West Germany (Germany),
  February 5, 1982

2008–09 OTT	50	3	3	6	26
NHL Totals	268	23	42	65	194

Schultz, Jeff   b. Calgary, Alberta, February 25, 1986

2008–09 WAS	64	1	11	12	21
NHL Totals	174	6	27	33	65

Schultz, Nick   b. Strasbourg, Saskatchewan, August 25, 1982

2008–09 MIN	79	2	9	11	31
NHL Totals	527	21	67	88	211

Schwarz, Marek b. Mlada Boleslav, Czechoslovakia (Czech Republic), April 1, 1986

| 2008–09 STL | 2 | 0–0–0–0 | 15 | 0 | 0 | 0.00 |
| NHL Totals | 6 | 0–2–0–0 | 125 | 9 | 0 | 4.32 |

Scott, John b. St. Catharines, Ontario, September 26, 1982

| 2008–09 MIN | 20 | 0 | 1 | 1 | 21 |
| NHL Totals | 20 | 0 | 1 | 1 | 21 |

Scuderi, Rob b. Syosset, New York, December 30, 1978

| 2008–09 PIT | 81 | 1 | 15 | 16 | 18 |
| NHL Totals | 300 | 3 | 36 | 39 | 112 |

Seabrook, Brent b. Richmond, British Columbia, April 20, 1985

| 2008–09 CHI | 82 | 8 | 18 | 26 | 62 |
| NHL Totals | 314 | 26 | 88 | 114 | 316 |

Sedin, Daniel b. Ornskoldsvik, Sweden, September 26, 1980

| 2008–09 VAN | 82 | 31 | 51 | 82 | 36 |
| NHL Totals | 642 | 179 | 283 | 462 | 264 |

Sedin, Henrik b. Ornskoldsvik, Sweden, September 26, 1980

| 2008–09 VAN | 82 | 22 | 60 | 82 | 48 |
| NHL Totals | 646 | 109 | 351 | 460 | 370 |

Segal, Brandon b. Richmond, British Columbia, July 12, 1983

| 2008–09 TB | 2 | 0 | 0 | 0 | 0 |
| NHL Totals | 2 | 0 | 0 | 0 | 0 |

Seidenberg, Dennis b. Schwenningen, West Germany (Germany), July 18, 1981

| 2008–09 CAR | 70 | 5 | 25 | 30 | 37 |
| NHL Totals | 295 | 14 | 70 | 84 | 113 |

Sekera, Andrej b. Bojnice, Czechoslovakia (Slovakia), June 8, 1986

2008–09 BUF	69	3	16	19	22
NHL Totals	108	5	22	27	40

Selanne, Teemu b. Helsinki, Finland, July 3, 1970

2008–09 ANA	65	27	27	54	36
NHL Totals	1,132	579	633	1,212	505

Semenov, Alexei b. Murmansk, Soviet Union (Russia), April 10, 1981

2008–09 SJ	47	1	7	8	57
NHL Totals	211	7	26	33	249

Semin, Alexander b. Krasjonarsk, Soviet Union (Russia), March 3, 1984

2008–09 WAS	62	34	45	79	77
NHL Totals	254	108	108	216	257

Sestito, Tim b. Rome, New York, August 28, 1984

2008–09 EDM	1	0	0	0	0
NHL Totals	1	0	0	0	0

Setoguchi, Devin b. Taber, Alberta, January 1, 1987

2008–09 SJ	81	31	34	65	25
NHL Totals	125	42	40	82	33

Shanahan, Brendan b. Mimico, Ontario, January 23, 1969

2008–09 NJ	34	6	8	14	29
NHL Totals	1,524	656	698	1,354	2,489

Shannon, Ryan b. Darien, Connecticut, March 2, 1983

2008–09 OTT	35	8	12	20	20
NHL Totals	115	15	29	44	36

Sharp, Patrick b. Thunder Bay, Ontario, December 27, 1981

2008–09 CHI	61	26	18	44	41
NHL Totals	337	101	78	179	273

Shelley, Jody b. Thompson, Manitoba, February 7, 1976

2008–09 SJ	70	2	2	4	116
NHL Totals	481	14	26	40	1,232

Sheppard, James b. Halifax, Nova Scotia, April 25, 1988

2008–09 MIN	82	5	19	24	41
NHL Totals	160	9	34	43	70

Sifers, Jamie b. Stratford, Connecticut, January 18, 1983

2008–09 TOR	23	0	2	2	18
NHL Totals	23	0	2	2	18

Sillinger, Mike b. Regina, Saskatchewan, June 29, 1971

2008–09 NYI	7	2	0	2	0
NHL Totals	1,049	240	308	548	644

Sim, Jon b. New Glasgow, Nova Scotia, September 29, 1977

2008–09 NYI	49	9	6	15	42
NHL Totals	358	61	52	113	248

Simmonds, Wayne b. Scarborough (Toronto), Ontario, August 26, 1988

2008–09 LA	82	9	14	23	73
NHL Totals	82	9	14	23	73

Sjostrom, Fredrik b. Fargelanda, Sweden, May 6, 1983

2008–09 NYR	79	7	6	13	30
NHL Totals	358	41	47	88	164

Skille, Jack b. Madison, Wisconsin, May 19, 1987

2008–09 CHI	8	1	0	1	5
NHL Totals	24	4	2	6	5

Skinner, Brett b. Brandon, Manitoba, June 28, 1983

2008–09 NYI	11	0	0	0	4
NHL Totals	11	0	0	0	4

Skoula, Martin b. Litomerice, Czechoslovakia (Czech Republic), October 28, 1979

2008–09 MIN	81	4	12	16	10
NHL Totals	724	41	144	185	318

Skrastins, Karlis b. Riga, Soviet Union (Latvia), July 9, 1974

2008–09 FLO	80	4	14	18	30
NHL Totals	679	27	88	115	313

Slater, Jim b. Petoskey, Michigan, December 9, 1982

2008–09 ATL	60	8	10	18	52
NHL Totals	274	31	39	70	201

Sloan, Tyler b. Calgary, Alberta, March 15, 1981

2008–09 WAS	26	1	4	5	14
NHL Totals	26	1	4	5	14

Sloane, David b. Ambler, Pennsylvania, April 6, 1985

2008–09 PHI	1	0	0	0	0
NHL Totals	1	0	0	0	0

Smaby, Matt b. Minneapolis, Minnesota, October 14, 1984

2008–09 TB	43	0	4	4	50
NHL Totals	57	0	4	4	62

Smid, Ladislav b. Frydlant, Czechoslovakia (Czech Republic), February 1, 1986

2008–09 EDM	60	0	11	11	57
NHL Totals	202	3	22	25	152

Smith, Jason   b. Calgary, Alberta, November 2, 1973

2008–09 OTT	63	1	0	1	47
NHL Totals	1,008	41	128	169	1,099

Smith, Mike   b. Kingston, Ontario, March 22, 1982

2008–09 TB	41	14–18–9–0	2,471	108	2	2.62
NHL Totals	98	41–41–11–0	5,630	237	8	2.53

Smith, Trevor   b. North Vancouver, British Columbia, February 8, 1985

2008–09 NYI	7	1	0	1	0
NHL Totals	7	1	0	1	0

Smith, Zach   b. Medicine Hat, Alberta, April 5, 1988

2008–09 OTT	1	0	0	0	0
NHL Totals	1	0	0	0	0

Smithson, Jerred   b. Vernon, British Columbia, February 4, 1979

2008–09 NAS	82	4	9	13	49
NHL Totals	323	21	37	58	220

Smolenak, Radek   b. Prague, Czechoslovakia (Czech Republic), December 3, 1986

2008–09 TB	6	0	1	1	10
NHL Totals	6	0	1	1	10

Smyth, Ryan   b. Banff, Alberta, February 21, 1976

2008–09 COL	77	26	33	59	62
NHL Totals	920	310	350	660	733

Sobotka, Vladimir   b. Trebic, Czechoslovakia (Czech Republic), July 2, 1987

2008–09 BOS	25	1	4	5	10
NHL Totals	73	2	10	12	34

Sopel, Brent b. Calgary, Alberta, January 7, 1977

2008–09 CHI	23	1	1	2	8
NHL Totals	515	41	162	203	259

Souray, Sheldon b. Elk Point, Alberta, July 13, 1976

2008–09 EDM	21	23	30	53	98
NHL Totals	613	92	157	249	955

Spacek, Jaroslav b. Rokycany, Czechoslovakia (Czech Republic), February 11, 1974

2008–09 BUF	80	8	37	45	38
NHL Totals	701	73	230	303	515

Spezza, Jason b. Mississauga, Ontario, June 13, 1983

2008–09 OTT	82	32	41	73	79
NHL Totals	404	148	270	418	302

Sprukts, Janis b. Riga, Soviet Union (Latvia), January 31, 1982

2008–09 FLO	1	0	0	0	0
NHL Totals	14	1	2	3	2

Staal, Eric b. Thunder Bay, Ontario, October 29, 1984

2008–09 CAR	82	40	35	75	50
NHL Totals	409	164	194	358	289

Staal, Jordan b. Thunder Bay, Ontario, September 10, 1988

2008–09 PIT	82	22	27	49	37
NHL Totals	245	63	56	119	116

Staal, Marc b. Thunder Bay, Ontario, January 13, 1987

2008–09 NYR	82	3	12	15	64
NHL Totals	162	5	20	25	106

Stafford, Drew b. Milwaukee, Wisconsin, October 30, 1985

2008–09 BUF	79	20	25	45	29
NHL Totals	184	49	61	110	113

Stafford, Garrett b. Los Angeles, California, January 28, 1980

| 2008–09 DAL | 3 | 0 | 2 | 2 | 0 |
| NHL Totals | 5 | 0 | 2 | 2 | 0 |

Staios, Steve b. Hamilton, Ontario, July 28, 1973

| 2008–09 EDM | 80 | 2 | 12 | 14 | 92 |
| NHL Totals | 839 | 52 | 140 | 192 | 1,170 |

Stajan, Matt b. Mississauga, Ontario, December 19, 1983

| 2008–09 TOR | 76 | 15 | 40 | 55 | 54 |
| NHL Totals | 390 | 71 | 111 | 182 | 217 |

Stamkos, Steve b. Markham, Ontario, February 7, 1960

| 2008–09 TB | 79 | 23 | 23 | 46 | 39 |
| NHL Totals | 79 | 23 | 23 | 46 | 39 |

Stapleton, Tim b. LaGrange, Illinois, July 9, 1982

| 2008–09 TOR | 4 | 1 | 0 | 1 | 0 |
| NHL Totals | 4 | 1 | 0 | 1 | 0 |

Stastny, Paul b. Quebec City, Quebec, December 27, 1985

| 2008–09 COL | 45 | 11 | 25 | 36 | 22 |
| NHL Totals | 193 | 63 | 122 | 185 | 88 |

Stastny, Yan b. Quebec City, Quebec, September 30, 1982

| 2008–09 STL | 34 | 3 | 4 | 7 | 20 |
| NHL Totals | 87 | 5 | 10 | 15 | 58 |

Staubitz, Brad b. Brights Grove, Ontario, July 28, 1984

| 2008–09 SJ | 35 | 1 | 2 | 3 | 76 |
| NHL Totals | 35 | 1 | 2 | 3 | 76 |

Steckel, David b. Milwaukee, Wisconsin, March 15, 1982

| 2008–09 WAS | 76 | 8 | 11 | 19 | 34 |
| NHL Totals | 155 | 13 | 18 | 31 | 70 |

Steen, Alexander b. Winnipeg, Manitoba, March 1, 1984

2008–09 TOR/STL	81	8	20	28	30
NHL Totals	314	56	94	150	130

• traded November 24, 2008, by Toronto to St. Louis with Carlo Colaiacovo for Lee Stempniak

Stempniak, Lee b. Buffalo, New York, February 4, 1983

2008–09 STL/TOR	75	14	30	44	33
NHL Totals	294	68	93	161	128

• traded November 24, 2008, by St. Louis to Toronto for Alexander Steen and Carlo Colaiacovo

Stephan, Tobias b. Zurich, Switzerland, January 21, 1984

2008–09 DAL	10	1–3–1–0	437	27	0	3.70
NHL Totals	11	1–3–2–0	498	29	0	3.49

Sterling, Brett b. Los Angeles, California, April 24, 1984

2008–09 ATL	6	1	0	1	2
NHL Totals	19	2	2	4	16

Stewart, Anthony b. LaSalle, Quebec, January 5, 1985

2008–09 FLO	59	2	5	7	34
NHL Totals	105	4	8	12	38

Stewart, Chris b. Toronto, Ontario, October 30, 1987

2008–09 COL	53	11	8	19	54
NHL Totals	53	11	8	19	54

Stewart, Gregory b. Kitchener, Ontario, May 21, 1986

2008–09 MON	20	0	1	1	32
NHL Totals	21	0	1	1	37

Stillman, Cory b. Peterborough, Ontario, December 20, 1973

2008–09 FLO	63	17	32	49	37
NHL Totals	902	251	400	651	443

St. Louis, Martin b. Laval, Quebec, June 18, 1975

2008–09 TB	82	30	50	80	14
NHL Totals	690	238	347	585	226

Stoll, Jarret b. Melville, Saskatchewan, June 25, 1982

2008–09 LA	74	18	23	41	68
NHL Totals	360	77	129	206	306

Stone, Ryan b. Calgary, Alberta, March 20, 1985

2008–09 PIT	2	0	0	0	2
NHL Totals	8	0	1	1	7

Stortini, Zachery b. Elliot Lake, Ontario, September 11, 1985

2008–09 EDM	52	6	5	11	181
NHL Totals	147	10	14	24	487

St. Pierre, Martin b. Ottawa, Ontario, August 11, 1983

2008–09 BOS	14	2	2	4	4
NHL Totals	35	3	5	8	12

Strachan, Tyson b. Melfort, Saskatchewan, October 30, 1984

2008–09 STL	30	0	3	3	39
NHL Totals	30	0	3	3	39

Stralman, Anton b. Tibro, Sweden, August 1, 1986

2008–09 TOR	38	1	12	13	20
NHL Totals	88	4	18	22	38

Streit, Mark b. Englisberg, Switzerland, December 11, 1977

2008–09 NYI	74	16	40	56	62
NHL Totals	279	41	124	165	132

Strudwick, Jason b. Edmonton, Alberta, July 17, 1975

2008–09 EDM	71	2	7	9	60
NHL Totals	559	13	34	47	738

Stuart, Brad b. Rocky Mountain House, Alberta, November 6, 1979

2008–09 DET	67	2	13	15	26
NHL Totals	646	61	183	244	398

Stuart, Colin b. Rochester, Minnesota, July 8, 1982

2008–09 ATL	33	5	3	8	18
NHL Totals	51	8	5	13	24

Stuart, Mark b. Rochester, Minnesota, April 27, 1984

2008–09 BOS	82	5	12	17	76
NHL Totals	196	10	18	28	181

Sturm, Marco b. Dingolfing, West Germany (Germany), September 8, 1978

2008–09 BOS	19	7	6	13	8
NHL Totals	779	212	217	429	368

Sullivan Steve b. Timmins, Ontario, July 6, 1974

2008–09 NAS	41	11	21	32	30
NHL Totals	764	239	370	609	480

Sulzer, Alexander b. Kaufbeuren, West Germany (Germany), May 30, 1984

2008–09 NAS	2	0	0	0	0
NHL Totals	2	0	0	0	0

Sundin, Mats b. Bromma, Sweden, February 13, 1971

2008–09 VAN	41	9	19	28	28
NHL Totals	1,346	564	785	1,349	1,093

Suter, Ryan   b. Madison, Wisconsin, January 21, 1985

2008–09 NAS	82	7	38	45	73
NHL Totals	311	23	93	116	264

Sutherby, Brian   b. Edmonton, Alberta, March 1, 1982

2008–09 ANA/DAL	59	8	7	15	71
NHL Totals	363	34	43	77	409

• traded December 14, 2008, by Anaheim to Dallas for David McIntyre and a conditional 6th-round draft choice in 2010

Sutter, Brandon   b. Huntington, New York, February 14, 1989

2008–09 CAR	50	1	5	6	16
NHL Totals	50	1	5	6	16

Sutter, Brett   b. Viking, Alberta, June 2, 1987

2008–09 CAL	4	1	0	1	2
NHL Totals	4	1	0	1	2

Sutton, Andy   b. Kingston, Ontario, March 10, 1975

2008–09 NYI	23	2	8	10	40
NHL Totals	513	30	93	123	911

Svatos, Marek   b. Kosice, Czechoslovakia (Slovakia), July 17, 1982

2008–09 COL	69	14	20	34	34
NHL Totals	262	89	64	153	172

Sydor, Darryl   b. Edmonton, Alberta, May 13, 1972

2008–09 PIT/DAL	73	3	12	15	18
NHL Totals	1,244	98	401	499	740

• traded November 16, 2008, by Pittsburgh to Dallas for Philippe Boucher

Sykora, Petr   b. Plzen, Czechoslovakia (Czech Republic), November 19, 1976

2008–09 PIT	76	25	21	46	36
NHL Totals	921	300	374	674	407

Syvret, Danny b. Millgrove, Ontario, June 13, 1985

2008–09 PHI	2	0	0	0	0
NHL Totals	28	0	1	1	12

Szczechura, Paul b. Brantford, Ontario, November 30, 1985

2008–09 TB	31	4	5	9	12
NHL Totals	31	4	5	9	12

Taffe, Jeff b. Hastings, Minnesota, February 19, 1981

2008–09 PIT	8	0	2	2	2
NHL Totals	153	20	22	42	36

Talbot, Maxime b. Lemoyne, Quebec, February 11, 1984

2008–09 PIT	75	12	10	22	63
NHL Totals	261	42	38	80	228

Tallackson, Barry b. Grafton, North Dakota, April 14, 1983

2008–09 NJ	4	0	0	0	0
NHL Totals	20	1	1	2	2

Tallinder, Henrik b. Stockholm, Sweden, January 10, 1979

2008–09 BUF	66	1	11	12	36
NHL Totals	386	16	72	88	246

Tambellini, Jeff b. Calgary, Alberta, April 13, 1984

2008–09 NYI	65	7	8	15	32
NHL Totals	144	11	21	32	56

Tanguay, Alex b. Ste. Justine, Quebec, November 21, 1979

2008–09 MON	50	16	25	41	34
NHL Totals	659	193	387	580	345

Tarnasky, Nick b. Rocky Mountain House, Alberta, November 25, 1984

2008–09 NAS/FLO	45	1	6	7	50	
NHL Totals	214	12	15	27	212	

• traded November 27, 2008, by Nashville to Florida for Wade Belak

Tellqvist, Mikael b. Sundbyberg, Sweden, September 19, 1979

2008–09 PHO/BUF	21	9–6–1–0	1,027	47	0	2.74
NHL Totals	113	45–41–8–2	6,033	303	6	3.01

• traded March 4, 2009, by Phoenix to Buffalo for a 4th-round draft choice in 2010

Theodore, Jose b. Laval, Quebec, September 13, 1976

2008–09 WAS	57	32–17–5–0	3,286	157	2	2.87
NHL Totals	501	215–214–15–30	28,411	1,266	28	2.67

Thomas, Bill b. Pittsburgh, Pennsylvania, June 20, 1983

2008–09 PIT	16	2	1	3	2
NHL Totals	56	11	9	20	12

Thomas, Tim b. Flint, Michigan, April 15, 1974

2008–09 BOS	54	36–11–7–0	3,258	114	5	2.10
NHL Totals	219	109–73–27–0	12,626	551	12	2.62

Thompson, Nate b. Anchorage, Alaska, October 5, 1984

2008–09 NYI	43	2	2	4	49
NHL Totals	47	2	2	4	49

Thorburn, Chris b. Sault Ste. Marie, Ontario, June 3, 1983

2008–09 ATL	82	7	8	15	104
NHL Totals	196	15	24	39	272

Thornton, Joe b. London, Ontario, July 2, 1979

2008–09 SJ	82	25	61	86	56
NHL Totals	836	265	577	842	831

Thornton, Shawn b. Oshawa, Ontario, July 23, 1977

2008–09 BOS	79	6	5	11	123
NHL Totals	216	14	16	30	355

Tikhonov, Viktor b. Riga, Soviet Union (Latvia), May 12, 1988

2008–09 PHO	61	8	8	16	20
NHL Totals	61	8	8	16	20

Timonen, Kimmo b. Kuopio, Finland, March 18, 1975

2008–09 PHI	77	3	40	43	54
NHL Totals	730	90	298	388	452

Tjarnqvist, Daniel b. Umea, Sweden, October 14, 1976

2008–09 COL	37	2	2	4	8
NHL Totals	352	18	72	90	130

Tkachuk, Keith b. Melrose, Massachusetts, March 28, 1972

2008–09 STL	79	25	24	49	61
NHL Totals	1,134	525	508	1,033	2,163

Tlusty, Jiri b. Slany, Czechoslovakia (Czech Republic), March 16, 1988

2008–09 TOR	14	0	4	4	0
NHL Totals	72	10	10	20	14

Toews, Jonathan b. Winnipeg, Manitoba, April 29, 1988

2008–09 CHI	82	34	35	69	51
NHL Totals	146	58	65	123	95

Tollefsen, Ole-Kristian b. Oslo, Norway, March 29, 1984

2008–09 CBJ	19	0	1	1	37
NHL Totals	145	4	6	10	273

Tootoo, Jordin b. Churchill, Manitoba, February 2, 1983

2008–09 NAS	72	4	12	16	124
NHL Totals	304	26	35	61	532

Tordjman, Josh   b. Montreal, Quebec, January 11, 1985

2008–09 PHO	2	0–2–0–0	117	8	0	4.07
NHL Totals	2	0–2–0–0	117	8	0	4.07

Torres, Raffi   b. Toronto, Ontario, October 8, 1981

2008–09 CBJ	51	12	8	20	23
NHL Totals	358	79	67	146	278

Toskala, Vesa   b. Tampere, Finland, May 20, 1977

2008–09 TOR	53	22–17–11–0	3,056	166	1	3.26
NHL Totals	234	120–70–22–5	13,162	586	12	2.67

Tucker, Darcy   b. Castor, Alberta, March 15, 1975

2008–09 COL	63	8	8	16	67
NHL Totals	876	205	247	452	1,363

Turco, Marty   b. Sault Ste. Marie, Ontario, August 13, 1975

2008–09 DAL	74	33–31–10–0	4,327	203	3	2.81
NHL Totals	456	240–134–26–26	25,976	978	36	2.26

Turris, Kyle   b. New Westminster, British Columbia, August 14, 1989

2008–09 PHO	63	8	12	20	21
NHL Totals	66	8	13	21	23

Tyutin, Fedor   b. Izhevsk, Soviet Union (Russia), July 19, 1983

2008–09 CBJ	82	9	25	34	81
NHL Totals	332	24	76	100	240

Umberger, R.J.   b. Pittsburgh, Pennsylvania, May 3, 1982

2008–09 CBJ	82	26	20	46	53
NHL Totals	310	75	87	162	131

Upshall, Scottie b. Fort McMurray, Alberta, October 7, 1983

2008–09 PHI/PHO	74	15	19	34	89
NHL Totals	230	46	60	106	223

• traded March 4, 2009, by Philadelphia to Phoenix with a 2nd-round draft choice in 2011 for Daniel Carcillo

Vaananen, Ossi b. Vantaa, Finland, August 18, 1980

2008–09 PHI/VAN	49	1	10	11	22
NHL Totals	479	13	55	68	482

• claimed off waivers by Vancouver from Philadelphia on February 27, 2009

Valabik, Boris b. Nitra, Czechoslovakia (Slovakia), February 14, 1986

2008–09 ATL	50	0	5	5	132
NHL Totals	57	0	5	5	174

Valiquette, Stephen b. Etobicoke (Toronto), Ontario, August 20, 1977

2008–09 NYR	15	5–5–2–0	823	39	1	2.84
NHL Totals	40	14–11–5–0	1,949	84	3	2.58

Van der Gulik, David b. Abbotsford, British Columbia, April 20, 1983

2008–09 CAL	6	0	2	2	0
NHL Totals	6	0	2	2	0

Vandermeer, Jim b. Caroline, Alberta, February 21, 1980

2008–09 CAL	45	1	6	7	108
NHL Totals	312	18	57	75	497

Vanek, Thomas b. Vienna, Austria, January 19, 1984

2008–09 BUF	73	40	24	64	44
NHL Totals	318	144	116	260	220

Van Ryn, Mike b. London, Ontario, May 14, 1979

2008–09 TOR	27	3	8	11	14
NHL Totals	353	30	99	129	260

Varlamov, Simeon b. Kuybyshev, Soviet Union (Russia), April 27, 1988

2008–09 WAS	6	4–0–1–0	328	13	0	2.37
NHL Totals	6	4–0–1–0	328	13	0	2.37

Veilleux, Stephane b. Beauceville, Quebec, November 16, 1981

2008–09 MIN	81	13	10	23	40
NHL Totals	361	43	47	90	254

Vermette, Antoine b. St. Agapit, Quebec, July 20, 1982

2008–09 OTT/CBJ	79	16	25	41	50
NHL Totals	376	87	93	180	213

• traded March 4, 2009, by Ottawa to Columbus for Pascal Leclaire and a 2nd-round draft choice in 2009

Vernace, Mike b. Toronto, Ontario, May 26, 1986

2008–09 COL	12	0	0	0	8
NHL Totals	12	0	0	0	8

Vertseeg, Kris b. Lethbridge, Alberta, May 13, 1986

2008–09 CHI	78	22	31	53	55
NHL Totals	91	24	33	57	61

Vesce, Ryan b. Lloyd Harbor, New York, April 7, 1982

2008–09 SJ	10	0	0	0	4
NHL Totals	10	0	0	0	4

Vishnevskiy, Ivan b. Barnaul, Soviet Union (Russia), February 18, 1988

2008–09 DAL	3	0	2	2	2
NHL Totals	3	0	2	2	2

Visnovsky, Lubomir b. Topolcany, Czechoslovakia (Slovakia), August 11, 1976

2008–09 EDM	50	8	23	31	30
NHL Totals	549	78	232	310	244

Vlasic, Marc-Edouard b. Montreal, Quebec, March 30, 1987

2008–09 SJ	82	6	30	36	42	
NHL Totals	245	11	65	76	84	

Vokoun, Tomas b. Karlovy Vary, Czechoslovakia (Czech Republic), July 2, 1976

2008–09 FLO	59	26–23–6–0	3,324	138	6	2.49
NHL Totals	512	217–211–25–35	29,163	1,244	31	2.56

Volchenkov, Anton b. Moscow, Soviet Union (Russia), February 25, 1982

2008–09 OTT	68	2	8	10	36
NHL Totals	364	12	68	80	259

Voracek, Jakub b. Kladno, Czechoslovakia (Czech Republic), August 15, 1989

2008–09 CBJ	80	9	29	38	44
NHL Totals	80	9	29	38	44

Voros, Aaron b. Vancouver, British Columbia, July 2, 1981

2008–09 NYR	54	8	8	16	122
NHL Totals	109	15	15	30	263

Vrana, Petr b. Sternberk, Czechoslovakia (Czech Republic), March 29, 1985

2008–09 NJ	16	1	0	1	2
NHL Totals	16	1	0	1	2

Vrbata, Radim b. Mlada Boleslav, Czechoslovakia (Czech Republic), June 13, 1981

2008–09 TB	18	3	3	6	8
NHL Totals	440	105	127	232	126

Wagner, Steve b. Grand Rapids, Minnesota, March 6, 1984

2008–09 STL	22	2	2	4	18
NHL Totals	46	4	8	12	26

Walker, Matt b. Beaverlodge, Alberta, April 7, 1980

2008–09 CHI	65	1	13	14	79
NHL Totals	240	2	23	25	354

Walker, Scott b. Cambridge, Ontario, July 19, 1973

2008–09 CAR	41	5	10	15	39
NHL Totals	787	146	243	389	1,130

Wallace, Tim b. Anchorage, Alaska, August 6, 1984

2008–09 PIT	16	0	2	2	7
NHL Totals	16	0	2	2	7

Wallin, Niclas b. Boden, Sweden, February 20, 1975

2008–09 CAR	64	2	8	10	42
NHL Totals	470	18	46	64	365

Walter, Ben b. Beaconsfield, Ontario, May 11, 1984

2008–09 NYI	4	0	0	0	0
NHL Totals	22	1	0	1	4

Wandell, Tom b. Sodertalje, Sweden, January 29, 1987

2008–09 DAL	14	1	2	3	4
NHL Totals	14	1	2	3	4

Ward, Aaron b. Windsor, Ontario, January 17, 1973

2008–09 BOS	65	3	7	10	44
NHL Totals	762	43	95	138	674

Ward, Cam b. Sherwood Park, Alberta, February 29, 1984

2008–09 CAR	68	39–23–5–0	3,928	160	6	2.44
NHL Totals	225	120–77–18–0	12,764	598	12	2.81

Ward, Jason b. Chapleau, Ontario, January 16, 1979

2008–09 TB	1	0	0	0	2
NHL Totals	336	36	45	81	171

Ward, Joel b. Toronto, Ontario, December 2, 1980

2008–09 NAS	79	17	18	35	29
NHL Totals	90	17	19	36	29

Weaver, Mike b. Bramalea, Ontario, May 2, 1978

2008–09 STL	58	0	7	7	12
NHL Totals	262	3	29	32	105

Weber, Mike b. Pittsburgh, Pennsylvania, December 16, 1987

2008–09 BUF	7	0	0	0	19
NHL Totals	23	0	3	3	33

Weber, Shea b. Sicamous, British Columbia, August 14, 1985

2008–09 NAS	81	23	30	53	80
NHL Totals	242	48	75	123	231

Weber, Yannick b. Morges, Switzerland, September 23, 1988

2008–09 MON	3	0	0	0	2
NHL Totals	3	0	0	0	2

Weekes, Kevin b. Toronto, Ontario, April 4, 1975

2008–09 NJ	16	7–5–0–0	794	32	0	2.42
NHL Totals	348	105–163–6–33	18,837	903	19	2.88

Weight, Doug b. Warren, Michigan, January 21, 1971

2008–09 NYI	53	10	28	38	55
NHL Totals	1,184	275	732	1,007	952

Weiss, Stephen b. Toronto, Ontario, April 3, 1983

2008–09 FLO	78	14	47	61	22
NHL Totals	401	75	149	224	139

Welch, Noah b. Brighton, Massachusetts, August 26, 1982

2008–09 FLO/TB	40	1	1	2	25
NHL Totals	73	4	5	9	58

• traded March 4, 2009, by Florida to Tampa Bay with a future 3rd-round draft choice for Steve Eminger

Weller, Craig b. Calgary, Alberta, January 17, 1981

2008–09 MIN	36	1	2	3	47
NHL Totals	95	4	10	14	127

Wellwood, Kyle b. Windsor, Ontario, May 16, 1983

2008–09 VAN	74	18	9	27	4
NHL Totals	263	49	86	135	18

Westgarth, Kevin b. Amherstburg, Ontario, February 7, 1984

2008–09 LA	9	0	0	0	9
NHL Totals	9	0	0	0	9

Wheeler, Blake b. Robbinsdale, Minnesota, August 31, 1986

2008–09 BOS	81	21	24	45	46
NHL Totals	81	21	24	45	46

White, Colin b. New Glasgow, Nova Scotia, December 12, 1977

2008–09 NJ	71	1	17	18	46
NHL Totals	593	18	89	107	754

White, Ian b. Winnipeg, Manitoba, June 4, 1984

2008–09 TOR	71	10	16	26	57
NHL Totals	240	19	60	79	151

White, Todd b. Kanata, Ontario, May 21, 1975

2008–09 ATL	82	22	51	73	24
NHL Totals	570	133	220	353	202

Whitfield, Trent b. Alameda, Saskatchewan, June 17, 1977

2008–09 STL	3	0	1	1	0
NHL Totals	177	11	17	28	97

Whitney, Ray b. Fort Saskatchewan, Alberta, May 8, 1972

2008–09 CAR	82	24	53	77	32
NHL Totals	992	303	508	811	369

Whitney, Ryan b. Boston, Massachusetts, February 19, 1983

2008–09 PIT/ANA	48	2	21	23	28
NHL Totals	273	34	126	160	235

• traded February 26, 2009, by Pittsburgh to Anaheim for Chris Kunitz and
Eric Tangradi

Wideman, Dennis b. Kitchener, Ontario, March 20, 1983

2008–09 BOS	79	13	37	50	34
NHL Totals	302	40	95	135	258

Williams, Jason b. London, Ontario, August 11, 1980

2008–09 ATL/CBJ	80	19	28	47	24
NHL Totals	376	85	120	205	139

• traded January 14, 2009, by Atlanta to Columbus for Clay Wilson and a
6th-round draft choice in 2009

Williams, Jeremy b. Regina, Saskatchewan, January 26, 1984

2008–09 TOR	11	5	2	7	2
NHL Totals	31	9	2	11	6

Williams, Justin b. Cobourg, Ontario, October 4, 1981

2008–09 CAR/LA	44	4	10	14	17
NHL Totals	503	125	195	320	333

• traded March 4, 2009, from Carolina to Los Angeles for Patrick O'Sullivan and a 2nd-round draft choice in 2009

Willsie, Brian b. London, Ontario, March 16, 1978

2008–09 COL	42	1	3	4	14
NHL Totals	376	52	56	108	217

Wilson, Clay b. Sturgeon Lake, Minnesota, April 5, 1983

2008–09 CBJ/ATL	7	0	1	1	0
NHL Totals	14	1	2	3	2

• traded January 14, 2009, from Columbus to Atlanta with a 6th-round draft choice in 2009, for Jason Williams

Wilson, Landon b. St. Louis, Missouri, March 13, 1975

2008–09 DAL	27	2	6	8	21
NHL Totals	375	53	66	119	352

Winchester, Brad b. Madison, Wisconsin, March 1, 1981

2008–09 STL	64	13	8	21	89
NHL Totals	183	18	16	34	242

Winchester, Jesse b. Long Sault, Ontario, October 4, 1983

2008–09 OTT	76	3	15	18	33
NHL Totals	77	3	15	18	35

Winnik, Daniel b. Toronto, Ontario, March 6, 1985

2008–09 PHO	49	3	4	7	63
NHL Totals	128	14	19	33	88

Wishart, Ty b. Belleville, Ontario, May 19, 1988

2008–09 TB	5	0	1	1	0
NHL Totals	5	0	1	1	0

Wisniewski, James b. Canton, Michigan, February 21, 1984

2008–09 CHI/ANA	48	3	21	24	30
NHL Totals	185	14	53	67	208

• traded March 4, 2009, by Chicago to Anaheim with Petri Kontiola for Samuel Pahlsson, Logan Stephenson, and a conditional 4th-round draft choice in 2009

Witt, Brendan b. Humboldt, Saskatchewan, February 20, 1975

2008–09 NYI	65	0	9	9	94
NHL Totals	848	23	93	116	1,379

Wolski, Wojtek b. Zabrze, Poland, February 24, 1986

2008–09 COL	78	14	28	42	28
NHL Totals	240	56	90	146	60

Woywitka, Jeff b. Vermilion, Alberta, September 1, 1983

2008–09 STL	65	3	15	18	57
NHL Totals	152	6	29	35	106

Wozniewski, Andy b. Buffalo Grove, Illinois, May 25, 1980

2008–09 STL	1	0	0	0	0
NHL Totals	77	2	10	12	81

Yandle, Keith b. Boston, Massachusetts, September 9, 1986

2008–09 PHO	69	4	26	30	37
NHL Totals	119	9	35	44	59

Yelle, Stephane b. Ottawa, Ontario, May 9, 1974

2008–09 BOS	77	7	11	18	32
NHL Totals	921	92	165	257	458

York, Mike b. Pontiac, Michigan, January 3, 1978

2008–09 CBJ	1	0	0	0	0
NHL Totals	579	127	195	322	135

Zajac, Travis   b. Winnipeg, Manitoba, May 13, 1985

2008–09 NJ	82	20	42	62	29
NHL Totals	244	51	87	138	76

Zanon, Greg   b. Burnaby, British Columbia, June 5, 1980

2008–09 NAS	82	4	7	11	38
NHL Totals	230	7	19	26	100

Zednik, Richard   b. Bystrica, Czechoslovakia (Slovakia),
    January 6, 1976

2008–09 FLO	70	17	16	33	46
NHL Totals	745	200	179	379	563

Zeiler, John   b. Pittsburgh, Pennsylvania, November 21, 1982

2008–09 LA	27	0	1	1	42
NHL Totals	86	1	4	5	87

Zetterberg, Henrik   b. Njurunda, Sweden, October 9, 1980

2008–09 DET	77	31	42	73	36
NHL Totals	432	183	222	405	158

Zherdev, Nikolai   b. Kiev, Soviet Union (Ukraine),
    November 5, 1984

2008–09 NYR	82	23	35	58	39
NHL Totals	365	99	140	239	203

Zidlicky, Marek   b. Most, Czechoslovakia (Czech Republic),
    February 3, 1977

2008–09 MIN	76	12	30	42	76
NHL Totals	383	47	170	217	375

Zigomanis, Mike b. North York (Toronto), Ontario, January 17, 1981

2008–09 PIT	22	2	4	6	27
NHL Totals	189	21	18	39	85

Zubov, Ilja b. Chelyabinsk, Soviet Union (Russia), February 14, 1987

2008–09 OTT	10	0	2	2	0
NHL Totals	11	0	2	2	0

Zubov, Sergei b. Moscow, Soviet Union (Russia), July 22, 1970

2008–09 DAL	10	0	4	4	0
NHL Totals	1,068	152	619	771	337

Zubrus, Dainius b. Eelektrenai, Soviet Union (Lithuania), June 16, 1978

2008–09 NJ	82	15	25	40	69
NHL Totals	853	166	272	438	556

COACHES' REGISTER, 2008–09

(OTL are listed in lost column)

	Games	W	L	T
Anderson, John b. Toronto, Ontario, March 28, 1957				
2008–09 ATL	82	35	41	6
NHL Totals	82	35	41	6
• hired June 20, 2008				
Babcock, Mike b. Manitouwadge, Ontario, April 29, 1963				
2008–09 DET	82	51	21	10
NHL Totals	492	282	139	71
• hired July 14, 2005				
Boudreau, Bruce b. Toronto, Ontario, January 9, 1955				
2008–09 WAS	82	50	24	8
NHL Totals	143	87	41	15
• hired November 22, 2007, replacing Glen Hanlon				
Bylsma, Dan b. Grand Haven, Michigan, September 19, 1970				
2008–09 PIT	25	18	3	4
NHL Totals	25	18	3	4
• hired February 15, 2009				
Carbonneau, Guy b. Sept-Iles, Quebec, March 18, 1960				
2008–09 MON	66	35	24	7
NHL Totals	230	124	83	23
• hired May 5, 2006; fired March 9, 2009				
Carlyle, Randy b. Sudbury, Ontario, April 19, 1956				
2008–09 ANA	82	42	33	7
NHL Totals	328	180	107	41
• hired August 1, 2005				

Clouston, Cory b. Viking, Alberta, September 19, 1969

| 2008–09 OTT | 34 | 19 | 11 | 4 |
| NHL Totals | 34 | 19 | 11 | 4 |

• hired February 2, 2009

Crawford, Marc b. Belleville, Ontario, February 13, 1961

| NHL Totals | 987 | 470 | 361 | 156 |

• hired by Dallas on June 4, 2009

DeBoer, Peter b. Dunnville, Ontario, June 13, 1968

| 2008–09 FLO | 82 | 41 | 30 | 11 |
| NHL Totals | 82 | 41 | 30 | 11 |

• hired June 13, 2008

Gainey, Bob b. Peterborough, Ontario, December 13, 1953

| 2008–09 MON | 16 | 6 | 6 | 4 |
| NHL Totals | 472 | 194 | 211 | 67 |

Gordon, Scott b. Easton, Massachusetts, February 6, 1963

| 2008–09 NYI | 82 | 26 | 47 | 9 |
| NHL Totals | 82 | 26 | 47 | 9 |

• hired August 12, 2008

Granato, Tony b. Downers Grove, Illinois, July 25, 1964

| 2008–09 COL | 82 | 32 | 45 | 5 |
| NHL Totals | 215 | 104 | 78 | 33 |

Gretzky, Wayne b. Brantford, Ontario, January 26, 1961

| 2008–09 PHO | 82 | 36 | 39 | 7 |
| NHL Totals | 328 | 143 | 161 | 24 |

• assumed coaching duties on August 8, 2005

Hartsburg, Craig b. Stratford, Ontario, June 29, 1959

| 2008–09 OTT | 48 | 17 | 24 | 7 |
| NHL Totals | 491 | 201 | 208 | 82 |

• hired June 13, 2008; fired February 2, 2009

Hitchcock, Ken b. Edmonton, Alberta, December 17, 1951

| 2008–09 CBJ | 82 | 41 | 31 | 10 |
| NHL Totals | 983 | 511 | 323 | 149 |

• fired by Philadelphia on October 22, 2006; hired by Columbus on November 21, 2006

Julien, Claude b. Orleans, Ontario, April 23, 1960

| 2008–09 BOS | 82 | 53 | 19 | 10 |
| NHL Totals | 402 | 213 | 134 | 55 |

• hired June 13, 2006; fired April 2, 2007

Keenan, Mike b. Bowmanville, Ontario, October 21, 1949

| 2008–09 CAL | 82 | 46 | 30 | 6 |
| NHL Totals | 1,386 | 672 | 531 | 183 |

• hired June 14, 2007, to replace Jim Playfair; fired May 22, 2009

Laviolette, Peter b. Norwood, Massachusetts, December 7, 1964

| 2008–09 CAR | 25 | 12 | 11 | 2 |
| NHL Totals | 487 | 244 | 184 | 59 |

• hired December 15, 2003, to replace Paul Maurice; fired December 3, 2008

Lemaire, Jacques b. LaSalle, Quebec, September 7, 1945

| 2008–09 MIN | 82 | 40 | 33 | 9 |
| NHL Totals | 1,131 | 540 | 414 | 177 |

• hired June 19, 2000; resigned April 12, 2009; hired by New Jersey on July 13, 2009

MacTavish, Craig b. London, Ontario, August 15, 1958

| 2008–09 EDM | 82 | 38 | 35 | 9 |
| NHL Totals | 656 | 301 | 252 | 103 |

• hired June 22, 2000; fired April 15, 2009

Martin, Jacques　b. St. Pascal, Ontario, October 1, 1952

NHL Totals	1,098	517	406	175

• hired by Montreal on June 1, 2009

Maurice, Paul　b. Sault Ste. Marie, Ontario, January 30, 1967

2008–09 CAR	57	33	19	5
NHL Totals	895	377	376	142

• hired December 3, 2008

McLellan, Todd　b. Melville, Saskatchewan, October 3, 1967

2008–09 SJ	82	53	18	11
NHL Totals	82	53	18	11

• hired June 11, 2008

Melrose, Barry　b. Kelvington, Saskatchewan, July 15, 1956

2008–09 TB	16	5	7	4
NHL Totals	225	84	108	33

• hired June 24, 2008; fired November 14, 2008

Murray, Andy　b. Gladstone, Manitoba, March 3, 1951

2008–09 STL	82	41	31	10
NHL Totals	700	316	261	123

• replaced Mike Kitchen on December 11, 2006

Murray, Terry　b. Shawville, Quebec, July 20, 1950

2008–09 LA	82	34	37	11
NHL Totals	819	394	314	111

• hired July 17, 2008

Quenneville, Joel　b. Windsor, Ontario, September 15, 1958

2008–09 CHI	78	45	22	11
NHL Totals	917	483	305	129

• hired October 16, 2008

Quinn, Pat b. Hamilton, Ontario, January 29, 1943

NHL Totals	1,318	657	481	180

• hired on May 26, 2009, by Edmonton

Renney, Tom b. Cranbrook, British Columbia, January 3, 1955

2008–09 NYR	61	31	23	7
NHL Totals	428	203	170	55

• hired February 25, 2004, to replace Glen Sather on an interim basis; fired
  February 23, 2009

Richards, Todd b. Crystal, Minnesota, October 20, 1966

• hired by Minnesota on June 16, 2009

Ruff, Lindy b. Warburg, Alberta, February 17, 1960

2008–09 BUF	82	41	32	9
NHL Totals	902	438	334	130

• hired July 21, 1997

Sacco, Joe b. Medford, Massachusetts, February 4, 1969

• hired by Colorado on June 4, 2009

Savard, Denis b. Pointe-Gatineau, Quebec, February 4, 1961

2008–09 CHI	4	1	2	1
NHL Totals	147	65	66	16

• replaced Trent Yawney on November 27, 2006; fired October 16, 2008, and
  replaced by Joel Quenneville

Stevens, John b. Campbellton, New Brunswick, May 4, 1966

2008–09 PHI	82	44	27	11
NHL Totals	238	107	98	33

• replaced Ken Hitchcock on October 22, 2006

Sutter, Brent b. Viking, Alberta, June 10, 1962

2008–09 NJ	82	51	27	4
NHL Totals	164	97	56	11

• hired July 13, 2007; resigned June 8, 2009; hired by Calgary on June 23, 2009

Therrien, Michel b. Montreal, Quebec, November 4, 1963

2008–09 PIT	57	27	25	5
NHL Totals	462	212	182	68

• named head coach on December 15, 2005; fired February 15, 2009

Tippett, Dave b. Moosomin, Saskatchewan, August 25, 1961

2008–09 DAL	82	36	35	11
NHL Totals	492	271	156	65

• hired May 16, 2002; fired June 10, 2009

Tocchet, Rick b. Toronto, Ontario, April 9, 1964

2008–09 TB	66	19	33	14
NHL Totals	66	19	33	14

• hired November 14, 2008

Tortorella, John b. Boston, Massachusetts, June 24, 1958

2008–09 NYR	21	12	7	2
NHL Totals	560	251	232	77

• hired February 23, 2009

Trotz, Barry b. Winnipeg, Manitoba, July 15, 1962

2008–09 NAS	82	40	34	8
NHL Totals	820	364	342	114

• hired August 6, 1997, a year before the Predators played their first NHL game

Vigneault, Alain b. Quebec City, Quebec, May 14, 1961

2008–09 VAN	82	45	27	10
NHL Totals	512	242	204	66

• hired June 20, 2006

Wilson, Ron b. Windsor, Ontario, May 28, 1955

2008–09 TOR	82	34	35	13
NHL Totals	1,173	552	461	160

• hired June 10, 2008

2009 NHL ENTRY DRAFT

First Round

1. NY Islanders—John Tavares (CAN)
2. Tampa Bay—Victor Hedman (SWE)
3. Colorado—Matt Duchene (CAN)
4. Atlanta—Evander Kane (CAN)
5. Los Angeles—Brayden Schenn (CAN)
6. Phoenix—Oliver Ekman-Larsson (SWE)
7. Toronto—Nazem Kadri (CAN)
8. Dallas—Scott Glennie (CAN)
9. Ottawa—Jared Cowen (CAN)
10. Edmonton—Magnus Paajarvi-Svensson (SWE)
11. Nashville—Ryan Ellis (CAN)
12. NY Islanders—Calvin de Haan (CAN)
13. Buffalo—Zack Kassian (CAN)
14. Florida—Dmitri Kulikov (RUS)
15. Anaheim—Peter Holland (CAN)
16. Minnesota—Nick Leddy (USA)
17. St. Louis—David Rundblad (SWE)
18. Montreal—Louis Leblanc (CAN)
19. NY Rangers—Chris Kreider (USA)
20. New Jersey—Jacob Josefsen (SWE)
21. Columbus—John Moore (USA)
22. Vancouver—Jordan Schroeder (USA)
23. Calgary—Tim Erixon (SWE)
24. Washington—Marcus Johansson (SWE)
25. Boston—Jordan Caron (CAN)
26. Anaheim—Kyle Palmieri (USA)
27. Carolina—Philippe Paradis (CAN)
28. Chicago—Dylan Olsen (CAN)
29. Tampa Bay—Carter Ashton (CAN)
30. Pittsburgh—Simon Despres (CAN)

Second Round

31. NY Islanders—Mikko Koskinen (FIN)
32. Detroit—Landon Ferraro (CAN)
33. Colorado—Ryan O'Reilly (CAN)
34. Atlanta—Carl Klingberg (SWE)
35. Los Angeles—Kyle Clifford (CAN)
36. Phoenix—Chris Brown (USA)
37. Anaheim—Matt Clark (USA)
38. Dallas—Alex Chiasson (CAN)
39. Ottawa—Jakob Silfverberg (SWE)
40. Edmonton—Anton Lander (SWE)
41. Nashville—Zack Budish (USA)
42. Nashville—Charles Olivier-Roussel (CAN)
43. San Jose—William Wrenn (USA)
44. Florida—Drew Shore (USA)
45. Atlanta—Jeremy Morin (USA)
46. Ottawa—Robin Lehner (SWE)
47. NY Rangers—Ethan Werek (CAN)
48. St. Louis—Brett Ponich (CAN)
49. Colorado—Stefan Elliott (CAN)
50. Toronto—Kenny Ryan (USA)
51. Carolina—Brian Dumoulin (USA)
52. Tampa Bay—Richard Panik (SVK)
53. Vancouver—Anton Rodin (SWE)
54. New Jersey—Eric Gelinas (CAN)
55. Washington—Dmitri Orlov (RUS)
56. Columbus—Kevin Lynch (USA)
57. San Jose—Taylor Doherty (CAN)
58. Toronto—Jesse Blacker (CAN)
59. Chicago—Brandon Pirri (CAN)
60. Detroit—Tomas Tatar (SVK)
61. Pittsburgh—Philip Samuelsson (SWE)

Third Round

62. NY Islanders—Anders Nilsson (SWE)
63. Pittsburgh—Ben Hanowski (USA)
64. Colorado—Tyson Barrie (CAN)
65. Montreal—Joonas Nattinen (FIN)
66. Buffalo—Brayden McNabb (CAN)
67. Florida—Josh Birkholz (USA)
68. Toronto—Jamie Devane (CAN)
69. Dallas—Reilly Smith (CAN)
70. Nashville—Taylor Beck (CAN)
71. Edmonton—Troy Hesketh (USA)
72. Nashville—Michael Latta (CAN)
73. New Jersey—Alexander Urbom (SWE)
74. Calgary—Ryan Howse (CAN)
75. Detroit—Andrej Nestrasil (CZE)
76. Anaheim—Igor Bobkov (RUS)
77. Minnesota—Matthew Hackett (CAN)
78. St. Louis—Sergei Andronov (RUS)
79. Montreal—Mac Bennett (USA)
80. NY Rangers—Ryan Bourque (USA)
81. Philadelphia—Adam Morrison (CAN)
82. Edmonton—Cameron Abney (CAN)
83. Vancouver—Kevin Connauton (CAN)
84. Los Angeles—Nicolas Deslauriers (CAN)
85. Washington—Cody Eakin (CAN)
86. Boston—Ryan Button (CAN)
87. Philadelphia—Simon Bertilsson (SWE)
88. Carolina—Mattias Lindstrom (SWE)
89. Chicago—Daniel Delisle (USA)
90. Detroit—Gleason Fournier (CAN)
91. NY Islanders—Michael Lee (USA)

Fourth Round

92. NY Islanders—Casey Cizikas (CAN)
93. Tampa Bay—Alex Hutchings (CAN)
94. Columbus—David Savard (CAN)
95. Los Angeles—Jean-Francois Berube (CAN)
96. Los Angeles—Linden Vey (CAN)
97. Phoenix—Jordan Szwarz (CAN)
98. Nashville—Craig Smith (USA)
99. Edmonton—Kyle Bigos (USA)
100. Ottawa—Chris Wideman (USA)
101. Edmonton—Toni Rajala (FIN)
102. Nashville—Mattias Ekholm (SWE)
103. Minnesota—Kristopher Foucault (CAN)
104. Buffalo—Marcus Foligno (USA)
105. Phoenix—Justin Weller (CAN)
106. Anaheim—Sami Vatanen (FIN)
107. Florida—Garrett Wilson (CAN)
108. St. Louis—Tyler Shattock (CAN)
109. Montreal—Alexander Avtsyn (RUS)
110. Nashville—Nick Oliver (USA)
111. Calgary—Henrik Bjorklund (SWE)
112. Boston—Lane MacDermid (USA)
113. Vancouver—Jeremy Price (CAN)
114. New Jersey—Seth Helgeson (USA)
115. Washington—Patrick Wey (USA)
116. Minnesota—Alexander Fallstrom (SWE)
117. Atlanta—Edward Pasquale (CAN)
118. Chicago—Byron Froese (CAN)
119. Toronto—revoked (improper signing of Jonas Frogren)
120. Atlanta—Ben Chiarot (CAN)
121. Pittsburgh—Nick Petersen (CAN)

Fifth Round

122. NY Islanders—Anton Klementyev (RUS)
123. Pittsburgh—Alex Velischek (CAN)
124. Colorado—Kieran Millan (CAN)
125. Atlanta—Cody Sol (CAN)
126. Los Angeles—David Kolomatis (USA)
127. NY Rangers—Roman Horak (CZE)
128. Toronto—Eric Knodel (USA)
129. Dallas—Tomas Vincour (CZE)
130. Ottawa—Mike Hoffman (CAN)
131. Carolina—Matt Kennedy (CAN)
132. Nashville—Gabriel Bourque (CAN)
133. Edmonton—Olivier Roy (CAN)
134. Buffalo—Mark Adams (USA)
135. Florida—Corban Knight (CAN)
136. Anaheim—Radoslav Illo (SVK)
137. Columbus—Thomas Larkin (GBR)
138. Florida—Wade Megan (USA)
139. Montreal—Gabriel Dumont (CAN)
140. NY Rangers—Scott Stajcer (CAN)
141. Calgary—Spencer Bennett (CAN)
142. Philadelphia—Nicola Riopel (CAN)
143. Vancouver—Peter Andersson (SWE)
144. New Jersey—Derek Rodwell (CAN)
145. Washington—Brett Flemming (CAN)
146. Ottawa—Jeff Costello (USA)
147. San Jose—Philip Varone (CAN)
148. Tampa Bay—Michael Zador (CAN)
149. Chicago—Markus Kruger (SWE)
150. Detroit—Nick Jensen (USA)
151. Pittsburgh—Andy Bathgate (CAN)

Sixth Round

152. NY Islanders—Anders Lee (USA)
153. Philadelphia—Dave Labrecque (CAN)
154. Colorado—Brandon Maxwell (USA)
155. Atlanta—Jimmy Bubnick (CAN)
156. Los Angeles—Michael Pelech (CAN)
157. Phoenix—Evan Bloodoff (CAN)
158. Toronto—Jerry D'Amigo (USA)
159. Dallas—Curtis McKenzie (CAN)
160. Ottawa—Corey Cowick (CAN)
161. Minnesota—Darcy Kuemper (CAN)
162. Tampa Bay—Jaroslav Janus (SVK)
163. Minnesota—Jere Sallinen (FIN)
164. Buffalo—Connor Knapp (USA)
165. Florida—Scott Timmins (CAN)
166. Anaheim—Scott Valentine (CAN)
167. Columbus—Anton Blomqvist (SWE)
168. St. Louis—David Shields (CAN)
169. Montreal—Dustin Walsh (CAN)
170. NY Rangers—Daniel Maggio (CAN)
171. Calgary—Joni Ortio (FIN)
172. Philadelphia—Eric Wellwood (CAN)
173. Vancouver—Joe Cannata (USA)
174. New Jersey—Ashton Bernard (CAN)
175. Washington—Garrett Mitchell (CAN)
176. Boston—Tyler Randell (CAN)
177. Chicago—David Pacan (CAN)
178. Carolina—Rasmus Rissanen (FIN)
179. Los Angeles—Brandon Kozun (USA)
180. Detroit—Mitchell Callahan (USA)
181. Pittsburgh—Viktor Ekbom (SWE)

Seventh Round

182. Minnesota—Erik Haula (FIN)
183. Tampa Bay—Kirill Gotovets (BLR)
184. Colorado—Gus Young (USA)
185. Atlanta—Levko Koper (CAN)
186. Los Angeles—Jordan Nolan (CAN)
187. Vancouver—Steven Anthony (CAN)
188. Toronto—Barron Smith (USA)
189. San Jose—Marek Viedensky (SVK)
190. Ottawa—Brad Peltz (USA)
191. Ottawa—Michael Sdao (USA)
192. Nashville—Cameron Reid (CAN)
193. Minnesota—Anthony Hamburg (USA)
194. Buffalo—Maxime Legault (CAN)
195. Chicago—Paul Phillips (USA)
196. Philadelphia—Oliver Lauridsen (DEN)
197. Columbus—Kyle Neuber (CAN)
198. Los Angeles—Nic Dowd (USA)
199. Montreal—Michael Cichy (USA)
200. NY Rangers—Mikhail Pashnin (RUS)
201. Calgary—Gaelan Patterson (CAN)
202. St. Louis—Maxwell Tardy (USA)
203. Atlanta—Jordan Samuels-Thomas (USA)
204. New Jersey—Curtis Gedig (CAN)
205. Washington—Benjamin Casavant (CAN)
206. Boston—Ben Sexton (CAN)
207. San Jose—Dominik Bielke (GER)
208. Carolina—Tommi Kivisto (FIN)
209. Chicago—David Gilbert (CAN)
210. Detroit—Adam Almqvist (SWE)
211. Montreal—Petteri Simila (FIN)

Notes:

- Brayden Schenn (5th overall, Los Angeles) is the brother of Luke
- Tim Erixon (23rd overall, Calgary) is the son of Jan
- Carter Ashton (29th overall, Tampa Bay) is the son of Brent
- Landon Ferraro (32nd overall, Detroit) is the son of Ray Ferraro
- Philip Samuelsson (61st overall, Pittsburgh) is the son of Ulf
- Tyson Barrie (64th overall, Colorado) is the son of Len
- Mac Bennett (79th overall, Montreal) is the grandson of Harvey
- Ryan Bourque (80th overall, NY Rangers) is the son of Ray
- Marcus Foligno (104th overall, Buffalo) is the son of Mike
- Lane MacDermid (112th overall, Boston) is the son of Paul
- Alex Velischek (123rd overall, Pittsburgh) is the son of Randy
- Andy Bathgate (151st overall, Pittsburgh) is the grandson of Andy Bathgate
- Brandon Maxwell (154th overall, Colorado) is the son of Brad
- Eric Wellwood (172nd overall, Philadelphia) is the brother of Kyle
- Jordan Nolan (186th overall, Los Angeles) is the son of Ted and brother of Brandon
- Barron Smith (188th overall, Toronto) is the son of Steve

ALL-TIME LEADERS

MOST GAMES

1,767	Gordie Howe
1,756	Mark Messier
1,731	Ron Francis
1,644	Chris Chelios
1,639	Dave Andreychuk

MOST POINTS, REGULAR SEASON

2,857	Wayne Gretzky
1,887	Mark Messier
1,850	Gordie Howe
1,798	Ron Francis
1,771	Marcel Dionne

MOST GOALS, REGULAR SEASON

894	Wayne Gretzky
801	Gordie Howe
741	Brett Hull
731	Marcel Dionne
717	Phil Esposito

MOST ASSISTS, REGULAR SEASON

1,963	Wayne Gretzky
1,249	Ron Francis
1,193	Mark Messier
1,169	Ray Bourque
1,135	Paul Coffey

MOST PENALTY MINUTES, REGULAR SEASON

3,966	Dave "Tiger" Williams
3,565	Dale Hunter

3,515	Tie Domi
3,381	Marty McSorley
3,300	Bob Probert

MOST GAMES, GOALIE, REGULAR SEASON

1,029	Patrick Roy
971	Terry Sawchuk
968	Martin Brodeur
963	Ed Belfour
922	Curtis Joseph

MOST WINS, GOALIE, REGULAR SEASON

557	Martin Brodeur
551	Patrick Roy
484	Ed Belfour
454	Curtis Joseph
447	Terry Sawchuk

MOST SHUTOUTS, GOALIE, REGULAR SEASON

103	Terry Sawchuk
101	Martin Brodeur
94	George Hainsworth
84	Glenn Hall
82	Jacques Plante

YEAR-BY-YEAR STANDINGS AND STANLEY CUP FINALS RESULTS

After playoff scores, goalies who have registered a shutout will appear in square brackets (i.e., [Broda] means Turk Broda registered a shutout). All overtime goals are also recorded.

1917–18

First Half	GP	W	L	GF	GA	PTS
Canadiens	14	10	4	81	47	20
Arenas	14	8	6	71	75	16
Ottawa	14	5	9	67	79	10
Wanderers⁺	6	1	5	17	35	2

Second Half	GP	W	L	GF	GA	PTS
Arenas	8	5	3	37	34	10
Ottawa	8	4	4	35	35	8
Canadiens	8	3	5	34	37	6

⁺ Wanderers' rink burned down on January 2, 1918, and team withdrew from league. Arenas and Canadiens each counted a win for defaulted games with the Wanderers.

* winner of first half played winner of second half in a two-game total-goals series for a place in the Stanley Cup finals against the winner of the Pacific Coast Hockey Association and the Western Canada Hockey League. If one team won both halves, it went to the best-of-five Stanley Cup finals automatically.

* from 1917–21 games were played until a winner decided

NHL Finals

March 11   Canadiens 3 at Arenas 7
March 13   Arenas 3 at Canadiens 4
Arenas won two-game total-goals series 10–7

Stanley Cup Finals
March 20   Vancouver 3 at Toronto 5
March 23   Vancouver 6 at Toronto 4
March 26   Vancouver 3 at Toronto 6
March 28   Vancouver 8 at Toronto 1
March 30   Vancouver 1 at Toronto 2
Toronto won best-of-five finals 3–2

1918–19

First Half

	GP	W	L	GF	GA	PTS
Canadiens	10	7	3	57	50	14
Ottawa	10	5	5	39	39	10
Arenas	10	3	7	42	49	6

Second Half

	GP	W	L	GF	GA	PTS
Ottawa	8	7	1	32	14	14
Canadiens	8	3	5	31	28	6
Arenas	8	2	6	22	43	4

* Spanish influenza epidemic caused the cancellation of the Stanley Cup finals
* the 1918–19 season was supposed to be, like the ones before and after it, a 24-game schedule. However, when Canadiens and Ottawa clinched first place in both halves early, Arenas manager Charlie Querrie refused to play the remaining games, fearing a lack of fan interest. The league almost sued the Arenas, but instead Canadiens and Ottawa played a best-of-seven, rather than a two-game total-goals series, to create extra home dates for the clubs.

NHL Finals
February 22   Ottawa 4 at Canadiens 8
February 27   Canadiens 5 at Ottawa 3
March 1   Ottawa 3 at Canadiens 6
March 3   Canadiens 3 at Ottawa 6
March 6   Ottawa 2 at Canadiens 4
Canadiens won best-of-seven series 4–1

Stanley Cup Finals

March 19   Canadiens 0 at Seattle 7 [Holmes]
March 22   Canadiens 4 at Seattle 2
March 24   Canadiens 2 at Seattle 7
March 26   Canadiens 0 at Seattle 0 (20:00 OT) [Vezina/Holmes]
March 30   Canadiens 4 at Seattle 3 (Odie Cleghorn 15:57 OT)

Finals cancelled after five games because of Spanish influenza and the death of Canadiens player Joe Hall

1919–20

First Half

	GP	W	L	GP	GA	PTS
Ottawa	12	9	3	59	23	18
Canadiens	12	8	4	62	51	16
St. Pats	12	5	7	52	62	10
Bulldogs	12	2	10	44	81	4

Second Half

Ottawa	12	10	2	62	41	20
St. Pats	12	7	5	67	44	14
Canadiens	12	5	7	67	62	10
Bulldogs	12	2	10	47	96	4

No NHL finals because Ottawa won both halves

Stanley Cup Finals

March 22   Seattle 2 at Ottawa 3
March 24   Seattle 0 at Ottawa 3 [Benedict]
March 27   Seattle 3 at Ottawa 1
March 30   Seattle 5 Ottawa 2*
April 1   Ottawa 6 Seattle 1*
Ottawa won best-of-five finals 3–2

* played in Toronto because of poor ice conditions in Ottawa

1920–21

First Half

	GP	W	L	GP	GA	PTS
Ottawa	10	8	2	49	23	16
St. Pats	10	5	5	39	47	10
Canadiens	10	4	6	37	51	8
Hamilton	10	3	7	34	38	6

Second Half

	GP	W	L			
St. Pats	14	10	4	66	53	20
Canadiens	14	9	5	75	48	18
Ottawa	14	6	8	48	52	12
Hamilton	14	3	11	58	94	6

NHL Finals

March 10   St. Pats 0 at Ottawa 5 [Benedict]
March 15   Ottawa 2 at St. Pats 0 [Benedict]
Ottawa won two-game total-goals series 7–0

Stanley Cup Finals

March 21   Ottawa 1 at Vancouver 3
March 24   Ottawa 4 at Vancouver 3
March 28   Ottawa 3 at Vancouver 2
March 31   Ottawa 2 at Vancouver 3
April 4   Ottawa 2 at Vancouver 1
Ottawa won best-of-five finals 3–2

1921–22

	GP	W	L	T	GF	GA	PTS
Ottawa	24	14	8	2	106	84	30
St. Pats	24	13	10	1	98	97	27
Canadiens	24	12	11	1	88	94	25
Hamilton	24	7	17	0	88	105	14

* overtime limited to 20 minutes (not sudden-death); minor penalties reduced from three to two minutes
* top two teams advance to playoffs; winner met the Pacific Coast Hockey Association–Western Canadian Hockey League Champion for the Stanley Cup

NHL Finals

March 11   Ottawa 4 at St. Pats 5
March 13   St. Pats 0 at Ottawa 0 [Roach/Benedict]
St. Pats won two-game total-goals series 5–4

Stanley Cup Finals

March 17   Vancouver 4 at St. Pats 3
March 21   Vancouver 1 at St. Pats 2   (Dye 4:50 OT)
March 23   Vancouver 3 at St. Pats 0 [Lehman]
March 25   Vancouver 0 at St. Pats 6 [Roach]
March 28   Vancouver 1 at St. Pats 5
St. Pats won best-of-five finals 3–2

1922–23

	GP	W	L	T	GF	GA	PTS
Ottawa	24	14	9	1	77	54	29
Canadiens	24	13	9	2	73	61	28
St. Pats	24	13	10	1	82	88	27
Hamilton	24	6	18	0	81	110	12

NHL Finals

March 7   Ottawa 2 at Canadiens 0 [Benedict]
March 9   Canadiens 2 at Ottawa 1
Ottawa won two-game total-goals series 3–2

Stanley Cup Playoffs

March 16   Ottawa 1 at Vancouver 0 [Benedict]
March 19   Ottawa 1 at Vancouver 4
March 23   Ottawa 3 at Vancouver 2
March 26   Ottawa 5 at Vancouver 1
Ottawa won best-of-five semifinals 3–1

Stanley Cup Finals
March 29   Ottawa 2 Edmonton 1 (Cy Denneny 2:08 OT)*
March 31   Ottawa 1 Edmonton 0 [Benedict]*
Ottawa won best-of-three finals 2–0

* games played at Vancouver

1923–24

	GP	W	L	T	GF	GA	PTS
Ottawa	24	16	8	0	74	54	32
Canadiens	24	13	11	0	59	48	26
St. Pats	24	10	14	0	59	85	20
Hamilton	24	9	15	0	63	68	18

NHL Finals
March 8   Ottawa 0 at Canadiens 1 [Vezina]
March 11   Canadiens 4 at Ottawa 2
Canadiens won two-game total-goals series 5–2

Stanley Cup Playoffs
March 18   Vancouver 2 at Canadiens 3
March 20   Vancouver 1 at Canadiens 2
Canadiens won best-of-three semifinals 2–0

Stanley Cup Finals
March 22   Calgary 1 at Canadiens 6
March 25   Canadiens 3 Calgary 0 [Vezina]*
Canadiens won best-of-three finals 2–0

* played at Ottawa

1924–25

	GP	W	L	T	GF	GA	PTS
Hamilton	30	19	10	1	90	60	39
St. Pats	30	19	11	0	90	84	38
Canadiens	30	17	11	2	93	56	36
Ottawa	30	17	12	1	83	66	35
Maroons	30	9	19	2	45	65	20
Boston	30	6	24	0	49	119	12

* the top two teams (Hamilton and Toronto) were supposed to compete for the NHL championship and the right to advance to the Stanley Cup Finals against the WCHL winners. However, the Tigers' players demanded more money for these extra games and the NHL simply disqualified the team. Thus, the St. Pats played the Canadiens.

NHL Finals
March 13   Canadiens 2 at St. Pats 0
March 19   St. Pats 2 at Canadiens 3
Canadiens won two-game total-goals series 5–2

Stanley Cup Finals
March 21   Canadiens 2 at Victoria 5
March 23   Canadiens 1 at Victoria 3*
March 27   Canadiens 4 at Victoria 2
March 30   Canadiens 1 at Victoria 6
Victoria won best-of-five finals 3–1

* played at Vancouver

1925–26

	GP	W	L	T	GF	GA	PTS
Ottawa	36	24	8	4	77	42	52
Maroons	36	20	11	5	91	73	45
Pirates	36	19	16	1	82	70	39
Boston	36	17	15	4	92	85	38
Americans	36	12	20	4	68	89	28

St. Pats	36	12	21	3	92	114	27
Canadiens	36	11	24	1	79	108	23

NHL Finals
March 25   Ottawa 1 at Maroons 1
March 27   Maroons 1 at Ottawa 0 [Benedict]
Maroons win two-game total-goals finals 2–1

Stanley Cup Finals

March 30   Victoria 0 at Maroons 3 [Benedict]
April 1   Victoria 0 at Maroons 3 [Benedict]
April 3   Victoria 3 at Maroons 2
April 6   Victoria 0 at Maroons 2 [Benedict]
Maroons won best-of-five finals 3–1

1926–27

Canadian Division

	GP	W	L	T	GF	GA	PTS
Ottawa	44	30	10	4	86	69	64
Canadiens	44	28	14	2	99	67	58
Maroons	44	20	20	4	71	68	44
Americans	44	17	25	2	82	91	36
Toronto*	44	15	24	5	79	94	35

American Division

Rangers	44	25	13	6	95	72	56
Boston	44	21	20	3	97	89	45
Chicago	44	19	22	3	115	116	41
Pirates	44	15	26	3	79	108	33
Cougars	44	12	28	4	76	105	28

* on February 14, 1927, the St. Pats changed their name to Maple Leafs

Stanley Cup Finals

April 7   Ottawa 0 at Boston 0* [Connell/Winkler]
April 9   Ottawa 3 at Boston 1
April 11   Boston 1 at Ottawa 1**
April 13   Boston 1 at Ottawa 3
Ottawa won best-of-five finals 2–0–2

* two 10-minute overtime periods
** one 20-minute overtime period

1927–28

Canadian Division

	GP	W	L	T	GF	GA	PTS
Canadiens	44	26	11	7	116	48	59
Maroons	44	24	14	6	96	77	54
Ottawa	44	20	14	10	78	57	50
Toronto	44	18	18	8	89	88	44
Americans	44	11	27	6	63	128	28

American Division

	GP	W	L	T	GF	GA	PTS
Boston	44	20	13	11	77	70	51
Rangers	44	19	16	9	94	79	47
Pirates	44	19	17	8	67	76	46
Cougars	44	19	19	6	88	79	44
Chicago	44	7	34	3	68	134	17

* overtime limited to 10 minutes of sudden-death; forward passing now allowed in defending zone

Finals

April 5   Rangers 0 at Maroons 2 [Benedict]
April 7   Rangers 2 at Maroons 1 (Frank Boucher 7:05 OT)
April 10   Rangers 0 at Maroons 2 [Benedict]

April 12   Rangers 1 at Maroons 0 [Miller]
April 14   Rangers 2 at Maroons 1
Rangers won best-of-five finals 3–2

1928–29

Canadian Division

	GP	W	L	T	GF	GA	PTS
Canadiens	44	22	7	15	71	43	59
Americans	44	19	13	12	53	53	50
Toronto	44	21	18	5	85	69	47
Ottawa	44	14	17	13	54	67	41
Maroons	44	15	20	9	67	65	39

American Division

	GP	W	L	T	GF	GA	PTS
Boston	44	26	13	5	89	52	57
Rangers	44	21	13	10	72	65	52
Cougars	44	19	16	9	72	63	47
Pirates	44	9	27	8	46	80	26
Chicago	44	7	29	8	33	85	22

* overtime set at 10 minutes without sudden-death; passing allowed into, but
  not within, the offensive zone
* the two division winners played a best-of-five and the two second place
  teams and third-place teams played two-game total-goals series. Those two
  winners then played to see who would play the winner of the two division
  champions' series.

Stanley Cup Finals
March 28   Rangers 0 at Boston 2 [Thompson]
March 29   Boston 2 at Rangers 1
Boston won best-of-three finals 2–0

1929–30

Canadian Division

	GP	W	L	T	GF	GA	PTS
Maroons	44	23	16	5	141	114	51
Canadiens	44	21	14	9	142	114	51
Ottawa	44	21	15	8	138	118	50
Toronto	44	17	21	6	116	124	40
Americans	44	14	25	5	113	161	33

American Division

	GP	W	L	T	GF	GA	PTS
Boston	44	38	5	1	179	98	77
Chicago	44	21	18	5	117	111	47
Rangers	44	17	17	10	136	143	44
Falcons	44	14	24	6	117	133	34
Pirates	44	5	36	3	102	185	13

* forward passing allowed in all three zones, producing twice the number of goals this season over last

Stanley Cup Finals

April 1   Canadiens 3 at Boston 0 [Hainsworth]
April 3   Boston 3 at Canadiens 4
Canadiens won best-of-three finals 2–0

1930–31

Canadian Division

	GP	W	L	T	GF	GA	PTS
Canadiens	44	26	10	8	129	89	60
Toronto	44	22	13	9	118	99	53
Maroons	44	20	18	6	105	106	46
Americans	44	18	16	10	76	74	46
Ottawa	44	10	30	4	91	142	24

American Division

Boston	44	28	10	6	143	90	62
Chicago	44	24	17	3	108	78	51
Rangers	44	19	16	9	106	87	47
Falcons	44	16	21	7	102	105	39
Quakers	44	4	36	4	76	184	12

Stanley Cup Finals

April 3	Canadiens 2 at Chicago 1
April 5	Canadiens 1 at Chicago 2 (24:50 OT)
April 9	Chicago 3 at Canadiens 2 (53:50 OT)
April 11	Chicago 2 at Canadiens 4
April 14	Chicago 0 at Canadiens 2 [Hainsworth]

Canadiens won best-of-five finals 3–2

1931–32

Canadian Division

	GP	W	L	T	GF	GA	PTS
Canadiens	48	25	16	7	128	111	57
Toronto	48	23	18	7	155	127	53
Maroons	48	19	22	7	142	139	45
Americans	48	16	24	8	95	142	40

American Division

Rangers	48	23	17	8	134	112	54
Chicago	48	18	19	11	86	101	47
Falcons	48	18	20	10	95	108	46
Boston	48	15	21	12	122	117	42

Stanley Cup Finals

April 5   Toronto 6 at Rangers 4
April 7   Toronto 6 at Rangers 2*
April 9   Rangers 4 at Toronto 6
Toronto won best-of-five finals 3–0

* played at Boston because Madison Square Garden unavailable April 7 because of circus. Because of the scores in the finals (6–4, 6–2, 6–4) this series has long been dubbed the "Tennis Series"
* all members of this Toronto team were given gold coins by Conn Smythe as lifetime passes to the Gardens

1932–33

Canadian Division

	GP	W	L	T	GF	GA	PTS
Toronto	48	24	18	6	119	111	54
Maroons	48	22	20	6	135	119	50
Canadiens	48	18	25	5	92	115	41
Americans	48	15	22	11	91	118	41
Ottawa	48	11	27	10	88	131	32

American Division

	GP	W	L	T	GF	GA	PTS
Boston	48	25	15	8	124	88	58
Detroit	48	25	15	8	111	93	58
Rangers	48	23	17	8	135	107	54
Chicago	48	16	20	12	88	101	44

Stanley Cup Finals

April 4   Toronto 1 at Rangers 5
April 8   Rangers 3 at Toronto 1
April 11   Rangers 2 at Toronto 3
April 13   Rangers 1 at Toronto 0 (Bill Cook 7:33 OT) [Aitkenhead]
Rangers won best-of-five finals 3–1

1933–34

Canadian Division

	GP	W	L	T	GF	GA	PTS
Toronto	48	26	13	9	174	119	61
Canadiens	48	22	20	6	99	101	50
Maroons	48	19	18	11	117	122	49
Americans	48	15	23	10	104	132	40
Ottawa	48	13	29	6	115	143	32

American Division

Detroit	48	24	14	10	113	98	58
Chicago	48	20	17	11	88	83	51
Rangers	48	21	19	8	120	113	50
Boston	48	18	25	5	111	130	41

Stanley Cup Finals

April 3   Chicago 2 at Detroit 1 (Paul Thompson 21:10 OT)
April 5   Chicago 4 at Detroit 1
April 8   Detroit 5 at Chicago 2
April 10   Detroit 0 at Chicago 1 (Mush March 30:05 OT) [Gardiner]
Chicago won best-of-five finals 3–1

1934–35

Canadian Division

	GP	W	L	T	GF	GA	PTS
Toronto	48	30	14	4	157	111	64
Maroons	48	24	19	5	123	92	53
Canadiens	48	19	23	6	110	145	44
Americans	48	12	27	9	100	142	33
Eagles	48	11	31	6	86	144	28

American Division

Boston	48	26	16	6	129	112	58
Chicago	48	26	17	5	118	88	57
Rangers	48	22	20	6	137	139	50
Detroit	48	19	22	7	127	114	45

Stanley Cup Finals

April 4   Maroons 3 at Toronto 2 (Dave Trottier 5:28 OT)
April 6   Maroons 3 at Toronto 1
April 9   Toronto 1 at Maroons 4
Maroons won best-of-five finals 3–0

1935–36
Canadian Division

	GP	W	L	T	GF	GA	PTS
Maroons	48	22	16	10	114	106	54
Toronto	48	23	19	6	126	106	52
Americans	48	16	25	7	109	122	39
Canadiens	48	11	26	11	82	123	33

American Division

Detroit	48	24	16	8	124	103	56
Boston	48	22	20	6	92	83	50
Chicago	48	21	19	8	93	92	50
Rangers	48	19	17	12	91	96	50

Stanley Cup Finals

April 5   Toronto 1 at Detroit 3
April 7   Toronto 4 at Detroit 9
April 9   Detroit 3 at Toronto 4 (Buzz Boll 0:31 OT)
April 11   Detroit 3 at Toronto 2
Detroit won best-of-five finals 3–1

1936–37

Canadian Division

	GP	W	L	T	GF	GA	PTS
Canadiens	48	24	18	6	115	111	54
Maroons	48	22	17	9	126	110	53
Toronto	48	22	21	5	119	115	49
Americans	48	15	29	4	122	161	34

American Division

	GP	W	L	T	GF	GA	PTS
Detroit	48	25	14	9	128	102	59
Boston	48	23	18	7	120	110	53
Rangers	48	19	20	9	117	106	47
Chicago	48	14	27	7	99	131	35

Stanley Cup Finals

April 6	Detroit 1 at Rangers 5
April 8	Rangers 2 at Detroit 4
April 11	Rangers 1 at Detroit 0 [Kerr]
April 13	Rangers 0 at Detroit 1 [Robertson]
April 15	Rangers 0 at Detroit 3 [Robertson]

Detroit won best-of-five finals 3–2

1937–38

Canadian Division

	GP	W	L	T	GF	GA	PTS
Toronto	48	24	15	9	151	127	57
Americans	48	19	18	11	110	111	49
Canadiens	48	18	17	13	123	128	49
Maroons	48	12	30	6	101	149	30

American Division

Boston	48	30	11	7	142	89	67
Rangers	48	27	15	6	149	96	60
Chicago	48	14	25	9	97	139	37
Detroit	48	12	25	11	99	133	35

Stanley Cup Finals

April 5   Chicago 3 at Toronto 1
April 7   Chicago 1 at Toronto 5
April 10   Toronto 1 at Chicago 2
April 12   Toronto 1 at Chicago 4
Chicago won best-of-five finals 3–1

1938–39

	GP	W	L	T	GF	GA	PTS
Boston	48	36	10	2	156	76	74
Rangers	48	26	16	6	149	105	58
Toronto	48	19	20	9	114	107	47
Americans	48	17	21	10	119	157	44
Detroit	48	18	24	6	107	128	42
Canadiens	48	15	24	9	115	146	39
Chicago	48	12	28	8	91	132	32

* only the last-place team did not qualify for the playoffs under the new one-division, 7–team format. The first- and second-place team played a best-of-seven to advance to the finals. The second played third and fourth played fifth in best-of-three, the two winners playing another best-of-three to advance to the finals.

Stanley Cup Finals

April 6   Toronto 1 at Boston 2
April 9   Toronto 3 at Boston 2 (Doc Romnes 10:38 OT)
April 11   Boston 3 at Toronto 1

April 13   Boston 2 at Toronto 0 [Brimsek]
April 16   Toronto 1 at Boston 3
Boston won best-of-seven finals 4–1

1939–40

	GP	W	L	T	GF	GA	PTS
Boston	48	31	12	5	170	98	67
Rangers	48	27	11	10	136	77	64
Toronto	48	25	17	6	134	110	56
Chicago	48	23	19	6	112	120	52
Detroit	48	16	26	6	90	126	38
Americans	48	15	29	4	106	140	34
Canadiens	48	10	33	5	90	167	25

Stanley Cup Finals

April 2   Toronto 1 at Rangers 2 (Alf Pike 15:30 OT)
April 3   Toronto 2 at Rangers 6
April 6   Rangers 1 at Toronto 2
April 9   Rangers 0 at Toronto 3 [Broda]
April 11   Rangers 2 at Toronto 1 (Muzz Patrick 31:43 OT)*
April 13   Rangers 3 at Toronto 2 (Bryan Hextall 2:07 OT)
Rangers won best-of-seven finals 4–2

* game could not be played at Madison Square Garden as it was previously
  booked for the circus

1940–41

	GP	W	L	T	GF	GA	PTS
Boston	48	27	8	13	168	102	67
Toronto	48	28	14	6	145	99	62
Detroit	48	21	16	11	112	102	53
Rangers	48	21	19	8	143	125	50
Chicago	48	16	25	7	112	139	39
Canadiens	48	16	26	6	121	147	38
Americans	48	8	29	11	99	186	27

Stanley Cup Finals

April 6   Detroit 2 at Boston 3
April 8   Detroit 1 at Boston 2
April 10   Boston 4 at Detroit 2
April 12   Boston 3 at Detroit 1
Boston won best-of-seven finals 4–0

1941–42

	GP	W	L	T	GF	GA	PTS
Rangers	48	29	17	2	177	143	60
Toronto	48	27	18	3	158	136	57
Boston	48	25	17	6	160	118	56
Chicago	48	22	23	3	145	155	47
Detroit	48	19	25	4	140	147	42
Canadiens	48	18	27	3	134	173	39
Brooklyn	48	16	29	3	133	175	35

Stanley Cup Finals

April 4   Detroit 3 at Toronto 2
April 7   Detroit 4 at Toronto 2
April 9   Toronto 2 at Detroit 5
April 12   Toronto 4 at Detroit 3
April 14   Detroit 3 at Toronto 9
April 16   Toronto 3 at Detroit 0 [Broda]
April 18   Detroit 1 at Toronto 3
Toronto won best-of-seven finals 4–3

* only time in NHL history that a team has trailed 3–0 in the finals and won
  the Stanley Cup

1942–43

	GP	W	L	T	GF	GA	PTS
Detroit	50	25	14	11	169	124	61
Boston	50	24	17	9	195	176	57
Toronto	50	22	19	9	198	159	53
Canadiens	50	19	19	12	181	191	50
Chicago	50	17	18	15	179	180	49
Rangers	50	11	31	8	161	253	30

* because of wartime restrictions on train schedules overtime was eliminated as of November 21, 1942
* the top four teams qualified for the playoffs in the six-team league, and both rounds were best-of-seven

Stanley Cup Finals

April 1   Boston 2 at Detroit 6
April 4   Boston 3 at Detroit 4
April 7   Detroit 4 at Boston 0 [Mowers]
April 8   Detroit 2 at Boston 0 [Mowers]
Detroit won best-of-seven finals 4–0

1943–44

	GP	W	L	T	GF	GA	PTS
Canadiens	50	38	5	7	234	109	83
Detroit	50	26	18	6	214	177	58
Toronto	50	23	23	4	214	174	50
Chicago	50	22	23	5	178	187	49
Boston	50	19	26	5	223	268	43
Rangers	50	6	39	5	162	310	17

Stanley Cup Finals

April 4   Chicago 1 at Canadiens 5
April 6   Canadiens 3 at Chicago 1
April 9   Canadiens 3 at Chicago 2
April 13   Chicago 4 at Canadiens 5 (Toe Blake 9:12 OT)
Canadiens won best-of-seven finals 4–0

1944–45

	GP	W	L	T	GF	GA	PTS
Canadiens	50	38	8	4	228	121	80
Detroit	50	31	14	5	218	161	67
Toronto	50	24	22	4	183	161	52
Boston	50	16	30	4	179	219	36
Chicago	50	13	30	7	141	194	33
Rangers	50	11	29	10	154	247	32

Stanley Cup Finals
April 6   Toronto 1 at Detroit 0 [McCool]
April 8   Toronto 2 at Detroit 0 [McCool]
April 12   Detroit 0 at Toronto 1 [McCool]
April 14   Detroit 5 at Toronto 3
April 19   Toronto 0 at Detroit 2 [Lumley]
April 21   Detroit 1 at Toronto 0 (Ed Bruneteau 14:16 OT) [Lumley]
April 22   Toronto 2 at Detroit 1
Toronto won best-of-seven finals 4–3

1945–46

	GP	W	L	T	GF	GA	PTS
Canadiens	50	28	17	5	172	134	61
Boston	50	24	18	8	167	156	56
Chicago	50	23	20	7	200	178	53
Detroit	50	20	20	10	146	159	50
Toronto	50	19	24	7	174	185	45
Rangers	50	13	28	9	144	191	35

Stanley Cup Finals
March 30   Boston 3 at Canadiens 4 (Maurice Richard 9:08 OT)
April 2   Boston 2 at Canadiens 3 (Jimmy Peters 16:55 OT)
April 4   Canadiens 4 at Boston 2

April 7   Canadiens 2 at Boston 3 (Terry Reardon 15:13 OT)
April 9   Boston 3 at Canadiens 6
Canadiens won best-of-seven finals 4–1

1946–47

	GP	W	L	T	GF	GA	PTS
Canadiens	60	34	16	10	189	138	78
Toronto	60	31	19	10	209	172	72
Boston	60	26	23	11	190	175	63
Detroit	60	22	27	11	190	193	55
Rangers	60	22	32	6	167	186	50
Chicago	60	19	37	4	193	274	42

Stanley Cup Finals

April 8   Toronto 0 at Canadiens 6 [Durnan]
April 10   Toronto 4 at Canadiens 0 [Broda]
April 12   Canadiens 2 at Toronto 4
April 15   Canadiens 1 at Toronto 2 (Syl Apps 16:36 OT)
April 17   Toronto 1 at Canadiens 3
April 19   Canadiens 1 at Toronto 2
Toronto won best-of-seven finals 4–2

1947–48

	GP	W	L	T	GF	GA	PTS
Toronto	60	32	15	13	182	143	77
Detroit	60	30	18	12	187	148	72
Boston	60	23	24	13	167	168	59
Rangers	60	21	26	13	176	201	55
Canadiens	60	20	29	11	147	169	51
Chicago	60	20	34	6	195	225	46

Stanley Cup Finals

April 7	Detroit 3 at Toronto 5
April 10	Detroit 2 at Toronto 4
April 11	Toronto 2 at Detroit 0 [Broda]
April 14	Toronto 7 at Detroit 2

Toronto won best-of-seven finals 4–0

1948–49

	GP	W	L	T	GF	GA	PTS
Detroit	60	34	19	7	195	145	75
Boston	60	29	23	8	178	163	66
Canadiens	60	28	23	9	152	126	65
Toronto	60	22	25	13	147	161	57
Chicago	60	21	31	8	173	211	50
Rangers	60	18	31	11	133	172	47

Stanley Cup Finals

April 8	Toronto 3 at Detroit 2 (Joe Klukay 17:31 OT)
April 10	Toronto 3 at Detroit 1
April 13	Detroit 1 at Toronto 3
April 16	Detroit 1 at Toronto 3

Toronto won best-of-seven finals 4–0

1949–50

	GP	W	L	T	GF	GA	PTS
Detroit	70	37	19	14	229	164	88
Canadiens	70	29	22	19	172	150	77
Toronto	70	31	27	12	176	173	74
Rangers	70	28	31	11	170	189	67
Boston	70	22	32	16	198	228	60
Chicago	70	22	38	10	203	244	54

Stanley Cup Finals

April 11	Rangers 1 at Detroit 4
April 13	Detroit 1 Rangers 3*
April 15	Detroit 4 Rangers 0*[Lumley]
April 18	Rangers 4 at Detroit 3 (Don Raleigh 8:34 OT)
April 20	Rangers 2 at Detroit 1 (Don Raleigh 1:38 OT)
April 22	Rangers 4 at Detroit 5
April 23	Rangers 3 at Detroit 4 (Pete Babando 28:31 OT)**

Detroit won best-of-seven finals 4–3

* played at Toronto because Madison Square Garden was previously booked for the circus. Games 6 and 7 played in Detroit because league by-laws stipulated a Stanley Cup-winning game cannot be played on neutral ice.

** first time in history the Cup was won on an OT goal in game 7

1950–51

	GP	W	L	T	GF	GA	PTS
Detroit	70	44	13	13	236	139	101
Toronto	70	41	16	13	212	138	95
Canadiens	70	25	30	15	173	184	65
Boston	70	22	30	18	178	197	62
Rangers	70	20	29	21	169	201	61
Chicago	70	13	47	10	171	280	36

Stanley Cup Finals

April 11	Canadiens 2 at Toronto 3 (Sid Smith 5:51 OT)
April 14	Canadiens 3 at Toronto 2 (Maurice Richard 2:55 OT)
April 17	Toronto 2 at Canadiens 1 (Ted Kennedy 4:47 OT)
April 19	Toronto 3 at Canadiens 2 (Harry Watson 5:15 OT)
April 21	Canadiens 2 at Toronto 3 (Bill Barilko 2:53 OT)

Toronto won best-of-seven finals 4–1

1951–52

	GP	W	L	T	GF	GA	PTS
Detroit	70	44	14	12	215	133	100
Canadiens	70	34	26	10	195	164	78
Toronto	70	29	25	16	168	157	74
Boston	70	25	29	16	162	176	66
Rangers	70	23	34	13	192	219	59
Chicago	70	17	44	9	158	241	43

Stanley Cup Finals

April 10   Detroit 3 at Canadiens 1
April 12   Detroit 2 at Canadiens 1
April 13   Canadiens 0 at Detroit 3 [Sawchuk]
April 15   Canadiens 0 at Detroit 3 [Sawchuk]
Detroit won best-of-seven finals 4–0

1952–53

	GP	W	L	T	GF	GA	PTS
Detroit	70	36	16	18	222	133	90
Canadiens	70	28	23	19	155	148	75
Boston	70	28	29	13	152	172	69
Chicago	70	27	28	15	169	175	69
Toronto	70	27	30	13	156	167	67
Rangers	70	17	37	16	152	211	50

Stanley Cup Finals

April 9   Boston 2 at Canadiens 4
April 11   Boston 4 at Canadiens 1
April 12   Canadiens 3 at Boston 0 [McNeil]
April 14   Canadiens 7 at Boston 3
April 16   Boston 0 at Canadiens 1 (Elmer Lach 1:22 OT) [McNeil]
Canadiens won best-of-seven finals 4–1

1953–54

	GP	W	L	T	GF	GA	PTS
Detroit	70	37	19	14	191	132	88
Canadiens	70	35	24	11	195	141	81
Toronto	70	32	24	14	152	131	78
Boston	70	32	28	10	177	181	74
Rangers	70	29	31	10	161	182	68
Chicago	70	12	51	7	133	242	31

Stanley Cup Finals

April 4	Canadiens 1 at Detroit 3
April 6	Canadiens 3 at Detroit 1
April 8	Detroit 5 at Canadiens 2
April 10	Detroit 2 at Canadiens 0 [Sawchuk]
April 11	Canadiens 1 at Detroit 0 (Ken Mosdell 5:45 OT) [McNeil]
April 13	Detroit 1 at Canadiens 4
April 16	Canadiens 1 at Detroit 2 (Tony Leswick 4:29 OT)

Detroit won best-of-seven finals 4–3

1954–55

	GP	W	L	T	GF	GA	PTS
Detroit	70	42	17	11	204	134	95
Canadiens	70	41	18	11	228	157	93
Toronto	70	24	24	22	147	135	70
Boston	70	23	26	21	169	188	67
Rangers	70	17	35	18	150	210	52
Chicago	70	13	40	17	161	235	43

Stanley Cup Finals

April 3	Canadiens 2 at Detroit 4
April 5	Canadiens 1 at Detroit 7
April 7	Detroit 2 at Canadiens 4
April 9	Detroit 3 at Canadiens 5

April 10   Canadiens 1 at Detroit 5
April 12   Detroit 3 at Canadiens 6
April 14   Canadiens 1 at Detroit 3
Detroit won best-of-seven finals 4–3

1955–56

	GP	W	L	T	GF	GA	PTS
Canadiens	70	45	15	10	222	131	100
Detroit	70	30	24	16	183	148	76
Rangers	70	32	28	10	204	203	74
Toronto	70	24	33	13	153	181	61
Boston	70	23	34	13	147	185	59
Chicago	70	19	39	12	155	216	50

Stanley Cup Finals

March 31   Detroit 4 at Canadiens 6
April 3   Detroit 1 at Canadiens 5
April 5   Canadiens 1 at Detroit 3
April 8   Canadiens 3 at Detroit 0 [Plante]
April 10   Detroit 1 at Canadiens 3
Canadiens won best-of-seven finals 4–1

1956–57

	GP	W	L	T	GF	GA	PTS
Detroit	70	38	20	12	198	157	88
Canadiens	70	35	23	12	210	155	82
Boston	70	34	24	12	195	174	80
Rangers	70	26	30	14	184	227	66
Toronto	70	21	34	15	174	192	57
Chicago	70	16	39	15	169	225	47

* penalized player allowed to return to the ice after a power-play goal has been
  scored by the opposition

Stanley Cup Finals

April 6	Boston 1 at Canadiens 5
April 9	Boston 0 at Canadiens 1 [Plante]
April 11	Canadiens 4 at Boston 2
April 14	Canadiens 0 at Boston 2 [Simmons]
April 16	Boston 1 at Canadiens 5

Canadiens won best-of-seven finals 4–1

1957–58

	GP	W	L	T	GF	GA	PTS
Canadiens	70	43	17	10	250	158	96
Rangers	70	32	25	13	195	188	77
Detroit	70	29	29	12	176	207	70
Boston	70	27	28	15	199	194	69
Chicago	70	24	39	7	163	202	55
Toronto	70	21	38	11	192	226	53

Stanley Cup Finals

April 8	Boston 1 at Canadiens 2
April 10	Boston 5 at Canadiens 2
April 13	Canadiens 3 at Boston 0 [Plante]
April 15	Canadiens 1 at Boston 3
April 17	Boston 2 at Canadiens 3 (Maurice Richard 5:45 OT)
April 20	Canadiens 5 at Boston 3

Canadiens won best-of-seven finals 4–2

1958–59

	GP	W	L	T	GF	GA	PTS
Canadiens	70	39	18	13	258	158	91
Boston	70	32	29	9	205	215	73
Chicago	70	28	29	13	197	208	69

Toronto	70	27	32	11	189	201	65
Rangers	70	26	32	12	201	217	64
Detroit	70	25	37	8	167	218	58

Stanley Cup Finals

April 9	Toronto 3 at Canadiens 5
April 11	Toronto 1 at Canadiens 3
April 14	Canadiens 2 at Toronto 3 (Dick Duff 10:06 OT)
April 16	Canadiens 3 at Toronto 2
April 18	Toronto 3 at Canadiens 5

Canadiens won best-of-seven finals 4–1

1959–60

	GP	W	L	T	GF	GA	PTS
Canadiens	70	40	18	12	255	178	92
Toronto	70	35	26	9	199	195	79
Chicago	70	28	29	13	191	180	69
Detroit	70	26	29	15	186	197	67
Boston	70	28	34	8	220	241	64
Rangers	70	17	38	15	187	247	49

Stanley Cup Finals

April 7	Toronto 2 at Canadiens 4
April 9	Toronto 1 at Canadiens 2
April 12	Canadiens 5 at Toronto 2
April 14	Canadiens 4 at Toronto 0 [Plante]

Canadiens won best-of-seven finals 4–0

1960–61

	GP	W	L	T	GF	GA	PTS
Canadiens	70	41	19	10	254	188	92
Toronto	70	39	19	12	234	176	90
Chicago	70	29	24	17	198	180	75

	GP	W	L	T	GF	GA	PTS
Detroit	70	25	29	16	195	215	66
Rangers	70	22	38	10	204	248	54
Boston	70	15	42	13	176	254	43

Stanley Cup Finals
April 6	Detroit 2 at Chicago 3
April 8	Chicago 1 at Detroit 3
April 10	Detroit 1 at Chicago 3
April 12	Chicago 1 at Detroit 2
April 14	Detroit 3 at Chicago 6
April 16	Chicago 5 at Detroit 1

Chicago won best-of-seven finals 4–2

1961–62

	GP	W	L	T	GF	GA	PTS
Canadiens	70	42	14	14	259	166	98
Toronto	70	37	22	11	232	180	85
Chicago	70	31	26	13	217	186	75
Rangers	70	26	32	12	195	207	64
Detroit	70	23	33	14	184	219	60
Boston	70	15	47	8	177	306	38

Stanley Cup Finals
April 10	Chicago 1 at Toronto 4
April 12	Chicago 2 at Toronto 3
April 15	Toronto 0 at Chicago 3 [Hall]
April 17	Toronto 1 at Chicago 4
April 19	Chicago 4 at Toronto 8
April 22	Toronto 2 at Chicago 1

Toronto won best-of-seven finals 4–2

1962–63

	GP	W	L	T	GF	GA	PTS
Toronto	70	35	23	12	221	180	82
Chicago	70	32	21	17	194	178	81
Canadiens	70	28	19	23	225	183	79
Detroit	70	32	25	13	200	194	77
Rangers	70	22	36	12	211	233	56
Boston	70	14	39	17	198	281	45

Stanley Cup Finals

April 9   Detroit 2 at Toronto 4
April 11   Detroit 2 at Toronto 4
April 14   Toronto 2 at Detroit 3
April 16   Toronto 4 at Detroit 2
April 18   Detroit 1 at Toronto 3
Toronto won best-of-seven finals 4–1

1963–64

	GP	W	L	T	GF	GA	PTS
Canadiens	70	36	21	13	209	167	85
Chicago	70	36	22	12	218	169	84
Toronto	70	33	25	12	192	172	78
Detroit	70	30	29	11	191	204	71
Rangers	70	22	38	10	186	242	54
Boston	70	18	40	12	170	212	48

Stanley Cup Finals

April 11   Detroit 2 at Toronto 3
April 14   Detroit 4 at Toronto 3 (Larry Jeffrey 7:52 OT)
April 16   Toronto 3 at Detroit 4
April 18   Toronto 4 at Detroit 2

April 21   Detroit 2 at Toronto 1
April 23   Toronto 4 at Detroit 3 (Bobby Baun 1:43 OT)
April 25   Detroit 0 at Toronto 4 [Bower]
Toronto won best-of-seven finals 4–3

1964–65

	GP	W	L	T	GF	GA	PTS
Detroit	70	40	23	7	224	175	87
Canadiens	70	36	23	11	211	185	83
Chicago	70	34	28	8	224	176	76
Toronto	70	30	26	14	204	173	74
Rangers	70	20	38	12	179	246	52
Boston	70	21	43	6	166	253	48

Stanley Cup Finals

April 17   Chicago 2 at Canadiens 3
April 20   Chicago 0 at Canadiens 2 [Worsley]
April 22   Canadiens 1 at Chicago 3
April 25   Canadiens 1 at Chicago 5
April 27   Chicago 0 at Canadiens 6 [Hodge]
April 29   Canadiens 1 at Chicago 2
May 1   Chicago 0 at Canadiens 4 [Worsley]
Canadiens won best-of-seven finals 4–3

1965–66

	GP	W	L	T	GF	GA	PTS
Canadiens	70	41	21	8	239	173	90
Chicago	70	37	25	8	240	187	82
Toronto	70	34	25	11	208	187	79
Detroit	70	31	27	12	221	194	74
Boston	70	21	43	6	174	275	48
Rangers	70	18	41	11	195	261	47

Stanley Cup Finals

April 24   Detroit 3 at Canadiens 2

April 26   Detroit 5 at Canadiens 2

April 28   Canadiens 4 at Detroit 2

May 1   Canadiens 2 at Detroit 1

May 3   Detroit 1 at Canadiens 5

May 5   Canadiens 3 at Detroit 2 (Henri Richard 2:20 OT)

Canadiens won best-of-seven finals 4–2

1966–67

	GP	W	L	T	GF	GA	PTS
Chicago	70	41	17	12	264	170	94
Canadiens	70	32	25	13	202	188	77
Toronto	70	32	27	11	204	211	75
Rangers	70	30	28	12	188	189	72
Detroit	70	27	39	4	212	241	58
Boston	70	17	43	10	182	253	44

Stanley Cup Finals

April 20   Toronto 2 at Canadiens 6

April 22   Toronto 3 at Canadiens 0 [Bower]

April 25   Canadiens 2 at Toronto 3 (Bob Pulford 28:26 OT)

April 27   Canadiens 6 at Toronto 2

April 29   Toronto 4 at Canadiens 1

May 2   Canadiens 1 at Toronto 3

Toronto won best-of-seven finals 4–2

1967–68

East Division

	GP	W	L	T	GF	GA	PTS
Canadiens	74	42	22	10	236	167	94
Rangers	74	39	23	12	226	183	90
Boston	74	37	27	10	259	216	84
Chicago	74	32	26	16	212	222	80
Toronto	74	33	31	10	209	176	76
Detroit	74	27	35	12	245	257	66

West Division

Philadelphia	74	31	32	11	173	179	73
Los Angeles	74	31	33	10	200	224	72
St. Louis	74	27	31	16	177	191	70
North Stars	74	27	32	15	191	226	69
Pittsburgh	74	27	34	13	195	216	67
Oakland	74	15	42	17	153	219	47

* top four teams in each division qualified for the playoffs

Stanley Cup Finals

May 5	Canadiens 3 at St. Louis 2 (Jacques Lemaire 1:41 OT)
May 7	Canadiens 1 at St. Louis 0 [Worsley]
May 9	St. Louis 3 at Canadiens 4 (Bobby Rousseau 1:13 OT)
May 11	St. Louis 2 at Canadiens 3

Canadiens won best-of-seven finals 4–0

1968–69

East Division

	GP	W	L	T	GF	GA	PTS
Canadiens	76	46	19	11	271	202	103
Boston	76	42	18	16	303	221	100
Rangers	76	41	26	9	231	196	91
Toronto	76	35	26	15	234	217	85
Detroit	76	33	31	12	239	221	78
Chicago	76	34	33	9	280	246	77

West Division

	GP	W	L	T	GF	GA	PTS
St. Louis	76	37	25	14	204	157	88
Oakland	76	29	36	11	219	251	69
Philadelphia	76	20	35	21	174	225	61
Los Angeles	76	24	42	10	185	260	58
Pittsburgh	76	20	45	11	189	252	51
North Stars	76	18	43	15	189	270	51

Stanley Cup Finals

April 27   St. Louis 1 at Canadiens 3
April 29   St. Louis 1 at Canadiens 3
May 1   Canadiens 4 at St. Louis 0 [Vachon]
May 4   Canadiens 2 at St. Louis 1
Canadiens won best-of-seven finals 4–0

1969–70

East Division

	GP	W	L	T	GF	GA	PTS
Chicago	76	45	22	9	250	170	99
Boston	76	40	17	19	277	216	99
Detroit	76	40	21	15	246	199	95
Rangers	76	38	22	16	246	189	92
Canadiens	76	38	22	16	244	201	92
Toronto	76	29	34	13	222	242	71

West Division

St. Louis	76	37	27	12	224	179	86
Pittsburgh	76	26	38	12	182	238	64
North Stars	76	19	35	22	224	257	60
Oakland	76	22	40	14	169	243	58
Philadelphia	76	17	35	24	197	225	58
Los Angeles	76	14	52	10	168	290	38

Stanley Cup Finals

May 3	Boston 6 at St. Louis 1
May 5	Boston 6 at St. Louis 2
May 7	St. Louis 1 at Boston 4
May 10	St. Louis 3 at Boston 4 (Bobby Orr 0:40 OT)

Boston won best-of-seven finals 4–0

1970–71

East Division

	GP	W	L	T	GF	GA	PTS
Boston	78	57	14	7	399	207	121
Rangers	78	49	18	11	259	177	109
Canadiens	78	42	23	13	291	216	97
Toronto	78	37	33	8	248	211	82
Buffalo	78	24	39	15	217	291	63
Vancouver	78	24	46	8	229	296	56
Detroit	78	22	45	11	209	308	55

West Division

Chicago	78	49	20	9	277	184	107
St. Louis	78	34	25	19	223	208	87
Philadelphia	78	28	33	17	207	225	73
North Stars	78	28	34	16	191	223	72
Los Angeles	78	25	40	13	239	303	63
Pittsburgh	78	21	37	20	221	240	62
California	78	20	53	5	199	320	45

Stanley Cup Finals

May 4	Canadiens 1 at Chicago 2 (Jim Pappin 21:11 OT)
May 6	Canadiens 3 at Chicago 5
May 9	Chicago 2 at Canadiens 4
May 11	Chicago 2 at Canadiens 5
May 13	Canadiens 0 at Chicago 2 [Esposito]
May 16	Chicago 3 at Canadiens 4
May 18	Canadiens 3 at Chicago 2

Canadiens won best-of-seven finals 4–3

1971–72

East Division

	GP	W	L	T	GF	GA	PTS
Boston	78	54	13	11	330	204	119
Rangers	78	48	17	13	317	192	109
Canadiens	78	46	16	16	307	205	108
Toronto	78	33	31	14	209	208	80
Detroit	78	33	35	10	261	262	76
Buffalo	78	16	43	19	203	289	51
Vancouver	78	20	50	8	203	297	48

West Division

	GP	W	L	T	GF	GA	PTS
Chicago	78	46	17	15	256	166	107
North Stars	78	37	29	12	212	191	86
St. Louis	78	28	39	11	208	247	67
Pittsburgh	78	26	38	14	220	258	66
Philadelphia	78	26	38	14	200	236	66
California	78	21	39	18	216	288	60
Los Angeles	78	20	49	9	206	305	49

Stanley Cup Finals

April 30	Rangers 5 at Boston 6
May 2	Rangers 1 at Boston 2
May 4	Boston 2 at Rangers 5
May 7	Boston 3 at Rangers 2
May 9	Rangers 3 at Boston 2
May 11	Boston 3 at Rangers 0 [Johnston]

Boston won best-of-seven finals 4–2

1972–73

East Division

	GP	W	L	T	GF	GA	PIM	PTS
Canadiens	78	52	10	16	329	184	783	120
Boston	78	51	22	5	330	235	1097	107
Rangers	78	47	23	8	297	208	765	102
Buffalo	78	37	27	14	257	219	940	88
Detroit	78	37	29	12	265	243	893	86
Toronto	78	27	41	10	247	279	716	64
Vancouver	78	22	47	9	233	339	943	53
Islanders	78	12	60	6	170	347	881	30

West Division

	GP	W	L	T	GF	GA	PIM	PTS
Chicago	78	42	27	9	284	225	864	93
Philadelphia	78	37	30	11	296	256	1756	85
North Stars	78	37	30	11	254	230	881	85
St. Louis	78	32	34	12	233	251	1195	76
Pittsburgh	78	32	37	9	257	265	866	73
Los Angeles	78	31	36	11	232	245	888	73
Flames	78	25	38	15	191	239	852	65
California	78	16	46	16	213	323	840	48

Stanley Cup Finals

April 29 Chicago 3 at Canadiens 8
May 1 Chicago 1 at Canadiens 4
May 3 Canadiens 4 at Chicago 7
May 6 Canadiens 4 at Chicago 0 [Dryden]
May 8 Chicago 8 at Canadiens 7
May 10 Canadiens 6 at Chicago 4
Canadiens won best-of-seven finals 4–2

1973–74

East Division

	GP	W	L	T	GF	GA	PTS
Boston	78	52	17	9	349	221	113
Canadiens	78	45	24	9	293	240	99
Rangers	78	40	24	14	300	251	94
Toronto	78	35	27	16	274	230	86
Buffalo	78	32	34	12	242	250	76
Detroit	78	29	39	10	255	319	68
Vancouver	78	24	43	11	224	296	59
Islanders	78	19	41	18	182	247	56

West Division

	GP	W	L	T	GF	GA	PTS
Philadelphia	78	50	16	12	273	164	112
Chicago	78	41	14	23	272	164	105
Los Angeles	78	33	33	12	233	231	78
Flames	78	30	34	14	214	238	74
Pittsburgh	78	28	41	9	242	273	65
St. Louis	78	26	40	12	206	248	64
North Stars	78	23	38	17	235	275	63
California	78	13	55	10	195	342	36

Stanley Cup Finals

May 7	Philadelphia 2 at Boston 3
May 9	Philadelphia 3 at Boston 2 (Bobby Clarke 12:01 OT)
May 12	Boston 1 at Philadelphia 4
May 14	Boston 2 at Philadelphia 4
May 16	Philadelphia 1 at Boston 5
May 19	Boston 0 at Philadelphia 1 [Parent]

Philadelphia won best-of-seven finals 4–2

1974–75

PRINCE OF WALES CONFERENCE
Adams Division

	GP	W	L	T	GF	GA	PTS
Buffalo	80	49	16	15	354	240	113
Boston	80	40	26	14	345	245	94
Toronto	80	31	33	16	280	309	78
California	80	19	48	13	212	316	51

Norris Division

	GP	W	L	T	GF	GA	PTS
Canadiens	80	47	14	19	374	225	113
Los Angeles	80	42	17	21	269	185	105
Pittsburgh	80	37	28	15	326	289	89
Detroit	80	23	45	12	259	335	58
Washington	80	8	67	5	181	446	21

CLARENCE CAMPBELL CONFERENCE
Patrick Division

	GP	W	L	T	GF	GA	PTS
Philadelphia	80	51	18	11	293	181	113
Rangers	80	37	29	14	319	276	88
Islanders	80	33	25	22	264	221	88
Flames	80	34	31	15	243	233	83

Smythe Division

	GP	W	L	T	GF	GA	PTS
Vancouver	80	38	32	10	271	254	86
St. Louis	80	35	31	14	269	267	84
Chicago	80	37	35	8	268	241	82
North Stars	80	23	50	7	221	341	53
Kansas City	80	15	54	11	184	328	41

* the top three teams in each division qualified for the playoffs. The four division champions received byes to the second round and all second- and third-place clubs were seeded 1–8 by points, #1 playing # 8, #2 and #7, etc. The first round was best-of-three, the subsequent rounds best-of-seven.

Stanley Cup Finals

May 15	Buffalo 1 at Philadelphia 4
May 18	Buffalo 1 at Philadelphia 2
May 20	Philadelphia 4 at Buffalo 5 (Rene Robert 18:29 OT)
May 22	Philadelphia 2 at Buffalo 4
May 25	Buffalo 1 at Philadelphia 5
May 27	Philadelphia 2 at Buffalo 0 [Parent]

Philadelphia won best-of-seven finals 4–2

1975–76

PRINCE OF WALES CONFERENCE

Adams Division

	GP	W	L	T	GF	GA	PTS
Boston	80	48	15	17	313	237	113
Buffalo	80	46	21	13	339	240	105
Toronto	80	34	31	15	294	276	83
California	80	27	42	11	250	278	65

Norris Division

	GP	W	L	T	GF	GA	PTS
Canadiens	80	58	11	11	337	174	127
Los Angeles	80	38	33	9	263	265	85
Pittsburgh	80	35	33	12	339	303	82
Detroit	80	26	44	10	226	300	62
Washington	80	11	59	10	224	394	32

CLARENCE CAMPBELL CONFERENCE

Patrick Division

	GP	W	L	T	GF	GA	PTS
Philadelphia	80	51	13	16	348	209	118
Islanders	80	42	21	17	297	190	101
Flames	80	35	33	12	262	237	82
Rangers	80	29	42	9	262	333	67

Smythe Division

Chicago	80	32	30	18	254	261	82
Vancouver	80	33	32	15	271	272	81
St. Louis	80	29	37	14	249	290	72
North Stars	80	20	53	7	195	303	47
Kansas City	80	12	56	12	190	351	36

Stanley Cup Finals

May 9	Philadelphia 3 at Canadiens 4
May 11	Philadelphia 1 at Canadiens 2
May 13	Canadiens 3 at Philadelphia 2
May 16	Canadiens 5 at Philadelphia 3

Canadiens won best-of-seven finals 4–0

1976–77

PRINCE OF WALES CONFERENCE

Adams Division

	GP	W	L	T	GF	GA	PTS
Boston	80	49	23	8	312	240	106
Buffalo	80	48	24	8	301	220	104
Toronto	80	33	32	15	301	285	81
Cleveland	80	25	42	13	240	292	63

Norris Division

Canadiens	80	60	8	12	387	171	132
Los Angeles	80	34	31	15	271	241	83
Pittsburgh	80	34	33	13	240	252	81
Washington	80	24	42	14	221	307	62
Detroit	80	16	55	9	183	309	41

CLARENCE CAMPBELL CONFERENCE

Patrick Division

Philadelphia	80	48	16	16	323	213	112
Islanders	80	47	21	12	288	193	106
Flames	80	34	34	12	264	265	80
Rangers	80	29	37	14	272	310	64

Smythe Division

St. Louis	80	32	39	9	239	276	73
North Stars	80	23	39	18	240	310	64
Chicago	80	26	43	11	240	298	63
Vancouver	80	25	42	13	235	294	63
Rockies	80	20	46	14	226	307	54

Stanley Cup Finals

May 7	Boston 3 at Canadiens 7
May 10	Boston 0 at Canadiens 3 [Dryden]
May 12	Canadiens 4 at Boston 2
May 14	Canadiens 2 at Boston 1

Canadiens won best-of-seven finals 4–0

1977–78

PRINCE OF WALES CONFERENCE

Adams Division

	GP	W	L	T	GF	GA	PTS
Boston	80	51	18	11	333	218	113
Buffalo	80	44	19	17	288	215	105
Toronto	80	41	29	10	271	237	92
Cleveland	80	22	45	13	230	325	57

Norris Division

Canadiens	80	59	10	11	359	183	129
Detroit	80	32	34	14	252	266	78
Los Angeles	80	31	34	15	243	245	77
Pittsburgh	80	25	37	18	254	321	68
Washington	80	17	49	14	195	321	48

CLARENCE CAMPBELL CONFERENCE

Patrick Division

Islanders	80	48	17	15	334	210	111
Philadelphia	80	45	20	15	296	200	105
Flames	80	34	27	19	274	252	87
Rangers	80	30	37	13	279	280	73

Smythe Division

Chicago	80	32	29	19	230	220	83
Rockies	80	19	40	21	257	305	59
Vancouver	80	20	43	17	239	320	57
St. Louis	80	20	47	13	195	304	53
North Stars	80	18	53	9	218	325	45

* all 1st- and 2nd-place teams qualified for playoffs and the next best four
regardless of division also qualified

Stanley Cup Finals

May 13	Boston 1 at Canadiens 4
May 16	Boston 2 at Canadiens 3 (Guy Lafleur 13:09 OT)
May 18	Canadiens 0 at Boston 4 [Cheevers]
May 21	Canadiens 3 at Boston 4 (Bobby Schmautz 6:22 OT)
May 23	Boston 1 at Canadiens 4
May 25	Canadiens 4 at Boston 1

Canadiens won best-of-seven finals 4–2

1978–79

PRINCE OF WALES CONFERENCE

Adams Division

	GP	W	L	T	GF	GA	PTS
Boston	80	43	23	14	316	270	100
Buffalo	80	36	28	16	280	263	88
Toronto	80	34	33	13	267	252	81
North Stars	80	28	40	12	257	289	68

Norris Division

	GP	W	L	T	GF	GA	PTS
Canadiens	80	52	17	11	337	204	115
Pittsburgh	80	36	31	13	281	279	85
Los Angeles	80	34	34	12	292	286	80
Washington	80	24	41	15	273	338	63
Detroit	80	23	41	16	252	295	62

CLARENCE CAMPBELL CONFERENCE

Patrick Division

	GP	W	L	T	GF	GA	PTS
Islanders	80	51	15	14	358	214	116
Philadelphia	80	40	25	15	281	248	95
Rangers	80	40	29	11	316	292	91
Flames	80	41	31	8	327	280	90

Smythe Division

	GP	W	L	T	GF	GA	PTS
Chicago	80	29	36	15	244	277	73
Vancouver	80	25	42	13	217	291	63
St. Louis	80	18	50	12	249	348	48
Rockies	80	15	53	12	210	331	42

Stanley Cup Finals

May 13	Rangers 4 at Canadiens 1
May 15	Rangers 2 at Canadiens 6
May 17	Canadiens 4 at Rangers 1

May 19   Canadiens 4 at Rangers 3 (Serge Savard 7:25 OT)
May 21   Rangers 1 at Canadiens 4
Canadiens won best-of-seven finals 4–1

1979–80

PRINCE OF WALES CONFERENCE
Adams Division

	GP	W	L	T	GF	GA	PTS
Buffalo	80	47	17	16	318	201	110
Boston	80	46	21	13	310	234	105
North Stars	80	36	28	16	311	253	88
Toronto	80	35	40	5	304	327	75
Quebec	80	25	44	11	248	313	61

Norris Division

	GP	W	L	T	GF	GA	PTS
Canadiens	80	47	20	13	328	240	107
Los Angeles	80	30	36	14	290	313	74
Pittsburgh	80	30	37	13	251	303	73
Hartford	80	27	34	19	303	312	73
Detroit	80	26	43	11	268	306	63

CLARENCE CAMPBELL CONFERENCE
Patrick Division

	GP	W	L	T	GF	GA	PTS
Philadelphia	80	48	12	20	327	254	116
Islanders	80	39	28	13	281	247	91
Rangers	80	38	32	10	308	284	86
Flames	80	35	32	13	282	269	83
Washington	80	27	40	13	261	293	67

Smythe Division

	GP	W	L	T	GF	GA	PTS
Chicago	80	34	27	19	241	250	87
St. Louis	80	34	34	12	266	278	80

Vancouver	80	27	37	16	256	281	70
Edmonton	80	28	39	13	301	322	69
Winnipeg	80	20	49	11	214	314	51
Rockies	80	19	48	13	234	308	51

* top four teams in each division qualified for the playoffs

Stanley Cup Finals

May 13	Islanders 4 at Philadelphia 3 (Denis Potvin 4:07 OT)
May 15	Islanders 3 at Philadelphia 8
May 17	Philadelphia 2 at Islanders 6
May 19	Philadelphia 2 at Islanders 5
May 22	Islanders 3 at Philadelphia 6
May 24	Philadelphia 4 at Islanders 5 (Bob Nystrom 7:11 OT)

Islanders won best-of-seven finals 4–2

1980–81

PRINCE OF WALES CONFERENCE
Adams Division

	GP	W	L	T	GF	GA	PTS
Buffalo	80	39	20	21	327	250	99
Boston	80	37	30	13	316	272	87
North Stars	80	35	28	17	291	263	87
Quebec	80	30	32	18	314	318	78
Toronto	80	28	37	15	322	367	71

Norris Division

Canadiens	80	45	22	13	332	232	103
Los Angeles	80	43	24	13	337	290	99
Pittsburgh	80	30	37	13	302	345	73
Hartford	80	21	41	18	292	372	60
Detroit	80	19	43	18	252	339	56

CLARENCE CAMPBELL CONFERENCE
Patrick Division
Islanders	80	48	18	14	355	260	110
Philadelphia	80	41	24	15	313	249	97
Calgary	80	39	27	14	329	298	92
Rangers	80	30	36	14	312	317	74
Washington	80	26	36	18	286	317	70

Smythe Division
St. Louis	80	45	18	17	352	281	107
Chicago	80	31	33	16	304	315	78
Vancouver	80	28	32	20	289	301	76
Edmonton	80	29	35	16	328	327	74
Rockies	80	22	45	13	258	344	57
Winnipeg	80	9	57	14	246	400	32

Stanley Cup Finals
May 12	North Stars 3 at Islanders 6
May 14	North Stars 3 at Islanders 6
May 17	Islanders 7 at North Stars 5
May 19	Islanders 2 at North Stars 4
May 21	North Stars 1 at Islanders 5

Islanders won best-of-seven finals 4–1

1981–82

CLARENCE CAMPBELL CONFERENCE
Norris Division
	GP	W	L	T	GF	GA	PTS
North Stars	80	37	23	20	346	288	94
Winnipeg	80	33	33	14	319	332	80
St. Louis	80	32	40	8	315	349	72
Chicago	80	30	38	12	332	363	72

Toronto	80	20	44	16	298	380	56
Detroit	80	21	47	12	270	351	54

Smythe Division

Edmonton	80	48	17	15	417	295	111
Vancouver	80	30	33	17	290	286	77
Calgary	80	29	34	17	334	345	75
Los Angeles	80	24	41	15	314	369	63
Rockies	80	18	49	13	241	362	49

PRINCE OF WALES CONFERENCE

Adams Division

Canadiens	80	46	17	17	360	223	109
Boston	80	43	27	10	323	285	96
Buffalo	80	39	26	15	307	273	93
Quebec	80	33	31	16	356	345	82
Hartford	80	21	41	18	264	351	60

Patrick Division

Islanders	80	54	16	10	385	250	118
Rangers	80	39	27	14	316	306	92
Philadelphia	80	38	31	11	325	313	87
Pittsburgh	80	31	36	13	310	337	75
Washington	80	26	41	13	319	338	65

Stanley Cup Finals

May 8	Vancouver 5 at Islanders 6 (Mike Bossy 19:58 OT)
May 11	Vancouver 4 at Islanders 6
May 13	Islanders 3 at Vancouver 0 [Smith]
May 16	Islanders 3 at Vancouver 1

Islanders won best-of-seven finals 4–0

1982–83

CLARENCE CAMPBELL CONFERENCE
Norris Division

	GP	W	L	T	GF	GA	PTS
Chicago	80	47	23	10	338	268	104
North Stars	80	40	24	16	321	290	96
Toronto	80	28	40	12	293	330	68
St. Louis	80	25	40	15	285	316	65
Detroit	80	21	44	15	263	344	57

Smythe Division

	GP	W	L	T	GF	GA	PTS
Edmonton	80	47	21	12	424	315	106
Calgary	80	32	34	14	321	317	78
Vancouver	80	30	35	15	303	309	75
Winnipeg	80	33	39	8	311	333	74
Los Angeles	80	27	41	12	308	365	66

PRINCE OF WALES CONFERENCE
Adams Division

	GP	W	L	T	GF	GA	PTS
Boston	80	50	20	10	327	228	110
Canadiens	80	42	24	14	350	286	98
Buffalo	80	38	29	13	318	285	89
Quebec	80	34	34	12	343	336	80
Hartford	80	19	54	7	261	403	45

Patrick Division

	GP	W	L	T	GF	GA	PTS
Philadelphia	80	49	23	8	326	240	106
Islanders	80	42	26	12	302	226	96
Washington	80	39	25	16	306	283	94

Rangers	80	35	35	10	306	287	80
New Jersey	80	17	49	14	230	338	48
Pittsburgh	80	18	53	9	257	394	45

Stanley Cup Finals

May 10	Islanders 2 at Edmonton 0 [Smith]
May 12	Islanders 6 at Edmonton 3
May 14	Edmonton 1 at Islanders 5
May 17	Edmonton 2 at Islanders 4

Islanders won best-of-seven finals 4–0

1983–84

CLARENCE CAMPBELL CONFERENCE

Norris Division

	GP	W	L	T	GF	GA	PTS
North Stars	80	39	31	10	345	344	88
St. Louis	80	32	41	7	293	316	71
Detroit	80	31	42	7	298	323	69
Chicago	80	30	42	8	277	311	68
Toronto	80	26	45	9	303	387	61

Smythe Division

Edmonton	80	57	18	5	446	314	119
Calgary	80	34	32	14	311	314	82
Vancouver	80	32	39	9	306	328	73
Winnipeg	80	31	38	11	340	374	73
Los Angeles	80	23	44	13	309	376	59

PRINCE OF WALES CONFERENCE

Adams Division

Boston	80	49	25	6	336	261	104
Buffalo	80	48	25	7	315	257	103
Quebec	80	42	28	10	360	278	94

Canadiens	80	35	40	5	286	295	75
Hartford	80	28	42	10	288	320	66

Patrick Division

Islanders	80	50	26	4	357	269	104
Washington	80	48	27	5	308	226	101
Philadelphia	80	44	26	10	350	290	98
Rangers	80	42	29	9	314	304	93
New Jersey	80	17	56	7	231	350	41
Pittsburgh	80	16	58	6	254	390	38

* five-minute sudden-death overtime introduced for regular-season games

Stanley Cup Finals

May 10	Edmonton 1 at Islanders 0 [Fuhr]
May 12	Edmonton 1 at Islanders 6
May 15	Islanders 2 at Edmonton 7
May 17	Islanders 2 at Edmonton 7
May 19	Islanders 2 at Edmonton 5

Edmonton won best-of-seven finals 4–1

1984–85

CLARENCE CAMPBELL CONFERENCE

Norris Division

	GP	W	L	T	GF	GA	PTS
St. Louis	80	37	31	12	299	288	86
Chicago	80	38	35	7	309	299	83
Detroit	80	27	41	12	313	357	66
North Stars	80	25	43	12	268	321	62
Toronto	80	20	52	8	253	358	48

Smythe Division

Edmonton	80	49	20	11	401	298	109
Winnipeg	80	43	27	10	358	332	96
Calgary	80	41	27	12	363	302	94
Los Angeles	80	34	32	14	339	326	82
Vancouver	80	25	46	9	284	401	59

PRINCE OF WALES CONFERENCE

Adams Division

Canadiens	80	41	27	12	309	262	94
Quebec	80	41	30	9	323	275	91
Buffalo	80	38	28	14	290	237	90
Boston	80	36	34	10	303	287	82
Hartford	80	30	41	9	268	318	69

Patrick Division

Philadelphia	80	53	20	7	348	241	113
Washington	80	46	25	9	322	240	101
Islanders	80	40	34	6	345	312	86
Rangers	80	26	44	10	295	345	62
New Jersey	80	22	48	10	264	346	54
Pittsburgh	80	24	51	5	276	385	53

Stanley Cup Finals

May 21	Edmonton 1 at Philadelphia 4
May 23	Edmonton 3 at Philadelphia 1
May 25	Philadelphia 3 at Edmonton 4
May 28	Philadelphia 3 at Edmonton 5
May 30	Philadelphia 3 at Edmonton 8

Edmonton won best-of-seven finals 4–1

1985–86

CLARENCE CAMPBELL CONFERENCE

Norris Division

	GP	W	L	T	GF	GA	PTS
Chicago	80	39	33	8	351	349	86
North Stars	80	38	33	9	327	305	85
St. Louis	80	37	34	9	302	291	83
Toronto	80	25	48	7	311	386	57
Detroit	80	17	57	6	266	415	40

Smythe Division

Edmonton	80	56	17	7	426	310	119
Calgary	80	40	31	9	354	315	89
Winnipeg	80	26	47	7	295	372	59
Vancouver	80	23	44	13	282	333	59
Los Angeles	80	23	49	8	284	389	54

PRINCE OF WALES CONFERENCE

Adams Division

Quebec	80	43	31	6	330	289	92
Canadiens	80	40	33	7	330	280	87
Boston	80	37	31	12	311	288	86
Hartford	80	40	36	4	332	302	84
Buffalo	80	37	37	6	296	291	80

Patrick Division

Philadelphia	80	53	23	4	335	241	110
Washington	80	50	23	7	315	272	107
Islanders	80	39	29	12	327	284	90
Rangers	80	36	38	6	280	276	78
Pittsburgh	80	34	38	8	313	305	76
New Jersey	80	28	49	3	300	374	59

Stanley Cup Finals

May 16	Canadiens 2 at Calgary 5
May 18	Canadiens 3 at Calgary 2 (Brian Skrudland 0:09 OT)
May 20	Calgary 3 at Canadiens 5
May 22	Calgary 0 at Canadiens 1 [Roy]
May 24	Canadiens 4 at Calgary 3

Canadiens won best-of-seven finals 4–1

1986–87

CLARENCE CAMPBELL CONFERENCE

Norris Division

	GP	W	L	T	GF	G	PTS
St. Louis	80	32	33	15	281	293	79
Detroit	80	34	36	10	260	274	78
Chicago*	80	29	37	14	290	310	72
Toronto	80	32	42	6	286	319	70
North Stars	80	30	40	10	296	314	70

Smythe Division

	GP	W	L	T	GF	G	PTS
Edmonton	80	50	24	6	372	284	106
Calgary	80	46	31	3	318	289	95
Winnipeg	80	40	32	8	279	271	88
Los Angeles	80	31	41	8	318	341	70
Vancouver	80	29	43	8	282	314	66

PRINCE OF WALES CONFERENCE

Adams Division

	GP	W	L	T	GF	G	PTS
Hartford	80	43	30	7	287	270	93
Canadiens	80	41	29	10	277	241	92
Boston	80	39	34	7	301	276	85
Quebec	80	31	39	10	267	276	72
Buffalo	80	28	44	8	280	308	64

Patrick Division

Philadelphia	80	46	26	8	310	245	100
Washington	80	38	32	10	285	278	86
Islanders	80	35	33	12	279	281	82
Rangers	80	34	38	8	307	323	76
Pittsburgh	80	30	38	12	297	290	72
New Jersey	80	29	45	6	293	368	64

* Chicago changed spelling of nickname from Black Hawks to Blackhawks at start of season

Stanley Cup Finals

May 17	Philadelphia 2 at Edmonton 4
May 20	Philadelphia 2 at Edmonton 3 (Jari Kurri 6:50 OT)
May 22	Edmonton 3 at Philadelphia 5
May 24	Edmonton 4 at Philadelphia 1
May 26	Philadelphia 4 at Edmonton 3
May 28	Edmonton 2 at Philadelphia 3
May 31	Philadelphia 1 at Edmonton 3

Edmonton won best-of-seven finals 4–3

1987–88

CLARENCE CAMPBELL CONFERENCE

Norris Division

	GP	W	L	T	GF	GA	PTS
Detroit	80	41	28	11	322	269	93
St. Louis	80	34	38	8	278	294	76
Chicago	80	30	41	9	284	326	69
Toronto	80	21	49	10	273	345	52
North Stars	80	19	48	13	242	349	51

Smythe Division

Calgary	80	48	23	9	397	305	105
Edmonton	80	44	25	11	363	288	99
Winnipeg	80	33	36	11	292	310	77
Los Angeles	80	30	42	8	318	359	68
Vancouver	80	25	46	9	272	320	59

PRINCE OF WALES CONFERENCE
Adams Division

Canadiens	80	45	22	13	298	238	103
Boston	80	44	30	6	300	251	94
Buffalo	80	37	32	11	283	305	85
Hartford	80	35	38	7	249	267	77
Quebec	80	32	43	5	271	306	69

Patrick Division

Islanders	80	39	31	10	308	267	88
Washington	80	38	33	9	281	249	85
Philadelphia	80	38	33	9	292	282	85
New Jersey	80	38	36	6	295	296	82
Rangers	80	36	34	10	300	283	82
Pittsburgh	80	36	35	9	319	316	81

Stanley Cup Finals

May 18	Boston 1 at Edmonton 2
May 20	Boston 2 at Edmonton 4
May 22	Edmonton 6 at Boston 3
May 24	Edmonton 3 at Boston 3*
May 26	Boston 3 at Edmonton 6

Edmonton won best-of-seven finals 4–0

* game suspended because of power failure but statistics counted (if necessary, this game would have been made up at the end of the series)

1988–89
CLARENCE CAMPBELL CONFERENCE
Norris Division

	GP	W	L	T	GF	GA	PTS
Detroit	80	34	34	12	313	316	80
St. Louis	80	33	35	12	275	285	78
North Stars	80	27	37	16	258	278	70

Chicago	80	27	41	12	297	335	66
Toronto	80	28	46	6	259	342	62

Smythe Division

Calgary	80	54	17	9	354	226	117
Los Angeles	80	42	31	7	376	335	91
Edmonton	80	38	34	8	325	306	84
Vancouver	80	33	39	8	251	253	74
Winnipeg	80	26	42	12	300	355	64

PRINCE OF WALES CONFERENCE

Adams Division

Canadiens	80	53	18	9	315	218	115
Boston	80	37	29	14	289	256	88
Buffalo	80	38	35	7	291	299	83
Hartford	80	37	38	5	299	290	79
Quebec	80	27	46	7	269	342	61

Patrick Division

Washington	80	41	29	10	305	259	92
Pittsburgh	80	40	33	7	347	349	87
Rangers	80	37	35	8	310	307	82
Philadelphia	80	36	36	8	307	285	80
New Jersey	80	27	41	12	281	325	66
Islanders	80	28	47	5	265	325	61

Stanley Cup Finals

May 14	Canadiens 2 at Calgary 3
May 17	Canadiens 4 at Calgary 2
May 19	Calgary 3 at Canadiens 4 (Ryan Walter 38:08 OT)
May 21	Calgary 4 at Canadiens 2
May 23	Canadiens 2 at Calgary 3
May 25	Calgary 4 at Canadiens 2

Calgary won best-of-seven finals 4–2

1989–90

CLARENCE CAMPBELL CONFERENCE

Norris Division

	GP	W	L	T	GF	GA	PTS
Chicago	80	41	33	6	316	294	88
St. Louis	80	37	34	9	295	279	83
Toronto	80	38	38	4	337	358	80
North Stars	80	36	40	4	284	291	76
Detroit	80	28	38	14	288	323	70

Smythe Division

Calgary	80	42	23	15	348	265	99
Edmonton	80	38	28	14	315	283	90
Winnipeg	80	37	32	11	298	290	85
Los Angeles	80	34	39	7	338	337	75
Vancouver	80	25	41	14	245	306	64

PRINCE OF WALES CONFERENCE

Adams Division

Boston	80	46	25	9	289	232	101
Buffalo	80	45	27	8	286	248	98
Canadiens	80	41	28	11	288	234	93
Hartford	80	38	33	9	275	268	85
Quebec	80	12	61	7	240	407	31

Patrick Division

Rangers	80	36	31	13	279	267	85
New Jersey	80	37	34	9	295	288	83
Washington	80	36	38	6	284	275	78

Islanders	80	31	38	11	281	288	73
Pittsburgh	80	32	40	8	318	359	72
Philadelphia	80	30	39	11	290	297	71

Stanley Cup Finals

May 15   Edmonton 3 at Boston 2 (Petr Klima 55:13 OT)
May 18   Edmonton 7 at Boston 2
May 20   Boston 2 at Edmonton 1
May 22   Boston 1 at Edmonton 5
May 24   Edmonton 4 at Boston 1
Edmonton won best-of-seven finals 4–1

1990–91

CLARENCE CAMPBELL CONFERENCE

Norris Division

	GP	W	L	T	GF	GA	PTS
Chicago	80	49	23	8	284	211	106
St. Louis	80	47	22	11	310	250	105
Detroit	80	34	38	8	273	298	76
North Stars	80	27	39	14	256	266	68
Toronto	80	23	46	11	241	318	57

Smythe Division

Los Angeles	80	46	24	10	340	254	102
Calgary	80	46	26	8	344	263	100
Edmonton	80	37	37	6	272	272	80
Vancouver	80	28	43	9	243	315	65
Winnipeg	80	26	43	11	260	288	63

PRINCE OF WALES CONFERENCE
Adams Division

Boston	80	44	24	12	299	264	100
Canadiens	80	39	30	11	273	249	89
Buffalo	80	31	30	19	292	278	81
Hartford	80	31	38	11	238	276	73
Quebec	80	16	50	14	236	354	46

Patrick Division

Pittsburgh	80	41	33	6	342	305	88
Rangers	80	36	31	13	297	265	85
Washington	80	37	36	7	258	258	81
New Jersey	80	32	33	15	272	264	79
Philadelphia	80	33	37	10	252	267	76
Islanders	80	25	45	10	223	290	60

Stanley Cup Finals

May 15	Minnesota 5 at Pittsburgh 4
May 17	Minnesota 1 at Pittsburgh 4
May 19	Pittsburgh 1 at Minnesota 3
May 21	Pittsburgh 5 at Minnesota 3
May 23	Minnesota 4 at Pittsburgh 6
May 25	Pittsburgh 8 at Minnesota 0 [Barrasso]

Pittsburgh won best-of-seven finals 4–2

1991–92
CLARENCE CAMPBELL CONFERENCE
Norris Division

	GP	W	L	T	GF	GA	PTS
Detroit	80	43	25	12	320	256	98
Chicago	80	36	29	15	257	236	87
St. Louis	80	36	33	11	279	266	83
North Stars	80	32	42	6	246	278	70
Toronto	80	30	43	7	234	294	67

Smythe Division

Vancouver	80	42	26	12	285	250	96
Los Angeles	80	35	31	14	287	296	84
Edmonton	80	36	34	10	295	297	82
Winnipeg	80	33	32	15	251	244	81
Calgary	80	31	37	12	296	305	74
San Jose	80	17	58	5	219	359	39

PRINCE OF WALES CONFERENCE

Adams Division

Canadiens	80	41	28	11	267	207	93
Boston	80	36	32	12	270	275	84
Buffalo	80	31	37	12	289	299	74
Hartford	80	26	41	13	247	283	65
Quebec	80	20	48	12	255	318	52

Patrick Division

Rangers	80	50	25	5	321	246	105
Washington	80	45	27	8	330	275	98
Pittsburgh	80	39	32	9	343	308	87
New Jersey	80	38	31	11	289	259	87
Islanders	80	34	35	11	291	299	79
Philadelphia	80	32	37	11	252	273	75

Stanley Cup Finals

May 26	Chicago 4 at Pittsburgh 5
May 28	Chicago 1 at Pittsburgh 3
May 30	Pittsburgh 1 at Chicago 0 [Barrasso]
June 1	Pittsburgh 6 at Chicago 5

Pittsburgh won best-of-seven finals 4–0

1992–93

CLARENCE CAMPBELL CONFERENCE
Norris Division

	GP	W	L	T	GF	GA	PTS
Chicago	84	47	25	12	279	230	106
Detroit	84	47	28	9	369	280	103
Toronto	84	44	29	11	288	241	99
St. Louis	84	37	36	11	282	278	85
North Stars	84	36	38	10	272	293	82
Tampa Bay	84	23	54	7	245	332	53

Smythe Division

	GP	W	L	T	GF	GA	PTS
Vancouver	84	46	29	9	346	278	101
Calgary	84	43	30	11	322	282	97
Los Angeles	84	39	35	10	338	340	88
Winnipeg	84	40	37	7	322	320	87
Edmonton	84	26	50	8	242	337	60
San Jose	84	11	71	2	218	414	24

PRINCE OF WALES CONFERENCE
Adams Division

	GP	W	L	T	GF	GA	PTS
Boston	84	51	26	7	332	268	109
Quebec	84	47	27	10	351	300	104
Canadiens	84	48	30	6	326	280	102
Buffalo	84	38	36	10	335	297	86
Hartford	84	26	52	6	284	369	58
Ottawa	84	10	70	4	202	395	24

Patrick Division

	GP	W	L	T	GF	GA	PTS
Pittsburgh	84	56	21	7	367	268	119
Washington	84	43	34	7	325	286	93
Islanders	84	40	37	7	335	297	87

	GP	W	L	T	GF	GA	PTS
New Jersey	84	40	37	7	308	299	87
Philadelphia	84	36	37	11	319	319	83
Rangers	84	34	39	11	304	308	79

Stanley Cup Finals

June 1	Los Angeles 4 at Canadiens 1
June 3	Los Angeles 2 at Canadiens 3 (Eric Desjardins 0:51 OT)
June 5	Canadiens 4 at Los Angeles 3 (John LeClair 0:34 OT)
June 7	Canadiens 3 at Los Angeles 2 (John LeClair 14:37 OT)
June 9	Los Angeles 1 at Canadiens 4

Canadiens won best-of-seven finals 4–1

1993–94

WESTERN CONFERENCE
Central Division

	GP	W	L	T	GF	GA	PTS
Detroit	84	46	30	8	356	275	100
Toronto	84	43	29	12	280	243	98
Dallas	84	42	29	13	286	265	97
St. Louis	84	40	33	11	270	283	91
Chicago	84	39	36	9	254	240	87
Winnipeg	84	24	51	9	245	344	57

Pacific Division

	GP	W	L	T	GF	GA	PTS
Calgary	84	42	29	13	302	256	97
Vancouver	84	41	40	3	279	276	85
San Jose	84	33	35	16	252	265	82
Anaheim	84	33	46	5	229	251	71
Los Angeles	84	27	45	12	294	322	66
Edmonton	84	25	45	14	261	305	64

EASTERN CONFERENCE

Northeast Division

Pittsburgh	84	44	27	13	299	285	101
Boston	84	42	29	13	289	252	97
Canadiens	84	41	29	14	283	248	96
Buffalo	84	43	32	9	282	218	95
Quebec	84	34	42	8	277	292	76
Hartford	84	27	48	9	227	288	63
Ottawa	84	14	61	9	201	397	37

Atlantic Division

Rangers	84	52	24	8	299	231	112
New Jersey	84	47	25	12	306	220	106
Washington	84	39	35	10	277	263	88
Islanders	84	36	36	12	282	264	84
Florida	84	33	34	17	233	233	83
Philadelphia	84	35	39	10	294	314	80
Tampa Bay	84	30	43	11	224	251	71

* the top eight teams in each conference qualified for the playoffs

Stanley Cup Finals

May 31	Vancouver 3 at Rangers 2 (Greg Adams 19:26 OT)
June 2	Vancouver 1 at Rangers 3
June 4	Rangers 5 at Vancouver 1
June 7	Rangers 4 at Vancouver 2
June 9	Vancouver 6 at Rangers 3
June 11	Rangers 1 at Vancouver 4
June 14	Vancouver 2 at Rangers 3

Rangers won best-of-seven finals 4–3

1994–95

WESTERN CONFERENCE

Central Division

	GP	W	L	T	GF	GA	PTS
Detroit	48	33	11	4	180	117	70
St. Louis	48	28	15	5	178	135	61
Chicago	48	24	19	5	156	115	53
Toronto	48	21	19	8	135	146	50
Dallas	48	17	23	8	136	135	42
Winnipeg	48	16	25	7	157	177	39

Pacific Division

	GP	W	L	T	GF	GA	PTS
Calgary	48	24	17	7	163	135	55
Vancouver	48	18	18	12	153	148	48
San Jose	48	19	25	4	129	161	42
Los Angeles	48	16	23	9	142	174	41
Edmonton	48	17	27	4	136	183	38
Anaheim	48	16	27	5	125	164	37

EASTERN CONFERENCE

Northeast Division

	GP	W	L	T	GF	GA	PTS
Quebec	48	30	13	5	185	134	65
Pittsburgh	48	29	16	3	181	158	61
Boston	48	27	18	3	150	127	57
Buffalo	48	22	19	7	130	119	51
Hartford	48	19	24	5	127	141	43
Canadiens	48	18	23	7	125	148	43
Ottawa	48	9	34	5	116	174	23

Atlantic Division

Philadelphia	48	28	16	4	150	132	60
New Jersey	48	22	18	8	136	121	52
Washington	48	22	18	8	136	120	52
Rangers	48	22	23	3	139	134	47
Florida	48	20	22	6	115	127	46
Tampa Bay	48	17	28	3	120	144	37
Islanders	48	15	28	5	126	158	35

Stanley Cup Finals

June 17	New Jersey 2 at Detroit 1
June 20	New Jersey 4 at Detroit 2
June 22	Detroit 2 at New Jersey 5
June 24	Detroit 2 at New Jersey 5

New Jersey won best-of-seven finals 4–0

1995–96

WESTERN CONFERENCE
Central Division

	GP	W	L	T	GF	GA	PTS
Detroit	82	62	13	7	325	181	131
Chicago	82	40	28	14	273	220	94
Toronto	82	34	36	12	247	252	80
St. Louis	82	32	34	16	219	248	80
Winnipeg	82	36	40	6	275	291	78
Dallas	82	26	42	14	227	280	66

Pacific Division

Colorado	82	47	25	10	326	240	104
Calgary	82	34	37	11	241	240	79
Vancouver	82	32	35	15	278	278	79
Anaheim	82	35	39	8	234	247	78
Edmonton	82	30	44	8	240	304	68
Los Angeles	82	24	40	18	256	302	66
San Jose	82	20	55	7	252	357	47

EASTERN CONFERENCE

Northeast Division

Pittsburgh	82	49	29	4	362	284	102
Boston	82	40	31	11	282	269	91
Canadiens	82	40	32	10	265	248	90
Hartford	82	34	39	9	237	259	77
Buffalo	82	33	42	7	247	262	73
Ottawa	82	18	59	5	191	291	41

Atlantic Division

Philadelphia	82	45	24	13	282	208	103
Rangers	82	41	27	14	272	237	96
Florida	82	41	31	10	254	234	92
Washington	82	39	32	11	234	204	89
Tampa Bay	82	38	32	12	238	248	88
New Jersey	82	37	33	12	215	202	86
Islanders	82	22	50	10	229	315	54

Stanley Cup Finals

June 4	Florida 1 at Colorado 3
June 6	Florida 1 at Colorado 8
June 8	Colorado 3 at Florida 2
June 10	Colorado 1 at Florida 0 (Uwe Krupp 44:31 OT) [Roy]

Colorado won best-of seven finals 4–0

1996–97

WESTERN CONFERENCE

Central Division

	GP	W	L	T	GF	GA	PTS
Dallas	82	48	26	8	252	198	104
Detroit	82	38	26	18	253	197	94
Phoenix	82	38	37	7	240	243	83
St. Louis	82	36	35	11	236	239	83
Chicago	82	34	35	13	223	210	81
Toronto	82	30	44	8	230	273	68

Pacific Division

	GP	W	L	T	GF	GA	PTS
Colorado	82	49	24	9	277	205	107
Anaheim	82	36	33	13	245	233	85
Edmonton	82	36	37	9	252	247	81
Vancouver	82	35	40	7	257	273	77
Calgary	82	32	41	9	214	239	73
Los Angeles	82	28	43	11	214	268	67
San Jose	82	27	47	8	211	278	62

EASTERN CONFERENCE

Northeast Division

	GP	W	L	T	GF	GA	PTS
Buffalo	82	40	30	12	237	208	92
Pittsburgh	82	38	36	8	285	280	84
Ottawa	82	31	36	15	226	234	77
Canadiens	82	31	36	15	249	276	77
Hartford	82	32	39	11	226	256	75
Boston	82	26	47	9	234	300	61

Atlantic Division

New Jersey	82	45	23	14	231	182	104
Philadelphia	82	45	24	13	274	217	103
Florida	82	35	28	19	221	201	89
Rangers	82	38	34	10	258	231	86
Washington	82	33	40	9	214	231	75
Tampa Bay	82	32	40	10	217	247	74
Islanders	82	29	41	12	240	250	70

Stanley Cup Finals

May 31	Detroit 4 at Philadelphia 2
June 3	Detroit 4 at Philadelphia 2
June 5	Philadelphia 1 at Detroit 6
June 7	Philadelphia 1 at Detroit 2

Detroit won best-of-seven finals 4–0

1997–98

WESTERN CONFERENCE

Central Division

	GP	W	L	T	GF	GA	PTS
Dallas	82	49	22	11	242	167	109
Detroit	82	44	23	15	250	196	103
St. Louis	82	45	29	8	256	204	98
Phoenix	82	35	35	12	224	227	82
Chicago	82	30	39	13	192	199	73
Toronto	82	30	43	9	194	237	69

Pacific Division

Colorado	82	39	26	17	231	205	95
Los Angeles	82	38	33	11	227	225	87
Edmonton	82	35	37	10	215	224	80
San Jose	82	34	38	10	210	216	78
Calgary	82	26	41	15	217	252	67
Anaheim	82	26	43	13	205	261	65
Vancouver	82	25	43	14	224	273	64

EASTERN CONFERENCE

Northeast Division

Pittsburgh	82	40	24	18	228	188	98
Boston	82	39	30	13	221	194	91
Buffalo	82	36	29	17	211	187	89
Canadiens	82	37	32	13	235	208	87
Ottawa	82	34	33	15	193	20	83
Carolina	82	33	41	8	200	219	74

Atlantic Division

New Jersey	82	48	23	11	225	166	107
Philadelphia	82	42	29	11	242	193	95
Washington	82	40	30	12	219	202	92
Islanders	82	30	41	11	212	225	71
Rangers	82	25	39	18	197	231	68
Florida	82	24	43	15	203	256	63
Tampa Bay	82	17	55	10	151	269	44

Stanley Cup Finals

June 9	Washington 1 at Detroit 2
June 11	Washington 4 at Detroit 5 (Kris Draper 15:24 OT)
June 13	Detroit 2 at Washington 1
June 16	Detroit 4 at Washington 1

Detroit won best-of-seven finals 4–0

1998–99

EASTERN CONFERENCE
Northeast Division

	GP	W	L	T	GF	GA	PTS
Ottawa	82	44	23	15	239	179	103
Toronto	82	45	30	7	268	231	97
Boston	82	39	30	13	214	181	91
Buffalo	82	37	28	17	207	175	91
Canadiens	82	32	39	11	184	209	75

Atlantic Division

	GP	W	L	T	GF	GA	PTS
New Jersey	82	47	24	11	248	196	105
Philadelphia	82	37	26	19	231	196	93
Pittsburgh	82	38	30	14	242	225	90
Rangers	82	33	38	11	217	227	77
Islanders	82	24	48	10	194	244	58

Southeast Division

	GP	W	L	T	GF	GA	PTS
Carolina	82	34	30	18	210	202	86
Florida	82	30	34	18	210	228	78
Washington	82	31	45	6	200	218	68
Tampa Bay	82	19	54	9	179	292	47

WESTERN CONFERENCE
Central Division

	GP	W	L	T	GF	GA	PTS
Detroit	82	43	32	7	245	202	93
St. Louis	82	37	32	13	237	209	87
Chicago	82	29	41	12	202	248	70
Nashville	82	28	47	7	190	261	63

Pacific Division

Dallas	82	51	19	12	236	168	114
Phoenix	82	39	31	12	205	197	90
Anaheim	82	35	34	13	215	206	83
San Jose	82	31	33	18	196	191	80
Los Angeles	82	32	45	5	189	222	69

Northwest Division

Colorado	82	44	28	10	239	205	98
Edmonton	82	33	37	12	230	226	78
Calgary	82	30	40	12	211	234	72
Vancouver	82	23	47	12	192	258	58

Stanley Cup Finals

June 8	Buffalo 3 at Dallas 2 (Jason Woolley 15:30 OT)
June 10	Buffalo 2 at Dallas 4
June 12	Dallas 2 at Buffalo 1
June 15	Dallas 1 at Buffalo 2
June 17	Buffalo 0 at Dallas 2 [Belfour]
June 19	Dallas 2 at Buffalo 1 (Brett Hull 54:51 OT)

Dallas won best-of-seven finals 4–2

1999–2000

EASTERN CONFERENCE

Northeast Division

	GP	W	L	T	OTL	GF	GA	PTS
Toronto	82	45	30	7	3	246	222	100
Ottawa	82	41	30	11	2	244	210	95
Buffalo	82	35	36	11	4	213	204	85
Canadiens	82	35	38	9	4	196	194	83
Boston	82	24	39	19	6	210	248	73

Atlantic Division

Philadelphia	82	45	25	12	3	237	179	105
New Jersey	82	45	29	8	5	251	203	103
Pittsburgh	82	37	37	8	6	241	236	88
Rangers	82	29	42	12	3	218	246	73
Islanders	82	24	49	9	1	194	275	58

Southeast Division

Washington	82	44	26	12	2	227	194	102
Florida	82	43	33	6	6	244	209	98
Carolina	82	37	35	10	0	217	216	84
Tampa Bay	82	19	54	9	7	204	309	54
Atlanta	82	14	61	7	4	170	313	39

WESTERN CONFERENCE

Central Division

St. Louis	82	51	20	11	1	248	165	114
Detroit	82	48	24	10	2	278	210	108
Chicago	82	33	39	10	2	242	245	78
Nashville	82	28	47	7	7	199	240	70

Northwest Division

Colorado	82	42	29	11	1	233	201	96
Edmonton	82	32	34	16	8	226	212	88
Vancouver	82	30	37	15	8	227	237	83
Calgary	82	31	41	10	5	211	256	77

Pacific Division

Dallas	82	43	29	10	6	211	184	102
Los Angeles	82	39	31	12	4	245	228	94
Phoenix	82	39	35	8	4	232	228	90
San Jose	82	35	37	10	7	225	214	87
Anaheim	82	34	36	12	3	217	227	83

Stanley Cup Finals

May 30	Dallas 3 at New Jersey 7
June 1	Dallas 2 at New Jersey 1
June 3	New Jersey 2 at Dallas 1
June 5	New Jersey 3 at Dallas 1
June 8	Dallas 1 at New Jersey 0 (Mike Modano 46:21 OT) [Belfour]
June 10	New Jersey 2 at Dallas 1 (Jason Arnott 28:20 OT)

New Jersey won best-of-seven finals 4–2

2000–01

EASTERN CONFERENCE

Northeast Division

	GP	W	L	T	OTL	GF	GA	PTS
Ottawa	82	48	21	9	4	274	205	109
Buffalo	82	46	30	5	1	218	184	98
Toronto	82	37	29	11	5	232	207	90
Boston	82	36	30	8	8	227	249	88
Montreal	82	28	40	8	6	206	232	70

Atlantic Division

	GP	W	L	T	OTL	GF	GA	PTS
New Jersey	82	48	19	12	3	295	195	111
Philadelphia	82	43	25	11	3	240	207	100
Pittsburgh	82	42	28	9	3	281	256	96
Rangers	82	33	43	5	1	250	290	72
Islanders	82	21	51	7	3	185	268	52

Southeast Division

	GP	W	L	T	OTL	GF	GA	PTS
Washington	82	41	27	10	4	233	211	96
Carolina	82	38	32	9	3	212	225	88
Florida	82	22	38	13	9	200	246	66
Atlanta	82	23	45	12	2	211	289	60
Tampa Bay	82	24	47	6	5	201	280	59

WESTERN CONFERENCE
Central Division

Detroit	82	49	20	9	4	253	202	111
St. Louis	82	43	22	12	5	249	195	103
Nashville	82	34	36	9	3	186	200	80
Chicago	82	29	40	8	5	210	246	71
Columbus	82	28	39	9	6	190	233	71

Northwest Division

Colorado	82	52	16	10	4	270	192	118
Edmonton	82	39	28	12	3	243	222	93
Vancouver	82	36	28	11	7	239	238	90
Calgary	82	27	36	15	4	197	236	73
Minnesota	82	25	39	13	5	168	210	68

Pacific Division

Dallas	82	48	24	8	2	241	187	106
San Jose	82	40	27	12	3	217	192	95
Los Angeles	82	38	28	13	3	252	228	92
Phoenix	82	35	27	17	3	214	212	90
Anaheim	82	25	41	11	5	188	245	66

Stanley Cup Finals

May 26	New Jersey 0 at Colorado 5 [Roy]
May 29	New Jersey 2 at Colorado 1
May 31	Colorado 3 at New Jersey 1
June 2	Colorado 2 at New Jersey 3
June 4	New Jersey 4 at Colorado 1
June 7	Colorado 4 at New Jersey 0 [Roy]
June 9	New Jersey 1 at Colorado 3

Colorado won best-of-seven finals 4–3

2001–02

EASTERN CONFERENCE
Northeast Division

	GP	W	L	T	OTL	GF	GA	PTS
Boston	82	43	24	6	9	236	201	101
Toronto	82	43	25	10	4	249	207	100
Ottawa	82	39	27	9	7	243	208	94
Montreal	82	36	31	12	3	207	209	87
Buffalo	82	35	35	11	1	213	200	82

Atlantic Division

	GP	W	L	T	OTL	GF	GA	PTS
Philadelphia	82	42	27	10	3	234	192	97
Islanders	82	42	28	8	4	239	220	96
New Jersey	82	41	28	9	4	205	187	95
Rangers	82	36	38	4	4	227	258	80
Pittsburgh	82	28	41	8	5	198	249	69

Southeast Division

	GP	W	L	T	OTL	GF	GA	PTS
Carolina	82	35	26	16	5	217	217	91
Washington	82	36	33	11	2	228	240	85
Tampa Bay	82	27	40	11	4	178	219	69
Florida	82	22	44	10	6	180	250	60
Atlanta	82	19	47	11	5	187	288	54

WESTERN CONFERENCE
Central Division

	GP	W	L	T	OTL	GF	GA	PTS
Detroit	82	51	17	10	4	251	187	116
St. Louis	82	43	27	8	4	227	188	98
Chicago	82	41	27	13	1	216	207	96
Nashville	82	28	41	13	0	196	230	69
Columbus	82	22	47	8	5	164	255	57

Pacific Division

San Jose	82	44	27	8	3	248	199	99
Phoenix	82	40	27	9	6	228	210	95
Los Angeles	82	40	27	11	4	214	190	95
Dallas	82	36	28	13	5	215	213	90
Anaheim	82	29	42	8	3	175	198	69

Northwest Division

Colorado	82	42	28	8	1	212	169	99
Vancouver	82	42	30	7	3	254	211	94
Edmonton	82	38	28	12	4	205	182	92
Calgary	82	32	35	12	3	201	220	79
Minnesota	82	26	35	12	9	195	238	73

Stanley Cup Finals

June 4	Carolina 3 at Detroit 2
June 6	Carolina 1 at Detroit 3
June 8	Detroit 3 at Carolina 2
June 10	Detroit 3 at Carolina 0
June 13	Carolina 1 at Detroit 3

Detroit won best-of-seven finals 4–1

2002–03

EASTERN CONFERENCE

Northeast Division

	GP	W	L	T	OTL	GF	GA	PTS
Ottawa	82	52	21	8	1	263	182	113
Toronto	82	44	28	7	3	236	208	98
Boston	82	36	31	11	4	245	237	87
Montreal	82	30	35	8	9	206	234	77
Buffalo	82	27	37	10	8	190	219	72

Atlantic Division

New Jersey	82	46	20	10	6	216	166	108
Philadelphia	82	45	20	13	4	211	166	107
Islanders	82	35	34	11	2	224	231	83
Rangers	82	32	36	10	4	210	231	78
Pittsburgh	82	27	44	6	5	189	255	65

Southeast Division

Tampa Bay	82	36	25	16	5	219	210	93
Washington	82	39	29	8	6	224	220	92
Atlanta	82	31	39	7	5	226	284	74
Florida	82	24	36	13	9	176	237	70
Carolina	82	22	43	11	6	171	240	61

WESTERN CONFERENCE

Central Division

Detroit	82	48	20	10	4	269	203	110
St. Louis	82	41	24	11	6	253	222	99
Chicago	82	30	33	13	6	207	226	79
Nashville	82	27	35	13	7	183	206	74
Columbus	82	29	42	8	3	213	263	69

Pacific Division

Dallas	82	46	17	15	4	245	169	111
Anaheim	82	40	27	9	6	203	193	95
Los Angeles	82	33	37	6	6	203	221	78
Phoenix	82	31	35	11	5	204	230	78
San Jose	82	28	37	9	8	214	239	73

Northwest Division

Colorado	82	42	19	13	8	251	194	105
Vancouver	82	45	23	13	1	264	208	104
Minnesota	82	42	29	10	1	198	178	95
Edmonton	82	36	26	11	9	231	230	92

| Calgary | 82 | 29 | 36 | 13 | 4 | 186 | 228 | 75 |

Stanley Cup Finals

May 27	Anaheim 0 at New Jersey 3 [Brodeur]
May 29	Anaheim 0 at New Jersey 3 [Brodeur]
May 31	New Jersey 2 at Anaheim 3 (Ruslan Salei 6:59 OT)
June 2	New Jersey 0 at Anaheim 1 (Steve Thomas 0:39 OT) [Giguere]
June 5	Anaheim 3 at New Jersey 6
June 7	New Jersey 2 at Anaheim 5
June 9	Anaheim 0 at New Jersey 3 [Brodeur]

New Jersey won best-of-seven finals 4–3

2003–04

EASTERN CONFERENCE

Atlantic Division

	GP	W	L	T	OTL	PTS	GF	GA
Philadelphia	82	40	21	15	6	101	229	186
New Jersey	82	43	25	12	2	100	213	164
Islanders	82	38	29	11	4	91	237	210
Rangers	82	27	40	7	8	69	206	250
Pittsburgh	82	23	47	8	4	58	190	303

Northeast Division

	GP	W	L	T	OTL	PTS	GF	GA
Boston	82	41	19	15	7	104	209	188
Toronto	82	45	24	10	3	103	242	204
Ottawa	82	43	23	10	6	102	262	189
Montreal	82	41	30	7	4	93	208	192
Buffalo	82	37	34	7	4	85	220	221

Southeast Division

Tampa Bay	82	46	22	8	6	106	245	192
Atlanta	82	33	37	8	4	78	214	243
Carolina	82	28	34	14	6	76	172	209
Florida	82	28	35	15	4	75	188	221
Washington	82	23	46	10	3	59	186	253

WESTERN CONFERENCE

Central Division

Detroit	82	48	21	11	2	109	255	189
St. Louis	82	39	30	11	2	91	191	198
Nashville	82	38	29	11	4	91	216	217
Columbus	82	25	45	8	4	62	177	238
Chicago	82	20	43	11	8	59	188	259

Northwest Division

Vancouver	82	43	24	10	5	101	235	194
Colorado	82	40	22	13	7	100	236	198
Calgary	82	42	30	7	3	94	200	176
Edmonton	82	36	29	12	5	89	221	208
Minnesota	82	30	29	20	3	83	188	183

Pacific Division

San Jose	82	43	21	12	6	104	219	183
Dallas	82	41	26	13	2	97	194	175
Los Angeles	82	28	29	16	9	81	205	217
Anaheim	82	29	35	10	8	76	184	213
Phoenix	82	22	36	18	6	68	188	245

Note: overtime losses (OTL) are worth one point in the standings and are not included in the loss column (L)

Stanley Cup Finals

May 25	Calgary 4 at Tampa Bay 1
May 27	Calgary 1 at Tampa Bay 4
May 29	Tampa Bay 0 at Calgary 3 [Kiprusoff]
May 31	Tampa Bay 1 at Calgary 0 (Richards 2:48 1st) [Khabibulin]
June 3	Calgary 3 at Tampa Bay 2 (Saprykin 14:40 OT)
June 5	Tampa Bay 3 at Calgary 2 (St. Louis 20:33 OT)
June 7	Calgary 1 at Tampa Bay 2

Tampa Bay won best-of-seven finals 4–3

Note: 2004–05 no season

2005–06

EASTERN CONFERENCE

Northeast Division	GP	W	L	OTL	SOL	GF	GA	P
Ottawa	82	52	21	3	6	314	211	113
Buffalo	82	52	24	1	5	281	239	110
Canadiens	82	42	31	6	3	243	247	93
Toronto	82	41	33	1	7	257	270	90
Boston	82	29	37	8	8	230	266	74

Atlantic Division								
New Jersey	82	46	27	5	4	242	229	101
Philadelphia	82	45	26	5	6	267	259	101
Rangers	82	44	26	8	4	257	215	100
Islanders	82	36	40	3	3	230	278	78
Pittsburgh	82	22	46	8	6	244	316	58

Southeast Division

	GP	W	L	OTL	SOL	GF	GA	P
Carolina	82	52	22	6	2	294	260	112
Tampa Bay	82	43	33	2	4	252	260	92
Atlanta	82	41	33	3	5	281	275	90
Florida	82	37	34	6	5	240	257	85
Washington	82	29	41	6	6	237	306	70

WESTERN CONFERENCE

Central Division

	GP	W	L	OTL	SOL	GF	GA	P
Detroit	82	58	16	5	3	305	209	124
Nashville	82	49	25	5	3	259	227	106
Columbus	82	35	43	1	3	223	279	74
Chicago	82	26	43	7	6	211	285	65
St. Louis	82	21	46	6	9	197	292	57

Northwest Division

	GP	W	L	OTL	SOL	GF	GA	P
Calgary	82	46	25	4	7	218	200	103
Colorado	82	43	30	3	6	283	257	95
Edmonton	82	41	28	4	9	256	251	95
Vancouver	82	42	32	4	4	256	255	92
Minnesota	82	38	36	5	3	231	215	84

Pacific Division

	GP	W	L	OTL	SOL	GF	GA	P
Dallas	82	53	23	5	1	265	218	112
San Jose	82	44	27	4	7	266	242	99
Anaheim	82	43	27	5	7	254	229	98
Los Angeles	82	42	35	4	1	249	270	89
Phoenix	82	38	39	2	3	246	271	81

Stanley Cup Finals

June 5	Edmonton 4 at Carolina 5
June 7	Edmonton 0 at Carolina 5 [Ward]
June 10	Carolina 1 at Edmonton 2
June 12	Carolina 2 at Edmonton 1
June 14	Edmonton 4 at Carolina 3 (Pisani 3:31 OT)]

June 17   Carolina 0 at Edmonton 4 [Ward]
June 19   Edmonton 1 at Carolina 3
Carolina won best-of-seven finals 4–3

2006–07

EASTERN CONFERENCE

Atlantic Division	GP	W	L	OT	GF	GA	P
New Jersey	82	49	24	9	216	201	107
Pittsburgh	82	47	24	11	277	246	105
Rangers	82	42	30	10	242	216	94
Islanders	82	40	30	12	248	240	92
Philadelphia	82	22	48	12	214	303	56

Northeast Division							
Buffalo	82	53	22	7	308	242	113
Ottawa	82	48	25	9	288	222	105
Toronto	82	40	31	11	258	269	91
Canadiens	82	42	34	6	245	256	90
Boston	82	35	41	6	219	289	76

Southeast Division							
Atlanta	82	43	28	11	246	245	97
Tampa Bay	82	44	33	5	253	261	93
Carolina	82	40	34	8	241	253	88
Florida	82	35	31	16	247	257	86
Washington	82	28	40	14	235	286	70

WESTERN CONFERENCE

Central Division							
Detroit	82	50	19	13	254	199	113
Nashville	82	51	23	8	272	212	110
St. Louis	82	34	35	13	214	254	81
Columbus	82	33	42	7	201	249	73
Chicago	82	31	42	9	201	258	71

Northwest Division

Vancouver	82	49	26	7	222	201	105
Minnesota	82	48	26	8	235	191	104
Calgary	82	43	29	10	258	226	96
Colorado	82	44	31	7	272	251	95
Edmonton	82	32	43	7	195	248	71

Pacific Division

Anaheim	82	48	20	14	258	208	110
San Jose	82	51	26	5	258	199	107
Dallas	82	50	25	7	226	197	107
Los Angeles	82	27	41	14	227	283	68
Phoenix	82	31	46	5	216	284	67

Stanley Cup Finals

May 28	Ottawa 2 at Anaheim 3
May 30	Ottawa 0 at Anaheim 1 (Pahlsson 14:15 3rd) [Giguere]
June 2	Anaheim 3 at Ottawa 5
June 4	Anaheim 3 at Ottawa 2
June 6	Ottawa 2 at Anaheim 6

Anaheim won best-of-seven 4–1

2007–08

EASTERN CONFERENCE

Northeast Division	GP	W	L	OT	GF	GA	P
Canadiens	82	47	25	10	262	222	104
Ottawa	82	43	31	8	261	247	94
Boston	82	41	29	12	212	222	94
Buffalo	82	39	31	12	255	242	90
Toronto	82	36	35	11	231	260	83

Atlantic Division

Pittsburgh	82	47	27	8	247	216	102
New Jersey	82	46	29	7	206	197	99
Rangers	82	42	27	13	213	199	97
Philadelphia	82	42	29	11	248	233	95
Islanders	82	35	38	9	194	243	79

Southeast Division

Washington	82	43	31	8	242	231	94
Carolina	82	43	33	6	252	249	92
Florida	82	38	35	9	216	226	85
Atlanta	82	34	40	8	216	272	76
Tampa Bay	82	31	42	9	223	267	71

WESTERN CONFERENCE

Central Division

Detroit	82	54	21	7	257	184	115
Nashville	82	41	32	9	230	229	91
Chicago	82	40	34	8	239	235	88
Columbus	82	34	36	12	193	218	80
St. Louis	82	33	36	13	205	237	79

Northwest Division	**GP**	**W**	**L**	**OT**	**GF**	**GA**	**P**
Minnesota	82	44	28	10	223	218	98
Colorado	82	44	31	7	231	219	95
Calgary	82	42	30	10	229	227	94
Edmonton	82	41	35	6	235	251	88
Vancouver	82	39	33	10	213	215	88

Pacific Division

San Jose	82	49	23	10	222	193	108
Anaheim	82	47	27	8	205	191	102
Dallas	82	45	30	7	242	207	97
Phoenix	82	38	37	7	214	231	83
Los Angeles	82	32	43	7	231	266	71

Stanley Cup Finals

Detroit vs. Pittsburgh

May 24	Pittsburgh 0 at Detroit 4 [Osgood]
May 26	Pittsburgh 0 at Detroit 3 [Osgood]
May 28	Detroit 2 at Pittsburgh 3
May 31	Detroit 2 at Pittsburgh 1
June 2	Pittsburgh 4 at Detroit 3 (Sykora 49:57 OT)
June 4	Detroit 3 at Pittsburgh 2

Detroit won best of seven 4–2

NHL AWARDS

Art Ross Trophy

1917–18	Joe Malone	Montreal Canadiens (48 points)
1918–19	Newsy Lalonde	Montreal Canadiens (32 points)
1919–20	Joe Malone	Quebec Bulldogs (49 points)
1920–21	Newsy Lalonde	Montreal Canadiens (43 points)
1921–22	Punch Broadbent	Ottawa Senators (46 points)
1922–23	Babe Dye	Toronto St. Pats (37 points)
1923–24	Cy Denneny	Ottawa Senators (24 points)
1924–25	Babe Dye	Toronto St. Pats (46 points)
1925–26	Nels Stewart	Montreal Maroons (42 points)
1926–27	Bill Cook	New York Rangers (37 points)
1927–28	Howie Morenz	Montreal Canadiens (51 points)
1928–29	Ace Bailey	Toronto Maple Leafs (32 points)
1929–30	Cooney Weiland	Boston Bruins (73 points)
1930–31	Howie Morenz	Montreal Canadiens (51 points)
1931–32	Busher Jackson	Toronto Maple Leafs (53 points)
1932–33	Bill Cook	New York Rangers (50 points)
1933–34	Charlie Conacher	Toronto Maple Leafs (52 points)
1934–35	Charlie Conacher	Toronto Maple Leafs (57 points)
1935–36	Sweeney Schriner	New York Americans (45 points)
1936–37	Sweeney Schriner	New York Americans (46 points)
1937–38	Gordie Drillon	Toronto Maple Leafs (52 points)
1938–39	Toe Blake	Montreal Canadiens (47 points)
1939–40	Milt Schmidt	Boston Bruins (52 points)
1940–41	Bill Cowley	Boston Bruins (62 points)
1941–42	Bryan Hextall	New York Rangers (56 points)
1942–43	Doug Bentley	Chicago Black Hawks (73 points)
1943–44	Herb Cain	Boston Bruins (82 points)
1944–45	Elmer Lach	Montreal Canadiens (80 points)
1945–46	Max Bentley	Chicago Black Hawks (61 points)
1946–47	Max Bentley	Chicago Black Hawks (72 points)

1947–48	Elmer Lach	Montreal Canadiens (61 points)
1948–49	Roy Conacher	Chicago Black Hawks (68 points)
1949–50	Ted Lindsay	Detroit Red Wings (78 points)
1950–51	Gordie Howe	Detroit Red Wings (86 points)
1951–52	Gordie Howe	Detroit Red Wings (86 points)
1952–53	Gordie Howe	Detroit Red Wings (95 points)
1953–54	Gordie Howe	Detroit Red Wings (81 points)
1954–55	Bernie Geoffrion	Montreal Canadiens (75 points)
1955–56	Jean Beliveau	Montreal Canadiens (88 points)
1956–57	Gordie Howe	Detroit Red Wings (89 points)
1957–58	Dickie Moore	Montreal Canadiens (84 points)
1958–59	Dickie Moore	Montreal Canadiens (96 points)
1959–60	Bobby Hull	Chicago Black Hawks (81 points)
1960–61	Bernie Geoffrion	Montreal Canadiens (95 points)
1961–62	Bobby Hull	Chicago Black Hawks (84 points)
1962–63	Gordie Howe	Detroit Red Wings (86 points)
1963–64	Stan Mikita	Chicago Black Hawks (89 points)
1964–65	Stan Mikita	Chicago Black Hawks (87 points)
1965–66	Bobby Hull	Chicago Black Hawks (97 points)
1966–67	Stan Mikita	Chicago Black Hawks (97 points)
1967–68	Stan Mikita	Chicago Black Hawks (87 points)
1968–69	Phil Esposito	Boston Bruins (126 points)
1969–70	Bobby Orr	Boston Bruins (120 points)
1970–71	Phil Esposito	Boston Bruins (152 points)
1971–72	Phil Esposito	Boston Bruins (133 points)
1972–73	Phil Esposito	Boston Bruins (130 points)
1973–74	Phil Esposito	Boston Bruins (145 points)
1974–75	Bobby Orr	Boston Bruins (135 points)
1975–76	Guy Lafleur	Montreal Canadiens (125 points)
1976–77	Guy Lafleur	Montreal Canadiens (136 points)
1977–78	Guy Lafleur	Montreal Canadiens (132 points)
1978–79	Bryan Trottier	New York Islanders (134 points)
1979–80	Marcel Dionne	Los Angeles Kings (137 points)
1980–81	Wayne Gretzky	Edmonton Oilers (164 points)

1981–82	Wayne Gretzky	Edmonton Oilers (212 points)
1982–83	Wayne Gretzky	Edmonton Oilers (196 points)
1983–84	Wayne Gretzky	Edmonton Oilers (205 points)
1984–85	Wayne Gretzky	Edmonton Oilers (208 points)
1985–86	Wayne Gretzky	Edmonton Oilers (215 points)
1986–87	Wayne Gretzky	Edmonton Oilers (183 points)
1987–88	Mario Lemieux	Pittsburgh Penguins (168 points)
1988–89	Mario Lemieux	Pittsburgh Penguins (199 points)
1989–90	Wayne Gretzky	Los Angeles Kings (142 points)
1990–91	Wayne Gretzky	Los Angeles Kings (163 points)
1991–92	Mario Lemieux	Pittsburgh Penguins (131 points)
1992–93	Mario Lemieux	Pittsburgh Penguins (160 points)
1993–94	Wayne Gretzky	Los Angeles Kings (130 points)
1994–95	Jaromir Jagr	Pittsburgh Penguins (70 points)
1995–96	Mario Lemieux	Pittsburgh Penguins (161 points)
1996–97	Mario Lemieux	Pittsburgh Penguins (122 points)
1997–98	Jaromir Jagr	Pittsburgh Penguins (102 points)
1998–99	Jaromir Jagr	Pittsburgh Penguins (127 points)
1999–00	Jaromir Jagr	Pittsburgh Penguins (96 points)
2000–01	Jaromir Jagr	Pittsburgh Penguins (121 points)
2001–02	Jarome Iginla	Calgary Flames (96 points)
2002–03	Peter Forsberg	Colorado Avalanche (106 points)
2003–04	Martin St. Louis	Tampa Bay Lightning (94 points)
2004–05	*no winner*	
2005–06	Joe Thornton	Boston Bruins/San Jose Sharks (125 points)
2006–07	Sidney Crosby	Pittsburgh Penguins (120 points)
2007–08	Alexander Ovechkin	Washington Capitals (112 points)
2008–09	Evgeni Malkin	Pittsburgh Penguins (113 points)

Hart Trophy

1923–24	Frank Nighbor	Ottawa Senators
1924–25	Billy Burch	Hamilton Tigers
1925–26	Nels Stewart	Montreal Maroons

1926–27	Herb Gardiner	Montreal Canadiens
1927–28	Howie Morenz	Montreal Canadiens
1928–29	Roy Worters	New York Americans
1929–30	Nels Stewart	Montreal Maroons
1930–31	Howie Morenz	Montreal Canadiens
1931–32	Howie Morenz	Montreal Canadiens
1932–33	Eddie Shore	Boston Bruins
1933–34	Aurel Joliat	Montreal Canadiens
1934–35	Eddie Shore	Boston Bruins
1935–36	Eddie Shore	Boston Bruins
1936–37	Babe Siebert	Montreal Canadiens
1937–38	Eddie Shore	Boston Bruins
1938–39	Toe Blake	Montreal Canadiens
1939–40	Ebbie Goodfellow	Detroit Red Wings
1940–41	Bill Cowley	Boston Bruins
1941–42	Tom Anderson	Brooklyn Americans
1942–43	Bill Cowley	Boston Bruins
1943–44	Babe Pratt	Toronto Maple Leafs
1944–45	Elmer Lach	Montreal Canadiens
1945–46	Max Bentley	Chicago Black Hawks
1946–47	Maurice Richard	Montreal Canadiens
1947–48	Buddy O'Connor	New York Rangers
1948–49	Sid Abel	Detroit Red Wings
1949–50	Chuck Rayner	New York Rangers
1950–51	Milt Schmidt	Boston Bruins
1951–52	Gordie Howe	Detroit Red Wings
1952–53	Gordie Howe	Detroit Red Wings
1953–54	Al Rollins	Chicago Black Hawks
1954–55	Ted Kennedy	Toronto Maple Leafs
1955–56	Jean Beliveau	Montreal Canadiens
1956–57	Gordie Howe	Detroit Red Wings
1957–58	Gordie Howe	Detroit Red Wings
1958–59	Andy Bathgate	New York Rangers
1959–60	Gordie Howe	Detroit Red Wings

1960–61	Bernie Geoffrion	Montreal Canadiens
1961–62	Jacques Plante	Montreal Canadiens
1962–63	Gordie Howe	Detroit Red Wings
1963–64	Jean Beliveau	Montreal Canadiens
1964–65	Bobby Hull	Chicago Black Hawks
1965–66	Bobby Hull	Chicago Black Hawks
1966–67	Stan Mikita	Chicago Black Hawks
1967–68	Stan Mikita	Chicago Black Hawks
1968–69	Phil Esposito	Boston Bruins
1969–70	Bobby Orr	Boston Bruins
1970–71	Bobby Orr	Boston Bruins
1971–72	Bobby Orr	Boston Bruins
1972–73	Bobby Clarke	Philadelphia Flyers
1973–74	Phil Esposito	Boston Bruins
1974–75	Bobby Clarke	Philadelphia Flyers
1975–76	Bobby Clarke	Philadelphia Flyers
1976–77	Guy Lafleur	Montreal Canadiens
1977–78	Guy Lafleur	Montreal Canadiens
1978–79	Bryan Trottier	New York Islanders
1979–80	Wayne Gretzky	Edmonton Oilers
1980–81	Wayne Gretzky	Edmonton Oilers
1981–82	Wayne Gretzky	Edmonton Oilers
1982–83	Wayne Gretzky	Edmonton Oilers
1983–84	Wayne Gretzky	Edmonton Oilers
1984–85	Wayne Gretzky	Edmonton Oilers
1985–86	Wayne Gretzky	Edmonton Oilers
1986–87	Wayne Gretzky	Edmonton Oilers
1987–88	Mario Lemieux	Pittsburgh Penguins
1988–89	Wayne Gretzky	Edmonton Oilers
1989–90	Mark Messier	Edmonton Oilers
1990–91	Brett Hull	St. Louis Blues
1991–92	Mark Messier	New York Rangers
1992–93	Mario Lemieux	Pittsburgh Penguins
1993–94	Sergei Fedorov	Detroit Red Wings

1994–95	Eric Lindros	Philadelphia Flyers
1995–96	Mario Lemieux	Pittsburgh Penguins
1996–97	Dominik Hasek	Buffalo Sabres
1997–98	Dominik Hasek	Buffalo Sabres
1998–99	Jaromir Jagr	Pittsburgh Penguins
1999–00	Chris Pronger	St. Louis Blues
2000–01	Joe Sakic	Colorado Avalanche
2001–02	Jose Theodore	Montreal Canadiens
2002–03	Peter Forsberg	Colorado Avalanche
2003–04	Martin St. Louis	Tampa Bay Lightning
2004–05	*no winner*	
2005–06	Joe Thornton	Boston Bruins/San Jose Sharks
2006–07	Sidney Crosby	Pittsburgh Penguins
2007–08	Alexander Ovechkin	Washington Capitals
2008–09	Alexander Ovechkin	Washington Capitals

Lady Byng Trophy

1924–25	Frank Nighbor	Ottawa Senators
1925–26	Frank Nighbor	Ottawa Senators
1926–27	Billy Burch	New York Americans
1927–28	Frank Boucher	New York Rangers
1928–29	Frank Boucher	New York Rangers
1929–30	Frank Boucher	New York Rangers
1930–31	Frank Boucher	New York Rangers
1931–32	Joe Primeau	Toronto Maple Leafs
1932–33	Frank Boucher	New York Rangers
1933–34	Frank Boucher	New York Rangers
1934–35	Frank Boucher	New York Rangers
1935–36	Doc Romnes	Chicago Black Hawks
1936–37	Marty Barry	Detroit Red Wings
1937–38	Gordie Drillon	Toronto Maple Leafs
1938–39	Clint Smith	New York Rangers
1939–40	Bobby Bauer	Boston Bruins
1940–41	Bobby Bauer	Boston Bruins

1941–42	Syl Apps	Toronto Maple Leafs
1942–43	Max Bentley	Chicago Black Hawks
1943–44	Clint Smith	Chicago Black Hawks
1944–45	Bill Mosienko	Chicago Black Hawks
1945–46	Toe Blake	Montreal Canadiens
1946–47	Bobby Bauer	Boston Bruins
1947–48	Buddy O'Connor	New York Rangers
1948–49	Bill Quackenbush	Detroit Red Wings
1949–50	Edgar Laprade	New York Rangers
1950–51	Red Kelly	Detroit Red Wings
1951–52	Sid Smith	Toronto Maple Leafs
1952–53	Red Kelly	Detroit Red Wings
1953–54	Red Kelly	Detroit Red Wings
1954–55	Sid Smith	Toronto Maple Leafs
1955–56	Dutch Reibel	Detroit Red Wings
1956–57	Andy Hebenton	New York Rangers
1957–58	Camille Henry	New York Rangers
1958–59	Alex Delvecchio	Detroit Red Wings
1959–60	Don McKenney	Boston Bruins
1960–61	Red Kelly	Toronto Maple Leafs
1961–62	Dave Keon	Toronto Maple Leafs
1962–63	Dave Keon	Toronto Maple Leafs
1963–64	Kenny Wharram	Chicago Black Hawks
1964–65	Bobby Hull	Chicago Black Hawks
1965–66	Alex Delvecchio	Detroit Red Wings
1966–67	Stan Mikita	Chicago Black Hawks
1967–68	Stan Mikita	Chicago Black Hawks
1968–69	Alex Delvecchio	Detroit Red Wings
1969–70	Phil Goyette	St. Louis Blues
1970–71	John Bucyk	Boston Bruins
1971–72	Jean Ratelle	New York Rangers
1972–73	Gilbert Perreault	Buffalo Sabres
1973–74	John Bucyk	Boston Bruins
1974–75	Marcel Dionne	Detroit Red Wings

1975–76	Jean Ratelle	New York Rangers/Boston Bruins
1976–77	Marcel Dionne	Los Angeles Kings
1977–78	Butch Goring	Los Angeles Kings
1978–79	Bob MacMillan	Atlanta Flames
1979–80	Wayne Gretzky	Edmonton Oilers
1980–81	Rick Kehoe	Pittsburgh Penguins
1981–82	Rick Middleton	Boston Bruins
1982–83	Mike Bossy	New York Islanders
1983–84	Mike Bossy	New York Islanders
1984–85	Jari Kurri	Edmonton Oilers
1985–86	Mike Bossy	New York Islanders
1986–87	Joe Mullen	Calgary Flames
1987–88	Mats Naslund	Montreal Canadiens
1988–89	Joe Mullen	Calgary Flames
1989–90	Brett Hull	St. Louis Blues
1990–91	Wayne Gretzky	Los Angeles Kings
1991–92	Wayne Gretzky	Los Angeles Kings
1992–93	Pierre Turgeon	New York Islanders
1993–94	Wayne Gretzky	Los Angeles Kings
1994–95	Ron Francis	Pittsburgh Penguins
1995–96	Paul Kariya	Mighty Ducks of Anaheim
1996–97	Paul Kariya	Mighty Ducks of Anaheim
1997–98	Ron Francis	Pittsburgh Penguins
1998–99	Wayne Gretzky	New York Rangers
1999–00	Pavol Demitra	St. Louis Blues
2000–01	Joe Sakic	Colorado Avalanche
2001–02	Ron Francis	Carolina Hurricanes
2002–03	Alexander Mogilny	Toronto Maple Leafs
2003–04	Brad Richards	Tampa Bay Lightning
2004–05	*no winner*	
2005–06	Pavel Datsyuk	Detroit Red Wings
2006–07	Pavel Datsyuk	Detroit Red Wings

| 2007–08 | Pavel Datsyuk | Detroit Red Wings |
| 2008–09 | Pavel Datsyuk | Detroit Red Wings |

Vezina Trophy

1926–27	George Hainsworth	Montreal Canadiens (1.47 GAA)
1927–28	George Hainsworth	Montreal Canadiens (1.05 GAA)
1928–29	George Hainsworth	Montreal Canadiens (0.92 GAA)
1929–30	Tiny Thompson	Boston Bruins (2.19 GAA)
1930–31	Roy Worters	New York Americans (1.61 GAA)
1931–32	Charlie Gardiner	Chicago Black Hawks (1.85 GAA)
1932–33	Tiny Thompson	Boston Bruins (1.76 GAA)
1933–34	Charlie Gardiner	Chicago Black Hawks (1.63 GAA)
1934–35	Lorne Chabot	Chicago Black Hawks (1.80 GAA)
1935–36	Tiny Thompson	Boston Bruins (1.68 GAA)
1936–37	Normie Smith	Detroit Red Wings (2.05 GAA)
1937–38	Tiny Thompson	Boston Bruins (1.80 GAA)
1938–39	Frank Brimsek	Boston Bruins (1.56 GAA)
1939–40	Dave Kerr	New York Rangers (1.54 GAA)
1940–41	Turk Broda	Toronto Maple Leafs (2.00 GAA)
1941–42	Frank Brimsek	Boston Bruins (2.35 GAA)
1942–43	Johnny Mowers	Detroit Red Wings (2.47 GAA)
1943–44	Bill Durnan	Montreal Canadiens (2.18 GAA)
1944–45	Bill Durnan	Montreal Canadiens (2.42 GAA)
1945–46	Bill Durnan	Montreal Canadiens (2.60 GAA)
1946–47	Bill Durnan	Montreal Canadiens (2.30 GAA)
1947–48	Turk Broda	Toronto Maple Leafs (2.38 GAA)
1948–49	Bill Durnan	Montreal Canadiens (2.10 GAA)
1949–50	Bill Durnan	Montreal Canadiens (2.20 GAA)
1950–51	Al Rollins	Toronto Maple Leafs (1.77 GAA)
1951–52	Terry Sawchuk	Detroit Red Wings (1.90 GAA)
1952–53	Terry Sawchuk	Detroit Red Wings (1.90 GAA)
1953–54	Harry Lumley	Toronto Maple Leafs (1.86 GAA)
1954–55	Terry Sawchuk	Detroit Red Wings (1.96 GAA)
1955–56	Jacques Plante	Montreal Canadiens (1.86 GAA)

1956–57	Jacques Plante	Montreal Canadiens (2.00 GAA)
1957–58	Jacques Plante	Montreal Canadiens (2.11 GAA)
1958–59	Jacques Plante	Montreal Canadiens (2.16 GAA)
1959–60	Jacques Plante	Montreal Canadiens (2.54 GAA)
1960–61	Johnny Bower	Toronto Maple Leafs (2.50 GAA)
1961–62	Jacques Plante	Montreal Canadiens (2.37 GAA)
1962–63	Glenn Hall	Chicago Black Hawks (2.47 GAA)
1963–64	Charlie Hodge	Montreal Canadiens (2.26 GAA)
1964–65	Terry Sawchuk	Toronto Maple Leafs (2.56 GAA)
	Johnny Bower	Toronto Maple Leafs (2.38 GAA)
1965–66	Gump Worsley	Montreal Canadiens (2.36 GAA)
	Charlie Hodge	Montreal Canadiens (2.58 GAA)
1966–67	Glenn Hall	Chicago Black Hawks (2.38 GAA)
	Denis DeJordy	Chicago Black Hawks (2.46 GAA)
1967–68	Gump Worsley	Montreal Canadiens (1.98 GAA)
	Rogie Vachon	Montreal Canadiens (2.48 GAA)
1968–69	Jacques Plante	St. Louis Blues (1.96 GAA)
	Glenn Hall	St. Louis Blues (2.17 GAA)
1969–70	Tony Esposito	Chicago Black Hawks (2.17 GAA)
1970–71	Ed Giacomin	New York Rangers (2.16 GAA)
	Gilles Villemure	New York Rangers (2.30 GAA)
1971–72	Tony Esposito	Chicago Black Hawks (1.77 GAA)
	Gary Smith	Chicago Black Hawks (2.42 GAA)
1972–73	Ken Dryden	Montreal Canadiens (2.26 GAA)
1973–74	Bernie Parent	Philadelphia Flyers (1.89 GAA)
	Tony Esposito	Chicago Black Hawks (2.04 GAA)
1974–75	Bernie Parent	Philadelphia Flyers (2.03 GAA)
1975–76	Ken Dryden	Montreal Canadiens (2.03 GAA)
1976–77	Ken Dryden	Montreal Canadiens (2.14 GAA)
	Michel Larocque	Montreal Canadiens (2.09 GAA)
1977–78	Ken Dryden	Montreal Canadiens (2.05 GAA)
	Michel Larocque	Montreal Canadiens (2.67 GAA)
1978–79	Ken Dryden	Montreal Canadiens (2.30 GAA)
	Michel Larocque	Montreal Canadiens (2.84 GAA)

1979–80	Bob Sauve	Buffalo Sabres (2.36 GAA)
	Don Edwards	Buffalo Sabres (2.57 GAA)
1980–81	Richard Sevigny	Montreal Canadiens (2.40 GAA)
	Denis Herron	Montreal Canadiens (3.50 GAA)
	Michel Larocque	Montreal Canadiens (3.03 GAA)
1981–82	Billy Smith	New York Islanders (2.97 GAA)
1982–83	Pete Peeters	Boston Bruins (2.36 GAA)
1983–84	Tom Barrasso	Buffalo Sabres (2.84 GAA)
1984–85	Pelle Lindbergh	Philadelphia Flyers (3.02 GAA)
1985–86	John Vanbiesbrouck	New York Rangers (3.32 GAA)
1986–87	Ron Hextall	Philadelphia Flyers (3.00 GAA)
1987–88	Grant Fuhr	Edmonton Oilers (3.43 GAA)
1988–89	Patrick Roy	Montreal Canadiens (2.47 GAA)
1989–90	Patrick Roy	Montreal Canadiens (2.53 GAA)
1990–91	Ed Belfour	Chicago Blackhawks (2.47 GAA)
1991–92	Patrick Roy	Montreal Canadiens (2.36 GAA)
1992–93	Ed Belfour	Chicago Blackhawks (2.59 GAA)
1993–94	Dominik Hasek	Buffalo Sabres (1.95 GAA)
1994–95	Dominik Hasek	Buffalo Sabres (2.11 GAA)
1995–96	Jim Carey	Washington Capitals (2.26 GAA)
1996–97	Dominik Hasek	Buffalo Sabres (2.27 GAA)
1997–98	Dominik Hasek	Buffalo Sabres (2.09 GAA)
1998–99	Dominik Hasek	Buffalo Sabres (1.87 GAA)
1999–00	Olaf Kolzig	Washington Capitals (2.24 GAA)
2000–01	Dominik Hasek	Buffalo Sabres (2.11 GAA)
2001–02	Jose Theodore	Montreal Canadiens (2.11 GAA)
2002–03	Martin Brodeur	New Jersey Devils (2.02 GAA)
2003–04	Martin Brodeur	New Jersey Devils (2.62 GAA)
2004–05	*no winner*	
2005–06	Miikka Kiprusoff	Calgary Flames (2.07 GAA)
2006–07	Martin Brodeur	New Jersey Devils (2.18 GAA)
2007–08	Martin Brodeur	New Jersey Devils (2.17 GAA)
2008–09	Tim Thomas	Boston Bruins (2.10 GAA)

Calder Memorial Trophy

1932–33	Carl Voss	Detroit Red Wings
1933–34	Russ Blinco	Montreal Maroons
1934–35	Sweeney Schriner	New York Americans
1935–36	Mike Karakas	Chicago Black Hawks
1936–37	Syl Apps	Toronto Maple Leafs
1937–38	Cully Dahlstrom	Chicago Black Hawks
1938–39	Frank Brimsek	Boston Bruins
1939–40	Kilby MacDonald	New York Rangers
1940–41	John Quilty	Montreal Canadiens
1941–42	Grant Warwick	New York Rangers
1942–43	Gaye Stewart	Toronto Maple Leafs
1943–44	Gus Bodnar	Toronto Maple Leafs
1944–45	Frank McCool	Toronto Maple Leafs
1945–46	Edgar Laprade	New York Rangers
1946–47	Howie Meeker	Toronto Maple Leafs
1947–48	Jim McFadden	Detroit Red Wings
1948–49	Pentti Lund	New York Rangers
1949–50	Jack Gelineau	Boston Bruins
1950–51	Terry Sawchuk	Detroit Red Wings
1951–52	Bernie Geoffrion	Montreal Canadiens
1952–53	Gump Worsley	New York Rangers
1953–54	Camille Henry	New York Rangers
1954–55	Ed Litzenberger	Chicago Black Hawks
1955–56	Glenn Hall	Detroit Red Wings
1956–57	Larry Regan	Boston Bruins
1957–58	Frank Mahovlich	Toronto Maple Leafs
1958–59	Ralph Backstrom	Montreal Canadiens
1959–60	Bill Hay	Chicago Black Hawks
1960–61	Dave Keon	Toronto Maple Leafs
1961–62	Bobby Rousseau	Montreal Canadiens
1962–63	Kent Douglas	Toronto Maple Leafs
1963–64	Jacques Laperriere	Montreal Canadiens
1964–65	Roger Crozier	Detroit Red Wings

1965–66	Brit Selby	Toronto Maple Leafs
1966–67	Bobby Orr	Boston Bruins
1967–68	Derek Sanderson	Boston Bruins
1968–69	Danny Grant	Minnesota North Stars
1969–70	Tony Esposito	Chicago Black Hawks
1970–71	Gilbert Perreault	Buffalo Sabres
1971–72	Ken Dryden	Montreal Canadiens
1972–73	Steve Vickers	New York Rangers
1973–74	Denis Potvin	New York Islanders
1974–75	Eric Vail	Atlanta Flames
1975–76	Bryan Trottier	New York Islanders
1976–77	Willi Plett	Atlanta Flames
1977–78	Mike Bossy	New York Islanders
1978–79	Bobby Smith	Minnesota North Stars
1979–80	Raymond Bourque	Boston Bruins
1980–81	Peter Stastny	Quebec Nordiques
1981–82	Dale Hawerchuk	Winnipeg Jets
1982–83	Steve Larmer	Chicago Black Hawks
1983–84	Tom Barrasso	Buffalo Sabres
1984–85	Mario Lemieux	Pittsburgh Penguins
1985–86	Gary Suter	Calgary Flames
1986–87	Luc Robitaille	Los Angeles Kings
1987–88	Joe Nieuwendyk	Calgary Flames
1988–89	Brian Leetch	New York Rangers
1989–90	Sergei Makarov	Calgary Flames
1990–91	Ed Belfour	Chicago Blackhawks
1991–92	Pavel Bure	Vancouver Canucks
1992–93	Teemu Selanne	Winnipeg Jets
1993–94	Martin Brodeur	New Jersey Devils
1994–95	Peter Forsberg	Quebec Nordiques
1995–96	Daniel Alfredsson	Ottawa Senators
1996–97	Bryan Berard	New York Islanders
1997–98	Sergei Samsonov	Boston Bruins
1998–99	Chris Drury	Colorado Avalanche

1999–00	Scott Gomez	New Jersey Devils
2000–01	Evgeni Nabokov	San Jose Sharks
2001–02	Danny Heatley	Atlanta Thrashers
2002–03	Barret Jackman	St. Louis Blues
2003–04	Andrew Raycroft	Boston Bruins
2004–05	*no winner*	
2005–06	Alexander Ovechkin	Washington Capitals
2006–07	Evgeni Malkin	Pittsburgh Penguins
2007–08	Patrick Kane	Chicago Blackhawks
2008–09	Steve Mason	Columbus Blue Jackets

James Norris Trophy

1953–54	Red Kelly	Detroit Red Wings
1954–55	Doug Harvey	Montreal Canadiens
1955–56	Doug Harvey	Montreal Canadiens
1956–57	Doug Harvey	Montreal Canadiens
1957–58	Doug Harvey	Montreal Canadiens
1958–59	Tom Johnson	Montreal Canadiens
1959–60	Doug Harvey	Montreal Canadiens
1960–61	Doug Harvey	Montreal Canadiens
1961–62	Doug Harvey	Montreal Canadiens
1962–63	Pierre Pilote	Chicago Black Hawks
1963–64	Pierre Pilote	Chicago Black Hawks
1964–65	Pierre Pilote	Chicago Black Hawks
1965–66	Jacques Laperriere	Montreal Canadiens
1966–67	Harry Howell	New York Rangers
1967–68	Bobby Orr	Boston Bruins
1968–69	Bobby Orr	Boston Bruins
1969–70	Bobby Orr	Boston Bruins
1970–71	Bobby Orr	Boston Bruins
1971–72	Bobby Orr	Boston Bruins
1972–73	Bobby Orr	Boston Bruins
1973–74	Bobby Orr	Boston Bruins

1974–75	Bobby Orr	Boston Bruins
1975–76	Denis Potvin	New York Islanders
1976–77	Larry Robinson	Montreal Canadiens
1977–78	Denis Potvin	New York Islanders
1978–79	Denis Potvin	New York Islanders
1979–80	Larry Robinson	Montreal Canadiens
1980–81	Randy Carlyle	Pittsburgh Penguins
1981–82	Doug Wilson	Chicago Black Hawks
1982–83	Rod Langway	Washington Capitals
1983–84	Rod Langway	Washington Capitals
1984–85	Paul Coffey	Edmonton Oilers
1985–86	Paul Coffey	Edmonton Oilers
1986–87	Raymond Bourque	Boston Bruins
1987–88	Raymond Bourque	Boston Bruins
1988–89	Chris Chelios	Montreal Canadiens
1989–90	Raymond Bourque	Boston Bruins
1990–91	Raymond Bourque	Boston Bruins
1991–92	Brian Leetch	New York Rangers
1992–93	Chris Chelios	Chicago Blackhawks
1993–94	Raymond Bourque	Boston Bruins
1994–95	Paul Coffey	Detroit Red Wings
1995–96	Chris Chelios	Chicago Blackhawks
1996–97	Brian Leetch	New York Rangers
1997–98	Rob Blake	Los Angeles Kings
1998–99	Al MacInnis	St. Louis Blues
1999–00	Chris Pronger	St. Louis Blues
2000–01	Nicklas Lidstrom	Detroit Red Wings
2001–02	Nicklas Lidstrom	Detroit Red Wings
2002–03	Nicklas Lidstrom	Detroit Red Wings
2003–04	Scott Niedermayer	New Jersey Devils
2004–05	*no winner*	
2005–06	Nicklas Lidstrom	Detroit Red Wings
2006–07	Nicklas Lidstrom	Detroit Red Wings
2007–08	Nicklas Lidstrom	Detroit Red Wings
2008–09	Zdeno Chara	Boston Bruins

Lester Patrick Trophy

1965–66	Jack Adams
1966–67	Gordie Howe
	Charles F. Adams
	James Norris, Sr.
1967–68	Tommy Lockhart
	Walter A. Brown
	Gen. John R. Kilpatrick
1968–69	Bobby Hull
	Ed Jeremiah
1969–70	Eddie Shore
	Jim Hendy
1970–71	Bill Jennings
	John B. Sollenberger
	Terry Sawchuk
1971–72	Clarence Campbell
	John A. Kelly
	Cooney Weiland
	James D. Norris
1972–73	Walter Bush, Jr.
1973–74	Alex Delvecchio
	Murray Murdoch
	Weston W. Adams Sr.
	Charles L. Crovat
1974–75	Donald M. Clark
	Bill Chadwick
	Tommy Ivan
1975–76	Stan Mikita
	George Leader
	Bruce A. Norris
1976–77	Johnny Bucyk
	Murray Armstrong
	John Mariucci

1977–78	Phil Esposito
	Tom Fitzgerald
	William T. Tutt
	Bill Wirtz
1978–79	Bobby Orr
1979–80	Bobby Clarke
	Ed Snider
	Fred Shero
	1980 U.S. Olympic Hockey Team
1980–81	Charles M. Schulz
1981–82	Emile Francis
1982–83	Bill Torrey
1983–84	John A. Ziegler Jr.
	Art Ross
1984–85	Jack Butterfield
	Arthur M. Wirtz
1985–86	John MacInnes
	Jack Riley
1986–87	Hobey Baker
	Frank Mathers
1987–88	Keith Allen
	Fred Cusick
	Bob Johnson
1988–89	Dan Kelly
	Lou Nanne
	Lynn Patrick
	Bud Poile
1989–90	Len Ceglarski
1990–91	Rod Gilbert
	Mike Ilitch
1991–92	Al Arbour
	Art Berglund
	Lou Lamoriello

1992–93	Frank Boucher
	Red Dutton
	Bruce McNall
	Gil Stein
1993–94	Wayne Gretzky
	Robert Ridder
1994–95	Joe Mullen
	Brian Mullen
	Bob Fleming
1995–96	George Gund
	Ken Morrow
	Milt Schmidt
1996–97	Seymour H. Knox III
	Bill Cleary
	Pat LaFontaine
1997–98	Peter Karmanos
	Neal Broten
	John Mayasich
	Max McNab
1998–99	Harry Sinden
	1998 U.S. Olympic Women's Hockey Team
1999–00	Mario Lemieux
	Craig Patrick
	Lou Vairo
2000–01	Scotty Bowman
	David Poile
	Gary Bettman
2001–02	1960 U.S. Olympic Team
	Herb Brooks
	Larry Pleau
2002–03	Ray Bourque
	Ron DeGregorio
	Willie O'Ree

2003–04	Mike Emrick
	John Davidson
	Ray Miron
2004–05	*none*
2005–06	Red Berenson
	Marcel Dionne
	Reed Larson
	Glen Sonmor
	Steve Yzerman
2006–07	Brian Leetch
	Cammi Granato
	John Halligan
	Stan Fischler
2007–08	Brian Burke
	Ted Lindsay
	Phil Housley
	Bob Naegele, Jr.

Conn Smythe Trophy

* indicates played for losing team

1964–65	Jean Beliveau	Montreal Canadiens
1965–66	Roger Crozier*	Detroit Red Wings
1966–67	Dave Keon	Toronto Maple Leafs
1967–68	Glenn Hall*	St. Louis Blues
1968–69	Serge Savard	Montreal Canadiens
1969–70	Bobby Orr	Boston Bruins
1970–71	Ken Dryden	Montreal Canadiens
1971–72	Bobby Orr	Boston Bruins
1972–73	Yvan Cournoyer	Montreal Canadiens
1973–74	Bernie Parent	Philadelphia Flyers
1974–75	Bernie Parent	Philadelphia Flyers
1975–76	Reggie Leach*	Philadelphia Flyers
1976–77	Guy Lafleur	Montreal Canadiens
1977–78	Larry Robinson	Montreal Canadiens

1978–79	Bob Gainey	Montreal Canadiens
1979–80	Bryan Trottier	New York Islanders
1980–81	Butch Goring	New York Islanders
1981–82	Mike Bossy	New York Islanders
1982–83	Billy Smith	New York Islanders
1983–84	Mark Messier	Edmonton Oilers
1984–85	Wayne Gretzky	Edmonton Oilers
1985–86	Patrick Roy	Montreal Canadiens
1986–87	Ron Hextall	Philadelphia Flyers
1987–88	Wayne Gretzky	Edmonton Oilers
1988–89	Al MacInnis	Calgary Flames
1989–90	Bill Ranford	Edmonton Oilers
1990–91	Mario Lemieux	Pittsburgh Penguins
1991–92	Mario Lemieux	Pittsburgh Penguins
1992–93	Patrick Roy	Montreal Canadiens
1993–94	Brian Leetch	New York Rangers
1994–95	Claude Lemieux	New Jersey Devils
1995–96	Joe Sakic	Colorado Avalanche
1996–97	Mike Vernon	Detroit Red Wings
1997–98	Steve Yzerman	Detroit Red Wings
1998–99	Joe Nieuwendyk	Dallas Stars
1999–00	Scott Stevens	New Jersey Devils
2000–01	Patrick Roy	Colorado Avalanche
2001–02	Nicklas Lidstrom	Detroit Red Wings
2002–03	J-S Giguere*	Mighty Ducks of Anaheim
2003–04	Brad Richards	Tampa Bay Lightning
2004–05	*no winner*	
2005–06	Cam Ward	Carolina Hurricanes
2006–07	Scott Niedermayer	Anaheim Ducks
2007–08	Henrik Zetterberg	Detroit Red Wings
2008–09	Evgeni Malkin	Pittsburgh Penguins

Bill Masterton Trophy

1967–68	Claude Provost	Montreal Canadiens

1968–69	Ted Hampson	Oakland Seals
1969–70	Pit Martin	Chicago Black Hawks
1970–71	Jean Ratelle	New York Rangers
1971–72	Bobby Clarke	Philadelphia Flyers
1972–73	Lowell MacDonald	Pittsburgh Penguins
1973–74	Henri Richard	Montreal Canadiens
1974–75	Don Luce	Buffalo Sabres
1975–76	Rod Gilbert	New York Rangers
1976–77	Ed Westfall	New York Islanders
1977–78	Butch Goring	Los Angeles Kings
1978–79	Serge Savard	Montreal Canadiens
1979–80	Al MacAdam	Minnesota North Stars
1980–81	Blake Dunlop	St. Louis Blues
1981–82	Glenn Resch	Colorado Rockies
1982–83	Lanny McDonald	Calgary Flames
1983–84	Brad Park	Detroit Red Wings
1984–85	Anders Hedberg	New York Rangers
1985–86	Charlie Simmer	Boston Bruins
1986–87	Doug Jarvis	Hartford Whalers
1987–88	Bob Bourne	Los Angeles Kings
1988–89	Tim Kerr	Philadelphia Flyers
1989–90	Gord Kluzak	Boston Bruins
1990–91	Dave Taylor	Los Angeles Kings
1991–92	Mark Fitzpatrick	New York Islanders
1992–93	Mario Lemieux	Pittsburgh Penguins
1993–94	Cam Neely	Boston Bruins
1994–95	Pat LaFontaine	Buffalo Sabres
1995–96	Gary Roberts	Calgary Flames
1996–97	Tony Granato	San Jose Sharks
1997–98	Jamie McLennan	St. Louis Blues
1998–99	John Cullen	Tampa Bay Lightning
1999–00	Ken Daneyko	New Jersey Devils
2000–01	Adam Graves	New York Rangers
2001–02	Saku Koivu	Montreal Canadiens

2002–03	Steve Yzerman	Detroit Red Wings
2003–04	Bryan Berard	Chicago Blackhawks
2004–05	*no winner*	
2005–06	Teemu Selanne	Mighty Ducks of Anaheim
2006–07	Phil Kessel	Boston Bruins
2007–08	Jason Blake	Toronto Maple Leafs
2008–09	Steve Sullivan	Nashville Predators

Jack Adams Award

1973–74	Fred Shero	Philadelphia Flyers
1974–75	Bob Pulford	Los Angeles Kings
1975–76	Don Cherry	Boston Bruins
1976–77	Scotty Bowman	Montreal Canadiens
1977–78	Bobby Kromm	Detroit Red Wings
1978–79	Al Arbour	New York Islanders
1979–80	Pat Quinn	Philadelphia Flyers
1980–81	Red Berenson	St. Louis Blues
1981–82	Tom Watt	Winnipeg Jets
1982–83	Orval Tessier	Chicago Black Hawks
1983–84	Bryan Murray	Washington Capitals
1984–85	Mike Keenan	Philadelphia Flyers
1985–86	Glen Sather	Edmonton Oilers
1986–87	Jacques Demers	Detroit Red Wings
1987–88	Jacques Demers	Detroit Red Wings
1988–89	Pat Burns	Montreal Canadiens
1989–90	Bob Murdoch	Winnipeg Jets
1990–91	Brian Sutter	St. Louis Blues
1991–92	Pat Quinn	Vancouver Canucks
1992–93	Pat Burns	Toronto Maple Leafs
1993–94	Jacques Lemaire	New Jersey Devils
1994–95	Marc Crawford	Quebec Nordiques
1995–96	Scotty Bowman	Detroit Red Wings
1996–97	Ted Nolan	Buffalo Sabres
1997–98	Pat Burns	Boston Bruins

1998–99	Jacques Martin	Ottawa Senators
1999–00	Joel Quenneville	St. Louis Blues
2000–01	Bill Barber	Philadelphia Flyers
2001–02	Bob Francis	Phoenix Coyotes
2002–03	Jacques Lemaire	Minnesota Wild
2003–04	John Tortorella	Tampa Bay Lightning
2004–05	*no winner*	
2005–06	Lindy Ruff	Buffalo Sabres
2006–07	Alain Vigneault	Vancouver Canucks
2007–08	Bruce Boudreau	Washington Capitals
2008–09	Claude Julien	Boston Bruins

Lester B. Pearson Award

1970–71	Phil Esposito	Boston Bruins
1971–72	Jean Ratelle	New York Rangers
1972–73	Bobby Clarke	Philadelphia Flyers
1973–74	Phil Esposito	Boston Bruins
1974–75	Bobby Orr	Boston Bruins
1975–76	Guy Lafleur	Montreal Canadiens
1976–77	Guy Lafleur	Montreal Canadiens
1977–78	Guy Lafleur	Montreal Canadiens
1978–79	Marcel Dionne	Los Angeles Kings
1979–80	Marcel Dionne	Los Angeles Kings
1980–81	Mike Liut	St. Louis Blues
1981–82	Wayne Gretzky	Edmonton Oilers
1982–83	Wayne Gretzky	Edmonton Oilers
1983–84	Wayne Gretzky	Edmonton Oilers
1984–85	Wayne Gretzky	Edmonton Oilers
1985–86	Mario Lemieux	Pittsburgh Penguins
1986–87	Wayne Gretzky	Edmonton Oilers
1987–88	Mario Lemieux	Pittsburgh Penguins
1988–89	Steve Yzerman	Detroit Red Wings
1989–90	Mark Messier	Edmonton Oilers
1990–91	Brett Hull	St. Louis Blues

1991–92	Mark Messier	New York Rangers
1992–93	Mario Lemieux	Pittsburgh Penguins
1993–94	Sergei Fedorov	Detroit Red Wings
1994–95	Eric Lindros	Philadelphia Flyers
1995–96	Mario Lemieux	Pittsburgh Penguins
1996–97	Dominik Hasek	Buffalo Sabres
1997–98	Dominik Hasek	Buffalo Sabres
1998–99	Jaromir Jagr	Pittsburgh Penguins
1999–00	Jaromir Jagr	Pittsburgh Penguins
2000–01	Joe Sakic	Colorado Avalanche
2001–02	Jarome Iginla	Calgary Flames
2002–03	Markus Naslund	Vancouver Canucks
2003–04	Martin St. Louis	Tampa Bay Lightning
2004–05	*no winner*	
2005–06	Jaromir Jagr	New York Rangers
2006–07	Sidney Crosby	Pittsburgh Penguins
2007–08	Alexander Ovechkin	Washington Capitals
2008–09	Alexander Ovechkin	Washington Capitals

Frank J. Selke Trophy

1977–78	Bob Gainey	Montreal Canadiens
1978–79	Bob Gainey	Montreal Canadiens
1979–80	Bob Gainey	Montreal Canadiens
1980–81	Bob Gainey	Montreal Canadiens
1981–82	Steve Kasper	Boston Bruins
1982–83	Bobby Clarke	Pittsburgh Penguins
1983–84	Doug Jarvis	Washington Capitals
1984–85	Craig Ramsay	Buffalo Sabres
1985–86	Troy Murray	Chicago Black Hawks
1986–87	Dave Poulin	Philadelphia Flyers
1987–88	Guy Carbonneau	Montreal Canadiens
1988–89	Guy Carbonneau	Montreal Canadiens
1989–90	Rick Meagher	St. Louis Blues
1990–91	Dirk Graham	Chicago Blackhawks

1991–92	Guy Carbonneau	Montreal Canadiens
1992–93	Doug Gilmour	Toronto Maple Leafs
1993–94	Sergei Fedorov	Detroit Red Wings
1994–95	Ron Francis	Pittsburgh Penguins
1995–96	Sergei Fedorov	Detroit Red Wings
1996–97	Michael Peca	Buffalo Sabres
1997–98	Jere Lehtinen	Dallas Stars
1998–99	Jere Lehtinen	Dallas Stars
1999–00	Steve Yzerman	Detroit Red Wings
2000–01	John Madden	New Jersey Devils
2001–02	Michael Peca	New York Islanders
2002–03	Jere Lehtinen	Dallas Stars
2003–04	Kris Draper	Detroit Red Wings
2004–05	*no winner*	
2005–06	Rod Brind 'Amour	Carolina Hurricanes
2006–07	Rod Brind 'Amour	Carolina Hurricanes
2007–08	Pavel Datsyuk	Detroit Red Wings
2008–09	Pavel Datsyuk	Detroit Red Wings

William M. Jennings Trophy

1981–82	Rick Wamsley & Denis Herron	Montreal Canadiens
1982–83	Rollie Melanson & Billy Smith	New York Islanders
1983–84	Al Jensen & Pat Riggin	Washington Capitals
1984–85	Tom Barrasso & Bob Sauve	Buffalo Sabres
1985–86	Bob Froese & Darren Jensen	Philadelphia Flyers
1986–87	Patrick Roy & Brian Hayward	Montreal Canadiens
1987–88	Patrick Roy & Brian Hayward	Montreal Canadiens
1988–89	Patrick Roy & Brian Hayward	Montreal Canadiens
1989–90	Andy Moog & Reggie Lemelin	Boston Bruins
1990–91	Ed Belfour	Chicago Blackhawks
1991–92	Patrick Roy	Montreal Canadiens
1992–93	Ed Belfour	Chicago Blackhawks
1993–94	Dominik Hasek & Grant Fuhr	Buffalo Sabres
1994–95	Ed Belfour	Chicago Blackhawks

1995–96	Chris Osgood & Mike Vernon	Detroit Red Wings
1996–97	Martin Brodeur & Mike Dunham	New Jersey Devils
1997–98	Martin Brodeur	New Jersey Devils
1998–99	Ed Belfour & Roman Turek	Dallas Stars
1999–00	Roman Turek	St. Louis Blues
2000–01	Dominik Hasek	Buffalo Sabres
2001–02	Patrick Roy	Colorado Avalanche
2002–03	Martin Brodeur	New Jersey Devils
	Roman Cechmanek	Philadelphia Flyers
	Robert Esche	Philadelphia Flyers
2003–04	Martin Brodeur	New Jersey Devils
2004–05	*no winner*	
2005–06	Miikka Kiprusoff	Calgary Flames
2006–07	Manny Fernandez & Niklas Backstrom	Minnesota Wild
2007–08	Chris Osgood & Dominik Hasek	Detroit Red Wings
2008–09	Tim Thomas & Manny Fernandez	Boston Bruins

King Clancy Memorial Trophy

1987–88	Lanny McDonald	Calgary Flames
1988–89	Bryan Trottier	New York Islanders
1989–90	Kevin Lowe	Edmonton Oilers
1990–91	Dave Taylor	Los Angeles Kings
1991–92	Raymond Bourque	Boston Bruins
1992–93	Dave Poulin	Boston Bruins
1993–94	Adam Graves	New York Rangers
1994–95	Joe Nieuwendyk	Calgary Flames
1995–96	Kris King	Winnipeg Jets
1996–97	Trevor Linden	Vancouver Canucks
1997–98	Kelly Chase	St. Louis Blues
1998–99	Rob Ray	Buffalo Sabres

1999–00	Curtis Joseph	Toronto Maple Leafs
2000–01	Shjon Podein	Colorado Avalanche
2001–02	Ron Francis	Carolina Hurricanes
2002–03	Brendan Shanahan	Detroit Red Wings
2003–04	Jarome Iginla	Calgary Flames
2004–05	*no winner*	
2005–06	Olaf Kolzig	Washington Capitals
2006–07	Saku Koivu	Montreal Canadiens
2007–08	Vincent Lecavalier	Tampa Bay Lightning
2008–09	Ethan Moreau	Edmonton Oilers

Rocket Richard Trophy

1998–99	Teemu Selanne	Mighty Ducks of Anaheim (47 goals)
1999–00	Pavel Bure	Florida Panthers (58 goals)
2000–01	Pavel Bure	Florida Panthers (59 goals)
2001–02	Jarome Iginla	Calgary Flames (52 goals)
2002–03	Milan Hejduk	Colorado Avalanche (50 goals)
2003–04	Rick Nash	Columbus Blue Jackets (41 goals)
	Jarome Iginla	Calgary Flames (41 goals)
	Ilya Kovalchuk	Atlanta Thrashers (41 goals)
2004–05	*no winner*	
2005–06	Jonathan Cheechoo	San Jose Sharks (56 goals)
2006–07	Vincent Lecavalier	Tampa Bay Lightning (52 goals)
2007–08	Alexander Ovechkin	Washington Capitals (65 goals)
2008–09	Alexander Ovechkin	Washington Capitals (56 goals)

HOCKEY HALLS OF FAME

Hockey Hall of Fame 2008 Elections, June 23, 2009
Notable eligible players not elected: Tom Barrasso, Pavel Bure, Doug Gilmour, Phil Housley, Alexander Mogilny, Adam Oates, Mike Richter

Inductees:

Players
Steve Yzerman
One of the greatest players ever to skate in the NHL, Yzerman was captain of the Detroit Red Wings for 20 years. No athlete in a major North American sport has been team leader for as long. Additionally, Yzerman played all of his 21 seasons with the same team, and soon after he retired in 2006, the Red Wings retired his number 19 to the rafters of the Joe Louis Arena. Yzerman led the team to three Stanley Cup victories, and his 1,755 points in the regular season rank sixth on the all-time list. He won the Lester B. Pearson Award in 1988–89 when he had 155 points, beating out both Wayne Gretzky and Mario Lemieux for the honour that year. Yzerman recorded 100 points or more in a season six straight years (1987–93) and had five 50-goal seasons during that span. He also helped Canada win gold at the 2002 Olympics and at the 1984 Canada Cup.

Luc Robitaille
The highest-scoring left winger in the history of the NHL, "Lucky Luc" played the game with class and dignity for 19 seasons. He won his only Stanley Cup with Detroit, in 2001–02, but he is better known as a long-time member of the Los Angeles Kings, for whom he had three stints totalling 14 years. Robitaille burst onto the NHL scene in 1986–87, scoring 45 goals and earning the Calder Trophy. The next year he had his first of three 50-goal and 100-point seasons. He played in eight All-Star Games and led Canada to victory at the 1994 World Championship, the first gold since 1961. It was his two goals in the

shootout over Finland that gave Canada the win. On January 20, 2007, his number 20 was retired by the Kings.

Brett Hull

Joining his father, Bobby, in the Hockey Hall of Fame puts the Hulls in a unique group of family members to be so honoured. Nicknamed "The Golden Brett" because of his blond hair and his father's nickname "The Golden Jet," Hull was best known for his quick snap shot from the off wing. By the time he retired, that shot had accounted for many of his 741 career goals in the regular season, third on the all-time list. Although born in Canada, Hull later represented the U.S. internationally, most famously in 1996 when USA beat Canada to win the inaugural World Cup of Hockey. He also won the Stanley Cup twice, first with Dallas in 1998–99 and three years later with Detroit. Hull's best year was 1990–91 when he scored 86 goals and 131 points and was given the Hart Trophy and Lester B. Pearson Award for his sensational season. He scored 50 goals in 50 games twice, an achievement accomplished more often only by Wayne Gretzky (three times).

Brian Leetch

One of a rare group of defencemen to record 1,000 points in a career, Brian Leetch might well be the finest American-born player in NHL history. A strong player in his own end, he was famous for his skating and offensive abilities in the model of Bobby Orr. He scored 23 goals as a rookie in 1988-89, a record that stands to this day, and won the Calder Trophy for his fine first season. He later recorded 102 points in 1991–92, becoming only the fifth defenceman to reach the 100-point plateau in a season. Leetch was part of the New York Rangers' historic Stanley Cup win in 1994. He won the Conn Smythe Trophy that spring, making him the only American player so honoured in the trophy's history. Two years later, he captained Team USA to victory in the World Cup of Hockey. He played the first 17 of his 19 NHL years with the Rangers, moving to Toronto and Boston for one year each at the end of his career.

Builders

Lou Lamoriello

The face of the New Jersey Devils since 1987, Lamoriello took a sad-sack franchise and built it into a Stanley Cup champion and perennial contender. He remains the longest-serving active GM with one team, and the Devils have now won the Cup three times under his leadership—1994–95, 1999–2000, and 2002–03. He is known for his acumen in assessing talent as well as his ability to convince players to buy into a team concept at contract time, often re-signing stars for less money than they could get elsewhere in exchange for the knowledge that every year the team stands a chance to win the Stanley Cup. Lamoriello brought strong defensive play to the team, something he was able to accomplish when he drafted goalie Martin Brodeur, who has gone on to become the winningest puck-stopper in NHL history.

Hockey Hall of Fame Honoured Members

(member, category, year inducted)

Sid Abel—Player, 1969

Charles Adams—Builder, 1960

Jack Adams—Player, 1959

Weston Adams—Builder, 1972

Frank Ahearn—Builder, 1962

Bunny Ahearne—Builder, 1977

Sir Montagu Allan—Builder, 1945

Keith Allen—Builder, 1992

Glenn Anderson—Player, 2008

Syl Apps—Player, 1961

Al Arbour—Builder, 1996

George Armstrong—Player, 1975

Neil Armstrong—Official, 1991

John Ashley—Official, 1981

Ace Bailey—Player, 1975

Dan Bain—Player, 1945

Hobey Baker—Player, 1945

Harold Ballard—Builder, 1977

Bill Barber—Player, 1990

Marty Barry—Player, 1965

Andy Bathgate—Player, 1978

Bobby Bauer—Player, 1996

Father David Bauer—Builder, 1989

Jean Beliveau—Player, 1972

Clint Benedict—Player, 1965

Doug Bentley—Player, 1964

Max Bentley—Player, 1966

Jack Bickell—Builder, 1978

Toe Blake—Player, 1966

Leo Boivin—Player, 1986

Dickie Boon—Player, 1952
Mike Bossy—Player, 1991
Butch Bouchard—Player, 1966
Frank Boucher—Player, 1958
George Boucher—Player, 1960
Ray Bourque—Player, 2004
Johnny Bower—Player, 1976
Russell Bowie—Player, 1945
Scotty Bowman—Builder, 1991
Frank Brimsek—Player, 1966
Punch Broadbent—Player, 1962
Turk Broda—Player, 1967
Herb Brooks—Builder, 2006
George Brown—Builder, 1961
Walter Brown—Builder, 1962
Frank Buckland—Builder, 1975
Johnny Bucyk—Player, 1981
Billy Burch—Player, 1974
Walter Bush—Builder, 2000
Jack Butterfield—Builder, 1980
Frank Calder—Builder, 1947
Harry Cameron—Player, 1962
Angus Campbell—Builder, 1964
Clarence Campbell—Builder, 1966
Joe Cattarinich—Builder, 1977
Bill Chadwick—Official, 1964
Gerry Cheevers—Player, 1985
Ed Chynoweth—Builder, 2008
King Clancy—Player, 1958
Dit Clapper—Player, 1947
Bobby Clarke—Player, 1987
Sprague Cleghorn—Player, 1958
Paul Coffey—Player, 2004
Neil Colville—Player, 1967

Charlie Conacher—Player, 1961
Lionel Conacher—Player, 1994
Roy Conacher—Player, 1998
Alex Connell—Player, 1958
Bill Cook—Player, 1952
Bun Cook—Player, 1995
Murray Costello—Builder, 2005
Art Coulter—Player, 1974
Yvan Cournoyer—Player, 1982
Bill Cowley—Player, 1968
Rusty Crawford—Player, 1962
John D'Amico—Official, 1993
Leo Dandurand—Builder, 1963
Jack Darragh—Player, 1962
Scotty Davidson—Player, 1950
Hap Day—Player, 1961
Alex Delvecchio—Player, 1977
Cy Denneny—Player, 1959
Frank Dilio—Builder, 1964
Marcel Dionne—Player, 1992
Gord Drillon—Player, 1975
Graham Drinkwater—Player, 1950
Ken Dryden—Player, 1983
George Dudley—Builder, 1958
Dick Duff—Player, 2006
Woody Dumart—Player, 1992
Tommy Dunderdale—Player, 1974
James Dunn—Builder, 1968
Bill Durnan—Player, 1964
Red Dutton—Player, 1958
Babe Dye—Player, 1970
Chaucer Elliott—Official, 1961
Tony Esposito—Player, 1988
Phil Esposito—Player, 1984

Art Farrell—Player, 1965
Bernie Federko—Player, 2002
Slava Fetisov—Player, 2001
Fern Flaman—Player, 1990
Cliff Fletcher—Builder, 2004
Frank Foyston—Player, 1958
Emile Francis—Builder, 1982
Ron Francis—Player, 2007
Frank Fredrickson—Player, 1958
Grant Fuhr—Player, 2003
Bill Gadsby—Player, 1970
Bob Gainey—Player, 1992
Chuck Gardiner—Player, 1945
Herb Gardiner—Player, 1958
Jimmy Gardner—Player, 1962
Mike Gartner—Player, 2001
Bernie Geoffrion—Player, 1972
Eddie Gerard—Player, 1945
Ed Giacomin—Player, 1987
Dr. Jack Gibson—Builder, 1976
Rod Gilbert—Player, 1982
Clark Gillies—Player, 2002
Billy Gilmour—Player, 1962
Moose Goheen—Player, 1952
Ebbie Goodfellow—Player, 1963
Tommy Gorman—Builder, 1963
Michel Goulet—Player, 1998
Mike Grant—Player, 1950
Shorty Green—Player, 1962
Jim Gregory—Builder, 2007
Wayne Gretzky—Player, 1999
Si Griffis—Player, 1950
Frank Griffiths—Builder, 1993
George Hainsworth—Player, 1961

Glenn Hall—Player, 1975
Joe Hall—Player, 1961
William Hanley—Builder, 1986
Doug Harvey—Player, 1973
Dale Hawerchuk—Player, 2001
Charles Hay—Builder, 1974
George Hay—Player, 1958
George Hayes—Official, 1988
Jim Hendy—Builder, 1968
Riley Hern—Player, 1962
Bobby Hewitson—Official, 1963
Foster Hewitt—Builder, 1965
William Hewitt—Builder, 1947
Bryan Hextall—Player, 1969
Harry Holmes—Player, 1972
Tom Hooper—Player, 1962
Red Horner—Player, 1965
Tim Horton—Player, 1977
Harley Hotchkiss—Builder, 2006
Gordie Howe—Player, 1972
Syd Howe—Player, 1965
Harry Howell—Player, 197
Bobby Hull—Player, 1983
Brett Hull—Player, 2009
Fred Hume—Builder, 1962
Bouse Hutton—Player, 1962
Harry Hyland—Player, 1962
Mike Ilitch—Builder, 2003
Punch Imlach—Builder, 1984
Mickey Ion—Official, 1961
Dick Irvin—Player, 1958
Tommy Ivan—Builder, 1974
Harvey Jackson—Player, 1971
William Jennings—Builder, 1975

Bob Johnson—Builder, 1992

Moose Johnson—Player, 1952

Ching Johnson—Player, 1958

Tom Johnson—Player, 1970

Aurel Joliat—Player, 1947

Gordon Juckes—Builder, 1979

Duke Keats—Player, 1958

Red Kelly—Player, 1969

Ted Kennedy—Player, 1966

Dave Keon—Player, 1986

Valeri Kharlamov—Player, 2005

Gen. John Reed Kilpatrick—
Builder, 1960

Brian Kilrea—Builder, 2003

Seymour Knox—Builder, 1993

Jari Kurri—Player, 2001

Elmer Lach—Player, 1966

Guy Lafleur—Player, 1988

Pat LaFontaine—Player, 2003

Newsy Lalonde—Player, 1950

Rod Langway—Player, 2002

Lou Lamoriello—Builder, 2009

Jacques Laperriere—Player, 1987

Guy Lapointe—Player, 1993

Edgar Laprade—Player, 1993

Igor Larionov—Player, 2008

Jack Laviolette—Player, 1962

George Leader—Builder, 1969

Robert LeBel—Builder, 1970

Brian Leetch—Player, 2009

Hugh Lehman—Player, 1958

Jacques Lemaire—Player, 1984

Mario Lemieux—Player, 1997

Percy LeSueur—Player, 1961

Herbie Lewis—Player, 1989

Ted Lindsay—Player, 1966

Tommy Lockhart—Builder, 1965

Paul Loicq—Builder, 1961

Harry Lumley—Player, 1980

Al MacInnis—Player, 2007

Mickey MacKay—Player, 1952

Frank Mahovlich—Player, 1981

Joe Malone—Player, 1950

Sylvio Mantha—Player, 1960

John Mariucci—Builder, 1985

Jack Marshall—Player, 1965

Frank Mathers—Builder, 1992

Steamer Maxwell—Player, 1962

Lanny McDonald—Player, 1992

Frank McGee—Player, 1945

Billy McGimsie—Player, 1962

Major Frederic McLaughlin—
Builder, 1963

George McNamara—Player, 1958

Mark Messier—Player, 2007

Stan Mikita—Player, 1983

Jake Milford—Builder, 1984

Hon. Hartland Molson—
Builder, 1973

Dickie Moore—Player, 1974

Paddy Moran—Player, 1958

Howie Morenz—Player, 1945

Scotty Morrison—Builder, 1999

Bill Mosienko—Player, 1965

Joe Mullen—Player, 2000

Larry Murphy—Player, 2004

Monsignor Athol Murray—
Builder, 1998

Cam Neely—Player, 2005

Roger Neilson—Builder, 2002

Francis Nelson—Builder, 1947

Frank Nighbor—Player, 1947

Reg Noble—Player, 1962

Bruce A. Norris—Builder, 1969

James Norris Jr.—Builder, 1962

James Norris Sr.—Builder, 1958

William Northey—Builder, 1947

Ambrose O'Brien—Builder, 1962

Buddy O'Connor—Player, 1988

Harry Oliver—Player, 1967

Bert Olmstead—Player, 1985

Brian O'Neill—Builder, 1994

Bobby Orr—Player, 1979

Fred Page—Builder, 1993

Bernie Parent—Player, 1984

Brad Park—Player, 1988

Craig Patrick—Builder, 2001

Frank Patrick—Builder, 1958

Lester Patrick—Player, 1947

Lynn Patrick—Player, 1980

Matt Pavelich—Official, 1987

Gilbert Perreault—Player, 1990

Tommy Phillips—Player, 1945

Allan Pickard—Builder, 1958

Pierre Pilote—Player, 1975

Rudy Pilous—Builder, 1985

Didier Pitre—Player, 1962

Jacques Plante—Player, 1978

Bud Poile—Builder, 1990

Sam Pollock—Builder, 1978

Denis Potvin—Player, 1991

Babe Pratt—Player, 1966

Joe Primeau—Player, 1963

Marcel Pronovost—Player, 1978

Bob Pulford—Player, 1991

Harvey Pulford—Player, 1945

Bill Quackenbush—Player, 1976

Frank Rankin—Player, 1961

Jean Ratelle—Player, 1985

Sen. Donat Raymond—
Builder, 1958

Chuck Rayner—Player, 1973

Ken Reardon—Player, 1966

Henri Richard—Player, 1979

Maurice Richard—Player, 1961

George Richardson—Player, 1950

Gordon Roberts—Player, 1971

John Ross Robertson—Builder, 1947

Claude Robinson—Builder, 1947

Larry Robinson—Player, 1995

Luc Robitaille—Player, 2009

Mike Rodden—Official, 1962

Art Ross—Player, 1945

Philip D. Ross—Builder, 1976

Patrick Roy—Player, 2006

Blair Russel—Player, 1965

Ernie Russell—Player, 1965

Jack Ruttan—Player, 1962

Dr. Gunther Sabetzki—
Builder, 1995

Borje Salming—Player, 1996

Glen Sather—Builder, 1997

Denis Savard—Player, 2000

Serge Savard—Player, 1986

Terry Sawchuk—Player, 1971

Fred Scanlan—Player, 1965

Ray Scapinello—Official, 2008

Milt Schmidt—Player, 1961

Sweeney Schriner—Player, 1962

Earl Seibert—Player, 1963

Oliver Seibert—Player, 1961

Frank Selke—Builder, 1960

Eddie Shore—Player, 1947

Steve Shutt—Player, 1993

Babe Siebert—Player, 1964

Joe Simpson—Player, 1962

Harry Sinden—Builder, 1983

Darryl Sittler—Player, 1989

Cooper Smeaton—Official, 1961

Alf Smith—Player, 1962

Billy Smith—Player, 1993

Clint Smith—Player, 1991

Frank Smith—Builder, 1962

Hooley Smith—Player, 1972

Tommy Smith—Player, 1973

Conn Smythe—Builder, 1958

Ed Snider—Builder, 1988

Allan Stanley—Player, 1981

Barney Stanley—Player, 1962

Peter Stastny—Player, 1998

Scott Stevens—Player, 2007

Jack Stewart—Player, 1964

Lord Stanley of Preston— Builder, 1945

Nels Stewart—Player, 1962

Red Storey—Official, 1967

Bruce Stuart—Player, 1961

Hod Stuart—Player, 1945

Capt. James T. Sutherland— Builder, 1947

Anatoli Tarasov—Builder, 1974

Cyclone Taylor—Player, 1947

Tiny Thompson—Player, 1959

Bill Torrey—Builder, 1995

Vladislav Tretiak—Player, 1989

Harry Trihey—Player, 1950

Bryan Trottier—Player, 1997

Lloyd Turner—Builder, 1958

William Tutt—Builder, 1978

Frank Udvari—Official, 1973

Norm Ullman—Player, 1982

Andy Van Hellemond— Official, 1999

Georges Vezina—Player, 1945

Carl Voss—Builder, 1974

Fred Waghorne—Builder, 1961

Jack Walker—Player, 1960

Marty Walsh—Player, 1962

Harry E. Watson—Player, 1962

Harry Watson—Player, 1994

Cooney Weiland—Player, 1971

Harry Westwick—Player, 1962

Fred Whitcroft—Player, 1962

Phat Wilson—Player, 1962

Arthur Wirtz—Builder, 1971

Bill Wirtz—Builder, 1976

Gump Worsley—Player, 1980

Roy Worters—Player, 1969

Steve Yzerman—Player, 2009

John Ziegler—Builder, 1987

IIHF Hall of Fame

(name, nationality, year inducted)

° denotes Referee; * denotes Builder; all others are Players

°Quido Adamec (Czech Republic), 2005

*John "Bunny" Ahearne (Great Britain), 1997

Veniamin Alexandrov (Russia), 2007

*Ernest Aljancic, Sr. (Slovenia), 2002

Helmut Balderis (Latvia), 1998

Rudi Ball (Germany), 2004

*Father David Bauer (Canada), 1997

Art Berglund (USA), 2008

*Curt Berglund (Sweden), 2003

Sven Bergqvist (Sweden), 1999

Lars Bjorn (Sweden), 1998

Vsevolod Bobrov (Russia), 1997

Vladimir Bouzek (Czech Republic), 2007

Roger Bourbonnais (Canada), 1999

Philippe Bozon (France), 2008

*Herb Brooks (USA), 1999

*Walter Brown (USA), 1997

Vlastimil Bubnik (Czech Republic), 1997

*Mike Buckna (Canada), 2004

*Ludek Bukac (Czech Republic), 2007

Walter Bush, Jr. (USA), 2009

*Enrico Calcaterra (Italy), 1999

Ferdinand Cattini (Switzerland), 1998

Hans Cattini (Switzerland), 1998

Josef Cerny (Czech Republic), 2007

*Arkady Chernyshev (Russia), 1999

Bill Christian (USA), 1998

Bill Cleary (USA), 1997

Gerry Cosby (USA), 1997

Jim Craig (USA), 1999

Mike Curran (USA), 1999

°Ove Dahlberg (Sweden), 2004

Vitali Davydov (Russia), 2004

Igor Dimitriev (Russia), 2007

Hans Dobida (Austria), 2007

Jaroslav Drobny (Czechoslovakia), 1997

Vladimir Dzurilla (Slovakia), 1998

*Rudolf Eklow (Sweden), 1999

Carl Erhardt (Great Britain), 1998

Slava Fetisov (Russia), 2005

Anatoli Firsov (Russia), 1998

Josef Golonka (Slovakia), 1998

Cammi Granato (USA), 2008

Wayne Gretzky (Canada), 2000

*Arne Grunander (Sweden), 1997

Henryk Gruth (Poland), 2006

*Bengt-Ake Gustafsson (Sweden), 2003

Karel Gut (Czech Republic), 1998

Geraldine Heaney (Canada), 2008

Anders Hedberg (Sweden), 1997

*Heinz Henschel (Germany), 2003

William Hewitt (Canada), 1998

Rudi Hiti (Slovenia), 2009

Ivan Hlinka (Czech Republic), 2002

Jiri Holecek (Czech Republic), 1998

Jiri Holik (Czech Republic), 1999

*Derek Holmes (Canada), 1999

Leif Holmqvist (Sweden), 1999

*Ladislav Horsky (Slovakia), 2004

Fran Huck (Canada), 1999

*Jorgen Hviid (Denmark), 2005

Gustav Jaenecke (Germany), 1998

Angela James (Canada), 2008

*Tore Johannessen (Norway), 1999

Mark Johnson (USA), 1999

Marshall Johnston (Canada), 1998

Tomas Jonsson (Sweden), 2000

Gord Juckes (Canada), 1997

Timo Jutila (Finland), 2003

°Yuri Karandin (Russia), 2004

Alexei Kasatonov (Russia), 2009

*Tsutomu Kawabuchi (Japan), 2004

Matti Keinonen (Finland), 2002

Valeri Kharlamov (Russia), 1998

*Anatoli Khorozov (Ukraine), 2006

Udo Kiessling (Germany), 2000

*Dave King (Canada), 2001

Jakob Kolliker (Switzerland), 2007

°Josef Kompalla (Germany), 2003

Viktor Konovalenko (Russia), 2007

*Vladimir Kostka (Czech Republic), 1997

Erich Kuhnhackl (Germany), 1997

Jari Kurri (Finland), 2000

Viktor Kuzkin (Russia), 2005

Jacques Lacarriere (France), 1998

Igor Larionov (Russia), 2008

*Bob Lebel (Canada), 1997

Mario Lemieux (Canada), 2008

*Harry Lindblad (Finland), 1999

Vic Lindquist (Canada), 1997

*Paul Loicq (Belgium), 1997

Konstantin Loktev (Russia), 2007

Hakan Loob (Sweden), 1998

*Cesar Luthi (Switzerland), 1998

Oldrich Machac (Czech Republic), 1999

Barry MacKenzie (Canada), 1999

Sergei Makarov (Russia), 2001

Josef Malecek (Czech Republic), 2003

Alexander Maltsev (Russia), 1999

*Louis Magnus (France), 1997

Pekka Marjamaki (Finland), 1998

Seth Martin (Canada), 1997

Vladimir Martinec (Czech Republic), 2001

John Mayasich (USA), 1997

Boris Mayorov (Russia), 1999

Jack McCartan (USA), 1998

Jack McLeod (Canada), 1999

Boris Mikhailov (Russia), 2000

Lou Nanne (USA), 2004

Mats Naslund (Sweden), 2005

Vaclav Nedomansky (Czech Republic), 1997

Kent Nilsson (Sweden), 2006

Nisse Nilsson (Sweden), 2002

Lasse Oksanen (Finland), 1999

Terry O'Malley (Canada), 1998

Eduard Pana (Romania), 1998

*Gyorgy Pasztor (Hungary), 2001

*Peter Patton (Great Britain), 2002

Esa Peltonen (Finland), 2007

Vladimir Petrov (Russia), 2006

Ronald Pettersson (Sweden), 2004

Frantisek Pospisil (Czech Republic), 1999

Sepp Puschnig (Austria), 1999

Alexander Ragulin (Russia), 1997

Hans Rampf (Germany), 2001

*Gord Renwick (Canada), 2002

*Bob Ridder (USA), 1998

*Jack Riley (USA), 1998

Thomas Rundquist (Sweden), 2007

*Gunther Sabetzki (Germany), 1997

Borje Salming (Sweden), 1998

Laszlo Schell (Hungary), 2009

Alois Schloder (Germany), 2005

Harry Sinden (Canada), 1997

Nikolai Sologubov (Russia), 2004

*Andrei Starovoitov (Russia), 1997

Vyacheslav Starshinov (Russia), 2007

*Jan Starsi (Slovakia), 1999

Peter Stastny (Slovakia), 2000

Ulf Sterner (Sweden), 2001

Roland Stoltz (Sweden), 1999

*Arne Stromberg (Sweden), 1998

*Goran Stubb (Finland), 2000

*Miroslav Subrt (Czech Republic), 2004

Jan Suchy (Czech Republic), 2009

*Anatoli Tarasov (Russia), 1997

Frantisek Tikal (Czech Republic), 2004

*Viktor Tikhonov (Russia), 1998

*Shoichi Tomita (Japan), 2006

Richard "Bibi" Torriani (Switzerland), 1997

Vladislav Tretiak (Russia), 1997

*Hal Trumble (USA), 1999

*Yoshiaki Tsutsumi (Japan), 1999

Sven Tumba (Sweden), 1997

*Thayer Tutt (USA), 2002

*Xaver Unsinn (Germany), 1998

Jorma Valtonen (Finland), 1999

Valeri Vasiliev (Russia), 1998

Juhani Wahlsten (Finland), 2006

*Walter Wasservogel (Austria), 1997

Harry Watson (Canada), 1998

°Unto Wiitala (Finland), 2003

Alexander Yakushev (Russia), 2003

Urpo Ylonen (Finland), 1997

*Vldimir Yurzinov (Russia), 2002

Vladimir Zabrodsky (Czech Republic), 1997

Joachim Ziesche (Germany), 1999

2009 WORLD JUNIOR CHAMPIONSHIP

Ottawa, CANADA, December 26, 2008–January 5, 2009

FINAL PLACINGS

GOLD MEDAL	Canada
SILVER MEDAL	Sweden
BRONZE MEDAL	Russia
Fourth Place	Slovakia
Fifth Place	United States
Sixth Place	Czech Republic
Seventh Place	Finland
Eighth Place	Latvia
Ninth Place	Germany
Tenth Place	Kazakhstan

All-Star Team

Goal	Jaroslav Janus (SVK)
Defence	P.K. Subban (CAN), Erik Karlsson (SWE)
Forward	John Tavares (CAN), Cody Hodgson (CAN), Nikita Filatov (RUS)

Directorate Awards

Best Goalie	Jacob Markstrom (SWE)
Best Defenceman	Erik Karlsson (SWE)
Best Forward	John Tavares (CAN)
Tournament MVP	John Tavares (CAN)

FINAL STANDINGS

**Preliminary Round
Group A**

	GP	W	OTW	OTL	L	GF	GA	P
Canada	4	4	0	0	0	35	6	12
United States	4	3	0	0	1	28	12	9
Czech Republic	4	2	0	0	2	20	14	6
Germany	4	1	0	0	3	12	19	3
Kazakhstan	4	0	0	0	4	2	46	0

December 26	United States 8/Germany 2
December 26	Canada 8/Czech Republic 1
December 27	Germany 9/Kazakhstan 0
December 28	Canada 15/Kazakhstan 0
December 28	United States 4/Czech Republic 3
December 29	Canada 5/Germany 1
December 30	Czech Republic 6/Germany 0
December 30	United States 12/Kazakhstan 0
December 31	Czech Republic 10/Kazakhstan 2
December 31	Canada 7/United States 4

Group B

	GP	W	OTW	OTL	L	GF	GA	P
Sweden	4	4	0	0	0	21	3	12
Russia	4	3	0	0	1	17	9	9
Slovakia	4	1	1	0	2	12	15	5
Finland	4	1	0	1	2	10	12	4
Latvia	4	0	0	0	4	5	26	0

December 26	Russia 4/Latvia 1
December 26	Sweden 3/Finland 1
December 27	Slovakia 7/Latvia 2
December 28	Russia 5/Finland 2

December 28	Sweden 3/Slovakia 1
December 29	Sweden 10/Latvia 1
December 30	Russia 8/Slovakia 1
December 30	Finland 5/Latvia 1
December 31	Sweden 5/Russia 0
December 31	Slovakia 3/Finland 2

Relegation Round

	GP	W	OTW	OTL	L	GF	GA	P
Finland	3	3	0	0	0	15	3	9
Latvia	3	2	0	0	1	15	7	6
Germany	3	1	0	0	2	11	10	3
Kazakhstan	3	0	0	0	3	2	23	0

Carry-over results

Germany 9/Kazakhstan 0
Finland 5/Latvia 1

January 2	Latvia 7/Germany 1
January 3	Finland 7/Kazakhstan 1
January 4	Finland 3/Germany 1
January 4	Latvia 7/Kazakhstan 1

Playoffs
Quarter-finals

January 2	Slovakia 5/United States 3
January 2	Russia 5/Czech Republic 1
January 3	Sweden 5/Slovakia 3
January 3	Canada 6/Russia 5 (10:00 OT/SO)

Fifth-place game

| January 4 | United States 3/Czech Republic 2 (OT) |

Bronze-Medal Game
January 5   Russia 5/Slovakia 2

Gold-Medal Game
January 5   Canada 5/Sweden 1

TEAM CANADA STATISTICS

	GP	G	A	P	Pim
Cody Hodgson	6	5	11	16	2
John Tavares	6	8	7	15	0
Jordan Eberle	6	6	7	13	2
P.K. Subban	6	3	6	9	6
Zack Boychuk	6	4	3	7	0
Tyler Ennis	6	3	4	7	0
Chris di Domenico	6	2	5	7	4
Ryan Ellis	6	1	6	7	0
Jamie Benn	6	4	2	6	4
Evander Kane	6	2	4	6	2
Angelo Esposito	6	3	1	4	4
Patrice Cormier	6	1	2	3	6
Alex Pietrangelo	6	1	2	3	0
Brett Sonne	6	1	2	3	0
Tom Hickey	6	0	3	3	2
Stefan della Rovere	6	1	1	2	26
Tyler Myers	6	1	0	1	2
Cody Goloubef	6	0	1	1	8
Keith Aulie	6	0	1	1	2
Colten Teubert	6	0	0	0	4
Dustin Tokarski	4	0	0	0	0
Chet Pickard	2	0	0	0	0

In Goal

	GP	W–L–T	Mins	GA	SO	GAA
Dustin Tokarski	4	4-0-0	248:41	11	0	2.65
Chet Pickard	2	2-0-0	120:00	1	1	0.50

2010 WORLD JUNIOR CHAMPIONSHIP SCHEDULE

Regina/Saskatoon, CANADA, December 26, 2009–January 5, 2010

Group A: Canada, Latvia, Slovakia, Switzerland, United States
Group B: Austria, Czech Republic, Finland, Russia, Sweden

Brandt Centre=Regina, Saskatchewan
Credit Union Centre=Saskatoon, Saskatchewan

December 26, 2009
Czech Republic–Sweden	Brandt Centre
Latvia–Canada	Credit Union Centre
Russia–Austria	Brandt Centre
Slovakia–United States	Credit Union Centre

December 27, 2009
Austria–Sweden	Brandt Centre
United States–Switzerland	Credit Union Centre
Czech Republic–Finland	Brandt Centre
Slovakia–Latvia	Credit Union Centre

December 28, 2009
Canada–Switzerland	Credit Union Centre
Finland–Russia	Brandt Centre

December 29, 2009
Austria–Czech Republic	Brandt Centre
Latvia–United States	Credit Union Centre
Sweden–Russia	Brandt Centre
Canada–Slovakia	Credit Union Centre

December 30, 2009
Finland–Austria   Brandt Centre
Switzerland–Latvia   Credit Union Centre

December 31, 2009
Sweden–Finland   Brandt Centre
Switzerland–Slovakia   Credit Union Centre
Russia–Czech Republic   Brandt Centre
United States–Canada   Credit Union Centre

January 1, 2010
NO GAMES

January 2, 2010
A4–B5 Relegation   Credit Union Centre
Quarter-final 1   Credit Union Centre
Quarter-final 2   Credit Union Centre

January 3, 2010
B4–A5 Relegation   Credit Union Centre
Semifinal 1   Credit Union Centre
Semifinal 2   Credit Union Centre

January 4, 2010
A4–B4 Relegation   Credit Union Centre
A5–B5 Relegation   Credit Union Centre
Fifth-Place Game   Credit Union Centre

January 5, 2010
Bronze-Medal Game   Credit Union Centre
Gold-Medal Game   Credit Union Centre

2009 WORLD MEN'S CHAMPIONSHIP

Zurich/Bern, SWITZERLAND, April 24–May 10, 2009

FINAL PLACINGS

GOLD MEDAL	Russia
SILVER MEDAL	Canada
BRONZE MEDAL	Sweden
Fourth Place	United States
Fifth Place	Finland
Sixth Place	Czech Republic
Seventh Place	Latvia
Eighth Place	Belarus
Ninth Place	Switzerland
Tenth Place	Slovakia
Eleventh Place	Norway
Twelfth Place	France
Thirteenth Place	Denmark
Fourteenth Place	Austria
Fifteenth Place	Germany
Sixteenth Place	Hungary

All-Star Team

Goal:	Andrei Mezin (BLR)
Defence:	Shea Weber (CAN), Kenny Jonsson (SWE)
Forward:	Martin St. Louis (CAN), Steve Stamkos (CAN), Ilya Kovalchuk (RUS)

Directorate Awards

Best Goalie	Andrei Mezin (BLR)
Best Defenceman	Shea Weber (CAN)
Best Forward	Ilya Kovalchuk (RUS)
Tournament MVP	Ilya Kovalchuk (RUS)

RESULTS & FINAL STANDINGS

Preliminary Round
Group A (Kloten)

	GP	W	OTW	OTL	L	GF	GA	P
Canada	3	3	0	0	0	22	4	9
Belarus	3	1	1	0	1	6	8	5
Slovakia	3	1	0	1	1	8	12	4
Hungary	3	0	0	0	3	4	16	0

April 24	Canada 6/Belarus 1
April 24	Slovakia 4/Hungary 3
April 26	Belarus 2/Slovakia 1 (5:00 OT/SO)
April 26	Canada 9/Hungary 0
April 28	Belarus 3/Hungary 1
April 28	Canada 7/Slovakia 3

Group B (Bern)

	GP	W	OTW	OTL	L	GF	GA	P
Russia	3	3	0	0	0	16	4	9
Switzerland	3	1	1	0	1	6	6	5
France	3	1	0	0	2	4	9	3
Germany	3	0	0	1	2	3	10	1

April 24	Russia 5/Germany 0
April 24	Switzerland 1/France 0
April 26	Switzerland 3/Germany 2 (OT)
April 26	Russia 7/France 2
April 28	Russia 4/Switzerland 2
April 28	France 2/Germany 1

Group C (Bern)

	GP	W	OTW	OTL	L	GF	GA	P
United States	3	2	0	1	0	15	9	7
Sweden	3	1	1	1	0	15	9	6
Latvia	3	1	1	0	1	7	6	5
Austria	3	0	0	0	3	2	15	0

April 25	United States 4/Latvia 2
April 25	Sweden 7/Austria 1
April 27	United States 6/Austria 1
April 27	Latvia 3/Sweden 2 (5:00 OT/SO)
April 29	Latvia 2/Austria 0
April 29	Sweden 6/United States 5 (OT)

Group D (Kloten)

	GP	W	OTW	OTL	L	GF	GA	P
Finland	3	3	0	0	0	14	4	9
Czech Republic	3	2	0	0	1	13	6	6
Norway	3	0	1	0	2	7	14	2
Denmark	3	0	0	1	2	5	15	1

April 25	Finland 5/Norway 0
April 25	Czech Republic 5/Denmark 0
April 27	Czech Republic 5/Norway 2
April 27	Finland 5/Denmark 1
April 29	Norway 5/Denmark 4 (OT)
April 29	Finland 4/Czech Republic 3

Qualification Round
Group E (Bern)

	GP	W	OTW	OTL	L	GF	GA	P
Russia	5	4	1	0	0	27	11	14
Sweden	5	2	1	2	0	23	18	10

	GP	W	OTW	OTL	L	GF	GA	P
United States	5	2	0	2	1	19	18	8
Latvia	5	1	2	0	2	15	14	7
Switzerland	5	1	1	1	2	9	13	6
France	5	0	0	0	5	8	27	0

April 30	Russia 6/Sweden 5 (OT)
April 30	Latvia 2/Switzerland 1
May 1	United States 6/France 2
May 2	Latvia 7/France 1
May 2	Russia 4/United States 1
May 3	Sweden 4/Switzerland 1
May 3	Russia 6/Latvia 1
May 4	Sweden 6/France 3
May 4	Switzerland 4/United States 3 (OT)

Group F (Kloten)

	GP	W	OTW	OTL	L	GF	GA	P
Canada	5	4	0	1	0	26	10	13
Finland	5	2	2	1	0	16	9	11
Czech Republic	5	3	0	0	2	20	11	9
Belarus	5	0	3	0	2	8	13	6
Slovakia	5	0	1	2	2	8	21	4
Norway	5	0	0	2	3	7	21	2

April 30	Belarus 3/Norway 2 (OT)
April 30	Canada 5/Czech Republic 1
May 1	Finland 2/Slovakia 1 (OT)
May 2	Czech Republic 8/Slovakia 0
May 2	Belarus 2/Finland 1 (5:00 OT/SO)
May 3	Canada 5/Norway 1
May 3	Czech Republic 3/Belarus 0
May 4	Slovakia 3/Norway 2 (OT)
May 4	Finland 4/Canada 3 (5:00 OT/SO)

Relegation Round
Group G

	GP	W	OTW	OTL	L	GF	GA	P
Denmark	3	3	0	0	0	13	4	9
Austria	3	2	0	0	1	9	5	6
Germany	3	1	0	0	2	3	5	3
Hungary	3	0	0	0	3	2	13	0

May 1	Bern	Denmark 3/Germany 1
May 1	Kloten	Austria 6/Hungary 0
May 3	Bern	Austria 1/Germany 0
May 3	Kloten	Denmark 5/Hungary 1
May 4	Bern	Germany 2/Hungary 1
May 4	Kloten	Denmark 5/Austria 2

Playoff Round (all games in Bern)
Quarter-finals

May 6	Russia 4/Belarus 3
May 6	United States 3/Finland 2
May 7	Canada 4/Latvia 2
May 7	Sweden 3/Czech Republic 1

Semifinals

May 8	Russia 3/United States 2
May 8	Canada 3/Sweden 1

Bronze-Medal Game

May 10	Sweden 4/United States 2

Gold-Medal Game

May 10	Russia 2/Canada 1

2009 WORLD WOMEN'S CHAMPIONSHIP

Hameenlinna, FINLAND, April 4–12, 2009

FINAL PLACINGS

GOLD MEDAL	United States
SILVER MEDAL	Canada
BRONZE MEDAL	Finland
Fourth Place	Sweden
Fifth Place	Russia
Sixth Place	Kazakhstan
Seventh Place	Switzerland
Eighth Place	Japan
Ninth Place	China

All-Star Team

Goal	Jesse Vetter (USA)
Defence	Carla MacLeod (CAN), Angela Ruggiero (USA)
Forward	Michelle Karvinen (FIN), Julie Chu (USA), Natalie Darwitz (USA)

Directorate Awards

Best Goalie	Charline Labonte (CAN)
Best Defenceman	Jenni Hiirikoski (FIN)
Best Forward	Hayley Wickenheiser (CAN)
Tournament MVP	Carla MacLeod (CAN)

RESULTS AND FINAL STANDINGS

Preliminary Round
Group A

	GP	W	OTW	OTL	L	GF	GA	P
United States	2	2	0	0	0	16	0	6
Russia	2	1	0	0	1	3	9	3
Japan	2	0	0	0	2	1	11	0

April 4	United States 8/Japan 0
April 5	Russia 3/Japan 1
April 6	United States 8/Russia 0

Group B

	GP	W	OTW	OTL	L	GF	GA	P
Canada	2	2	0	0	0	20	1	6
Sweden	2	1	0	0	1	6	8	3
China	2	0	0	0	2	2	19	0

April 4	Canada 13/China 1
April 5	Sweden 6/China 1
April 6	Canada 7/Sweden 0

Group C

	GP	W	OTW	OTL	L	GF	GA	P
Finland	2	2	0	0	0	13	3	6
Kazakhstan	2	0	1	0	1	2	8	2
Switzerland	2	0	0	1	1	4	8	1

April 4	Finland 7/Kazakhstan 0
April 5	Kazakhstan 2/Switzerland 1
April 6	Finland 6/Switzerland 3

Qualifying Round
Group D

	GP	W	OTW	OTL	L	GF	GA	P
Canada	2	2	0	0	0	10	1	6
United States	2	1	0	0	1	8	2	3
Finland	2	0	0	0	2	0	15	0

April 8	Canada 8/Finland 0
April 9	United States 7/Finland 0
April 10	Canada 2/United States 1

Group E

	GP	W	OTW	OTL	L	GF	GA	P
Sweden	2	2	0	0	0	17	0	6
Russia	2	1	0	0	1	9	10	3
Kazakhstan	2	0	0	0	2	2	18	0

April 8	Sweden 9/Kazakhstan 0
April 9	Russia 9/Kazakhstan 2
April 10	Sweden 8/Russia 0

Relegation Round
Group E

	GP	W	OTW	OTL	L	GF	GA	P
Switzerland	2	1	1	0	0	8	6	5
Japan	2	1	0	0	1	4	4	3
China	2	0	0	1	1	5	7	1

April 8	Switzerland 5/China 4
April 9	Switzerland 3/Japan 2
April 10	Japan 2/China 1

Bronze-Medal Game

April 12   Finland 4/Sweden 1

Gold-Medal Game

April 12   United States 4/Canada 1

VICTORIA CUP

PostFinance Arena, Bern, SWITZERLAND, October 1, 2008
NEW YORK RANGERS 4, METALLURG MAGNITOGORSK 3

Ryan Callahan scored the game-winning goal with only 20 seconds left in regulation time to give the New York Rangers a 4–3 victory over Metallurg Magnitogorsk in the inaugural Victoria Cup game. An impressive crowd of 13,794 at PostFinance Arena in Bern watched the entertaining game.

The goal capped an impressive comeback from 3–0 down late in the second period. Most of the first two periods were dominated by the Russians, as they capitalized on their scoring chances in the offensive end and moved the puck quickly out of their own end to prevent the Rangers from applying sustained pressure.

But Rangers coach Tom Renney made some adjustments during the second intermission. Most importantly, he changed strategy between the blue lines, where Metallurg had been so effective in stopping New York's attack. As a result, the third period was dominated by the NHL team.

Callahan's goal was the result of a horrific giveaway by Metallurg defenceman Vladimir Malenkikh. He tried to make a pass across to his defensive partner at the blue line, but Callahan intercepted the pass and went in alone on goalie Andrei Mezin. Callahan made a great deke and tucked the puck into the open net for the winning goal.

The Rangers had defeated the local SC Bern Bears 8–1 the previous night in an exhibition tune-up.

Lineups

New York Rangers—Goal: Henrik Lundqvist, Stephen Valiquette (DNP); Defence: Dan Girardi, Dmitri Kalinin, Paul Mara, Wade Redden, Michal Rozsival, Marc Staal; Forward: Blair Betts, Ryan Callahan, Nigel Dawes, Chris Drury, Brandon Dubinsky, Dan Fritsche, Scott Gomez, Lauri Korpikoski, Markus Naslund, Petr Prucha, Pat Rismiller, Fredrik Sjostrom, Aaron Voros, Nikolai Zherdev; Coach: Tom Renney.

Metallurg Magnitogorsk—Goal: Andrei Mezin, Ilya Proskuryakov (DNP); Defence: Vitali Atyushov, Evgeni Biryukov, Vladislav Bulin, Rinat Ibragimov, Vladimir Malenkikh, Karel Pilar, Alexander Seluyanov, Evgeni Varlamov; Forward: Stanislav Chistov, Vadim Ermolayev, Evgeni Fedorov, Ravil Gusmanov, Alexei Kaigorodov, Denis Khlystov, Jaroslav Kudrna, Jan Marek, Igor Mirnov, Denis Platonov, Tomas Rolinek, Alexei Simakov, Nikolai Zavarukhin; Coach: Valeri Belousov.

Game Summary
First Period

0–1	Metallurg, Platonov (Chistov)	1:28
0–2	Metallurg, Malenkikh (unassisted)	18:07 (pp)

Penalties: Fritsche (NYR, 2:39), Ermolayev (MM, 6:23), Naslund (NYR, 9:43), Mara (NYR, 16:19)

Second Period

0–3	Metallurg, Zavarukhin (Atyushov, Marek)	10:20 (pp)
1–3	NY Rangers, Drury (Zherdev)	19:37 (pp)

Penalties: Simakov (MM, 0:26), Biryukov (MM, 6:27), Prucha

(NYR, 9:17), Ermolayev (MM, 11:48), Naslund (NYR, 12:17), Redden (NYR, 14:09), Kaigorodov (MM, 19:25), Zavarukhin (MM, 19:28)

Third Period

2–3	NY Rangers, Fritsche (Rozsival) 5:45	
3–3	NY Rangers, Drury (Gomez, Naslund) 10:13 (pp)	
4–3	NY Rangers, Callahan (unassisted) 19:40	

Penalties: Varlamov (MM, 10:50), Callahan (NYR, 13:37), Pilar (MM, 13:37)

In Goal

NYR—Lundqvist

MET—Mezin

Shots on Goal

NYR	11	14	19	44
MM	7	12	6	25

Attendance

13,794

CHAMPIONS HOCKEY LEAGUE, 2008–09

New to the international hockey schedule for 2008–09 was the Champions Hockey League, which replaced the European Champions Cup. This new venture, developed by the IIHF, was important for several reasons. First, the format drew from the successful Champions League football competition (that is, teams played each opponent once at home and once away, and all games were played on Wednesday nights throughout the season).

Second, it offered some 10 million euros in prize money, and games were televised throughout every major hockey nation in Europe. Third, the winner automatically qualified for the Victoria Cup game against an NHL opponent.

The inaugural season of the CHL featured the champions and runners-up from the top seven European hockey nations: Russia, Sweden, Finland, Czech Republic, Germany, Switzerland and Slovakia.

The top team in each group advanced to a home-and-home semifinal, and these two winners met for a final home-and-home series to determine the champion.

Points are awarded on a three-point system. A victory earns three points and a defeat zero. All games have a decisive outcome—if a game is tied at the end of regulation play, there is no extra time: the game is decided immediately by a shootout (three shots per side). The shootout winner receives two points and the shootout loser receives one point.

RESULTS
Group A
Teams: MET=Metallurg Magnitogorsk (Russia); EIS=Eisbären Berlin (Germany); KAR=Karpat Oulu (Finland)

	GP	W	L	OTW	OTL	GF	GA	P
MET	4	3	1	0	0	11	5	9
EIS	4	2	1	1	0	10	10	8
KAR	4	0	3	0	1	5	11	1

October 8, 2008	KAR 2 at EIS 3 (O2 World Arena, Berlin, Germany)
October 22, 2008	MET 2 at KAR 0 (Oulun Energia Arena, Oulu, Finland)
October 29, 2008	EIS 2 at MET 5 (Arena Metallurg, Magnitogorsk, Russia)
November 12, 2008	EIS 3 at KAR 2 (OT) (Oulun Energia Arena, Oulu, Finland)
November 19, 2008	KAR 1 at MET 3 (Arena Metallurg, Magnitogorsk, Russia)
December 3, 2008	MET 1 at EIS 2 (O2 World Arena, Berlin, Germany)

Group B
Teams: HV71=HV 71 Jonkoping (Sweden); BLU=Espoo Blues (Finland); SCB=SC Bern Bears (Switzerland)

	GP	W	L	OTW	OTL	GF	GA	P
BLU	4	4	0	0	0	14	4	12
HV71	4	1	3	0	0	13	18	3
SCB	4	1	3	0	0	11	16	3

October 8, 2008	SCB 2 at HV71 6 (Kinnarps Arena, Jonkoping, Sweden)

October 22, 2008	BLU 3 at SCB 1 (PostFinance Arena, Bern, Switzerland)
October 29, 2008	HV71 2 at BLU 3 (LansiAuto Arena, Espoo, Finland)
November 12, 2008	HV71 5 at SCB 7 (PostFinance Arena, Bern, Switzerland)
November 19, 2008	SCB 1 at BLU 2 (LansiAuto Arena, Espoo, Finland)
December 3, 2008	BLU 6 at HV71 0 (Kinnarps Arena, Jonkoping, Sweden)

Group C

Teams: SYU=Salavat Yulayev Ufa (Russia); MCB=Mountfield Ceske Budejovice (Czech Republic); SLO= Slovan Bratislava (Slovakia)

	GP	W	L	OTW	OTL	GF	GA	P
SYU	4	4	0	0	0	22	5	12
SLO	4	1	3	0	0	11	20	3
MCB	4	1	3	0	0	9	17	3

October 8, 2008	MCB 1 at SYU 7 (Ufa Arena, Ufa, Russia)
October 22, 2008	SLO 2 at MCB 5 (Budvar Arena, Ceske Budejovice, Czech)
October 29, 2008	SYU 4 at SLO 2 (Zimny Stadion, Bratislava, Slovakia)
November 12, 2008	SYU 3 at MCB 0 (Budvar Arena, Ceske Budejovice, Czech)
November 19, 2008	MCB 3 at SLO 5 (Zimny Stadion, Bratislava, Slovakia)
December 3, 2008	SLO 2 at SYU 8 (Ufa Arena, Ufa, Russia)

Group D

Teams: ZHC=ZHC Lions Zurich (Switzerland); SLA=Slavia Prague (Czech Republic); LHC= Linkopings HC (Sweden)

	GP	W	L	OTW	OTL	GF	GA	P
ZHC	4	3	0	0	1	20	11	10
SLA	4	2	1	1	0	15	15	8
LHC	4	0	4	0	0	11	20	0

October 8, 2008	LHC 2 at SLA 4 (O2 Arena, Prague, Czech Republic)
October 22, 2008	ZHC 7 at LHC 2 (Cloetta Centre, Linkoping, Sweden)
October 29, 2008	SLA 5 at ZSC 4 (OT) (Hallenstadion, Zurich, Switzerland)
November 12, 2008	SLA 5 at LHC 4 (Cloetta Centre, Linkoping, Sweden)
November 19, 2008	LHC 3 at ZHC 4 (Hallenstadion, Zurich, Switzerland)
December 3, 2008	ZSC 5 at SLA 1 (O2 Arena, Prague, Czech Republic)

SEMIFINALS

Teams: MET=Metallurg Magnitogork (Russia); SYU=Salavat Yulayev Ufa (Russia)

	GP	W	L	OTW	OTL	GF	GA	P
MET	2	1	1	0	0	4	3	3
SYU	2	1	1	0	0	3	4	3

December 10, 2008	SYU 2 at MET 1 (Arena Metallurg, Magnitogorsk, Russia)
January 7, 2009	MET 3 at SYU 1 (Ufa Arena, Ufa, Russia)

• Metallurg Magnitogorsk won a tie-breaking shootout after the second game, 2–0. Jan Marek and Igor Mirnov scored for Metallurg; Alexei Tereshenko and Alexander Perezhogin missed for Ufa.

Teams: BLU=Espoo Blues (Finland); ZSC= ZHC Lions Zurich (Switzerland)

	GP	W	L	OTW	OTL	GF	GA	P
ZSC	2	2	0	0	0	10	4	6
BLU	2	0	2	0	0	4	10	0

December 10, 2008   BLU 3 at ZSC 6 (Diners Club Arena, Rapperswil, Switzerland)

January 7, 2009   ZSC 4 at BLU 1 (LansiAuto Arena, Espoo, Finland)

Championship Finals

	GP	W	T	L	GF	GA	P
ZSC	2	1	1	0	7	2	4
MET	2	0	1	1	2	7	1

January 21, 2008   ZSC 2 at MET 2 (Arena Metallurg, Magnitogorsk, Russia)

January 28, 2008   MET 0 at ZSC 5 (Diners Club Arena, Rapperswil, Switzerland)

• ZSC Lions Zurich qualify to play in 2009 Victoria Cup game vs. Chicago Blackhawks on September 29, 2009.

PRO CLASSICS RESULTS

1972 Summit Series
Canada/Moscow, September 2–28, 1972

	GP	W	L	T	GF	GA	P
Canada	8	4	3	1	31	32	9
Soviet Union	8	3	4	1	32	31	7

Results

Game 1	September 2	Montreal	Soviet Union 7/Canada 3
Game 2	September 4	Toronto	Canada 4/Soviet Union 1
Game 3	September 6	Winnipeg	Canada 4/Soviet Union 4
Game 4	September 8	Vancouver	Soviet Union 5/Canada 3

Exhibition	September 16	Stockholm	Canada 4/Swedish Nationals 1
Exhibition	September 17	Stockholm	Canada 4/Swedish Nationals 4

Game 5	September 22	Moscow	Soviet Union 5/Canada 4
Game 6	September 24	Moscow	Canada 3/Soviet Union 2
Game 7	September 26	Moscow	Canada 4/Soviet Union 3
Game 8	September 28	Moscow	Canada 6/Soviet Union 5

(Paul Henderson scores series winner at 19:26 of 3rd)

Exhibition	September 30	Prague	Canada 3/Czech Nationals 3

1976 Canada Cup
Canada, September 2–15, 1976
Series MVP: Bobby Orr (Canada)

Team MVPs

Canada	Rogie Vachon
Czechoslovakia	Milan Novy
Soviet Union	Alexander Maltsev
Sweden	Borje Salming
United States	Robbie Ftorek
Finland	Matti Hagman

Final Standings Round Robin

	GP	W	L	T	GF	GA	P
Canada	5	4	1	0	22	6	8
Czechoslovakia	5	3	1	1	19	9	7
Soviet Union	5	2	2	1	23	14	5
Sweden	5	2	2	1	16	18	5
United States	5	1	3	1	14	21	3
Finland	5	1	4	0	16	42	2

Results

September 2	Ottawa	Canada 11/Finland 2
September 3	Toronto	Sweden 5/United States 2
	Montreal	Czechoslovakia 5/Soviet Union 3
September 5	Montreal	Canada 4/United States 2
	Montreal	Soviet Union 3/Sweden 3
	Toronto	Czechoslovakia 8/Finland 0
September 7	Toronto	Canada 4/Sweden 0
	Montreal	Soviet Union 11/Finland 3
	Philadelphia	Czechoslovakia 4/United States 4
September 9	Montreal	Czechoslovakia 1/Canada 0
	Winnipeg	Finland 8/Sweden 6
	Philadelphia	Soviet Union 5/United States 0

September 11	Toronto	Canada 3/Soviet Union 1
	Quebec City	Sweden 2/Czechoslovakia 1
	Montreal	United States 6/Finland 3

FINALS (best two-of-three)

September 13	Toronto	Canada 6/Czechoslovakia 0
September 15	Montreal	Canada 5/Czechoslovakia 4
		(Sittler 11:33 OT)

1981 Canada Cup

Canada, September 1–13, 1981

Tournament MVP: Vladislav Tretiak

Team Canada MVP: Mike Bossy

All-Star Team

Goal	Vladislav Tretiak (Soviet Union)
Defence	Alexei Kasatonov (Soviet Union)
	Arnold Kadlec (Czechoslovakia)
Forward	Gil Perreault (Canada)
	Mike Bossy (Canada)
	Sergei Shepelev (Soviet Union)

Final Standings Round Robin

	GP	W	L	T	GF	GA	P
Canada	5	4	0	1	32	13	9
Soviet Union	5	3	1	1	20	13	7
Czechoslovakia	5	2	1	2	21	13	6
United States	5	2	2	1	17	19	5
Sweden	5	1	4	0	13	20	2
Finland	5	0	4	1	6	31	1

Results

September 1	Edmonton	Canada 9/Finland 0
	Edmonton	United States 3/Sweden 1
	Winnipeg	Czechoslovakia 1/Soviet Union 1
September 3	Edmonton	Canada 8/United States 3
	Edmonton	Czechoslovakia 7/Finland 1
	Winnipeg	Soviet Union 6/Sweden 3
September 5	Winnipeg	Canada 4/Czechoslovakia 4
	Winnipeg	Sweden 5/Finland 0
	Edmonton	Soviet Union 4/United States 1
September 7	Montreal	Canada 4/Sweden 3
	Winnipeg	Soviet Union 6/Finland 1
	Montreal	United States 6/Czechoslovakia 2
September 9	Montreal	Canada 7/Soviet Union 3
	Ottawa	Czechoslovakia 7/Sweden 1
	Montreal	Finland 4/United States 4

Semifinals

September 11	Montreal	Canada 4/United States 1
	Ottawa	Soviet Union 4/Czechoslovakia 1

Finals

September 13	Montreal	Soviet Union 8/Canada 1

1984 Canada Cup
Canada, September 1–18, 1984
Tournament MVP: John Tonelli

All-Star Team
Goal	Vladimir Myshkin (Soviet Union)
Defence	Paul Coffey (Canada)
	Rod Langway (United States)
Forward	Wayne Gretzky (Canada)
	John Tonelli (Canada)
	Sergei Makarov (Soviet Union)

Final Standings Round Robin
	GP	W	L	T	GF	GA	P
Soviet Union	5	5	0	0	22	7	10
United States	5	3	1	1	21	13	7
Sweden	5	3	2	0	15	16	6
Canada	5	2	2	1	23	18	5
West Germany	5	0	4	1	13	29	1
Czechoslovakia	5	0	4	1	10	21	1

Results
September 1	Montreal	Canada 7/West Germany 2
	Halifax	United States 7/Sweden 1
September 2	Montreal	Soviet Union 3/Czechoslovakia 0
September 3	Montreal	Canada 4/United States 4
September 4	London	Czechoslovakia 4/West Germany 4
	Calgary	Soviet Union 3/Sweden 2
September 6	Vancouver	Sweden 4/Canada 2
	Edmonton	Soviet Union 8/West Germany 1
	Buffalo	United States 3/Czechoslovakia 2
September 8	Calgary	Canada 7/Czechoslovakia 2
	Calgary	Sweden 4/West Germany 2
	Edmonton	Soviet Union 2/United States 1

September 10	Edmonton	Soviet Union 6/Canada 3
	Vancouver	Sweden 4/Czechoslovakia 2
	Calgary	United States 6/West Germany 4

Semifinals

September 12	Edmonton	Sweden 9/United States 2
September 13	Calgary	Canada 3/Soviet Union 2
		(Bossy 12:29 OT)

Finals (best two-of-three)

| September 16 | Calgary | Canada 5/Sweden 2 |
| September 18 | Edmonton | Canada 6/Sweden 5 |

1987 Canada Cup
Canada, August 28–September 15, 1987

Tournament All-Star Team

Goal	Grant Fuhr (Canada)
Defence	Ray Bourque (Canada)
	Viacheslav Fetisov (Soviet Union)
Forward	Mario Lemieux (Canada)
	Wayne Gretzky (Canada)
	Vladimir Krutov (Soviet Union)

Final Standings Round Robin

	GP	W	L	T	GF	GA	P
Canada	5	3	0	2	19	13	8
Soviet Union	5	3	1	1	22	13	7
Sweden	5	3	2	0	17	14	6
Czechoslovakia	5	2	2	1	12	15	5
United States	5	2	3	0	13	14	4
Finland	5	0	5	0	9	23	0

Results

August 28	Calgary	Canada 4/Czechoslovakia 4
	Hartford	United States 4/Finland 1
August 29	Calgary	Sweden 5/Soviet Union 3
August 30	Hamilton	Canada 4/Finland 1
August 31	Regina	Soviet Union 4/Czechoslovakia 0
	Hamilton	United States 5/Sweden 2
September 2	Halifax	Soviet Union 7/Finland 4
	Hamilton	Canada 3/United States 2
	Regina	Sweden 4/Czechoslovakia 0
September 4	Hartford	Soviet Union 5/United States 1
	Sydney	Czechoslovakia 5/Finland 2
	Montreal	Canada 5/Sweden 3
September 6	Sydney	Sweden 3/Finland 1
	Sydney	Czechoslovakia 3/United States 1
	Hamilton	Canada 3/Soviet Union 3
September 8	Hamilton	Soviet Union 4/Sweden 2
	Montreal	Canada 5/Czechoslovakia 3

Finals (best two-of-three)

September 11	Montreal	Soviet Union 6/Canada 5 (Semak 5:33 OT)
September 13	Hamilton	Canada 6/Soviet Union 5 (Mario Lemieux 30:07 OT)
September 15	Hamilton	Canada 6/Soviet Union 5 (Lemieux scores winner at 18:34 of 3rd)

1991 Canada Cup

Canada, August 31–September 16, 1991

Tournament All-Star Team

Goal	Bill Ranford (Canada)
Defence	Al MacInnis (Canada)
	Chris Chelios (United States)

Forward   Wayne Gretzky (Canada)
             Jeremy Roenick (United States)
             Mats Sundin (Sweden)

Final Standings Round Robin

	GP	W	L	T	GF	GA	P
Canada	5	3	0	2	21	11	8
United States	5	4	1	0	19	15	8
Finland	5	2	2	1	10	13	5
Sweden	5	2	3	0	13	17	4
Soviet Union	5	1	3	1	14	14	3
Czechoslovakia	5	1	4	0	11	18	2

Results

August 31	Toronto	Canada 2/Finland 2
	Saskatoon	Czechoslovakia 5/Soviet Union 2
	Pittsburgh	United States 6/Sweden 3
September 2	Hamilton	Canada 6/United States 3
	Montreal	Sweden 3/Soviet Union 2
	Saskatoon	Finland 1/Czechoslovakia 0
September 5	Toronto	Canada 4/Sweden 1
	Hamilton	Soviet Union 6/Finland 1
	Detroit	United States 4/Czechoslovakia 2
September 7	Montreal	Canada 6/Czechoslovakia 2
	Toronto	Finland 3/Sweden 1
	Chicago	United States 2/Soviet Union 1
September 9	Quebec City	Canada 3/Soviet Union 3
	Toronto	Sweden 5/Czechoslovakia 2
	Chicago	United States 4/Finland 3

Semifinals

September 11	Hamilton	United States 7/Finland 3
September 12	Toronto	Canada 4/Sweden 0

Finals (best two-of-three)

| September 14 | Montreal | Canada 4/United States 1 |
| September 16 | Hamilton | Canada 4/United States 2 |

World Cup of Hockey 2004
Canada/Europe/United States, August 30–September 14, 2004

FINAL STANDINGS ROUND ROBIN
North American Pool

	GP	W	L	T	GF	GA	P
United States	3	3	0	0	19	8	6
Canada	3	2	1	0	11	10	4
Russia	3	1	2	0	12	14	2
Slovakia	3	0	3	0	9	19	0

European Pool

	GP	W	L	T	GF	GA	P
Sweden	3	3	0	0	14	3	6
Finland	3	2	1	0	17	11	4
Germany	3	1	2	0	11	15	2
Czech Republic	3	0	3	0	4	17	0

Results

August 26	Stockholm	Sweden 6/Germany 1
August 27	Helsinki	Finland 7/Czech Republic 3
August 28	Helsinki	Finland 8/Germany 3
	Prague	Sweden 3/Czech Republic 0
	Vancouver	Canada 5/Russia 3
August 31	Philadelphia	United States 5/Canada 3
	Garmisch	Germany 7/Czech Republic 1
	Montreal	Russia 7/Slovakia 4
September 1	Ottawa	Canada 3/Slovakia 2
	Stockholm	Sweden 5/Finland 2

September 2	New York	United States 5/Russia 2
September 3	New York	United States 9/Slovakia 3

Quarter-finals

September 5	Montreal	Canada 4/Germany 1
September 6	Ottawa	Russia 5/Finland 0

Semifinals

September 7	Philadelphia	Canada 3/Sweden 2 (Fleury 39:47 OT)
September 8	Ottawa	United States 5/Russia 2

Finals (best two-of-three)

September 10	Philadelphia	Canada 4/United States 3 (Yzerman 19:53 OT)
September 12	Montreal	United States 5/Canada 2
September 14	Montreal	United States 5/Canada 2

World Cup of Hockey 2004
August 30–September 14, 2004
Tournament MVP: Vincent Lecavalier (CAN)

All-Tournament Team

Goal	Martin Brodeur (CAN)
Defence	Adam Foote (CAN)
	Kimmo Timonen (FIN)
Forward	Vincent Lecavalier (CAN)
	Fredrik Modin (SWE)
	Saku Koivu (FIN)

PRELIMINARY ROUND STANDINGS
European Pool

	GP	W	L	T	GF	GA	P
Finland	3	2	0	1	11	4	5
Sweden	3	2	0	1	13	9	5
Czech Republic	3	1	2	0	10	10	2
Germany	3	0	3	0	4	15	0

August 30	Helsinki	Finland 4/Czech Republic 0
August 31	Stockholm	Sweden 5/Germany 2
September 1	Stockholm	Sweden 4/Czech Republic 3
September 2	Cologne	Finland 3/Germany 0
September 3	Prague	Czech Republic 7/Germany 2
September 4	Helsinki	Finland 4/Sweden 4 (5:00 OT)

North American Pool

	GP	W	L	T	GF	GA	P
Canada	3	3	0	0	10	3	6
Russia	3	2	1	0	9	6	4
USA	3	1	2	0	5	6	2
Slovakia	3	0	3	0	4	13	0

August 31	Montreal	Canada 2/USA 1
September 1	Montreal	Canada 5/Slovakia 1
September 2	St. Paul	Russia 3/USA 1
September 3	St. Paul	USA 3/Slovakia 1
September 4	Toronto	Canada 3/Russia 1
September 5	Toronto	Russia 5/Slovakia 2

Quarter-finals

September 6	Helsinki	Finland 2/Germany 1
September 7	Stockholm	Czech Republic 6/Sweden 1

September 7   St. Paul   USA 5/Russia 2
September 8   Toronto   Canada 5/Slovakia 1

Semifinals
September 11   St. Paul   Finland 2/USA 1
September 12   Toronto   Canada 4/Czech Republic 3
                              (Vincent Lecavalier 3:45 OT)

Finals
September 14   Toronto   Canada 3/Finland 2

WORLD CHAMPIONSHIPS, 1930–2008

January 31–February 10, 1930
Chamonix, France/Berlin, Germany/Vienna, Austria

GOLD MEDAL	Canada
SILVER MEDAL	Germany
BRONZE MEDAL	Switzerland
Fourth Place	Austria
Fifth Place	Poland
Sixth Place (tie)	Czechoslovakia
	France
	Hungary
	Japan
Tenth Place (tie)	Belgium
	Great Britain
	Italy

March 1–8, 1931
Krynica, Poland

GOLD MEDAL	Canada
SILVER MEDAL	United States
BRONZE MEDAL	Austria
Fourth Place	Poland
Fifth Place	Czechoslovakia
Sixth Place	Sweden
Seventh Place	Hungary
Eighth Place	Great Britain
Ninth Place	France
Tenth Place	Romania

February 18–26, 1933

Prague, Czechoslovakia

GOLD MEDAL	United States
SILVER MEDAL	Canada
BRONZE MEDAL	Czechoslovakia
Fourth Place	Austria
Fifth Place (tie)	Germany
	Switzerland
Seventh Place (tie)	Hungary
	Poland
Ninth Place	Romania
Tenth Place	Latvia
Eleventh Place	Italy
Twelfth Place	Belgium

February 3–11, 1934

Milan, Italy

GOLD MEDAL	Canada
SILVER MEDAL	United States
BRONZE MEDAL	Germany
Fourth Place	Switzerland
Fifth Place	Czechoslovakia
Sixth Place	Hungary
Seventh Place	Austria
Eighth Place	Great Britain
Ninth Place	Italy
Tenth Place	Romania
Eleventh Place	France
Twelfth Place	Belgium

January 19–27, 1935

Davos, Switzerland

GOLD MEDAL	Canada
SILVER MEDAL	Switzerland
BRONZE MEDAL	Great Britain
Fourth Place	Czechoslovakia
Fifth Place	Sweden
Sixth Place	Austria
Seventh Place	France
Eighth Place	Italy
Ninth Place	Germany
Tenth Place	Poland
Eleventh Place (tie)	Hungary
	Romania
Thirteenth Place	Latvia
Fourteenth Place	Belgium
	Netherlands

February 17–27, 1937

London, Great Britain

GOLD MEDAL	Canada
SILVER MEDAL	Great Britain
BRONZE MEDAL	Switzerland
Fourth Place	Germany
Fifth Place	Hungary
Sixth Place	Czechoslovakia
Seventh Place	France
Eighth Place	Poland
Ninth Place (tie)	Norway
	Romania
	Sweden

February 11–20, 1938

Prague, Czechoslovakia

GOLD MEDAL	Canada
SILVER MEDAL	Great Britain
BRONZE MEDAL	Czechoslovakia
Fourth Place	Germany
Fifth Place	Sweden
Sixth Place	Switzerland
Seventh Place (tie)	Hungary
	Poland
	United States
Tenth Place (tie)	Austria
	Latvia
	Lithuania
Thirteenth Place (tie)	Norway
	Romania

February 3–12, 1939

Basel/Zurich, Switzerland

GOLD MEDAL	Canada
SILVER MEDAL	United States
BRONZE MEDAL	Switzerland
Fourth Place	Czechoslovakia
Fifth Place	Germany
Sixth Place	Poland
Seventh Place	Hungary
Eighth Place	Great Britain
Ninth Place	Italy
Tenth Place	Latvia
Eleventh Place (tie)	Belgium
	Netherlands
Thirteenth Place	Finland
	Yugoslavia

February 15–23, 1947

Prague, Czechoslovakia

GOLD MEDAL	Czechoslovakia
SILVER MEDAL	Sweden
BRONZE MEDAL	Austria
Fourth Place	Switzerland
Fifth Place	United States
Sixth Place	Poland
Seventh Place	Romania
Eighth Place	Belgium

February 12–20, 1949

Stockholm, Sweden

GOLD MEDAL	Czechoslovakia
SILVER MEDAL	Canada
BRONZE MEDAL	United States
Fourth Place	Sweden
Fifth Place	Switzerland
Sixth Place	Austria
Seventh Place	Finland
Eighth Place	Norway
Ninth Place	Belgium
Tenth Place	Denmark

March 13–22, 1950

London, Great Britain

GOLD MEDAL	Canada
SILVER MEDAL	United States
BRONZE MEDAL	Switzerland
Fourth Place	Great Britain
Fifth Place	Sweden
Sixth Place	Norway

Seventh Place	Belgium
Eighth Place	Netherlands
Ninth Place	France

March 9–17, 1951

Paris, France

GOLD MEDAL	Canada
SILVER MEDAL	Sweden
BRONZE MEDAL	Switzerland
Fourth Place	Norway
Fifth Place	Great Britain
Sixth Place	United States
Seventh Place	Finland

March 6–15, 1953

Zurich/Basel, Switzerland

GOLD MEDAL	Sweden
SILVER MEDAL	West Germany
BRONZE MEDAL	Switzerland
Fourth Place	Czechoslovakia

February 26–March 7, 1954

Stockholm, Sweden

GOLD MEDAL	Soviet Union
SILVER MEDAL	Canada
BRONZE MEDAL	Sweden
Fourth Place	Czechoslovakia
Fifth Place	West Germany
Sixth Place	Finland
Seventh Place	Switzerland
Eighth Place	Norway

February 25–March 6, 1955

Düsseldorf, West Germany

GOLD MEDAL	Canada
SILVER MEDAL	Soviet Union
BRONZE MEDAL	Czechoslovakia
Fourth Place	United States
Fifth Place	Sweden
Sixth Place	West Germany
Seventh Place	Poland
Eighth Place	Switzerland
Ninth Place	Finland

February 24–March 5, 1957

Moscow, Soviet Union

GOLD MEDAL	Sweden
SILVER MEDAL	Soviet Union
BRONZE MEDAL	Czechoslovakia
Fourth Place	Finland
Fifth Place	West Germany
Sixth Place	Poland
Seventh Place	Austria
Eighth Place	Japan

To protest the suppression of the Hungarian revolution by Soviet forces, Canadian Prime Minister Louis St. Laurent refused to allow a Canadian team to travel to Moscow to play at the World Championships.

February 25–March 9, 1958

Oslo, Norway

GOLD MEDAL	Canada
SILVER MEDAL	Soviet Union
BRONZE MEDAL	Sweden

Fourth Place	Czechoslovakia
Fifth Place	United States
Sixth Place	Finland
Seventh Place	Norway
Eighth Place	Poland

March 9–15, 1959

Prague, Czechoslovakia

GOLD MEDAL	Canada
SILVER MEDAL	Soviet Union
BRONZE MEDAL	Czechoslovakia
Fourth Place	United States
Fifth Place	Sweden
Sixth Place	Finland
Seventh Place	West Germany
Eighth Place	Norway
Ninth Place	East Germany
Tenth Place	Italy
Eleventh Place	Poland
Twelfth Place	Switzerland
Thirteenth Place	Romania
Fourteenth Place	Hungary
Fifteenth Place	Austria

March 1–12, 1961

Geneva/Lausanne, Switzerland

GOLD MEDAL	Canada
SIVER MEDAL	Czechoslovakia
BRONZE MEDAL	Soviet Union
Fourth Place	Sweden
Fifth Place	East Germany

Sixth Place | United States
Seventh Place | Finland
Eighth Place | West Germany

May 8–18, 1962

Colorado Springs, United States

GOLD MEDAL | Sweden
SILVER MEDAL | Canada
BRONZE MEDAL | United States
Fourth Place | Finland
Fifth Place | Norway
Sixth Place | West Germany
Seventh Place | Switzerland
Eighth Place | Great Britain

March 7–17, 1963

Stockholm, Sweden

GOLD MEDAL | Soviet Union
SILVER MEDAL | Sweden
BRONZE MEDAL | Czechoslovakia
Fourth Place | Canada
Fifth Place | Finland
Sixth Place | East Germany
Seventh Place | West Germany
Eighth Place | United States

March 3–14, 1965

Tampere, Finland

GOLD MEDAL | Soviet Union
SILVER MEDAL | Czechoslovakia
BRONZE MEDAL | Sweden

Fourth Place	Canada
Fifth Place	East Germany
Sixth Place	United States
Seventh Place	Finland
Eighth Place	Norway

March 3–14, 1966

Ljubljana, Yugoslavia

GOLD MEDAL	Soviet Union
SILVER MEDAL	Czechoslovakia
BRONZE MEDAL	Canada
Fourth Place	Sweden
Fifth Place	East Germany
Sixth Place	United States
Seventh Place	Finland
Eighth Place	Poland

March 18–29, 1967

Vienna, Austria

GOLD MEDAL	Soviet Union
SILVER MEDAL	Sweden
BRONZE MEDAL	Canada
Fourth Place	Czechoslovakia
Fifth Place	United States
Sixth Place	Finland
Seventh Place	West Germany
Eighth Place	East Germany

March 15–30, 1969

Stockholm, Sweden

GOLD MEDAL	Soviet Union

SILVER MEDAL   Sweden
BRONZE MEDAL   Czechoslovakia
Fourth Place   Canada
Fifth Place   Finland
Sixth Place   United States

To protest the ineligibility of professionals from the World Championships according to IIHF rules, Canada did not compete in IIHF sanctioned tournaments from 1970 through 1976.

March 14–30, 1970

Stockholm, Sweden

GOLD MEDAL   Soviet Union
SILVER MEDAL   Sweden
BRONZE MEDAL   Czechoslovakia
Fourth Place   Finland
Fifth Place   East Germany
Sixth Place   Poland

March 19–April 3, 1971

Bern/Geneva, Switzerland

GOLD MEDAL   Soviet Union
SILVER MEDAL   Czechoslovakia
BRONZE MEDAL   Sweden
Fourth Place   Finland
Fifth Place   East Germany
Sixth Place   United States

April 7–22, 1972

Prague, Czechoslovakia

GOLD MEDAL   Czechoslovakia
SILVER MEDAL   Soviet Union

BRONZE MEDAL	Sweden
Fourth Place	Finland
Fifth Place	East Germany
Sixth Place	Switzerland

March 31–April 15, 1973

Moscow, Soviet Union

GOLD MEDAL	Soviet Union
SILVER MEDAL	Sweden
BRONZE MEDAL	Czechoslovakia
Fourth Place	Finland
Fifth Place	Poland
Sixth Place	East Germany

April 5–20, 1974

Helsinki, Finland

GOLD MEDAL	Soviet Union
SILVER MEDAL	Czechoslovakia
BRONZE MEDAL	Sweden
Fourth Place	Finland
Fifth Place	Poland
Sixth Place	East Germany

April 3–19, 1975

Munich/Düsseldorf, West Germany

GOLD MEDAL	Soviet Union
SILVER MEDAL	Czechoslovakia
BRONZE MEDAL	Sweden
Fourth Place	Finland
Fifth Place	Poland
Sixth Place	United States

April 8–25, 1976

Katowice, Poland

GOLD MEDAL	Czechoslovakia
SILVER MEDAL	Soviet Union
BRONZE MEDAL	Sweden
Fourth Place	United States
Fifth Place	Finland
Sixth Place	West Germany
Seventh Place	Poland
Eighth Place	East Germany

April 21–May 8, 1977

Vienna, Austria

GOLD MEDAL	Czechoslovakia
SILVER MEDAL	Sweden
BRONZE MEDAL	Soviet Union
Fourth Place	Canada
Fifth Place	Finland
Sixth Place	United States
Seventh Place	West Germany
Eighth Place	Romania

April 25–May 8, 1978

Prague, Czechoslovakia

GOLD MEDAL	Soviet Union
SILVER MEDAL	Czechoslovakia
BRONZE MEDAL	Canada
Fourth Place	Sweden
Fifth Place	West Germany
Sixth Place	USA
Seventh Place	Finland
Eighth Place	East Germany

April 14–27, 1979

Moscow, Soviet Union

GOLD MEDAL	Soviet Union
SILVER MEDAL	Czechoslovakia
BRONZE MEDAL	Sweden
Fourth Place	Canada
Fifth Place	Finland
Sixth Place	West Germany
Seventh Place	United States
Eighth Place	Poland

April 12–26, 1981

Gothenburg/Stockholm, Sweden

GOLD MEDAL	Soviet Union
SILVER MEDAL	Sweden
BRONZE MEDAL	Czechoslovakia
Fourth Place	Canada
Fifth Place	United States
Sixth Place	Finland
Seventh Place	West Germany
Eighth Place	Netherlands

April 15–29, 1982

Helsinki/Tampere, Finland

GOLD MEDAL	Soviet Union
SILVER MEDAL	Czechoslovakia
BRONZE MEDAL	Canada
Fourth Place	Sweden
Fifth Place	Finland
Sixth Place	West Germany
Seventh Place	Italy
Eighth Place	United States

April 16–May 2, 1983

Dortmund/Düsseldorf/Munich, West Germany

GOLD MEDAL	Soviet Union
SILVER MEDAL	Czechoslovakia
BRONZE MEDAL	Canada
Fourth Place	Sweden
Fifth Place	East Germany
Sixth Place	West Germany
Seventh Place	Finland
Eighth Place	Italy

April 17–May 3, 1985

Prague, Czechoslovakia

GOLD MEDAL	Czechoslovakia
SILVER MEDAL	Canada
BRONZE MEDAL	Soviet Union
Fourth Place	United States
Fifth Place	Finland
Sixth Place	Sweden
Seventh Place	East Germany
Eighth Place	West Germany

April 12–28, 1986

Moscow, Soviet Union

GOLD MEDAL	Soviet Union
SILVER MEDAL	Sweden
BRONZE MEDAL	Canada
Fourth Place	Finland
Fifth Place	Czechoslovakia
Sixth Place	United States
Seventh Place	East Germany
Eighth Place	Poland

April 17–May 3, 1987

Vienna, Austria

GOLD MEDAL	Sweden
SILVER MEDAL	Soviet Union
BRONZE MEDAL	Czechoslovakia
Fourth Place	Canada
Fifth Place	Finland
Sixth Place	West Germany
Seventh Place	United States
Eighth Place	Switzerland

April 15–May 1, 1989

Stockholm, Sweden

GOLD MEDAL	Soviet Union
SILVER MEDAL	Canada
BRONZE MEDAL	Czechoslovakia
Fourth Place	Sweden
Fifth Place	Finland
Sixth Place	United States
Seventh Place	West Germany
Eighth Place	Poland

April 16–May 2, 1990

Bern, Switzerland

GOLD MEDAL	Soviet Union
SILVER MEDAL	Sweden
BRONZE MEDAL	Czechoslovakia
Fourth Place	Canada
Fifth Place	United States
Sixth Place	Finland
Seventh Place	West Germany
Eighth Place	Norway

April 14–May 5, 1991

Helsinki, Finland

GOLD MEDAL	Sweden
SILVER MEDAL	Canada
BRONZE MEDAL	Soviet Union
Fourth Place	United States
Fifth Place	Finland
Sixth Place	Czechoslovakia
Seventh Place	Switzerland
Eight Place	Germany

April 28–May 10, 1992

Prague/Bratislava, Czechoslovakia

GOLD MEDAL	Sweden
SILVER MEDAL	Finland
BRONZE MEDAL	Czechoslovakia
Fourth Place	Switzerland
Fifth Place	Russia
Sixth Place	Germany
Seventh Place	United States
Eighth Place	Canada
Ninth Place	Italy
Tenth Place	Norway
Eleventh Place	France
Twelfth Place	Poland

April 18–May 2, 1993

Munich, Germany

GOLD MEDAL	Russia
SILVER MEDAL	Sweden
BRONZE MEDAL	Czech Republic
Fourth Place	Canada

Fifth Place	Germany
Sixth Place	United States
Seventh Place	Finland
Eighth Place	Italy
Ninth Place	Austria
Tenth Place	France
Eleventh Place	Norway
Twelfth Place	Switzerland

April 25–May 8, 1994

Bolzano, Italy

GOLD MEDAL	Canada
SILVER MEDAL	Finland
BRONZE MEDAL	Sweden
Fourth Place	United States
Fifth Place	Russia
Sixth Place	Italy
Seventh Place	Czech Republic
Eighth Place	Austria
Ninth Place	Germany
Tenth Place	France
Eleventh Place	Norway
Twelfth Place	Great Britain

April 23–May 7, 1995

Stockholm/Gavle, Sweden

GOLD MEDAL	Finland
SILVER MEDAL	Sweden
BRONZE MEDAL	Canada
Fourth Place	Czech Republic
Fifth Place	Russia
Sixth Place	United States
Seventh Place	Italy

Eighth Place   France
Ninth Place   Germany
Tenth Place   Norway
Eleventh Place   Austria
Twelfth Place   Switzerland

April 21–May 5, 1996

Vienna, Austria

GOLD MEDAL   Czech Republic
SILVER MEDAL   Canada
BRONZE MEDAL   United States
Fourth Place   Russia
Fifth Place   Finland
Sixth Place   Sweden
Seventh Place   Italy
Eighth Place   Germany
Ninth Place   Norway
Tenth Place   Slovakia
Eleventh Place   France
Twelfth Place   Austria

April 26–May 14, 1997

Helsinki/Tampere/Turku, Finland

GOLD MEDAL   Canada
SILVER MEDAL   Sweden
BRONZE MEDAL   Czech Republic
Fourth Place   Russia
Fifth Place   Finland
Sixth Place   United States
Seventh Place   Latvia
Eighth Place   Italy
Ninth Place   Slovakia
Tenth Place   France

Eleventh Place	Germany
Twelfth Place	Norway

May 1–17, 1998

Zurich, Switzerland

GOLD MEDAL	Sweden
SILVER MEDAL	Finland
BRONZE MEDAL	Czech Republic
Fourth Place	Switzerland
Fifth Place	Russia
Sixth Place	Canada
Seventh Place	Slovakia
Eighth Place	Belarus
Ninth Place	Latvia
Tenth Place	Italy
Eleventh Place	Germany
Twelfth Place	United States

May 1–16, 1999

Oslo/Hamar/Lillehammer, Norway

GOLD MEDAL	Czech Republic
SILVER MEDAL	Finland
BRONZE MEDAL	Sweden
Fourth Place	Canada
Fifth Place	Russia
Sixth Place	United States
Seventh Place	Slovakia
Eighth Place	Switzerland
Ninth Place	Belarus
Tenth Place	Austria
Eleventh Place	Latvia
Twelfth Place	Norway
Thirteenth Place	Italy

Fourteenth Place   Ukraine
Fifteenth Place   France
Sixteenth Place   Japan

April 29–May 14, 2000

St. Petersburg, Russia

GOLD MEDAL   Czech Republic
SILVER MEDAL   Slovakia
BRONZE MEDAL   Finland
Fourth Place   Canada
Fifth Place   United States
Sixth Place   Switzerland
Seventh Place   Sweden
Eighth Place   Latvia
Ninth Place   Belarus
Tenth Place   Norway
Eleventh Place   Russia
Twelfth Place   Italy
Thirteenth Place   Austria
Fourteenth Place   Ukraine
Fifteenth Place   France
Sixteenth Place   Japan

April 28–May 13, 2001

Hanover/Cologne/Nuremberg, Germany

GOLD MEDAL   Czech Republic
SILVER MEDAL   Finland
BRONZE MEDAL   Sweden
Fourth Place   United States
Fifth Place   Canada
Sixth Place   Russia
Seventh Place   Slovakia

Eighth Place	Germany
Ninth Place	Switzerland
Tenth Place	Ukraine
Eleventh Place	Austria
Twelfth Place	Italy
Thirteenth Place	Latvia
Fourteenth Place	Belarus
Fifteenth Place	Norway
Sixteenth Place	Japan

April 26–May 11, 2002

Gothenburg/Karlstad/Jonkoping, Sweden

GOLD MEDAL	Slovakia
SILVER MEDAL	Russia
BRONZE MEDAL	Sweden
Fourth Place	Finland
Fifth Place	Czech Republic
Sixth Place	Canada
Seventh Place	United States
Eighth Place	Germany
Ninth Place	Ukraine
Tenth Place	Switzerland
Eleventh Place	Latvia
Twelfth Place	Austria
Thirteenth Place	Slovenia
Fourteenth Place	Poland
Fifteenth Place	Italy
Sixteenth Place	Japan

April 27–May 11, 2003

Helsinki/Tampere/Turku, Finland

GOLD MEDAL	Canada
SILVER MEDAL	Sweden

BRONZE MEDAL	Slovakia
Fourth Place	Czech Republic
Fifth Place	Finland
Sixth Place	Germany
Seventh Place	Russia
Eighth Place	Switzerland
Ninth Place	Latvia
Tenth Place	Austria
Eleventh Place	Denmark
Twelfth Place	Ukraine
Thirteenth Place	United States
Fourteenth Place	Belarus
Fifteenth Place	Slovenia
Sixteenth Place	Japan

April 24–May 9, 2004

Prague/Ostrava, Czech Republic

GOLD MEDAL	Canada
SILVER MEDAL	Sweden
BRONZE MEDAL	United States
Fourth Place	Slovakia
Fifth Place	Czech Republic
Sixth Place	Finland
Seventh Place	Latvia
Eighth Place	Switzerland
Ninth Place	Germany
Tenth Place	Russia
Eleventh Place	Austria
Twelfth Place	Denmark
Thirteenth Place	Kazakhstan
Fourteenth Place	Ukraine
Fifteenth Place	Japan
Sixteenth Place	France

April 30–May 15, 2005

Vienna/Innsbruck, Austria

GOLD MEDAL	Czech Republic
SILVER MEDAL	Canada
BRONZE MEDAL	Russia
Fourth Place	Sweden
Fifth Place	Slovakia
Sixth Place	United States
Seventh Place	Finland
Eighth Place	Switzerland
Ninth Place	Latvia
Tenth Place	Belarus
Eleventh Place	Ukraine
Twelfth Place	Kazakhstan
Thirteenth Place	Slovenia
Fourteenth Place	Denmark
Fifteenth Place	Germany
Sixteenth Place	Austria

May 5–May 21, 2006

Riga, Latvia

GOLD MEDAL	Sweden
SILVER MEDAL	Czech Republic
BRONZE MEDAL	Finland
Fourth Place	Canada
Fifth Place	Russia
Sixth Place	Belarus
Seventh Place	United States
Eighth Place	Slovakia
Ninth Place	Switzerland
Tenth Place	Latvia
Eleventh Place	Norway
Twelfth Place	Ukraine

Thirteenth Place   Denmark
Fourteenth Place   Italy
Fifteenth Place   Kazakhstan
Sixteenth Place   Slovenia

April 24–May 10, 2007

Moscow/Mytischi, Russia

GOLD MEDAL   Canada
SILVER MEDAL   Finland
BRONZE MEDAL   Russia
Fourth Place   Sweden
Fifth Place   United States
Sixth Place   Slovakia
Seventh Place   Czech Republic
Eighth Place   Switzerland
Ninth Place   Germany
Tenth Place   Denmark
Eleventh Place Belarus
Twelfth Place   Italy
Thirteenth Place Latvia
Fourteenth Place Norway
Fifteenth Place Austria
Sixteenth Place Ukraine

May 2–May18, 2008

Halifax/Quebec City, Canada

GOLD MEDAL   Russia
SILVER MEDAL   Canada
BRONZE MEDAL   Finland
Fourth Place   Sweden
Fifth Place   Czech Republic

Sixth Place	United States
Seventh Place	Switzerland
Eighth Place	Norway
Ninth Place	Belarus
Tenth Place	Germany
Eleventh Place	Latvia
Twelfth Place	Denmark
Thirteenth Place	Slovakia
Fourteenth Place	France
Fifteenth Place	Slovenia
Sixteenth Place	Italy

WORLD JUNIOR CHAMPIONSHIPS, 1977–2008

ALL MEDAL WINNERS BY CUMULATIVE STANDINGS (1977–2008)

Country	Gold	Silver	Bronze	Total
Canada	14	7	3	24
Soviet Union	9	3	2	14
Russia	3	6	4	13
Finland	2	4	6	12
Sweden	1	8	3	12
Czechoslovakia	0	4	6	10
United States	1	1	3	5
Czech Republic	2	0	2	4
Slovakia	0	0	1	1
Switzerland	0	0	1	1

1977 WORLD JUNIOR CHAMPIONSHIPS

CZECHOSLOVAKIA, DECEMBER 22, 1976–JANUARY 2, 1977

FINAL PLACINGS

GOLD MEDAL	Soviet Union
SILVER MEDAL	Canada
BRONZE MEDAL	Czechoslovakia
Fourth Place	Finland
Fifth Place	Sweden
Sixth Place	West Germany
Seventh Place	United States
Eighth Place	Poland*

* relegated to 'B' pool for 1978

ALL-STAR TEAM

Goal	Alexander Tyznych (Soviet Union)
Defence	Risto Siltanen (Finland)
	Lubos Oslizlo (Czechoslovakia)
Forward	Dale McCourt (Canada)
	Bengt-Ake Gustafsson (Sweden)
	Igor Romasin (Soviet Union)

DIRECTORATE AWARDS

BEST GOALIE	Jan Hrabak (Czechoslovakia)
BEST DEFENCEMAN	Viacheslav Fetisov (Soviet Union)
BEST FORWARD	Dale McCourt (Canada)

1978 WORLD JUNIOR CHAMPIONSHIPS

CANADA, DECEMBER 22, 1977–JANUARY 3, 1978

FINAL PLACINGS

GOLD MEDAL	Soviet Union
SILVER MEDAL	Sweden
BRONZE MEDAL	Canada
Fourth Place	Czechoslovakia
Fifth Place	United States
Sixth Place	Finland
Seventh Place	West Germany
Eighth Place	Switzerland*

* promoted from 'B' pool in 1977; relegated to 'B' pool for 1979

ALL-STAR TEAM

Goal	Alexander Tyznych (Soviet Union)
Defence	Risto Siltanen (Finland)
	Viacheslav Fetisov (Soviet Union)
Forward	Wayne Gretzky (Canada)
	Mats Naslund (Sweden)
	Anton Stastny (Czechoslovakia)

DIRECTORATE AWARDS

BEST GOALIE	Alexander Tyzhnych (Soviet Union)
BEST DEFENCEMAN	Viacheslav Fetisov (Soviet Union)
BEST FORWARD	Wayne Gretzky (Canada)

1979 WORLD JUNIOR CHAMPIONSHIPS

SWEDEN, DECEMBER 27, 1978–JANUARY 3, 1979

FINAL PLACINGS

GOLD MEDAL	Soviet Union
SILVER MEDAL	Sweden
BRONZE MEDAL	Czechoslovakia
Fourth Place	Finland
Fifth Place	Canada
Sixth Place	United States
Seventh Place	West Germany
Eighth Place	Norway*

* promoted from 'B' pool in 1978; relegated to 'B' pool for 1980

ALL-STAR TEAM

Goal	Pelle Lindbergh (Sweden)
Defence	Ivan Cerny (Czechoslovakia)
	Alexei Kasatonov (Soviet Union)
Forward	Anatoli Tarasov (Soviet Union)
	Thomas Steen (Sweden)
	Vladimir Krutov (Soviet Union)

DIRECTORATE AWARDS

BEST GOALIE	Pelle Lindbergh (Sweden)
BEST DEFENCEMAN	Alexei Kasatonov (Soviet Union)
BEST FORWARD	Vladimir Krutov (Soviet Union)

1980 WORLD JUNIOR CHAMPIONSHIPS

FINLAND, DECEMBER 27, 1979–JANUARY 2, 1980

FINAL PLACINGS

GOLD MEDAL	Soviet Union
SILVER MEDAL	Finland
BRONZE MEDAL	Sweden
Fourth Place	Czechoslovakia
Fifth Place	Canada
Sixth Place	West Germany
Seventh Place	United States
Eighth Place	Switzerland*

* promoted from 'B' pool in 1979; relegated to 'B' pool for 1981

ALL-STAR TEAM

Goal	Jari Paavola (Finland)
Defence	Reijo Ruotsalainen (Finland)
	Tomas Jonsson (Sweden)
Forward	Hakan Loob (Sweden)
	Igor Larionov (Soviet Union)
	Vladimir Krutov (Soviet Union)

DIRECTORATE AWARDS

BEST GOALIE	Jari Paavola (Finland)
BEST DEFENCEMAN	Reijo Ruotsalainen (Finland)
BEST FORWARD	Vladimir Krutov (Soviet Union)

1981 WORLD JUNIOR CHAMPIONSHIPS

WEST GERMANY, DECEMBER 27, 1980–JANUARY 2, 1981

FINAL PLACINGS

GOLD MEDAL	Sweden
SILVER MEDAL	Finland
BRONZE MEDAL	Soviet Union
Fourth Place	Czechoslovakia
Fifth Place	West Germany
Sixth Place	United States
Seventh Place	Canada
Eighth Place	Austria*

* promoted from 'B' pool in 1980; relegated to 'B' pool for 1982

ALL-STAR TEAM

Goal	Lars Eriksson (Sweden)
Defence	Miloslav Horava (Czechoslovakia)
	Hakan Nordin (Sweden)
Forward	Ari Lahteenmaki (Finland)
	Patrik Sundstrom (Sweden)
	Jan Erixon (Sweden)

DIRECTORATE AWARDS

BEST GOALIE	Lars Eriksson (Sweden)
BEST DEFENCEMAN	Miloslav Horava (Czechoslovakia)
BEST FORWARD	Patrik Sundstrom (Sweden)

1982 WORLD JUNIOR CHAMPIONSHIPS

UNITED STATES, DECEMBER 22, 1981–JANUARY 2, 1982
(some games played in Canada)

FINAL PLACINGS

GOLD MEDAL	Canada
SILVER MEDAL	Czechoslovakia
BRONZE MEDAL	Finland
Fourth Place	Soviet Union
Fifth Place	Sweden
Sixth Place	United States
Seventh Place	West Germany
Eighth Place	Switzerland*

* promoted from 'B' pool in 1981; relegated to 'B' pool for 1983

ALL-STAR TEAM

Goal	Mike Moffat (Canada)
Defence	Gord Kluzak (Canada)
	Ilya Biakin (Soviet Union)
Forward	Mike Moller (Canada)
	Petri Skriko (Finland)
	Vladimir Ruzicka (Czechoslovakia)

DIRECTORATE AWARDS

BEST GOALIE	Mike Moffat (Canada)
BEST DEFENCEMAN	Gord Kluzak (Canada)
BEST FORWARD	Petri Skriko (Finland)

1983 WORLD JUNIOR CHAMPIONSHIPS
SOVIET UNION, DECEMBER 26, 1982–JANUARY 4, 1983

FINAL PLACINGS
GOLD MEDAL	Soviet Union
SILVER MEDAL	Czechoslovakia
BRONZE MEDAL	Canada
Fourth Place	Sweden
Fifth Place	United States
Sixth Place	Finland
Seventh Place	West Germany
Eighth Place	Norway*

* promoted from 'B' pool in 1982; relegated to 'B' pool for 1984

ALL-STAR TEAM
Goal	Matti Rautiainen (Finland)
Defence	Ilya Biakin (Soviet Union)
	Simo Saarinen (Finland)
Forward	Tomas Sandstrom (Sweden)
	Vladimir Ruzicka (Czechoslovakia)
	German Volgin (Soviet Union)

DIRECTORATE AWARDS
BEST GOALIE	Dominik Hasek (Czechoslovakia)
BEST DEFENCEMAN	Ilya Biakin (Soviet Union)
BEST FORWARD	Tomas Sandstrom (Sweden)

1984 WORLD JUNIOR CHAMPIONSHIPS

SWEDEN, DECEMBER 25, 1983–JANUARY 3, 1984

FINAL PLACINGS

GOLD MEDAL	Soviet Union
SILVER MEDAL	Finland
BRONZE MEDAL	Czechoslovakia
Fourth Place	Canada
Fifth Place	Sweden
Sixth Place	United States
Seventh Place	West Germany
Eighth Place	Switzerland*

* promoted from 'B' pool in 1983; relegated to 'B' pool for 1985

ALL-STAR TEAM

Goal	Evgeny Belosheikin (Soviet Union)
Defence	Alexei Gusarov (Soviet Union)
	Frantisek Musil (Czechoslovakia)
Forward	Petr Rosol (Czechoslovakia)
	Raimo Helminen (Finland)
	Nikolai Borschevsky (Soviet Union)

DIRECTORATE AWARDS

BEST GOALIE	Alan Perry (United States)
BEST DEFENCEMAN	Alexei Gusarov (Soviet Union)
BEST FORWARD	Raimo Helminen (Finland)

1985 WORLD JUNIOR CHAMPIONSHIPS

FINLAND, DECEMBER 23, 1984–JANUARY 1, 1985

FINAL PLACINGS

GOLD MEDAL	Canada
SILVER MEDAL	Czechoslovakia
BRONZE MEDAL	Soviet Union

Fourth Place	Finland
Fifth Place	Sweden
Sixth Place	United States
Seventh Place	West Germany
Eighth Place	Poland*

* promoted from 'B' pool in 1984; relegated to 'B' pool for 1986

ALL-STAR TEAM

Goal	Timo Lehkonen (Finland)
Defence	Bobby Dollas (Canada)
	Mikhail Tatarinov (Soviet Union)
Forward	Mikko Makela (Finland)
	Michal Pivonka (Czechoslovakia)
	Esa Tikkanen (Finland)

DIRECTORATE AWARDS

BEST GOALIE	Craig Billington (Canada)
BEST DEFENCEMAN	Vesa Salo (Finland)
BEST FORWARD	Michal Pivonka (Czechoslovakia)

1986 WORLD JUNIOR CHAMPIONSHIPS

CANADA, DECEMBER 26, 1985–JANUARY 4, 1986

FINAL PLACINGS

GOLD MEDAL	Soviet Union
SILVER MEDAL	Canada
BRONZE MEDAL	United States
Fourth Place	Czechoslovakia
Fifth Place	Sweden

Sixth Place	Finland
Seventh Place	Switzerland*
Eighth Place	West Germany**

* promoted from 'B' pool in 1985
** relegated to 'B' pool for 1987

ALL-STAR TEAM

Goal	Evgeny Belosheikin (Soviet Union)
Defence	Sylvain Cote (Canada)
	Mikhail Tatarinov (Soviet Union)
Forward	Shayne Corson (Canada)
	Igor Viazmikin (Soviet Union)
	Michal Pivonka (Czechoslovakia)

DIRECTORATE AWARDS

BEST GOALIE	Evgeny Belosheikin (Soviet Union)
BEST DEFENCEMAN	Mikhail Tatarinov (Soviet Union)
BEST FORWARD	Jim Sandlak (Canada)

1987 WORLD JUNIOR CHAMPIONSHIPS

CZECHOSLOVAKIA, DECEMBER 26, 1986–JANUARY 4, 1987

FINAL PLACINGS

GOLD MEDAL	Finland
SILVER MEDAL	Czechoslovakia
BRONZE MEDAL	Sweden
Fourth Place	United States
Fifth Place	Poland*
Sixth Place	Switzerland**

Canada and the Soviet Union were disqualified

* promoted from 'B' pool in 1986
** relegated to 'B' pool for 1988

ALL-STAR TEAM

Goal	Sam Lindstahl (Sweden)
Defence	Jiri Latal (Czechoslovakia)
	Brian Leetch (United States)
Forward	Ulf Dahlen (Sweden)
	Juraj Jurik (Czechoslovakia)
	Scott Young (United States)

DIRECTORATE AWARDS

BEST GOALIE	Markus Ketterer (Finland)
BEST DEFENCEMAN	Calle Johansson (Sweden)
BEST FORWARD	Robert Kron (Czechoslovakia)

1988 WORLD JUNIOR CHAMPIONSHIPS

RUSSIA, DECEMBER 26, 1987–JANUARY 4, 1988

FINAL PLACINGS

GOLD MEDAL	Canada
SILVER MEDAL	Soviet Union
BRONZE MEDAL	Finland
Fourth Place	Czechsloavkia
Fifth Place	Sweden
Sixth Place	United States
Seventh Place	West Germany*
Eighth Place	Poland**

* promoted from 'B' pool in 1987
** relegated to 'B' pool for 1989

ALL-STAR TEAM

Goal	Jimmy Waite (Canada)
Defence	Greg Hawgood (Canada)
	Teppo Numminen (Finland)

Forward   Theoren Fleury (Canada)
           Alexander Mogilny (Soviet Union)
           Petr Hrbek (Czechoslovakia)

DIRECTORATE AWARDS
BEST GOALIE   Jimmy Waite (Canada)
BEST DEFENCEMAN   Teppo Numminen (Finland)
BEST FORWARD   Alexander Mogilny (Soviet Union)

1989 WORLD JUNIOR CHAMPIONSHIPS
UNITED STATES, DECEMBER 26, 1988–JANUARY 4, 1989

FINAL PLACINGS
GOLD MEDAL   Soviet Union
SILVER MEDAL   Sweden
BRONZE MEDAL   Czechoslovakia
Fourth Place   Canada
Fifth Place   United States
Sixth Place   Finland
Seventh Place   Norway*
Eighth Place   West Germany**

* promoted from 'B' pool in 1988
** relegated to 'B' pool for 1990

ALL-STAR TEAM
Goal   Alexei Ivashkin (Soviet Union)
Defence   Rickard Persson (Sweden)
           Milan Tichy (Czechoslovakia)
Forward   Niklas Eriksson (Sweden)
           Pavel Bure (Soviet Union)
           Jeremy Roenick (United States)

DIRECTORATE AWARDS
BEST GOALIE   Alexei Ivashkin (Soviet Union)
BEST DEFENCEMAN   Rickard Persson (Sweden)
BEST FORWARD   Pavel Bure (Soviet Union)

1990 WORLD JUNIOR CHAMPIONSHIPS
FINLAND, DECEMBER 26, 1989–JANUARY 4, 1990

FINAL PLACINGS
GOLD MEDAL   Canada
SILVER MEDAL   Soviet Union
BRONZE MEDAL   Czechoslovakia
Fourth Place   Finland
Fifth Place   Sweden
Sixth Place   Norway
Seventh Place   United States
Eighth Place   Poland*

* promoted from 'B' pool in 1989; relegated to 'B' pool for 1991

ALL-STAR TEAM
Goal   Stephane Fiset (Canada)
Defence   Alexander Godynyuk (Soviet Union)
           Jiri Slegr (Czechoslovakia)
Forward   Dave Chyzowski (Canada)
           Jaromir Jagr (Czechoslovakia)
           Robert Reichel (Czechoslovakia)

DIRECTORATE AWARDS
BEST GOALIE   Stephane Fiset (Canada)
BEST DEFENCEMAN   Alexander Godynyuk (Soviet Union)
BEST FORWARD   Robert Reichel (Czechoslovakia)

1991 WORLD JUNIOR CHAMPIONSHIPS

CANADA, DECEMBER 26, 1990–JANUARY 4, 1991

FINAL PLACINGS

GOLD MEDAL	Canada
SILVER MEDAL	Soviet Union
BRONZE MEDAL	Czechoslovakia
Fourth Place	United States
Fifth Place	Finland
Sixth Place	Sweden
Seventh Place	Switzerland*
Eighth Place	Norway**

* promoted from 'B' pool in 1990
** relegated to 'B' pool for 1992

ALL-STAR TEAM

Goal	Pauli Jaks (Switzerland)
Defence	Dmitri Yushkevich (Soviet Union)
	Scott Lachance (United States)
Forward	Mike Craig (Canada)
	Eric Lindros (Canada)
	Martin Rucinsky (Czechoslovakia)

DIRECTORATE AWARDS

BEST GOALIE	Pauli Jaks (Switzerland)
BEST DEFENCEMAN	Jiri Slegr (Czechoslovakia)
BEST FORWARD	Eric Lindros (Canada)

1992 WORLD JUNIOR CHAMPIONSHIPS

GERMANY, DECEMBER 26, 1991–JANUARY 4, 1992

FINAL PLACINGS

GOLD MEDAL	Commonwealth of Independent States
SILVER MEDAL	Sweden
BRONZE MEDAL	United States
Fourth Place	Finland
Fifth Place	Czechoslovakia
Sixth Place	Canada
Seventh Place	Germany*
Eighth Place	Switzerland**

* promoted from 'B' pool in 1991
** relegated to 'B' pool for 1993

ALL-STAR TEAM

Goal	Mike Dunham (United States)
Defence	Scott Niedermayer (Canada)
	Janne Gronvall (Finland)
Forward	Alexei Kovalev (CIS)
	Michael Nylander (Sweden)
	Peter Ferraro (United States)

DIRECTORATE AWARDS

BEST GOALIE	Mike Dunham (United States)
BEST DEFENCEMAN	Darius Kasparaitis (CIS)
BEST FORWARD	Michael Nylander (Sweden)

1993 WORLD JUNIOR CHAMPIONSHIPS

SWEDEN, DECEMBER 26, 1992–JANUARY 4, 1993

FINAL PLACINGS

GOLD MEDAL	Canada
SILVER MEDAL	Sweden
BRONZE MEDAL	Czech Republic
Fourth Place	United States
Fifth Place	Finland
Sixth Place	Russia
Seventh Place	Germany
Eighth place	Japan*

* promoted from 'B' pool in 1992; relegated to 'B' pool for 1994

ALL-STAR TEAM

Goal	Manny Legace (Canada)
Defence	Brent Tully (Canada)
	Kenny Jonsson (Sweden)
Forward	Paul Kariya (Canada)
	Markus Naslund (Sweden)
	Peter Forsberg (Sweden)

DIRECTORATE AWARDS

BEST GOALIE	Manny Legace (Canada)
BEST DEFENCEMAN	Janne Gronvall (Finland)
BEST FORWARD	Peter Forsberg (Sweden)

1994 WORLD JUNIOR CHAMPIONSHIPS
CZECH REPUBLIC, DECEMBER 26, 1993–JANUARY 4, 1994

FINAL PLACINGS
GOLD MEDAL	Canada
SILVER MEDAL	Sweden
BRONZE MEDAL	Russia
Fourth Place	Finland
Fifth Place	Czech Republic
Sixth Place	United States
Seventh Place	Germany
Eighth Place	Switzerland*

* promoted from 'B' pool in 1993; relegated to 'B' pool for 1995

ALL-STAR TEAM
Goal	Evgeny Riabchikov (Russia)
Defence	Kenny Jonsson (Sweden)
	Kimmo Timonen (Finland)
Forward	Niklas Sundstrom (Sweden)
	Valeri Bure (Russia)
	David Vyborny (Czech Republic)

DIRECTORATE AWARDS
BEST GOALIE	Jamie Storr (Canada)
BEST DEFENCEMAN	Kenny Jonsson (Sweden)
BEST FORWARD	Niklas Sundstrom (Sweden)

1995 WORLD JUNIOR CHAMPIONSHIPS

CANADA, DECEMBER 26, 1994–JANUARY 4, 1995

FINAL PLACINGS

GOLD MEDAL	Canada
SILVER MEDAL	Russia
BRONZE MEDAL	Sweden
Fourth Place	Finland
Fifth Place	United States
Sixth Place	Czech Republic
Seventh Place	Germany
Eighth Place	Ukraine*

* promoted from 'B' pool in 1994

Note: no team was relegated to 'B' pool from this year's tournament because in 1996 the 'A' pool expanded to ten teams and a new round-robin format

ALL-STAR TEAM

Goal	Igor Karpenko (Ukraine)
Defence	Bryan McCabe (Canada)
	Anders Eriksson (Sweden)
Forward	Jason Allison (Canada)
	Eric Daze (Canada)
	Marty Murray (Canada)

DIRECTORATE AWARDS

BEST GOALIE	Evgeny Tarasov (Russia)
BEST DEFENCEMAN	Bryan McCabe (Canada)
BEST FORWARD	Marty Murray (Canada)

1996 WORLD JUNIOR CHAMPIONSHIPS

UNITED STATES, DECEMBER 26, 1995–JANUARY 4, 1996

FINAL PLACINGS

GOLD MEDAL	Canada
SILVER MEDAL	Sweden
BRONZE MEDAL	Russia
Fourth Place	Czech Republic
Fifth Place	United States
Sixth Place	Finland
Seventh Place	Slovakia*
Eighth Place	Germany
Ninth Place	Switzerland*
Tenth Place	Ukraine**

* promoted from 'B' pool in 1995
** relegated to 'B' pool for 1997

ALL-STAR TEAM

Goal	Jose Theodore (Canada)
Defence	Nolan Baumgartner (Canada)
	Mattias Ohlund (Sweden)
Forward	Jarome Iginla (Canada)
	Johan Davidsson (Sweden)
	Alexei Morozov (Russia)

DIRECTORATE AWARDS

BEST GOALIE	Jose Theodore (Canada)
BEST DEFENCEMAN	Mattias Ohlund (Sweden)
BEST FORWARD	Jarome Iginla (Canada)

1997 WORLD JUNIOR CHAMPIONSHIPS

SWITZERLAND, DECEMBER 26, 1996–JANUARY 4, 1997

FINAL PLACINGS

GOLD MEDAL	Canada
SILVER MEDAL	United States
BRONZE MEDAL	Russia
Fourth Place	Czech Republic
Fifth Place	Finland
Sixth Place	Slovakia
Seventh Place	Switzerland
Eighth Place	Sweden
Ninth Place	Germany
Tenth Place	Poland*

* promoted from 'B' pool in 1996; relegated to 'B' pool for 1998

ALL-STAR TEAM

Goal	Brian Boucher (United States)
Defence	Chris Phillips (Canada)
	Mark Streit (Switzerland)
Forward	Christian Dube (Canada)
	Sergei Samsonov (Russia)
	Michael York (United States)

DIRECTORATE AWARDS

BEST GOALIE	Marc Denis (Canada)
BEST DEFENCEMAN	Joseph Corvo (United States)
BEST FORWARD	Alexei Morozov (Russia)

1998 WORLD JUNIOR CHAMPIONSHIPS

FINLAND, DECEMBER 25, 1997–JANUARY 3, 1998

FINAL PLACINGS

GOLD MEDAL	Finland
SILVER MEDAL	Russia
BRONZE MEDAL	Switzerland
Fourth Place	Czech Republic
Fifth Place	United States
Sixth Place	Sweden
Seventh Place	Kazakhstan*
Eighth Place	Canada
Ninth Place	Slovakia
Tenth Place	Germany**

* promoted from 'B' pool in 1997
** relegated to 'B' pool for 1999

ALL-STAR TEAM

Goal	David Aebischer (Switzerland)
Defence	Pierre Hedin (Sweden)
	Andrei Markov (Russia)
Forward	Olli Jokinen (Finland)
	Eero Somervuori (Finland)
	Maxim Balmochnykh (Russia)

DIRECTORATE AWARDS

BEST GOALIE	David Aebischer (Switzerland)
BEST DEFENCEMAN	Pavel Skrbek (Czech Republic)
BEST FORWARD	Olli Jokinen (Finland)

1999 WORLD JUNIOR CHAMPIONSHIPS

CANADA, DECEMBER 26, 1998–JANUARY 5, 1999

FINAL PLACINGS

GOLD MEDAL	Russia
SILVER MEDAL	Canada
BRONZE MEDAL	Slovakia
Fourth Place	Sweden
Fifth Place	Finland
Sixth Place	Kazakhstan
Seventh Place	Czech Republic
Eighth Place	United States
Ninth Place	Switzerland
Tenth Place	Belarus*

* promoted from 'B' pool in 1998; relegated to 'B' pool for 2000

ALL-STAR TEAM

Goal	Roberto Luongo (Canada)
Defence	Vitali Vishnevsky (Russia)
	Brian Campbell (Canada)
Forward	Daniel Tkachuk (Canada)
	Brian Gionta (United States)
	Maxim Balmochnykh (Russia)

DIRECTORATE AWARDS

BEST GOALIE	Roberto Luongo (Canada)
BEST DEFENCEMAN	Maxim Afinigenov (Russia)
BEST FORWARD	Vitali Vishnevski (Russia)

2000 WORLD JUNIOR CHAMPIONSHIPS

SWEDEN, DECEMBER 25, 1999–JANUARY 4, 2000

FINAL PLACINGS

GOLD MEDAL	Czech Republic
SILVER MEDAL	Russia
BRONZE MEDAL	Canada
Fourth Place	United States
Fifth Place	Sweden
Sixth Place	Switzerland
Seventh Place	Finland
Eighth Place	Kazakhstan
Ninth Place	Slovakia
Tenth Place	Ukraine*

* promoted from 'B' pool in 1999; demoted to 'B' pool for 2001

ALL-STAR TEAM

Goal	Rick DiPietro (United States)
Defence	Mathieu Biron (Canada)
	Alexander Rjasantsev (Russia)
Forward	Milan Kraft (Czech Republic)
	Alexei Tereschenko (Russia)
	Evgeny Muratov (Russia)

DIRECTORATE AWARDS

BEST GOALIE	Rick DiPietro (United States)
BEST DEFENCEMAN	Alexander Rjasantsev (Russia)
BEST FORWARD	Milan Kraft (Czech Republic)

2001 WORLD JUNIOR CHAMPIONSHIPS

RUSSIA, DECEMBER 26, 2000–JANUARY 5, 2001

FINAL PLACINGS

GOLD MEDAL	Czech Republic
SILVER MEDAL	Finland
BRONZE MEDAL	Canada
Fourth Place	Sweden
Fifth Place	United States
Sixth Place	Switzerland
Seventh Place	Russia
Eighth Place	Slovakia
Ninth Place	Belarus*
Tenth Place	Kazakhstan**

* promoted from 'B' pool in 2000
** demoted to 'B' pool for 2002

ALL-STAR TEAM

Goal	Ari Ahonen (Finland)
Defence	Rostislav Klesla (Czech Republic)
	Tuukka Mantyla (Finland)
Forward	Jason Spezza (Canada)
	Jani Rita (Finland)
	Pavel Brendl (Czech Republic)

DIRECTORATE AWARDS

BEST GOALIE	Tomas Duba (Czech Republic)
BEST DEFENCEMAN	Rostislav Klesla (Czech Republic)
BEST FORWARD	Pavel Brendl (Czech Republic)

2002 WORLD JUNIOR CHAMPIONSHIPS

CZECH REPUBLIC, DECEMBER 25, 2001–JUANUARY 4, 2002

FINAL PLACINGS

GOLD MEDAL	Russia
SILVER MEDAL	Canada
BRONZE MEDAL	Finland
Fourth Place	Switzerland
Fifth Place	United States
Sixth Place	Sweden
Seventh Place	Czech Republic
Eighth Place	Slovakia
Ninth Place	Belarus
Tenth Place	France*

* promoted from 2001; demoted for 2003

ALL-STAR TEAM

Goal	Pascal Leclaire (Canada)
Defence	Jay Bouwmeester (Canada)
	Igor Knyazev (Russia)
Forward	Mike Cammalleri (Canada)
	Marek Svatos (Canada)
	Stanislav Chistov (Russia)

DIRECTORATE AWARDS

BEST GOALIE	Kari Lehtonen (Finland)
BEST DEFENCEMAN	Igor Knyazev (Russia)
BEST FORWARD	Mike Cammalleri (Canada)

2003 WORLD JUNIOR CHAMPIONSHIPS

CANADA, DECEMBER 26, 2002–JANUARY 5, 2003

FINAL PLACINGS

GOLD MEDAL	Russia
SILVER MEDAL	Canada
BRONZE MEDAL	Finland
Fourth Place	United States
Fifth Place	Slovakia
Sixth Place	Czech Republic
Seventh Place	Switzerland
Eighth Place	Sweden
Ninth Place	Germany*
Tenth Place	Belarus**

* promoted from 2002
** demoted for 2004

ALL-STAR TEAM

Goal	Marc-Andre Fleury (Canada)
Defence	Carlo Colaiacovo (Canada)
	Joni Pitkanen (Finland)
Forward	Scottie Upshall (Canada)
	Igor Grigorenko (Russia)
	Yuri Trubachev (Russia)

DIRECTORATE AWARDS

BEST GOALIE	Marc-Andre Fleury (Canada)
BEST DEFENCEMAN	Joni Pitkanen (Finland)
BEST FORWARD	Igor Grigorenko (Russia)

2004 WORLD JUNIOR CHAMPIONSHIPS

FINLAND, DECEMBER 26, 2003–JANUARY 6, 2004

FINAL PLACINGS

GOLD MEDAL	United States
SILVER MEDAL	Canada
BRONZE MEDAL	Finland
Fourth Place	Czech Republic
Fifth Place	Russia
Sixth Place	Slovakia
Seventh Place	Sweden
Eighth Place	Switzerland
Ninth Place	Austria*
Tenth Place	Ukraine**

* promoted from 2003
** demoted for 2005

ALL-STAR TEAM

Goal	Al Montoya (United States)
Defence	Dion Phaneuf (Canada)
	Sami Lepisto (Finland)
Forward	Jeff Carter (Canada)
	Valtteri Filppula (Finland)
	Zach Parise (United States)

DIRECTORATE AWARDS

BEST GOALIE	Al Montoya (United States)
BEST DEFENCEMAN	Sami Lepisto (Finland)
BEST FORWARD	Zach Parise (United States)

2005 WORLD JUNIOR CHAMPIONSHIP

UNITED STATES, December 25, 2004–January 4, 2005

FINAL PLACINGS

GOLD MEDAL	Canada
SILVER MEDAL	Russia
BRONZE MEDAL	Czech Republic
Fourth Place	United States
Fifth Place	Finland
Sixth Place	Sweden
Seventh Place	Slovakia
Eighth Place	Switzerland
Ninth Place	Germany*
Tenth Place	Belarus*

* promoted from 2004; demoted for 2006

ALL-STAR TEAM

Goal	Marek Schwarz (Czech Republic)
Defence	Dion Phaneuf (Canada)
	Gary Suter (United States)
Forward	Patrice Bergeron (Canada)
	Jeff Carter (Canada)
	Alexander Ovechkin (Russia)

DIRECTORATE AWARDS

BEST GOALIE	Marek Schwarz (Czech Republic)
BEST DEFENCEMAN	Dion Phaneuf (Canada)
BEST FORWARD	Alexander Ovechkin (Russia)

2006 WORLD JUNIOR CHAMPIONSHIP

CANADA, December 26, 2005–January 5, 2006

FINAL PLACINGS

GOLD MEDAL	Canada
SILVER MEDAL	Russia
BRONZE MEDAL	Finland
Fourth Place	United States
Fifth Place	Sweden
Sixth Place	Czech Republic
Seventh Place	Switzerland
Eighth Place	Slovakia
Ninth Place	Latvia*
Tenth Place	Norway*

* promoted from 2005; demoted for 2007

ALL-STAR TEAM

Goal	Tuukka Rask (Finland)
Defence	Luc Bourdon (Canada)
	Jack Johnson (United States)
Forward	Steve Downie (Canada)
	Evgeni Malkin (Russia)
	Lauri Tukonen (Finland)

DIRECTORATE AWARDS

BEST GOALIE	Tuukka Rask (Finland)
BEST DEFENCEMAN	Marc Staal (Canada)
BEST FORWARD	Evgeni Malkin (Russia)

2007 WORLD JUNIOR CHAMPIONSHIP

SWEDEN, December 26, 2006–January 5, 2007

FINAL PLACINGS

GOLD MEDAL	Canada
SILVER MEDAL	Russia
BRONZE MEDAL	United States
Fourth Place	Sweden
Fifth Place	Czech Republic
Sixth Place	Finland
Seventh Place	Switzerland
Eighth Place	Slovakia
Ninth Place	Germany
Tenth Place	Belarus

ALL-STAR TEAM

Goal	Carey Price (Canada)
Defence	Kristopher Letang (Canada)
	Erik Johnson (United States)
Forward	Jonathan Toews (Canada)
	Alexei Cherepanov (Russia)
	Patrick Kane (United States)

DIRECTORATE AWARDS

BEST GOALIE	Carey Price (Canada)
BEST DEFENCEMAN	Erik Johnson (United States)
BEST FORWARD	Alexi Cherepanov (Russia)
TOURNAMENT MVP	Carey Price (Canada)

2008 WORLD JUNIOR CHAMPIONSHIP

CZECH REPUBLIC, December 26, 2007–January 5, 2008

FINAL PLACINGS

GOLD MEDAL	Canada
SILVER MEDAL	Sweden
BRONZE MEDAL	Russia
Fourth Place	United States
Fifth Place	Czech Republic
Sixth Place	Finland
Seventh Place	Slovakia
Eighth Place	Kazakhstan
Ninth Place	Switzerland
Tenth Place	Denmark

ALL-STAR TEAM

Goal	Steve Mason (Canada)
Defence	Drew Doughty (Canada)
	Victor Hedman (Sweden)
Forward	Viktor Tikhonov (Russia)
	Patrik Berglund (Sweden)
	James van Remsdyk (United States)

DIRECTORATE AWARDS

BEST GOALIE	Steve Mason (Canada)
BEST DEFENCEMAN	Drew Doughty (Canada)
BEST FORWARD	Viktor Tikhonov (Russia)
TOURNAMENT MVP	Steve Mason (Canada)

WORLD WOMEN'S CHAMPIONSHIPS, 1990–2008

1990 World Women's Championship

CANADA, March 19–25, 1990

FINAL PLACINGS

GOLD MEDAL	Canada
SILVER MEDAL	United States
BRONZE MEDAL	Finland
Fourth Place	Sweden
Fifth Place	Switzerland
Sixth Place	Norway
Seventh Place	Germany
Eighth Place	Japan

1992 World Women's Championship

FINLAND, April 20–26, 1992

FINAL PLACINGS

GOLD MEDAL	Canada
SILVER MEDAL	United States
BRONZE MEDAL	Finland
Fourth Place	Sweden
Fifth Place	China
Sixth Place	Norway
Seventh Place	Denmark
Eighth Place	Switzerland

DIRECTORATE AWARDS

BEST GOALIE	Annica Ahlen (Sweden)
BEST DEFENCEMAN	Geraldine Heaney (Canada)
BEST FORWARD	Cammi Granato (United States)

1994 World Women's Championship

UNITED STATES, April 11–17, 1994

FINAL PLACINGS

GOLD MEDAL	Canada
SILVER MEDAL	United States
BRONZE MEDAL	Finland
Fourth Place	China
Fifth Place	Sweden
Sixth Place	Norway
Seventh Place	Switzerland
Eighth Place	Germany

DIRECTORATE AWARDS

BEST GOALIE	Erin Whitten (United States)
BEST DEFENCEMAN	Geraldine Heaney (Canada)
BEST FORWARD	Riikka Nieminen (Finland)

1997 World Women's Championship

CANADA, March 31–April 6, 1997

FINAL PLACINGS

GOLD MEDAL	Canada
SILVER MEDAL	United States
BRONZE MEDAL	Finland
Fourth Place	China
Fifth Place	Sweden
Sixth Place	Russia
Seventh Place	Switzerland
Eighth Place	Norway

DIRECTORATE AWARDS

None awarded

1999 World Women's Championship

FINLAND, March 8–14, 1999

FINAL PLACINGS

GOLD MEDAL	Canada
SILVER MEDAL	United States
BRONZE MEDAL	Finland
Fourth Place	Sweden
Fifth Place	China
Sixth Place	Russia
Seventh Place	Germany
Eighth Place	Switzerland

DIRECTORATE AWARDS

BEST GOALIE	Sami Jo Small (Canada)
BEST DEFENCEMAN	Kirsi Hanninen (Finland)
BEST FORWARD	Jenny Schmidgall (United States)

2000 World Women's Championship

CANADA, April 3–9, 2000

FINAL PLACINGS

GOLD MEDAL	Canada
SILVER MEDAL	United States
BRONZE MEDAL	Finland
Fourth Place	Sweden
Fifth Place	Russia
Sixth Place	China
Seventh Place	Germany
Eighth Place	Japan

DIRECTORATE AWARDS

BEST GOALIE	Sami Jo Small (Canada)
BEST DEFENCEMAN	Angela Ruggiero (United States)
BEST FORWARD	Katja Riipi (Finland)

2001 World Women's Championship

UNITED STATES, April 2–8, 2001

FINAL PLACINGS

GOLD MEDAL	Canada
SILVER MEDAL	United States
BRONZE MEDAL	Russia
Fourth Place	Finland
Fifth Place	Sweden
Sixth Place	Germany
Seventh Place	China
Eighth Place	Kazakhstan

DIRECTORATE AWARDS

BEST GOALIE	Kim St. Pierre (Canada)
BEST DEFENCEMAN	Karyn Bye (United States)
BEST FORWARD	Jennifer Botterill (Canada)
MVP	Jennifer Botterill (Canada)

2003 World Women's Championship

CHINA, April 3–9, 2003

CANCELLED DUE TO SARS OUTBREAK

2004 World Women's Championship

CANADA, March 30–April 6, 2004

FINAL PLACINGS

GOLD MEDAL	Canada
SILVER MEDAL	United States
BRONZE MEDAL	Finland
Fourth Place	Sweden
Fifth Place	Russia

Sixth Place	Germany
Seventh Place	China
Eighth Place	Switzerland
Ninth Place	Japan

DIRECTORATE AWARDS

BEST GOALIE	Kim St. Pierre (Canada)
BEST DEFENCEMAN	Angela Ruggiero (United States)
BEST FORWARD	Jayna Hefford (Canada)
MVP	Jennifer Botterill (Canada)

ALL-STAR TEAM

Goal	Pam Dreyer (United States)
Defence	Gunilla Andersson (Sweden), Angela Ruggiero (United States)
Forward	Jayna Hefford (Canada), Jennifer Botterill (Canada), Natalie Darwitz (United States)

2005 World Women's Championship

SWEDEN, April 2–9, 2005

FINAL PLACINGS

GOLD MEDAL	United States
SILVER MEDAL	Canada
BRONZE MEDAL	Sweden
Fourth Place	Finland
Fifth Place	Germany
Sixth Place	China
Seventh Place	Kazakhstan
Eighth Place	Russia

DIRECTORATE AWARDS

| BEST GOALIE | Chanda Gunn (United States) |
| BEST DEFENCEMAN | Angela Ruggiero (United States) |

BEST FORWARD   Jayna Hefford (Canada)
MVP   Krissy Wendell (United States)

ALL-STAR TEAM
Goalie   Natalya Turnova (Kazakhstan)
Defence   Cheryl Pounder (Canada),
          Angela Ruggiero (United States)
Forward   Hayley Wickenheiser (Canada),
          Maria Rooth (Sweden),
          Krissy Wendell (United States)

2007 World Women's Championship
CANADA, April 3–10, 2007

FINAL PLACINGS
GOLD MEDAL   Canada
SILVER MEDAL   United States
BRONZE MEDAL   Sweden
Fourth Place   Finland
Fifth Place   Switzerland
Sixth Place   China
Seventh Place   Russia
Eighth Place   Germany
Ninth Place   Kazakhstan

DIRECTORATE AWARDS
BEST GOALIE   Noora Raty (Finland)
BEST DEFENCEMAN   Molly Engstrom (United States)
BEST FORWARD   Hayley Wickenheiser (Canada)
MVP   Hayley Wickenheiser (Canada)

ALL-STAR TEAM
Goalie   Kim St. Pierre (Canada)
Defence   Delaney Collins (Canada)

Forward	Angela Ruggiero (United States)
	Natalie Darwitz (United States)
	Krissy Wendell (United States)
	Hayley Wickenheiser (Canada)

2008 World Women's Championship

CHINA, April 4–12, 2008

FINAL PLACINGS

GOLD	United States
SILVER	Canada
BRONZE	Finland
Fourth Place	Switzerland
Fifth Place	Sweden
Sixth Place	Russia
Seventh Place	Japan
Eighth Place	China
Ninth Place	Germany

All-Star Team

Goalie	Noora Raty (Finland)
Defence	Emma Laaksonen (Finland)
	Julie Chu (United States)
Forward	Hayley Wickenheiser (Canada)
	Natalie Darwitz (United States)
	Jayne Hefford (Canada)

Directorate Awards

Best Goalie	Noora Raty (Finland)
Best Defenceman	Angela Ruggiero (United States)
Best Forward	Natalie Darwitz (United States)
MVP	Noora Raty (Finland)

NATIONAL & CANADIAN WOMEN'S HOCKEY LEAGUES, 1999–2008

ALL-TIME STANDINGS

1999–2000
Eastern Division

	GP	W	L	T	GF	GA	P
Sainte Julie Pantheres	35	20	8	7	109	68	47
Montreal Wingstar	35	18	7	10	116	62	46
Ottawa Raiders	35	9	20	6	61	109	24
Laval Le Mistral	35	7	23	5	78	177	19

Western Division

	GP	W	L	T	GF	GA	P
Beatrice Aeros	40	35	3	2	217	37	72
Brampton Thunder	40	29	5	6	208	64	64
Mississauga Chiefs	40	21	13	6	133	79	48
Clearnet Lightning	40	4	33	3	44	249	11
Scarborough Sting	40	3	34	3	49	170	9

CHAMPIONSHIP FINALS

March 18   Sainte Julie Pantheres 2/Beatrice Aeros 2
March 19   Beatrice Aeros 1/Sainte Julie Pantheres 0
Beatrice wins championship 3–1 in points

2000–01
Eastern Division

	GP	W	L	T	GF	GA	P
Montreal Wingstar	40	30	6	4	163	63	64
Sainte Julie Pantheres	40	22	15	3	168	102	47
Ottawa Raiders	40	11	25	4	78	150	26
Laval Le Mistral	40	5	33	2	68	261	12

Western Division

Beatrice Aeros	40	35	2	3	222	46	73
Brampton Thunder	40	30	7	3	223	82	63
Mississauga Ice Bears	40	21	16	3	107	97	45
Toronto Sting	40	8	29	3	82	168	19
Clearnet Lightning	40	5	34	1	77	219	11
Vancouver Griffins	18	14	4	0	91	43	28

CHAMPIONSHIP FINALS

Beatrice Aeros 2/Sainte Julie Pantheres 2
Beatrice Aeros 8/Sainte Julie Pantheres 1
Beatrice wins championship 3–1 in points

2001–02

Eastern Division

	GP	W	L	T	GF	GA	P
Ottawa Raiders	30	14	10	6	71	72	34
Montreal Wingstar	30	11	14	5	66	78	27
Le Cheyenne de la Metropol	30	11	15	4	73	85	26

Western Division

Beatrice Aeros	30	23	2	5	149	39	51
Mississauga Ice Bears	30	12	10	8	82	81	32
Brampton Thunder	30	8	14	8	73	97	24
Telus Lightning	30	4	18	8	59	120	16

Pacific Division

Vancouver Griffins	31	27	4	0	84	14	54

CHAMPIONSHIP FINALS

Beatrice Aeros 3/Brampton Thunder 2 (OT)

2002–03
Eastern Division

	GP	W	L	T	OTL	GF	GA	P
Montreal Wingstar	36	18	15	3	0	83	81	39
Ottawa Raiders	36	13	20	1	2	96	122	29
Quebec Avalanche	36	10	20	5	1	87	120	26

Central Division

	GP	W	L	T	OTL	GF	GA	P
Beatrice Aeros	36	32	3	1	0	201	54	65
Brampton Thunder	36	27	9	0	0	152	71	54
Mississauga Ice Bears	36	19	13	3	1	122	111	42
Telus Lightning	36	0	34	1	1	54	236	2

Western Division

	GP	W	L	T	OTL	GF	GA	P
Calgary X-Treme	24	23	1	0	0	144	37	46
Vancouver Griffins	24	10	13	0	1	82	92	21
Edmonton Chimos	24	3	20	0	1	35	132	7

CHAMPIONSHIP FINALS
Calgary X-Treme 3/Beatrice Aeros 0

2003–04
Eastern Division

	G	W	L	T	OTL	GF	GA	P
Montreal Axion	36	20	10	5	1	113	84	46
Ottawa Raiders	36	9	23	4	0	85	144	22
Quebec Avalanche	36	4	28	2	2	65	163	12

Central Division

	G	W	L	T	OTL	GF	GA	P
Toronto Aeros	36	33	2	1	0	197	42	67
Brampton Thunder	36	28	6	2	0	190	72	58
Oakville Ice	36	17	17	2	0	118	99	36
Telus Lightning	36	8	28	0	0	66	224	16

Western Division

Calgary X-Treme	12	11	1	0	0	64	9	22
Edmonton Chimos	12	1	11	0	0	9	64	2

CHAMPIONSHIP FINALS

Calgary X-Treme 5/Brampton Thunder 4 (OT/SO)

2004–05

Eastern Division

	G	W	L	T	OTL	GF	GA	P
Montreal Axion	36	24	9	2	1	140	85	51
Ottawa Raiders	36	14	19	2	1	101	128	31
Quebec Avalanche	36	5	25	4	2	53	132	16

Central Division

	G	W	L	T	OTL	GF	GA	P
Brampton Thunder	36	30	3	2	1	165	70	63
Toronto Aeros	36	24	6	4	2	142	68	54
Oakville Ice	36	13	15	6	2	97	99	34
Telus Lightning	36	4	28	4	0	72	189	12

CHAMPIONSHIP FINALS

Toronto Aeros 5/Montreal Axion 4 (OT)

2005–06

Eastern Division

	G	W	L	T	OTL	GF	GA	P
Ottawa Raiders	36	21	8	4	3	122	77	49
Montreal Axion	36	14	17	3	2	100	122	33
Quebec Avalanche	36	4	28	2	2	58	135	12

Central Division

	G	W	L	T	OTL	GF	GA	P
Durham Lightning	36	23	6	5	2	107	74	53
Brampton Thunder	36	19	12	5	0	113	97	43
Oakville Ice	36	20	14	1	1	118	100	42
Toronto Aeros	36	13	17	4	2	114	127	32

CHAMPIONSHIP FINALS
April 15   Montreal Axion 1/Brampton Thunder 0

2006–07

	G	W	L	T	OTL	GF	GA	P
Etobicoke Dolphins	20	15	1	2	2	87	66	64
Mississauga Aeros	21	15	5	0	1	107	51	31
Brampton Thunder	16	8	8	0	0	71	66	16
Oakville Ice	17	6	8	1	2	40	53	15
Montreal Axion	13	6	6	0	0	66	56	13
Quebec Avalanche	12	2	8	2	0	41	91	6
Ottawa Raiders	11	2	8	0	0	25	54	5

CHAMPIONSHIP FINALS
April 14   Brampton Thunder 4/Montreal Axion 0

Note: the NWHL was replaced by the CWHL in 2007

2007–08
Central Division

	GP	W	L	OT	GF	GA	P
Brampton Canadette-Thunder	30	22	7	1	111	59	45
Mississauga Chiefs	30	21	8	1	115	61	43
Vaughan Flames	30	12	16	2	69	101	26
Burlington Barracudas	30	11	18	1	76	98	23

Eastern Division

	GP	W	L	OT	GF	GA	P
Montreal Stars	28	21	6	1	112	55	43
Ottawa Capital-Canucks	28	8	17	3	58	102	19
Quebec Phoenix	28	8	21	1	56	121	17

PLAYOFFS

Burlington 2 at Ottawa 1
(Burlington advanced)

Mississauga 6 at Vaughan 2
Mississauga 6 at Vaughan 2

Mississauga 4 at Montreal 3
Mississauga 1 at Montreal 4
(Mississauga won tie-breaker)

Burlington 2 at Brampton 5
Burlington 3 at Brampton 3
(Brampton advanced)

CHAMPIONSHIP FINALS

Mississauga Chiefs 3/Brampton Canadette-Thunder 2 (OT)

CANADIAN & WESTERN WOMEN'S HOCKEY LEAGUES, 2008–09

CWHL Regular-Season Standings

	GP	W	L	P
Montreal Stars	28	24	3	49
Brampton Thunder	26	19	6	39
Mississauga Chiefs	26	16	8	34
Burlington Barracudas	25	10	13	22
Vaughan Flames	25	4	19	10
Ottawa Senators	24	4	20	8

League Playoffs

(best-of-two plus sudden-death OT in case of tie)

March 14   Brampton 3/Mississauga 2
March 15   Mississauga 4/Brampton 1
OT tie-breaker: Brampton, Jayna Hefford
Brampton Thunder advance to Clarkson Cup finals

March 14   Montreal 6/Burlington 1
March 15   Burlington 3/Montreal 1
OT tie-breaker: Montreal, Noemie Marin
Montreal Stars advance to Clarkson Cup finals

WWHL Regular-Season Standings

	GP	W	L	OTL	P
Calgary Oval X-Treme	23	20	2	1	42
Minnesota Whitecaps	22	18	3	1	38
Edmonton Chimos	24	14	10	0	28
Strathmore Rockies	23	6	16	1	13
B.C. Breakers	24	0	22	2	2

League Playoffs
Semifinals
March 7   Calgary 9/Strathmore 0
March 7   Minnesota 4/Edmonton 0

Finals
March 8   Minnesota 2/Calgary 0

Both finalists advance to Clarkson Cup finals

CLARKSON CUP FINALS
(Kingston, Ontario)

Round Robin
March 19   Minnesota 4/Montreal 3
March 19   Brampton 4/Calgary 3

Semifinals
March 20   Montreal 4/Brampton 1
March 20   Minnesota 2/Calgary 1

Finals
March 21   Montreal 3   Minnesota 1

HOCKEY POOL NOTES

HOCKEY POOL NOTES

HOCKEY POOL NOTES

HOCKEY POOL NOTES

HOCKEY POOL NOTES

HOCKEY POOL NOTES

HOCKEY POOL NOTES

HOCKEY POOL NOTES

HOCKEY POOL NOTES

HOCKEY POOL NOTES

HOCKEY POOL NOTES

HOCKEY POOL NOTES